Classics of American Literature

Arnold Weinstein, Ph.D.

THE
GREAT
COURSES

PUBLISHED BY:

THE GREAT COURSES
Corporate Headquarters
4840 Westfields Boulevard, Suite 500
Chantilly, Virginia 20151-2299
Phone: 1-800-832-2412
Fax: 703-378-3819
www.thegreatcourses.com

Arnold Weinstein, Ph.D.

Edna and Richard Salomon Distinguished Professor
and Professor of Comparative Literature
Brown University

Arnold Weinstein was born in Tennessee in 1940 and received his undergraduate degree in romance languages from Princeton University in 1962. He studied at Université de Paris in 1960–1961 and at Freie Universitat, Berlin, in 1962–1963. He received his master's and doctorate in comparative literature from Harvard University in 1964 and 1968, respectively.

Dr. Weinstein has been teaching courses on European, English, and American literature at Brown University since 1968. In addition, he is the sponsor of Swedish Studies at Brown. He has been the chairperson of the Advisory Council on Comparative Literature at Princeton University and is actively involved in the American Comparative Literature Association.

Among the many academic honors, research grants, and fellowships he has received include research grants from the American Council of Learned Societies and the National Endowment for the Humanities. In 1983 he was visiting professor of American Literature at Stockholm University, where he received the Fulbright Senior Lecturer Award. He is currently a member of the Academy of Literary Studies and the director of an NEH-funded program in great books. In 1995 he was named Brown University's best teacher in the humanities. He is the recipient of a National Endowment for the Humanities Award for University Teachers for 1998–1999 for his work in literature and medicine.

Dr. Weinstein is the author of *Vision and Response in Modern Fiction* (1984), *Fictions of the Self: 1550–1800* (1981), *The Fiction of Relationship* (1988), and *Nobody's Home: Speech, Self, and Place in American Fiction from Hawthorne to DeLillo* (1993). He is working in the fields of literature and medicine, with a view toward a book-length study of the relationship between the two, especially concerning the issues of diagnosis and interpretation.

Table of Contents
Classics of American Literature

Table of Contents
Classics of American Literature

Classics of American Literature

Scope:

We all read many books over our lifetimes, but how many of them do we really remember? We have all heard of the great names in American literature—Emerson, Thoreau, Poe, Hawthorne, Melville, Whitman, Dickinson, Twain, James, Hemingway, Fitzgerald, Faulkner, Eliot, O'Neill, Morrison—but do we know why they are great? Do we truly savor these books in such a way that they are a part of our inner landscape, part of the way we now see America and ourselves?

Of course, many of the books that are considered classics of American literature are part of everyone's repertory. But have we made them into personal knowledge? We know that Rip Van Winkle falls asleep for 20 years for some mysterious reason—but what exactly? Why did Emerson believe in "self-reliance," and why do we? Thoreau went to Walden Pond to force nature into utterance. Is this a victory? An escape? A fiction? Melville's Ahab does war with the white whale. Is his struggle heroic or sacrilegious? Mad or impotent? Whitman celebrates the common man, the great city, even life and death. But is he believable? Stowe shows us Uncle Tom, black slave turned into Christ figure—how much has changed since then? Dickinson, the recluse of Amherst, writes the most explosive verse of the century—how could she know what she knew? Twain, our greatest showman, tells a story with an inkling of Peter Pan: Tom Sawyer never does grow up, but Huck Finn must face the racism of the South and somehow get past his own polluted conscience—can he do it? James brings American innocents to Europe for them to inherit the world—but do they?

In the 20th century, Hemingway speaks for a lost generation of American writers who discovered Paris but lost home and self in the bargain. Fitzgerald's Gatsby is the crown prince of capitalism, the hero of self-invention. He finishes up poorly, but Willy Loman, Arthur Miller's salesman-hero, finishes even worse as the American dream turns into a nightmare—have we lost our truest faith? Faulkner's decaying South is alive with ghosts—can there be a future if we are all ghost-ridden? Ellison writes the epic story of an entire race in the adventures of his "invisible man," and Morrison harks all the way back to the horrors of slavery in *Beloved*, joining Stowe, Twain, and Faulkner to remind us, just as the stories of the concentration camps remind us, that even carnage may be survivable. But at what cost?

American classics are wonderfully rich fare. These books are often the sites of great conflict—political, racial, sexual, and moral. More than any other modern nation, America is a mythic land, a place with a sense of its own destiny and promise, a place that has experienced bloody wars to achieve that destiny. The events of American history shimmer forth in our classics. The Puritan origins and the Revolutionary War have pride of place in much of Hawthorne. The search for an American language—for the great American theme of freedom—is at the core of Emerson, Thoreau, and Whitman. The nightmares of slavery and fratricide, inseparable from the Civil War, inform the vision not only of Stowe, Melville, and Twain, but also of Faulkner and Morrison. America's loss of innocence in World War I, coupled with its enduring belief in the self-made man, reappear as both fact and fiction, as promises that may be unkeepable, in Hemingway, Fitzgerald, T. S. Eliot, and Arthur Miller. Somewhat like a great voyage across the United States, then, especially a voyage in time, we explore our country in these books, an exploration unimaginable in any other form.

Objectives—Upon completion of this course, you should be able to:

1. Explain the role of "self-reliance" and the "self-made man" in the evolution of American literature;

2. Identify the central tenets of American Romanticism;

3. Describe the evolution of the American ghost story, from Poe and Hawthorne to James and Morrison;

4. Outline the epic strain in American literature, from Melville and Whitman to Faulkner and Ellison;

5. Explain the importance of slavery as a critical subject matter for Stowe, Twain, Faulkner, and Morrison;

6. Summarize the perspective on nature revealed in such seminal poets as Whitman, Dickinson, Frost, and Eliot;

7. Identify the main tenets of Modernism in the work of Eliot, Fitzgerald, Hemingway, and Faulkner;

8. Identify the major contributions of O'Neill, Miller, and Williams to American theater; and

9. Summarize the major threads of the complex relationship between America's great writers and the past.

Lecture Forty-Three
The Turn of the Screw—Do You Believe in Ghosts?

Scope: As an author obsessed with issues of consciousness and communication, James seems fated to have tackled the genre of ghost stories. *The Turn of the Screw* is a candidate for the greatest horror story in literature, even though it has none of the Gothic features we remember in Poe. Instead, it deals with the themes of innocence and guilt, understood spiritually as the exit from Eden, actualized narratively as drama of perception. The horror of the story derives from its choice of protagonists: two children who are suspected of being in communication with evil ghosts from the past. This bristling scenario comes to us via the vision of the governess-narrator who is to protect these children from harm. This story has been subject to some famous critical theories, and they all add up to one thing: What do we see in what we see? Or, no less strikingly: How do we read?

Objectives—Upon completion of this lecture, you should be able to:

1. Summarize the "straight" and "Freudian" readings of *The Turn of the Screw*;

2. Explain how James renders vision to be inherently ambiguous in *The Turn of the Screw*; and

3. Describe how James's depiction of Miles and Flora offended the Victorian sensibilities of his day.

Outline

I. *The Turn of the Screw* constitutes a *cause célèbre* in literary criticism. James's text has caused consternation since its appearance in 1898.

A. At the time of its publication, James's story was seen as shocking and awful. It is the account, offered by a heroic governess, of two innocent children hounded by evil ghosts. James offended the Victorian belief in childhood purity; his story of corruption was considered ghastly.

B. *The Turn of the Screw* is elaborately outfitted with metaphors of innocence and corruption, and its images make it clear that James is telling a story of the proverbial Fall.

    1. The children, Miles and Flora, are easily understood as symbolic figures: Miles as soldier and essential male, and Flora as flower and essential female.

    2. This is a pastoral reading: The story begins in June, when all is in bloom, and finishes in November, in darkness. The children are themselves "aged" by the text, as the story continues.

    3. The Fall—the children's loss of innocence—is to be understood as the cost of knowledge, especially sexual knowledge.

    4. The Fall is also the arrival of death onto the scene.

    5. The governess exercises a priestly function in that she valiantly does battle with the evil ghosts who want to claim the children. She presses Miles to confess his contact with the ghosts; only when he confesses can he be saved.

C. This version of events, a version most readers subscribe to, is now regarded as the "straight reading." In 1934, Edmund Wilson published a famous alternative in his essay, "The Ambiguity of Henry James." Enter the notorious "Freudian reading," in which the reader discovers more than just a surface meaning.

    1. In one view of the story, the children are not in cahoots with the ghosts and have no visions at all; in fact, no one other than the governess ever actually *sees* the ghosts.

    2. The governess sees the ghosts because she is having hallucinations, and she is having hallucinations because she is sexually repressed. Hence, the ghosts, Quint and Jessel, are "projected" by the governess, even though she truly believes that they are real and that the children see them.

    3. Textual evidence buttresses this theory, indicating that the governess is infatuated with the master/uncle who entrusts her with the children, and this infatuation generates her visions.

    4. Quint and Jessel, former menial and governess, make their ghostly appearances in strikingly symbolic fashion: Quint appears on a tower, Jessel by a lake. The Freudian doctrine easily translates this into symbols of male and female sexuality. Other scenes also have a powerful sexual dimension to them, and there is a growing sense that they represent sexual experience in multiple ways, resulting in an evil impact on the children.

5. Yet this reading flies in the face of James's claim that the governess has no "subjective complications" of her own. James himself specified what kind of ghost story he was writing: not the "case-study" type, but the one evoking "sacred terror." There is much horror in this reading, since we now have to imagine innocent children subjected to a mad governess who is seeing ghosts.

D. There are still other interesting readings. Some suspect the housekeeper, Mrs. Grose, of being the villain; others have argued that our categories of innocence and experience need to be rethought. After all, both the straight and the Freudian readings presuppose utterly innocent children who are destroyed either by the ghosts or the governess. But are children utterly innocent? What about infantile sexuality? What about Victorian priggishness?

E. Nonetheless, the reader is obliged to choose between two divergent interpretations: (1) The ghosts are real, we trust the governess, and the story is a sacrificial parable of the Fall; or (2) The governess is delusional or mad, she invents the ghosts, and we see this because we distrust her account.

II. At issue in this critical crossroads is the status of vision. Does the governess *see* or *invent/produce* the ghosts? The ramifications of this question are enormous.

A. Remember the lesson of Melville's "Benito Cereno": Vision can be culturally constructed. What might a sheltered and repressed Victorian woman see?

B. The initial Freudian premise is that the governess is projecting her desire for the master into a vision of Quint (as a "lower" version of master) and Jessel (as a consenting version of herself). But the screw turns still further: Is the governess projecting her desire *onto the children*? There is much evidence to buttress this view as well.

C. Finally, what does it actually mean to choose between the straight and the Freudian readings?

1. Who would choose the "straight" reading? It is a gullible, naïve, duped, gross reading of events.

2. Conversely, the Freudian reading is seductive because it is suspicious and sophisticated; we must invest in "reading" the governess and "interpreting" her account rather than simply believing it.

3. Freud, arriving for his first visit in America, joked that he brought the plague with him. He did, indeed. "Plague" is the era of suspicion, the very project of psychoanalysis whereby what you "say" does not mean what you really think. Here is the distinction between manifest (surface) meanings and latent (deeper) meanings. Only a fool believes in the surface and trusts the appearances; we like to probe, translate, and uncover what is hidden.

4. These issues are at the core of literature and reading. To distrust the governess's account is to critique, to rewrite, to decode. Hence, the status of vision in literature turns out to be inseparable from the status of language and reading. This is not simply a question of literature; it translates into our everyday lives as well: How do we "read" the newspapers? The language of friends and loved ones?

D. And yet, to *translate* the story of the governess—a story of evil ghosts corrupting innocent children—into a story of sexual repression and projection is to do to her what she does to the children: to extort her secret, to label her story a cover story. She insists on seeing evil in the children; we insist on seeing evil in her. Isn't this the reductive and coercive procedure that psychoanalysis can fall into, a bullying vision that says, "I know you better than you know yourself; I can decode your secrets; I can translate you; I make it possible for you to confess."

Lecture Forty-Three—Transcript
The Turn of the Screw—Do You Believe in Ghosts?

This is Lecture Forty-Three, and it's the first of two lectures on James' story, "The Turn of the Screw," which—quite simply—I take to be the best ghost story in the English language. These are large claims that I'll try to make good on. This story picks up all the issues of interpretation that we have seen in James' Corpus but it gives them a kind of urgency, I think, and a kind of reach that we don't quite expect. This story has been subject to several different kinds of interpretations itself, and it will be fun to go through that. It poses the question, again, as I alluded earlier, what happens when someone sees ghosts? Do we take that as a kind of credible vision? Do we take that as a mirror that tells us about the speaker? What do we make of it, we, as readers, living in a time where we may or may not believe in ghosts?

James' story created quite a row when it first came out. It's a kind of harrowing story of evil, and there was a lot of consternation in the public. I'm going to read you one particularly violent reaction to it.

> *The Turn of the Screw* is the most hopelessly evil story that we have ever read in any literature, ancient or modern. How Mr. James could or any man or woman could choose to make such a study
> of infernal human debauchery—for it is nothing else—is unaccountable. It is the story of two orphaned children, mere infants, whose guardian leaves them in a lonely English country house. The little boy and the little girl, at the toddling period of life, when they are but helpless babes, fall under the influence of a governess and her lover who poison the very core of their conscience and character and defile their souls in a way and by means darkly and subtly hinted rather than portrayed by Mr. James. The study, while it exhibits Mr. James' genius in a powerful light, affects the reader with a disgust that is not to be expressed. The feeling, after perusal of this horrible story, is that one has been assisting in an outrage upon the holiest and sweetest fountain of human innocence and helping to debauch, at least by helplessly standing by, the pure and trusting nature of children. Human imagination can go no further into infamy.

Literary art could not be used with more refined subtlety of spiritual defilement.

The point that is left out of that description of the story is that these two figures, the governess and her lover, who poison the children, are ghosts. They're both dead when the story starts and the governess sees them. So the story flaunts Victorian pieties in a sense. It's about desecrating innocents and children. This a particularly, I think, sensitive issue for the Victorians. Children were considered pure. There's a kind of idyllic representation of the children, and the story comes across then, the governess who sees these two ghosts who want to somehow possess the children, becomes a kind of allegory of evil. There are a lot of interesting inter-readings along those lines and James' story completely responds to that, that the children are initially presented, in the story, as beatific, angelic, pure, beautiful. They are smitten, as the story goes, and we watch them age.

I'm going to read you some of the terms that are used so you'll see just how thorough going this is. The girl's name is Flora; the boy's name is Miles. Flora has extraordinary charm. She is most beautiful. Miles is incredibly beautiful. Both have "the bloom of health and happiness." Miles is too fine and fair for the world. He is a beautiful little boy. The governess is "dazzled by their loveliness." They're "most loveable" in their "helplessness" touching their "fragrant faces," one can only believe "their incapacity and their beauty." Miles is a "prodigy of delightful, loveable goodness." Flora is described in terms that are like "rosy, Rosalie, the golden clove, her curls, her loveliest, eagerest simplicity, the excess of something beautiful that's shown out of the blue, the lovely little lighted face, beauty and amiability, happiness and cleverness." Miles has "a wonderful smile, the beautiful eye of a little fairy prince."

This is pretty consistent—persistent—moreover, the names themselves. Miles seems to be a kind of faint, symbolic notion of *miles,* the little male: the archetypal little soldier. Flora: the flower, the essential female. All of this leads to a view of the story, that it's a kind of pastoral tragedy of sorts. It's about these innocent, idyllic children who are then beset upon by these ghosts; and, it's important to realize just how much evil is packed into the ghosts. On the one hand, the ghosts themselves are linked. It's Miss Jessel and Peter Quint. Peter Quint was a former menial servant at the place and Miss Jessel is the former governess, which is the position that the narrator moves into. She becomes the governess. We are to understand that they, themselves, had an elicit sex affair—love affair—and that the governess,

Miss Jessel, committed suicide because she was pregnant. There's a sexual secret between these two that is particularly odious vis-à-vis the children. That is to say, this is part of the corruption, part of the degrading that's going on with the children.

It gets even worse than that. There is the implication as well that Peter Quint takes the boy aside and Jessel takes the girl aside, and so you get the hint that there's a kind of homosexual debauchery going on, too. So, these innocent children are really, you know, being undone and corrupted, in complex ways, in lots of different ways. The exposure to this couple, also kind of private lessons in sexual education; all of this is a kind of pastoral story of leaving the Garden of Eden and being exposed, initiated into sexual knowledge at a time that's far too early. The story is also set, in terms of its timeframe, it begins in June, spring is at its full, and it closes in November, darkness and cold. There's a focus on dead leaves and wind and rain. It's a story of the fall. It's a story, again, of the loss of innocence and the moving towards winter and death. In the story, the description of the children changes. Miles becomes aged as the story goes, as does Flora. At certain points in the later part of the story, her face is described as that of a little old woman. She starts cursing in the late part of the story and the governess says, "Where could she have ever learned these words, etc." So, you know, it's unmistakably an allegory about the loss of innocence. I think that anybody who can't see that doesn't know how to read. It is there.

So, what's the role of the governess? She's the one who inherits the situation. She comes into this country house—large estate—and her job is to take care of these two children. Flora's already there and Miles is coming home from his boarding school. Well, her function is fundamentally priestly. She is the one who's going to try to do battle with these forces of evil that are corrupting the children. There's one critic, Robert Heilman, who's given us a very good, I think, definition of what her job is. "The governess' priestly function is made still more explicit by the fact that she comes, ultimately, to act as confessor and to use every possible means to bring Miles to confession." She wants him to admit that he sees the ghosts because she sees them. She sees them preying on the children, and they will not own up to the fact that they are having this intercourse with the ghosts. She doesn't want to speak their name. She wants the children to come out and admit what's going on.

The long final scene, which is a scene between the governess and Miles really takes place in the confessional with the governess as priest endeavoring, by both word and gesture, to protect her charge against the

9

evil force whose invasion has, with consummate irony, carried even there. In one sense, the governess must elicit confession because, in her need for objective reassurance, she will not take the lead as accuser; but, securing the confession is, more importantly, a mitigation of Miles' own pride, his self-will. It could soften him and make him accessible to grace. The experience has a clear, sacramental quality. The governess says that Miles since has 'the need of confession. He'll confess. "If he confesses, he's saved." That's from the story. And it's when he begins to break and confess that 'the white face of damnation ..." which is the way the text describes the face of the ghost, Peter Quint, "... becomes baffled and, in a vital moment, retreats."

So that is the reading. The first reaction that I read to you—that reviewer said this is one of the most horrible things that I've ever seen in literature, these beautiful, angelic children being completely corrupted by these ghosts and no one seems to be able to stop it, the governess heroically tries to—that reading—this story was published in 1898—for decades, that is the way everybody read it.

In 1934, Edmund Wilson, a very distinguished American man of letters, published an essay called, "The Ambiguity of Henry James," at which time he essentially threw out that reading and said that reading is an illusion. He says there aren't any ghosts. The children are not in cahoots with the ghosts or with evil. The children never mention the ghosts because they don't see the ghosts, nor does anybody else see the ghosts except the governess. She sees them because she invents them and she invents them because she's sexually repressed. This is the famous Freudian reading of the story. She's having hallucinations. She's seeing Quint and Jessel and believes, truly believes, that the children see them, too. This is buttressed and motivated by the fact that the governess is clearly—even though she's alone at this mansion, this house—she is offered this job by this very dashing, attractive master, the uncle of the children. This reading then says that she is infatuated with him and projects her own romantic feelings for him, the absent master, onto Quint, in some sense, as a kind of configuration of the master, and then Jessel, I suppose, as a kind of version of herself as governess.

I'll read you a couple of passages where you can get a feeling for her sense of the master. When she got the job, he was

> A gentleman, a bachelor in the prime of life, such a figure as had never risen, save in a dream or an old novel, before a fluttered, anxious girl out of a Hampshire vicarage. One could easily fix his

type; it never, happily, dies out. He was handsome and bold and pleasant, offhand and gay and kind.

That's the man who offers her the job and she thinks about him when she meets, for example, Mrs. Grose, who is the housekeeper, a much lower figure in the social order here. She says, "To be carried away, I'm afraid, that's what I came for. I'm rather easily carried away. I was carried away in London." There are other passages as well where we sense that he is very present in her mind. She never says he's behind what she sees; but, once she has, [she] is out there trying to take charge and care of these young children and she can't help but feel that this is going to earn her credit in the right quarter. That's what she said, "I saw that I had been asked for a service, admirable and difficult, and there would be greatness in letting it be seen, oh, in the right quarter, that I could succeed where many another girl might have failed." I'm just giving you a few of the passages, where we know that this master is much in her mind and that she's drawn to him. Now, of course, Wilson makes the huge jump beyond that to say that it's this infatuation, that she's a very naïve young girl, she's coming out of a vicarage, she has had very little experience in life. It's this that produces the visions themselves.

Well, let's talk about the ghosts a little bit, Peter Quint and Miss Jessel. As I said, they are formerly the people who were at the house, so Mrs. Grose knows who they were. The children have, obviously, had contact with them when they were living. They appear in forms that are classic Freudian forms, that we first see Peter Quint on top of a tower, a crenulated tower, and we first see Jessel appear at the side of the lake. The Freudian doctrine says, "Ah ha! Tower, lake, well, we know what we've got there, we've got clear kinds of sexual images here, uterus and penis and things like that." Wilson is not quite that crude, but he's backing up his reading by saying that all of the pieces are in place here for this kind of an interpretation. Likewise, when the governess first sees Jessel at the lake, she also is there looking after Flora. Flora is performing a very unusual kind of activity. I'd like to describe it to you because I think you need to know this.

> She had picked up a small flat piece of wood, which happened to have in it a little hole that had evidently suggested to her the idea of sticking in another fragment that might figure as a mast and make the thing a boat. This second morsel, as I watched her, she was very markedly and intently attempting to tighten in its place.

Now critics have looked at that, you know. What's going on here? Right when the narrator is going to perceive—knows—that Jessel is there, at the other side of this lake, little Flora is there with two pieces of wood and one is being screwed into the other. That's where the title of this story comes from, "The Turn of the Screw." We all know that "screw" has a very obvious kind of sexual connotation, and that's clearly an inference. James won't say much about it but that's an inference there that, yes, the ghost is there and, in a sense, the corollary is that the child is already showing some kind of sexual curiosity, imitating sexual activity there. The story has hints like this. These are the kinds of things that the critic goes to buttress this case. This has been the action of the ghost; this is their evil impact.

Now, it's worth thinking about these matters because James wrote prefaces to almost all of his books. He would come back and write the prefaces later and he, in particular, talked about this story and he said that, if you listen to him, there's no way that this could be the imagination of the governess. He says, for example:

> Of course I had, about my woman, to take a very sharp line. The grotesque business I had to make her picture and the childish psychology I had to make her trace and present, were, for me at least, a very difficult job, in which absolute lucidity and logic, a singleness of effect, were imperative. Therefore I had to (and listen carefully) rule out subjective complications of her own.

You couldn't say it more clearly. James is making it clear here. There are *No* subjective complications here on the part of the governess. He also, later, defined the kind of ghost story he was trying to write, this is in 1898 when he wrote this thing. He talks about the new type of ghost story, which is not what he wants.

> The new type, indeed, the mere modern 'psychical' case, washed clean of all queerness as by an exposure to a flowing laboratory tap, and equipped with credentials vouching for this. The new type clearly promised very little for the more it was respectably certified the less it seemed of a nature to rouse the dear old sacred terror.

That's the old kind of ghost story, the one that rouses the dear old sacred terror. That's what he wants to write. So he tells us, there are no subjective complications and none of the new type of psychical analysis or anything such as that, just the old sacred terror. I think it's crucial that we reflect on these matters. What are we supposed to believe here? Do we want to entertain the view that ghosts are real? Or, that the governess is deluded or hallucinating? Ultimately, anything that you read is going to have a lot to do with what you can take to be credible, and this story really puts it on our plate. Which is more credible? Obviously, we will buttress whichever reading with as much evidence as we can find in the text. James seems to say it's off limits to read this as a story about her subjective complications. In a large, cultural sense, it's off limits for us to read it as a bona fide ghost story, too, if we don't believe in ghosts. It depends. I don't know who does and who doesn't.

It's a horror story, the sacred terror, in either version. The earlier reading of it, which is that these sexual ghosts have come to corrupt the innocent children that is a terrible, horrible story. But, the other version, that this woman, herself, is seeing and imagining these ghosts, is no less horrible because she too is involved with the children. And, what is happening to the children may, in fact, have even more terror in it. Imagine, for a moment, that Wilson is right and that this woman is not only deluded but also mad. Just think, for a moment, about a situation in which young children are entrusted to a mad governess, that, in itself is a more terrifying situation. You could think more horrors in that scenario than in the more traditional, biblical, pastoral reading that this is an allegory about the loss of innocence and that these ghosts represent a kind of sexual initiation.

We'll see these issues later in this course when we get to *The Yellow Wallpaper*. We're going to get the same issue of a woman's vision and we're going to have to determine whether this is clairvoyant, visionary, or mad. Those are the questions that, ultimately, there are no outside panel to adjudicate. Every reader has to, in some sense, make up his or her mind about those issues. There are other readings that have been published, too. Some of them are crazy but they're funny. One of them is that Mrs. Grose did it, the housekeeper. And they say, you know—Grose? She's called Mrs. Grose? There's the first clue right there. Then you've got this maniacal reading that says that everything that's being written about in the story, Mrs. Grose is behind. You know, she's somehow masterminding the entire series of events. That's not a very serious reading.

A very interesting alternative reading is "Why should we accept these two polarized readings that, one, the children are innocent and then corrupted by these evil ghosts or, the Freudian reading, the children are innocent and then put upon by the mad governess?" Are children innocent? Are we so sure of that? Whose belief is that? Would that have, perhaps, made more sense in mid-Victorian culture than it might today? What do we know about Freud and infantile sexuality? In other words, the terms of that story, really, they start to move once you start situating it within its own cultural moment. James may be toying with precisely some of the pieties, some of the fixed ideas of his own moment.

Having said that, I still want to return to the fun in the story, the conflict between the "straight" reading, that's what it's called now, and the Freudian reading. That raises the great critical question which, I think, we need to talk about—which I'm going to talk about. One, the straight reading: The ghosts are real. We trust the governess. We trust the text is what I'm saying, that's what the text tells us. She's the speaker. She's the narrator. She tells us, "I saw the ghosts. They were out there, I could see [them trying] to claim the souls of the children." It's a sacrificial story of evil. The other reading is the governess is delusional or mad. She invents the ghosts, not knowing it, but she's doing it. This is a different reading altogether. We are suspicious of her. It's about the status of vision. Does the governess see or does she invent and produce what she sees?

We have seen these issues in this course. "Benito Cereno" was about the same thing. What is Delano going to make of this strange ship, that he enters with these black people positioned in these strange positions, and this strange Spanish captain? We'll see that he is going to foist onto what he sees, all of his own ideas about blacks, which are they're like Newfoundland dogs, and the black women are like does. He cannot see that there has been a slave revolt here and a mutiny. He's not culturally able to process it that way. Well, what would a sheltered, repressed young woman in the Victorian Age see? What would the world look like to her? The issue is very much about what you see *in* what you see. It's interesting too, that this has been made into a film, several films, actually. One of the old classics is *The Innocents* with Deborah Carr and I think it shows the poverty of film versus the richness of language. That's because I teach literature.

You can keep the ambiguity in the written text. Language allows us to process it. Once you have to put it into visual language, you have to fish or cut bait. There's either going to be a ghost or there's not. You know, that's why I called it the *impoverishment* of film. It cannot deal with what people themselves conjecture and create. Of course, that's Henry James' territory. This is an aside—all of the beautiful films that are made of James' novels disappoint. *Merchant Ivory* is great as are a lot of the other people making these splendid films. They're beautiful period pieces, they're not James. James is about the fabric of thinking. He's about speculation. He's about conjecture. He's about the mental constructs, not about the beautiful late Victorian settings and furnishings and appointments of these houses, which, of course, many people go to now because we're in such a mood to see the grand finish of the 19th century. I think that Jane Austen has a revival in a similar way and you miss the point there too, frequently. In any event, ghosts are most pointedly what would be hard to get across this way.

The question that's raised here is, "Is what you see not only what you're culturally constructed to see but what you desire?" Because, that's the second shoe that drops with the Freudian reading, you're projecting this vision. Is the governess libidinally engaged here? Does she project onto Peter Quint her desire for the master, or onto Jessel her self-image? Or is it worse still? Let's continue these displacements and substitutions. Is she somehow co-opting the children into her own scenario? That is to say, that the children, Flora and Miles, are playing out a role as well for her that she can't see. All she says is, "I'm trying to save them. I'm trying to shield them from evil." But we've sensed that maybe she has encroachments on them in a different way. Maybe little Miles, the little boy, is a stand-in also for his uncle, the master, or for Peter Quint.

These terms, straight versus Freudian, are loaded. I've said, this is what's on your plate. You have to choose; and, what I want now to say is, it's an unfair choice. No one is going to choose the straight reading. There is nothing sexy about the straight reading. No pizzazz there at all. If you choose the straight reading, which is that, "Yes, the ghosts are real," then you are essentially a kind of bad reader. You've missed the point. You're gullible. You're naïve. You take what the governess says at her word. You are gross, like Mrs. Grose, and Mrs. Grose, in this story, cannot read and, literally, she can't read and she can't write. Freudian is seductive because it's suspicious. It's because you read the story and you say, "Ah ha! Wait a minute! I can see what's going on underneath the surface here." You read the governess, and then I take that word read and I bracket it. You [read] the governess, you interpret the governess, you decipher the governess.

When Freud came to America for the only time, and gave his lecture at Clarke, in Worcester, he joked, he said, "I've brought the plague with me." And I think he was right because what he brought was the era of suspicion that goes with psychoanalysis. Psychoanalysis says, every time you speak, you're revealing volumes about your libidinal life, about your desires that you don't know. You don't know it. I do. That's what I'm trained to read. That's what a psychoanalyst does. I take your language— whether you're paying me X hundred dollars an hour on a couch or whatever—and I tell you what it means. Just open your mouth. I'll hear the words and I will decode it for you. You know how the psychoanalytic tradition goes. Likewise, what about the jokes that you make? "Ah ha! A joke is a slip of the tongue. I know what's being expressed. Your dreams? Dreams, you say! Well, we know [what] that is, that's where all of the repressed gets reconfigured; and there, too, I've got lots of lights for you, I've got lots of skill."

So, this era of suspicion quite simply means that, what you say is only the surface. It's the manifest meaning, not the latent meaning. What really is being signified is what you can't say, what you don't even know but is there, nonetheless. It's what's underneath. Think of our own terms. The word "surface" is usually a kind of derogatory term; whereas, the word "depth" and "deep," what's underneath, we credit that with somehow being more genuine, being more authentic, being more serious. Layers, layers of depth that are underneath obvious surfaces, we are all taught to read that way, whether we're talking about reading novels and poems. Every time you read a text, you say, "Well, I know what the words say but what do they mean?" There's something else going on here. We privilege that. We say, "That's, what's exciting." But the same is true when you read the newspapers. The same is true when you listen to conversations. What did he really mean? What was the real point here? What is it that's being concealed? What's coming out? All of this is the plague. All of this is what Freud essentially brought. I mean, Freud didn't create this; ever since there's been human communication, this has existed.

I'm trying to say that this business of being suspicious of the surface, and going under to find out what's really concealed or hidden or behind, this is something that is an absolute meat and potatoes issue. We deal with it all the time. That's what criticism means. What do you think this course is except me standing up here and doing that with every text that we look at? I say, "Ah ha! You've just read the surface here. Now I'm going to tell you, I'm going to unpack this text, tell you all the things that are under it." It also means not to be duped by the surface, okay? But, what it also does is it rewrites it's translates, it takes that text and it turns it into something else, which is what I will call the meaning of the text. The story is about all of those issues. It's about not just the status of vision; but it's about how we read, how we decipher, how we make sense of things. And, as I say, this isn't just literature. This is how we deal with our friends and loved ones. It's the nature of communication.

This is James' field. That is what James is so great at. It's showing you what a minefield communication is, what complex operations go on when we speak to one another and think about what people are saying. The last point I want to make here, however, is that, if we do that to this story, if we take the governess' story—which is a pastoral story of trying to shield these children from evil—and we translate it into a story of her somehow hounding these children, of her being deluded, of her hallucinating, we are doing to her what she's doing to the children. We are twisting her the same way she's twisting them. We're trying to extort her secret, what she won't tell us, which is exactly what she's doing to the children. I want you to hear the power dynamic, the interpretation of that aggression.

Lecture Forty-Four
Turning the Screw of Interpretation

Scope: How can one get past the critical impasse of the two opposed readings of *The Turn of the Screw*? Are there ultimate guidelines for reading properly? Will the text "tell" us its true meaning? These questions seem to be about issues of literary and critical procedure, but they lead us to other, still deeper issues of how we negotiate our world, how we see and assess our experience. James's story is a haunting one, not because it deals with ghosts, but because it displays with awesome purity the moral stakes of interpretation. Once again, we realize how social, ethical, and "relational" interpretation is; it does not take place in a vacuum but involves our judgment of others, indeed our treatment of others. James will show us that interpretation can be lethal.

Objectives—Upon completion of this lecture, you should be able to:

1. Summarize the role of "subjective complications" in *The Turn of the Screw*;

2. Explain the role that love plays in the James novel; and

3. Describe, according to James, the nature of human vision.

Outline

I. We have become familiar with the notion of reading as detective work. All texts require deciphering, and many texts centralize that activity and make us grasp its enormity.

   A. Getting to the hidden truth is not a benign operation. The prodigious example of Roger Chillingworth "working" on Arthur Dimmesdale in *The Scarlet Letter* speaks volumes to us about the ethical transgressions involved in such "sleuthing."

   B. Hawthorne's playful manner—his mixing of registers and his profusion of possible meanings for the "A"—suggests that single meanings and right answers may not be what literature and life offer.

1. We need to reconsider James's notion of authority here. The master is absent from the scene in *The Turn of the Screw*. All we can have are partial versions of events.
2. More urgently, how do we go about interpreting children, who cannot interpret themselves? *Infans* means "speechless." What does it mean to get at their infantile secrets? Could there be an analogy here with the unconscious, which is inherently resistant to language?

C. James claimed that "subjective complications" were ruled out in his story. Is this possible? What about criticism itself? Is it free of subjective complications? Should it be?

II. James is showing us, on every page of this text, that all thinking and all utterance is "governed" by subjective complications.

A. Stories do not "speak." They must be spoken. The elaborate frame of *The Turn of the Screw* underscores the contingency of narrative, its status as personal utterance.
1. The narrator learns of the story from Douglas, who wants to share it with friends.
2. Douglas got it from an older woman, his sister's governess (with whom he seems to have been in love), who died and left him the story. The parallels between Miles and the governess of the narrative are unmistakable.
3. This story has an ominous feel to it of a deadly form of chain letters; in dying, someone bequeaths this horrible account of children and ghosts, and it moves from speaker to speaker. We recall Poe's interest in voices beyond the grave. We also might consider the possibility that a story can kill—you could die of fright. As we will see, that notion will return within the story itself.

B. James repeatedly shows us the collusion between vision and speech that characterizes human utterance (at least in this story).
1. Douglas seems to speak of what he imagines, not what he sees.
2. We also learn that love is inseparable from this narrative: the beloved governess told Douglas the original story; the story itself is about love as a filter of language.

3.   In a number of key scenes within the story, we see a kind of slippage and fluidity that again display the hold of fantasy, of all language being scripted by inner drives.

III. As James's story delves ever deeper into the nature of vision, of what goes into what we see, a very central issue comes into focus: the significance of the unseen, the reign of the invisible.

    A. We hear over and over about the governess's "inner certainty," her powerful intuition about what is happening, versus a visual account of events.

        1. The governess even says that the ghosts are not there if she doesn't see them, and we sense a kind of umbilical cord between them and her.

        2. The governess's apprehension of the ghosts is also motivated by an odd desire to see them, to have them appear. And each time they do appear, we have a clear notation of "collusion" with the governess herself.

        3. The plot thickens, however, when the governess moves from her own "vision" of the ghosts to her indictment of the children for denying that they also see the ghosts. What do they see? What do we see?

        4. Quickly enough, the governess moves from conjecture to certainty, even though the "visual evidence" is open-ended. This is an intriguing issue in that we are accustomed to crediting all intuitions as prophetic and truthful *when they appear in literature.* In real life we are much less credulous, more dependent on empirical data. One thinks also of the Emersonian doctrine of self-reliance and spontaneity, which celebrates "inner certainty" at the expense of everything else. Is this a formula for disaster in the public world of interpersonal relations?

    B. In a central image, the governess describes her role as a *shield.* We need to mull over this image.

        1. The governess wants, laudably, to protect the children from ghosts.

        2. It follows that she therefore needs to know everything about the ghosts, and she is worried if she doesn't see them. Is this an invitation?

3. Regarding the shield, we cannot know whether the children see the ghosts, but we do know they see the governess. In short, the shield itself is visible.
4. What kind of a shield is this? Consider the language by which the governess describes her activities with the children. We must realize that she is a player in these events, not simply an objective narrator.
5. The "activist" nature of the governess is most fully on show in two key scenes with Flora and Miles—when the governess points out the presence of Jessel, but Flora looks at the governess, and in the governess's bedside interview with Miles.

C. At what point must all our guessing games stop? Do issues of epistemology—which remain undecided—yield to issues of ethics which we simply must decide? Consider, in this regard, a key scene in which the governess watches the children at play and then describes to Mrs. Grose what she really sees. What do you see?

D. We finally attend to the central issue here: Is there a ghost in this text?
1. Watch the actual behavior of the governess. Who does things like this?
2. How would you imagine a ghost in action? We need to take a careful look at the harrowing final pages of this narrative, in which the governess fatefully seeks to get at Miles's secret. Here is where all the Jamesian issues—getting at the truth, projecting one's own feelings, creating ghosts—are on show, and there is little in literature that matches this for beauty and horror. Poe would have been proud.

Essential Readings:

James, *The Turn of the Screw* (Norton Critical Edition, 1966).

Recommended Readings:

Essays by Heilman and Spilka in the Norton edition of *The Turn of the Screw* (1966).

James, *The Ambassadors* (Norton Critical Edition, 1964).

———, "The Aspern Papers."

———, "The Beast in the Jungle."

Wilson, "The Ambiguity of Henry James."

Topics for Further Consideration:

1. Identify some of the technical innovations that Henry James brings to the art of the novel.

2. Summarize the questions that *The Turn of the Screw* raises about both "reader suspicion" and the "ethics" of reading.

Lecture Forty-Four—Transcript
Turning the Screw of Interpretation

This is Lecture Forty-Four, and it's the second lecture on James' story, "The Turn of the Screw." After having sort of established the two polar readings—of the straight and the Freudian reading—I want to delve still further into the issue of interpretation. As we've seen, that's the terrain that James really works in; and, he shows us what a rich and deep and conflicted terrain it is. He shows us how social it is. What happens if we take interpretation and rephrase it as a search for truth? I do that devil's advocate. If you say, "search for truth," it sounds like we're talking about philosophy. It sounds like we're talking about a kind of objective pursuit. If you think of the search for truth in interpersonal terms as the search for someone else's truth, then we're back to interpretation, but we now realize that that quest, which as I say, seems admirable, laudable, clean, that quest can be very dirty and can be very damaging as well. It can involve a kind of power play or a kind of aggression that we exercise on others. I want to try to make good on those claims.

We've seen already in this course a lot of evidence that the idea of getting to people's secrets can be thought of as exploitative and invasive. One of the beautiful texts we have on that is *The Scarlet Letter*. Chillingworth is one of our classic characters, which sort of worms his way into someone else to try to get at their concealed secret. As I've indicated, that is the classic posture of the novelist. That's what writers do. They produce characters and they have that kind of curiosity to show what's inside of them. What happens if there is no single secret inside of a character or inside of a person? In this story, the master has vacated the premises. He's left the governess to manage everything. There is no authority in place. I want you to think about what I'm saying here. There is no authority. There is no omniscient view. There is no certainty about what the right answer is in this story. You can't get outside of the story to see it as God might and to say, "Well who's telling the truth and who's lying?"

This text, like the "A" in Hawthorne's story, is susceptible to many different meanings, many different interpretations. Perhaps we have to respect its mystery. Perhaps children are not going to own up. Our term "infans" which is where we get infants from, and it means speechless. We know that babies can't speak. Maybe young children can't tell us all the things that are really in them. The text may not say what its core is, or it may not have a single core. This is analogous to the unconscious, which is resistant as well, if it exists, to language, or to somehow being corralled into plain light.

Another question is, and here I come back to that notion of let's think of interpretation as the search for the truth. The search for the truth, in all those works can be capitalized, that sounds like a kind of clean, but objective enterprise. That's of course what philosophy as a discipline prides itself on. Philosophy is, by definition, the disinterested pursuit of truth. All of the terms that would complicate that, like bias, subjectivity, emotion, libido, all of those are just the things that the philosopher and the clear-thinking person tries to rule out of his or her procedures. Literature indulges in those things. It takes them to its bosom in some sense, because it, in fact, knows that all human utterance is always surrounded by affect, it's surrounded by bias, and by subjectivity. This text tells us that there can't be statements that have a bottom line to them, that they're always somehow conditioned by feeling. There are lots of instances in it.

For example, I started the other lecture on this text by reading you that critique. That review that was published at the same time the text appeared. Could you hear the heat and rage of that man? He kept saying, "This is the most evil story ever written." That wasn't a philosophical remark. He was showing that this story angered him. That's the way we respond to most things: We like them; we hate them. Whatever. The notion of there being some sort of cool, lucid, objective medium out there that we are working in when we express our judgments, that may be a fiction as well, a fiction that some disciplines like to maintain. The sciences in general like to maintain that and that maybe others that are suspicious of.

James situates this story in such a way as to make us suspicious of that. The story is packaged in an elaborate frame. It's told by this man Douglas, who comes to share it with friends and tells it to the narrator. Douglas himself has heard this story from someone else. He says he got it from the woman who was the governess. Yet this woman is dead now and has left him, at her death, this story. She was governess, he says, of his own sister. We're led to think that maybe Douglas is Miles—even though Miles dies in the story— and that maybe the sister was Flora. We get a sense that there's a whole sort of chain of people here. They have to go back and search for the actual written document. It comes in and then it is read to people around a fireplace. As I said, it's like a lethal chain letter. It's as if this story is connected to dying, that the governess has died and has left the story and now it comes to this group of people.

Moreover, it raises the question, "Could a story be lethal?" Could listening to a story about ghosts somehow kill you? There is an expression to die of fright. Could that happen? There will be a death at the end of this story. You might well think that it comes from that. There's also as I say a key sort of collusion between language and feeling, language and vision as well. James emphasizes that. When Douglas is speaking, James writes, "He took no notice of her. He looked at me, but as if instead of me he saw what he spoke of." It's like somehow what you see, what you say, they're all sort of brought in together. They're not easily cleared out from each other. Likewise we're told that love is going to be part of this story. "She was in love," that's the governess they're referring to, that is, "she had been came out." She couldn't tell her story without its coming out, that your feelings are somehow going to also surface in anything that you say. That again brings me back to this point that our desire for objectivity or for disinterested narrative may be a naïve desire. In fact, it's a desire rather than a fact. Literature centralizes affect, bias, interest, unlike philosophy, unlike the sciences.

Now where do these things get play in this particular story? There are a number of references, for example, parts of the story where we see something of the fluidity, where things sort of change their position, where they're given it first as fact and then they come to us as fiction. For example, at one point the governess is teaching a lesson of geography to Flora and the geography lesson involves the Sea of Azov. It's just a reference to the lesson. The next paragraph goes like this. "Suddenly, amid these elements, I became aware that on the other side of the Sea of Azov we had an interested spectator." That's going to be the figure of Jessel; but now, the lake that's at the property has become the Sea of Azov. That's the kind of fluidity of this piece. Things just sort of become one another.

One of the most intriguing, threatening versions of that is at the end of the story when the governess now has the boy Miles sort of alone to herself and they are having dinner together. This is how James writes it. "We continued silent while the maid was with us, as silent it whimsically occurred to me as some young couple who on their wedding journey at the end feel shy in the presence of the waiter. He turned around only when the waiter had left. Well, so we're alone." Did you hear it? There's a maid there, then there's a reference. The metaphor or the simile is the wedding couple shy in the presence of the waiter, and in the next sentence says there's no maid anymore. It's a waiter. There's a sex change of this figure. We know sort of we've glided into another realm here. We've glided into the realm of feeling, into the realm of analogy, of metaphor. Of course the reference to a young couple on their wedding journey is not entirely innocent either in the relationship between this governess and this young boy.

The text is about the power of feeling as it somehow shapes vision, and as all of that is coated into language. This text is effectively about the centrality of the unseen, of the things that somehow govern, as it were, to take a term from this text, and coerce the way we speak. For example, as the governess becomes aware of these ghosts, she's working predominantly by a kind of sense of feeling, that she *feels* them before she sees them. She even says at one point that, "If I didn't feel them, they weren't there." She has a kind of privileged relationship to the ghosts. I want to read you the first vision of Peter Quint, when she first sees him. She's taking a little stroll on the grounds of the property and she's thinking that, "It would be as charming as a charming story suddenly to meet someone. Someone would appear there at the turn of a path and would stand before me and smile and approve." You know that she's thinking about the master, the uncle. I read this as a lead-in to what will happen. Sure enough, she will meet someone. "She has a sense that her imagination had in a flash turned real. He did stand there." That's the reference to the tower where she first sees Peter Quint. It's not who she's expecting. What I want to suggest to you is, that we're supposed to I think feel that she has produced him in some sense, that she is hoping that maybe some prince charming would appear, and lo and behold here's a vision of a man standing in the tower.

There's a sense of a self-fulfilling prophecy in this story. She says she wants to shield the children. She says:

> I had an absolute certainty that I should see again what I had already seen, but something within me said that by offering myself bravely as the sole subject of such experience, by accepting, by inviting, by surmounting it all, I should serve as an expiatory victim and guard the tranquility of the rest of the household.

She will take the place of the children. But can you see too that that is a kind of invitation? "I would accept, I would invite, I would surmount." She is asking for this kind of encounter, intercourse of sorts, with the ghost. She says, "That way I can protect the children. They'll just sort of batten to me instead." The vision of Jessel the first time is comparably I think suggestive here. That's right after that passage about the Sea of Azov. There's an interested spectator. You get this language of inner certainty, of intuition. "I began to take in with certitude, and yet without direct vision, the presence a good way off of a third person." It's a strong feeling. Of course, we have those feelings. We sense that there's somebody behind us, or somebody standing on the side when we're not looking. James stresses that she's not looking. James doesn't say she sees somebody else. She feels that somebody else is there.

I want again to suggest that maybe this is a form of production, because later, that whole segment of the story ends up with the description of the little girl, that she is looking at, putting the piece of wood into the other piece of wood. After she looks at that, she says, "I felt I was ready for more. Then I again shifted my face, my eyes. I faced what I had to face." End segment. That's where it stops. The next segment starts with her talking to Mrs. Grose and explaining what she saw. The reader never sees her seeing anything. She says, "I saw it. I saw with my own eyes." And she says, "I saw that she was perfectly aware," Flora. "I saw that Flora knew." What the text has shown us is that Flora's back is to this figure. Flora's busy working with the pieces of wood there. That's not what the governess says: "I saw she was perfectly aware."

There are depths in this. "The more I go over it, the more I see in it, the more I see in it, and the more I fear. I don't know what I don't see, what I don't fear." She says at one point, "What I'm worried about is of not seeing her. As long as I see them I'm sort of controlling them. Maybe they're going to somehow get beyond even my visual field." Well this builds up to an obvious kind of certainty and conviction on the part of the governess. She now knows. Every time she watches the children, she knows what's really going on. It's not what you or I would see. She, because of this new kind of privileged vision that she's got she can see what's going on. So she tells Mrs. Grose, "I simply make it out." The four, depend on it, perpetually meet the two children and the two ghosts.

> If on either of these last nights you had been with either child, you'd have clearly understood. The more I've watched and waited the more I've felt that if there were nothing else to make it sure it would be made so by the systematic silence of each.

Watch what we're into here. The less they say the more certain I am they're concealing it. And, you know, it's really dicey when you start saying, "Silence means." Silence is silence. It's not language. She knows what it means.

> "Never, by a slip of the tongue, have they so much as alluded to either of their old friends, any more than Miles has alluded to his

expulsion. [Because he's been kicked out of school. He hasn't said anything about that either.] Oh, yes, we may sit here and look at them, and they may show off to us there to their fill; but even while they pretend to be lost in their fairytale they're steeped in their vision of the dead restored. He's not reading to her," [What you see now is Miles reading to Flora] I declared; "they're talking of them—[Now we are just reading this text; we have no access, we're just reading what she's saying] they're talking horrors! I go on, I know, as if I were crazy; it's a wonder I'm not. What I've seen would have made you so; but it's only made me more lucid, made me get hold of still other things."

This book begins to build more and more on her intuition, her inner conviction, and her certainty that what she's seeing behind the façade of their apparent behavior is actually their exchanges with the ghosts. Mind you, Mrs. Grose can't see any of that. She can't see. No one in the text sees the ghosts except for the governess.

I want to make a couple of observations here. When you read a work of literature, and a character says, "I had a strong intuition that," or, "It suddenly became clear to me that," we underline it. We write it out in the margin and we say, "Yes, this will come true. This is an omen." This is what we call foreshadowing. Does that work like that in life? Do your foreshadowings come true? Do your intuitions come true? In general, in life we are much more, much more demanding. We do not privilege foreshadowings, intuition and private personal conviction in the same way. If you tell me, "I really do have a feeling that the world is going to end tomorrow," I may say, "Well that may be your sense of it, but it doesn't particularly have any, you know, relevance for me." In general, we require empirical data before we're willing to validate things in our own public worlds, in our worlds beyond art, whereas in art, these things have a kind of aura to them.

When a character says, "Intuition, ah, yes, intuition," that's truth. It comes out of the tradition we're talking about. That's what Emerson said. "Trust yourself. Self reliance." It's in your intuitions that you have access to the truth. Now what I want to tell you is that in a public world, in a world of interpersonal relationships, this can be a formula for disaster. People can have intuitions and visions, and often we end up locking them up because of it, because nobody else has the same ones. They end up acting on their intuitions and visions. We know what the damage could be in cases like that. This text I think shows an awareness of those matters. He wants to measure the social inter-relational possibilities of these issues. What happens when someone has a clear conviction and is working with others?

Already we know that she's convinced the children see the ghosts as well. She says she wants to protect the children from the ghosts. She wants to be, in her own words, a shield. She wants to shield them from the ghosts. They of course never acknowledge that there are any ghosts. We will never know, when we read this text, whether or not the children see the ghosts. We do know that they see the shield. They see her. She is their constant companion. She describes herself as their jailer. After all, she knows, as far as she's concerned, that they are having commerce with ghosts. Therefore she's onto them. She's watching them like a hawk. Try for a moment to imagine this story from outside of her perspective.

Try to imagine it from the perspective of one of the children, or from Mrs. Grose, or anybody else, what this woman's behavior must be like. We see her grabbing these children. She says, "It's amazing they didn't scream out against me. I press them so close all the time." I want you, in other words, to think of her not just as a narrator who's the conduit for the story and the authority of the story, but also as a player, as a character, as someone who is having an impact on events and not just a kind of window to the truth. I want to show you how the story pushes you in that direction. For example, when she has her showdown with Flora, she finally lets it out to Flora. She says, "Where, my pet, is Miss Jessel?" That's where she breaks the rules. She finally sounds the name of the dead woman. It really produces quite a reaction in the girl.

"The quick, smitten glare with which the child's face now received it fairly likened my breach of the silence to the smash of a pane of glass." It's like she's broken glass. At this point the governess is seeing Jessel. Mrs. Grose is there. She's not seeing anything. Flora is there. Instead of Flora looking over there at Jessel, that's not what happens.

> To see her, without a convulsion of her small pink face, not even feign to glance in the direction of the prodigy I announced, (Jessel) but only, instead of that, turn at me an expression of hard, still gravity, an expression absolutely new and unprecedented and that appeared to read and accuse and judge me—this was a stroke that somehow converted the little girl herself into a figure portentous.

She's not looking at anybody else; she's looking at the governess. The governess has said, "There's Jessel." Now again, imagine to yourself, "There's the woman who's dead, who was your governess," and the child looks at her, she looks at her with this very strange face, and it's a face later we're told of an old, old woman. Then Mrs. Grose comes in and says, "I see nothing, Miss. What are you talking about?" But I want you to think about why James has put it this way. The child looks instead at the governess. This story is about ghosts all right. It's about tracking them. They may not be where they're pointed, they may be in other places altogether.

Likewise the interest in Miles is equally damaging it seems to me; that she is tracking Miles, she wants him to finally confess. He keeps saying, "I think I need to get away," to get away really from his governess. She keeps throwing herself.

> I threw myself upon him and in the tenderness of my pity I embraced him. "Dear little Miles, dear little Miles—!" My face was close to his, and he let me kiss him, simply taking it with indulgent good humor. 'Well, old, lady,' he says. 'Is there nothing—nothing at all that you want to tell me?' … [And finally he says] ever so gently, "To let me alone."

And then she hugs him again. She feels a quaver of consenting consciousness, "That made me drop on my knees beside the bed." Try to visualize this; that this woman, much older, and a small boy sort of embracing him at the bed, and sees once more the chance of possessing him. "Dear little Miles. Dear little Miles, if you knew how I want to help you. I want you to help me to save you." And at that point, he gives a high loud shriek, and the lights go out, the candle goes out. He says, "It's I who blew it, dear." It's like blowing a fuse. This is getting too hot. He knows he is under threat here. Well the story ends with the governess essentially closing in on Miles.

I want you to pay attention to this. I'm going to read you through some of these last pages. This whole text has been about, as I said, what we see and what we see. The governess looks at these children and she sees commerce with the ghosts, with evil. She tells Mrs. Grose that you look at them; you think they're just playing, but that's not true. It's just

> To gaze into the depths of blue of the child's eyes and pronounce their loveliness a trick of premature cunning was to be guilty of a cynicism. … But nonetheless, I couldn't endure it from merely wanting to, but I had to repeat to Mrs. Grose—as I did there, over and over, that with our small friends' voices in the air, their pressure on one's heart, and their fragrant faces against one's cheek, we only saw their incapacity and their beauty. It was a

pity that, somehow, to settle this once and for all, I had to re-enumerate the signs of subtly that had made a miracle my self-possession. It's a pity to be obliged to reinvestigate the certitude of the moment itself.

In other words, she's going to say, "I want you to realize that they look deceptive here. They look innocent. They look like they're playing, but it's not the case. It's not the case." Now again, I've been talking about inner vision. What do you make of children playing? You say, "Well, it's a fraud. It's a deception," is what she makes of it. That language, by the way, it's repeated several times. "It's a pity. It's a pity." I think it's Shakespearean and I think it's the reference to Othello's lines of pity over Iago, the pity of it. That is a play also about misperception, about thinking that someone who is in fact innocent, you think she's guilty and you end up killing her, which is pretty much what this text is about.

The last part of this text is the final rendezvous between the governess and the little boy. It starts after the passage I read to you about the maid who then becomes transformed into the waiter. Then the two of them are alone together. It really is quite an astonishing sequence. She keeps telling him, "Don't you remember how when I came and sat on your bed on the night of the storm there was nothing in the world I wouldn't do for you?" And the text says he's getting more and more visibly nervous. She senses that he's getting ready to yield. She talks about an implication of surrender so faint.

This continues. We watch this and we watch the language of it as she feels like she's just merely reaching port. Then she says this too gives her pause.

> To do it any way was an act of violence, (to get to his secret, to make him speak) for what did it consist of but the obtrusion of the idea of grossness and guilt on a small helpless creature who had been for me a revelation of the possibilities of beautiful intercourse?

That's the term that James used. I think he projects on to it the sense that there's closeness here, that there's a kind of involvement, investment on the part of the governess with this boy. Well it closes in. She realizes that she must make him speak. She must make him admit that he has seen the ghosts—or in this case as well that he's told lies—and he must own up to it. He's stolen a letter. He must own up to that. The language of it is very vampirish, "The face that was close to mine was as white as the face against the glass, and out of it presently came a sound, not low nor weak, but as if from much further away that I drank like a weft of fragrance." I feel sucked in here. By the way, the face on the glass that she alludes to is the face of Peter Quint.

In this scene, you've got to see what's happening. She is trying to get this boy to finally confess his evil. At the same time the ghost is appearing. The ghost is at the window. He admits that he stole the letter.

> "I took it." At this, with a moan of joy, I enfolded him, I drew him close; and while I held him to my breast, where I could feel in the sudden fever of his little body the tremendous pulse of his little heart, I kept my eyes on the thing at the window and saw it move and shift its posture. I have likened it to a sentinel, but its slow wheel, for the moment, was rather the prowl of battled beast.

She knows that there's not much time here to get Miles to own up. She wants him to confess. He must confess. All he can say is, "I said things."

> "What were those things?" (After continuing to press him) My sternness was all for his judge, his executioner; and yet it made him avert himself again, and that movement made me, with a single bound and irrepressible cry, spring straight upon him. (And she grabs the boy. She enfolds him because there she sees at the window again the ghost.) ... "No more, no more, no more!" I shrieked to my visitant as I tried to press him against me. (Miles has heard from Flora already about that this ghost Jessel has been talked about.)

> "Is she here?" Miles panted as he caught with his sealed eyes the direction of my words. Then as his strange "she" staggered me, and with a gasp, I echoed it, "Miss Jessel, Miss Jessel!" he with a sudden fury gave me back. I seized, stupefied, his supposition—some sequel to what we had done to Flora, but this made me only want to show him that it was better still than that. (Like, Jessel was the ghost for your sister. We've got the real ghost for you. This is going to be Quint.) "It's not Miss Jessel! But it's at the window—straight before us. It's there—the coward horror, there for the last time!" At this, after a second in which his head made the movement of baffled dog's on a scent and then gave a frantic little shake for air and light, he was at me in a white rage, bewildered, glaring vainly over the place and missing wholly, though it now, to my sense, filled the room like the taste of poison, the wide, overwhelming presence. "It's he," the boy says.

I was so determined to have all my proof that I flashed into ice to challenge him. "Whom do you mean by 'he'?"

"Peter Quint—you devil!" His face gave again, round the room, its convulsed supplication. "Where?"

They are still in my ears, his supreme surrender of the name and his tribute to my devotion. "What does he matter now, my own?— what will he ever matter? I have you." I launched at the beast, "but he has lost you forever!" Then, for the demonstration of my work, "There, there!" I said to Miles. But he had already jerked round, stared, glared again, and seen but the quiet day. With the stroke of the loss I was so proud of he uttered the cry of a creature hurled over an abyss, and the grasp with which I recovered him might have been that of catching him in his fall. I caught him, yes, I held him—it may be imagined with what a passion; but at the end of a minute I began to feel what it truly was that I held. We were alone with the quiet day, and his little heart, dispossessed, had stopped.

That's the story that has been read straight-wise as saving this child from evil. Now I read you all of that last sequence for you to see, insofar as you can see words, this woman encroaching further and further and further on this little boy, who senses the encroachment. Her project, her sincere project, is to shield this child from sexual knowledge. What I have tried to convey in reading it to you is what I think James is showing us, [that] she is, in some sense, the sexual threat she's trying to shield him from. He does die. He dies in an embrace from this older woman who is telling him that this ghost is at the window that he still can't see. That is how interpretation becomes social, inter-relational. She is motivated by goodwill. She kills him nonetheless.

Lecture Forty-Five
Stephen Crane and the Literature of War

Scope: Stephen Crane's meteoric career and brief life constitute a very pure and luminous moment in American literature. This young man, who died at the age of 28, bore witness to a radically changing world in the 1890s. He witnessed the epic changes that took place in the Civil War, and indeed the gruesome spate of wars that mark our 20th century, and he did so in language that remains as fresh, startling, and vivid today as it was a century ago. Crane's *Red Badge of Courage* is not only the best account we have of the Civil War (written by someone who had never seen a war before), but it also introduces a new style in our literary tradition: images of unheard-of violence and distortion, cacophony of noise, and a rendition of events that brings the objectivity of journalism and the immediacy of experience into narrative discourse. Crane points directly to Hemingway's efforts to render the moment, to tell American readers about conflicts all over the globe as well as right here at home. But he prefigures the war literature of others as well, including Mailer, Heller, and the literature of Vietnam. But Crane is more than *The Red Badge*; he is also the author of some of the finest short stories we possess: the account of four shipwrecked men surviving in an "open boat" (based on Crane's real experience), the report of a fatal altercation in a Nebraska town in arctic winter, and the astonishing portrayal of an idyllic small-town in America going terribly sour. Here, as everywhere, Crane emerges as the implacably lucid observer of violence, of the human subject under stress, of the war that is life.

Crane is the great youth of our literature; he tore through his life and burned out, like a comet going across the sky, dying of tuberculosis at the age of 28. His integrity, his fearlessness, his lucidity, his restless desire to see and report on the violence that subtends life—all this puts him in the company of other visionary writers who died young, including Georg Büchner and Arthur Rimbaud. Starting his career with exposés of brutal life in the Bowery, Crane moves prophetically to his great subject of war in *The Red Badge of Courage*, the book that took the world by storm and made the 23-year-old writer a celebrity overnight. Crane's rendition of the Civil War is unprecedented in its immediacy, and his account of the true proportions of war lays forever to rest any lingering views of battle as noble, grand, or even coherent. With this text we witness the birth of a new kind of American writing: the unflinching, quasi-journalistic report of violent conflicts, rendering both the individual subject and the harsh setting in ways never before attempted.

Objectives—Upon completion of this lecture, you should be able to:

1. Summarize in what ways Crane is and is not a naturalist;

2. Give examples of why *The Red Badge of Courage* was considered by many critics to have been a clear break with the literature of Europe; and

3. Explain, according to Crane, the relationship between fiction and journalism.

Outline

I. A new phase in American literature begins with *The Red Badge of Courage*. Contemporary critics considered it a break with the European past. Stephen Crane's "freshness" is to be understood as part of his youthful genius, as if he came fully into his powers without the need for education or training.

  A. It is instructive to compare his career to that of the equally precocious German playwright Georg Büchner, who had a comparably clinical view of human emotions under great stress and who left us the single greatest play about the French Revolution (a parallel text, of sort, to *The Red Badge*), *Danton's Death*.

  B. Crane's career was tragically brief, but the curve in it is suggestive: from home to world, from privilege to responsibility.

   1. Crane was born in 1871 in Newark, New Jersey, the son of a Methodist minister, in a very large family.

   2. Interested in athletics more than academics, Crane was an erratic, "sometime" student at both Lafayette College and Syracuse University, but he spent most of his time in New York, studying the life in saloons and flophouses in the Bowery. From this experience, he wrote his first major text,

Maggie: A Girl of the Streets, a brutal "naturalist" account of prostitution and sordidness in the modern urban setting. Crane published this piece at his own expense.

3. Crane established contact with the leaders of American Realism, Hamlin Garland and William Dean Howells. In 1895, *The Red Badge of Courage* was published, and it was a sensation, especially in England. It made Crane famous overnight.

4. Crane continued to defend the victims of urban culture against the authorities. On December 31, 1896, he departed on the steamship *Commodore* to deliver arms to Cuban rebels, but the ship sank, and Crane left his record of surviving at sea in his masterful story, "The Open Boat."

5. Crane lived with Cora Taylor, an older woman who was a war correspondent. Crane covered the Greco-Turkish War in 1897 as a war correspondent, then moved to England with Cora, covered the Spanish-American War, traveled to Cuba and to Puerto Rico, and came under fire at Gauntanamo and San Juan Hill. He was exhausted and ill.

6. Crane returned to England in 1899, enjoyed a circle of distinguished British writers as friends, and continued to publish war stories and children's stories. Then he suffered his first tuberculosis attack. Crane traveled by litter in 1900 to a sanitarium in the Black Forest, where he died the same year.

C. Many consider Crane a naturalist, though he did not hold to the tenets of determinism. William Dean Howells's comment that Crane "had sprung into literature fully armed" speaks volumes about Crane's precociousness and also his subject matter.

1. The two decades of world peace following the Franco-Prussian War in 1871 come to a close in the 1890s, a time of constant hostilities. Crane seemed magnetically drawn to these far-flung sites of conflict and carnage. In this way, he anticipated writers such as Hemingway and Malraux, great adventurer-journalists who felt compelled to give testimony. He also anticipates our century of war-related horrors.

2. Crane's education in "war" began in New York. His critical experiences were in the Bowery, and he saw, in the lives of laborers and prostitutes, the principles of violence and conflict that are common to the modern city and the modern war.

Crane carries out the naturalist mission here, in depicting the brutal industrial machinery that grinds up human lives.

3. Crane's own upbringing, in a good family with station and means, suggests that his early experiences were perhaps a form of "slumming." Yet there is nothing condescending or sensationalist in his accounts of "the other side," and his great work invariably sets out to dismantle pretension, to stab through inflated rhetoric, to expose hyperbole. He turns out to be deeply "countercultural."

II. *The Red Badge of Courage* is Crane's most famous contribution to American literature, and it constitutes our premier literary account of the Civil War, seen from the battlefield itself.

A. The book was a sensation, an immediate bestseller, especially in England, and Crane became a celebrity overnight.

1. Critics felt that this was the first truly indigenous work of American literature, that earlier 19th-century writers had been responding in some fashion to Europe, whereas Crane was working new ground.

2. Crane is said to have written his book in 10 feverish nights. Astonishingly enough, this 23-year-old writer described the war without ever having seen a battle. He later claimed that his knowledge of conflict came from his background in athletics, and it gave him great pleasure that war veterans assumed him to have "been there." Once he did actually encounter war, he was especially pleased to have "gotten it right" beforehand.

3. Getting it right meant, for Crane, to report on the actual experience, rather than repeating the rhetoric. It is instructive to see how national leaders at the time described the Spanish-American War, when looking at Crane's version of the Civil War. Political rhetoric of the day was naïve and jingoistic.

B. Crane's sole creed was to be faithful to what he *saw*. He would appear to have gone too far with *Maggie*, but *The Red Badge* was a perfect hit. Here was a war story that needed telling.

1. Crane's protagonist, Henry Fleming, senses that the age of epic warfare is already over.

2. Yet Henry is a young romantic, hungering for glamour and glory, expecting grand events, wanting to believe in heroism.

3. Crane deflates these expectations over and over. Henry's mother initially sounds this cautionary note, and periodically throughout his experience, Henry himself, by the end of the novel, sees clearly this flaw in his vision, this need to idealize and romanticize war.
4. Crane's true subject is not so much war itself as crisis, a set of violent circumstances in which a human being is placed. Crane was the lucid observer of what is virtually a laboratory procedure. We come to realize that human behavior is fundamentally a question mark.
5. Hence, Henry Fleming does not *know* how he will react to battle. His own future behavior is a riddle, and he is obsessed to find out the answer; this is the scientific realm of the text.
6. Crane is perhaps best defined as an impressionist, not a naturalist.

Lecture Forty-Five—Transcript
Stephen Crane and the Literature of War

This is Lecture Forty-Five, and it's the first of three lectures on Stephen Crane. I'll spend the first two lectures talking about the book that everybody knows of Crane's, which is *The Red Badge of Courage*, and then a final lecture as well on some of Crane's really quite astounding short stories.

The Red Badge of Courage really marks a new phase of American literature. It's published in the mid 1890s; and, I think it's still regarded as one of our great texts about war. It has a kind of immediacy on the one hand, and a kind of journalistic brilliance on the other hand, that point to figures like Hemmingway. I think, in fact, Hemmingway's almost incomprehensible without thinking of Crane as his precursor. Crane wrote *The Red Badge of Courage*. He'd never been to war. He was born in 1871. He didn't know anything about war firsthand, experientially. It's a kind of astounding text from that point of view as well.

Crane is a figure who really has a kind of remarkable career, partly for its brevity. He dies at the ripe age of twenty-eight. He's like a comet, a meteor. He burns out. He lives too hard. He reminds me a great deal of some European figures, like Gerhard Büchner in Germany, who only lived to be 29 and also has a kind of incredible intensity in his work and the same kind of scientific regard for things, a way of looking at critical, violent situations with the kind of anatomy look of a scientist about how to see what kinds of principles are at work here. He, [Crane] however, combines the kind of Büchner scientific gaze with the kind of visionary imagination that one finds in another child writer, Rimbaud, the great French visionary poet, whose greatest poems were written really before he was 20 years old.

In this lecture, I want to try to frame the Crane career a bit and close with some initial comments on *The Red Badge of Courage*; and, in the next lecture [we will] look more carefully at *The Red Badge of Courage*. This book changes the way people think about war. As I said, it marks a new phase in American literature. It was understood that way then. This isn't just the result of modern criticism. Critics, contemporaries, felt that this was absolutely new material, a new way of seeing things. It was felt that Crane breaks with the European models that he had been exposed to.

Let me talk about the brief phase of his career—insofar as he had one. He was born in New Jersey, in Newark, in 1871, from a well-to-do family. He was the child of a Methodist minister, a large family with lots of children. As a young boy, he was a very good athlete—interested in athletics—although he was small in stature. He was a middling student, went to several schools, and was a special student at Syracuse University. The family, as I say, was prominent. Syracuse University had been co-founded by his mother's uncle. Most of the time, rather than being in school, he's in New York "checking things out." He is spending time looking at speakeasies, at saloons, flophouses, the bowery, slums. He has this insatiable curiosity about the way the underclass lives; a kind of lifestyle, a kind of rhythm of life, a kind of routine violence and excitement that is quite different from what he saw in his own middle-class environment.

As a very young person, he writes the draft—even then as a student—of his first novel, *Maggie*, which he published in 1893 at his own expense. It was complete flop. Nobody wanted to read Maggie. It's a very, straight-on account of life in the bowery. It's a story of the slums. It did allow him to make the acquaintance of the leaders of American realism, in particular Hamlin Garland and William Dean Howell. So early on, he becomes established as a kind of promising figure in this new school of American Realism, which is meant to break with the kind of belletristic, flighty literature of the past, to be a much more of a kind of journalistic, tough-minded, lucid approach to the sort of quickness and nitty-gritty of life in the streets and in the cities.

He publishes *The Red Badge of Courage* in 1895. As I say, he'd never been to war. He did some research, but this book is an overnight bestseller. He becomes famous immediately, and particularly in England. He continues to spend time in the New York area. He becomes involved with social causes. He defends the down and out. He is interested in the sort of rough fate of prostitutes. He takes stands against the police. His life is filled with adventure. In 1896, he departs on the steamship *Commodore* on December 31st, which is carrying arms for Cuban rebels. The boat goes down, it sinks. Crane has an ordeal at sea. He spends 30 hours in a tiny little boat, which is the substance of one of his great stories that I'll talk about later, "The Open Boat."

He goes on to live, unmarried, with this older woman, Cora Taylor, who was a war correspondent, which is what he then became. He covers the Greco-Turkish war in 1897. He moves to England. His health begins to fail. He also covers the Spanish-American war. He goes to Cuba. He's under fire at Guantanamo, San Juan Hill. He has a first flare-up of TB. He returns to England in 1899 where he lives in this very large manor house, has a circle of very distinguished friends who were English writers: H.G. Wells, Conrad, Henry James. He continues to write—even in these years—children's stories, war stories. He writes his astonishing short piece called "The Blue Hotel," which we'll talk about. He has his first TB attack. In 1900, he's carried by litter to a sanitarium in the Black Forest in Germany, where he dies.

I said, it's a burnout life. It's a life that is too intense. He's drawn, really, like a moth to light, to wars, to critical hotspots across the globe. This is a form of behavior that is familiar to us today. We think of Hemingway, we think of Malraux, we think of Norman Mailer, we think of a lot of 20th century writers; but Crane is the first to start this. It's a kind of American posture in a sense, of going where the action is, of then writing about it for the folks back home. It's the kind of lure, the appeal, the siren song of a certain kind of journalism.

Crane, I think, has to be understood too as being situated within the Naturalist literary movement. I called him realist in the sense that he knows people like Howells and Garland, but naturalist is a tougher movement. It's a movement that believes more in determinism. It's a movement that in France is sort of epitomized by the work of Zola, and in America it leads to writers like Dreiser, Norris, and Upton Sinclair. I think Crane can be seen as really the first of the American naturalists. He's not a card-carrying naturalist. He doesn't subscribe in the same entirely philosophical way to the tenets of determinism. On the other hand, he's drawn by the same kinds of forces. He's drawn to situations where human beings are coerced, squeezed. He wants to write about the fictions of willpower, the myth that people have some sort of control over their lives. He's interested in situations where there are explosive forces out there that buffet the human subject.

Howells himself commented once that Crane, I quote, "Had sprung into literature fully armed." It's a marvelous metaphor, "fully armed," because it really does characterize the subject of so much of Crane's work, which is war. You have to place this. The last war that people really talked about was the war in 1871, when the Prussians invaded France. There had been peace up until the 1890s. The 1890s were the decade when war returns to the European scene and to the American scene. It's an outbreak of constant hostilities. As I said, Crane is drawn to them. He can't seem to stay away from this. Also, the 1890s anticipates our own century of continuous warfare. It's as if those two decades between the 1870s and the 1890s look very, very much nostalgic to us today.

Crane's education began in New York, visiting the bowery, the flophouses. A comment he made to James Huneker, "I told the seemingly sane man that I got my artistic education on the bowery." He said, 'Oh really? So they have a school of fine arts there?'" He obviously meant a different kind of education. He saw the modern city as a place of war, that the plight of the laborers, the prostitutes—they were living in the conditions of war already. To write about the Civil War, in some ways, is to return to an earlier scene where he'd already encountered, in his own modern environment, something of the violence, something of the coerciveness that [one] obtains in war. In particular, the city is the place where you discover the new industrial machine that grinds up people. This is that Naturalist vision that I alluded to, this is what he could have found in Zola and what you would see in Dreiser just a few years later.

If you remember that Crane himself comes from a very proper family, it's very easy to take the view that he was slumming. He was just out there checking out what was going on in the bowery—the lives of prostitutes— totally different from the kind of really, well heeled background from which he came. I think that it's worth mentioning that, just to essentially discredit it. One of the great things about Crane is his integrity, his heart. He really feels for what he sees, and he can't help the fact that he comes from a different kind of background. There is nothing condescending about Crane's work, it seems to me. He can be very severe on people who are puffed up and inflated and pious. He's severe on sentimentalism. There's a kind of sharp, stabbing rhythm to Crane's work where it's deflating all the time. It's puncturing the kinds of illusory notions of grandeur about life and about things such as war. Crane is capable of a great deal of heroism, and the people who knew him felt that.

There's a tribute that H.G. Wells gave of Crane, which I'd like to quote, which I think captures something of the kind of radical nature of this man.

> He was the expression in literary art of certain enormous repudiations. It's as if the racial thought and tradition had been raised from his mind, and it's site plowed and salted. It's as if he just simply erased his entire background; the social amenities he was accustomed to, so that he could look at things with utter neutrality. He could actually take in the newness of a world around him, which was quite different from the genteel age that had just passed.

His great theme is that of dismantling pretension, of going through, stabbing through inflated rhetoric, of exposing hyperbole. As I said, *The Red Badge of Courage* made him an overnight celebrity. Many people considered it the first American text about American themes. It was written it is thought, in 10 days, or 10 nights. I suppose feverish nights of writing. He'd never seen a war before. He once gave a very funny remark about where he learned about violence. It won't surprise you. He says, "Of course I've never been in a battle, but I believe that I got my sense of the rage of conflict on the football field, or else fighting is a hereditary instinct, and I wrote intuitively." His athletic background plays into this; that he understood something of the antics of people rushing at each other, hurting each other, killing each other, in some senses.

There is also a feeling that *The Red Badge of Courage* is located not only in the Civil War, but is located in the moment that Crane himself is inaugurating, which is a moment in which violence and brutality and physical conflict seem to sort of saturate the culture. I want to read you a criticism. This is written in the 1930s about *The Red Badge of Courage* and about Crane's own moment.

> He lived in the dime novel days, when the public fevers with prosperity and indifferent to the defects of this massive country, demanded fiction of a similar quality in which quote, men were men, quote, shot at the drop of a hat, and quote, died in their boots. It was significantly enough, the age of dawning pugilism, of Sullivan of Corbett, Fitzsimmons, Jeffries and Johnson. The old frontier had gone to be sure, but new ones were springing up in the Klondike, Mexico, the trenches of Cuba, the bowery, the wheat pit in Chicago, and the open sea where men still live by craft and brute strength, where the strong devoured the puny, bravery counted for more than mercy, and reason chose nature, amoral and impulsive, for its guide.

It's a sense of the kind of brutality of this moment, and the way it's sort of showing up throughout different aspects of American culture. The interest in boxing, and things like that, comes at the same time.

So Crane has this sense of the role of conflict, the role of physical, bruising conflict in life. He has to have wondered how could he possibly succeed in writing a story about a war when he'd never been to war. I mean, he was just a kid when he wrote this thing. He was in his early 20s. Yet, everybody who read this story assumed that Crane was some grizzled veteran; and veterans themselves would come to him, and they'd see what a young person he was, "How could you have known these things?" This pleased him enormously, that people who had themselves, had gone through war would read his text and feel that he had gotten it right. When later—and of course we don't have a lot later in his life, he didn't live long, but he certainly lived to see a number of wars after writing *The Red Badge*—when he saw them, he also patted himself on the back that he had gotten it right, that he had not exaggerated. That he hadn't cheated was what most concerned him. He wanted to get it right.

That's really what people were struck by in this text. It didn't just get it right, it told a story about war that no one had ever told. War had been presented in a completely different fashion prior to that. Moreover, in the moment in which Crane is writing about war, the moment of the Spanish-American conflict, the moment of the Cuban conflict, the Greco-Turkish conflicts, the rhetoric that is heard about war is very different from what Crane is writing.

I'm going to read you a couple of passages about the sort of national discourse on war at the time that Crane is writing. This is President McKinley who's justifying the seizure of the Philippines. This is what McKinley wrote:

> I am not ashamed to tell you, gentlemen, that I went down on my knees and prayed to Almighty God for light and guidance that one night. And one night late it came to me this way. ... There was nothing left for us to do but to take them all, (this is the Philippines) and to educate the Filipinos and uplift and civilize and Christianize them, and by God's grace do the very best we could by them, as our fellow men for whom Christ also died.

This is the rhetoric that's invoked for the seizure of the Philippines. Here's what Henry Cabot Lodge said about the Spanish-American War.

> What a wonderful war it has been. What a navy we've got. what good fighters our soldiers are. Nothing but victory, and at such small cost.

Or this is John Hay's letter from the American Embassy in London on July 27th, 1898 congratulating Theodore Roosevelt on the war that Roosevelt, who was the Assistant Secretary of the Navy, had helped to start. This is Hay.

It has been a splendid little war; begun with the highest motives, carried on with magnificent intelligence and spirit, favored by that fortune which loves the brave. It is now to be concluded I hope with that fine, good nature, which is after all the distinguishing trait of the American character.

This is the kind of mush, the kind of inflated rhetoric that Crane is nauseated by, sickened by. Other critics of the time did not buy this rhetoric either. William James was part of an anti-imperialist league at the same time, and he called the seizure of the Philippines quote "The bloodiest colonial war in proportion to population ever fought by a white power in Asia." What prophetic lines. This is in the late 1890s.

Crane is writing against a particular ethos as well, a particular kind of language and a particular kind of softness. That's what people saw in the text. Ford Madox Ford, who is a very distinguished writer himself, wrote that Crane's depiction of the war forever changed the way at least writers could think about war. He said all of us had thought about war, but the images we had were really from the post-medieval period. I quote,

> Suddenly there was *The Red Badge of Courage* showing us, to our absolute conviction, how the normal absolutely undistinguished, essentially civilian man from the street had behaved in a terrible and prolonged war, without distinction, without military qualities, without special courage, without even any profound apprehension of or passion to the causes of the struggle in which almost without will he was engaged.

And he goes on to say that this is exactly in fact how people will perform in the wars to come.

> Is it beside the mark to note that this was exactly how we all did take it 20 years later, from the English Channel to the frontiers of Italy? The point was that with *The Red Badge* in the 90s, we were provided with a map showing us our own hearts. If before that date we'd been asked how we should behave in a war, we should no doubt have answered, "We should behave like demi-gods with all the memorial attributes of war, memorials."

After that we realized that this was not likely to be the case. What do you bring with you to war? You bring with you your own eyes. That's what Crane always said. It's your eyes that you've got. Crane, when he had written the book *Maggie*, it was not a popular success. People mocked the author; they mocked the text. Crane wrote this to a friend in 1898.

> When I was the mark for every humorist in the country, I went ahead. Now, when I am the mark for only 50 percent of the humorists in the country, I go ahead. If I understand that a man is born into this world with his own pair of eyes, and that he is not at all responsible for his vision, he's merely responsible for his quality of personal honesty. To keep close to this personal honesty is my supreme ambition. *Maggie* was too harsh. It was too melodramatic an account of life in the slums. *The Red Badge of Courage* was a perfect hit. (Perhaps it's because it was writing about a war that was already 30 years past.)

His character, Henry Fleming, also begins the story with epic expectations of what war is:

> He had, of course, dreamed of battles all his life—of vague and bloody conflicts that had thrilled him with their sweep and fire. In visions he had seen himself in many struggles. He had imagined people secure in the shadow of his eagle-eyed prowess. (That's how he had dreamed. He had sensed that this wasn't the case) … From his home his youthful eyes had looked upon the war in his own country with distrust. It must be some sort of a play affair. He had long despaired of witnessing a Greeklike struggle. Such would be no more, he said. Men were better, or more timid. Secular and religious education had effaced their throat-grappling instinct, or else firm finance held in check the passions.

So, this is a young man who feels like he's been cheated out of the great wars. It's belated. It's too late for it to happen. But he goes to this one thinking, nonetheless, this might be my chance. There is a lot of romantic expectation in this text. He hopes nonetheless for his moment of glory on the field. He even imagines a kind of glorious, dramatic, very dashing death.

> A blue desperate figure leading lurid charges with one knee forward and a broken blade high—a blue, determined figure standing before a crimson and steel assault, getting calmly killed on a high place before the eyes of all. He thought of the magnificent pathos of his dead body.

And yet, what marks this text, of course, is the contrapuntal rhythm of it. This is the text that is going to forever deflate the kind of noble rhetoric of war. Henry Fleming comes with this view, and yet in the course of the story he will learn that this is not going to happen. It's not going to be done that way. Even early on, when he tells his mother that he is going to enlist in the Civil War, Crane writes, "He had privately primed himself for a beautiful scene. He had prepared certain sentences which he thought could be used with touching effect." But this is what his mom says. "You watch out Henry, and take good care of yourself in this here fighting business. You watch out. Don't go a-thinking you can lick the whole rebel army at the start, 'cause you can't. You're just one little feller amongst a whole lot of others." "Just one little feller amongst a whole lot of others." Thanks, mom. I mean, that's what she's going to tell him from the beginning. That's what he's going to learn over and over in this text, that his group, his unit, his fighting, his exploits don't count for much in the larger scheme of things.

> They had taken themselves and the enemy very seriously and had imagined they were deciding the war. Individuals must have supposed that they were cutting the letters of their names deep into everlasting tablets of brass, or enshrining their reputations forever in the hearts of their countrymen, while, as to fact, the affair would appear in printed reports under a meek and immaterial title.

By the end of this text, he comes to a very famous kind of resolution that these grand, noble expectations will not come too much.

> He found that he could look back upon the brass and bombast of his earlier gospels and see them truly. (And then the final note of maturity)... He knew that he would no longer quail before his guides wherever they should point. He had been to touch the great death, and found that, after all, it was but the great death. He was a man.

That's how the text closes. How do you get there? How do you make it to that kind of sense of equilibrium and harmony and seeing through bombast and seeing through illusion?

It's in the trip to that conclusion that the story achieves its greatness. Crane gives us a kind of "first time view," that we don't know what human nature is. We don't know how we're going to react. We don't know what crisis will bring out in us. This will be, I think, the starting point of writers like Hemmingway. Hemmingway's great phrase is "Grace under pressure." There's not much grace in Crane, but there's a lot of pressure. Behavior, as

I said, is a question mark. It's a riddle. The most remarkable things about this story are the way in which Henry Fleming sees his own life in front of him as guesswork. Will he or will he not bolt under pressure? How do you know if you're a coward? How can you tell until you've been tested?

> He tried to mathematically prove to himself that he would not run from a battle. ... Here he was confronted with a thing of moment. It suddenly appeared to him that perhaps in a battle he might run. He was forced to admit that as far as war was concerned he knew nothing of himself. ... He sprang from the bunk and began to pace nervously to and fro. "Good Lord, what's the matter with me?" he said. He felt that in this crisis his laws of life were useless. Whatever he had learned of himself was here of no avail. He was an unknown quantity.

I want you to hear the scientism here. This is a laboratory experiment. He was an unknown quantity.

> He saw that he would again be obliged to experiment as he had in early youth. He must accumulate information of himself, and meanwhile he resolved to remain close upon his guard lest those qualities of which he knew nothing should everlastingly disgrace him.

What if the surprise is dreadful? What if all of a sudden you become a figure that you've never anticipated? There is a kind of maturity here, in knowing that you don't know. In crisis, under stress, a metamorphosis can take place. Anything can come. There's this emphasis on experimentation itself. As you know, etymologically, the word experience is linked back to experiment. They have to do with the same thing. It's open-ended. You don't know.

> He finally concluded that the only way to prove himself was to go into the blaze, (This is, I think, very close to Conrad too) and then figuratively to watch his legs to discover their merits and faults. (See if they're running backwards or forwards, which way you're going, into the battle or out of the battle) He reluctantly admitted that he could not sit still and with a mental slate and pencil derive an answer. (You can study military warfare; that ain't going to tell you anything) To gain it, (the answer) he must have blaze, blood, and danger, (and hear the scientific analogy here) even as a chemist requires this, that, and the other. So he fretted for the opportunity.

That's the scientism here. That's the rigor, that's the honesty of this text, is that you don't know what you're going to do, which is tantamount to saying that you don't know who you are, which is tantamount to saying that when crisis comes, when emergencies come, you become other. The human being is a much less noble creature than we could ever figure out in our leisure, sitting at our desk, or in the lab, before the experiment is concluded.

Even that scientism doesn't take the measure of what Crane's greatness is. As I said in my initial remarks, he gives us the immediacy of things. He is a journalist in a sense that he can write down what war looks like, but he's also a great writer. I think the literary movement that we should most align him with is not Naturalism, but Impressionism. Impressionism is the brilliance of images. So this is the last passage I'll read to you about how Fleming sees Crane.

> In the darkness he saw visions of a thousand-tongued fear that would babble at his back and cause him to flee, while others were going coolly about their country's business. He admitted he would not be able to cope with this monster. He felt every nerve in his body would be an ear to hear the voices, while other men would remain stolid and deaf.

That's not scientific anymore at all, "A thousand-tongued fear." Hear that extraordinary image. "And in him an ear to hear every one of these voices." This is the remarkable sensitivity, the poetic sensitivity of this man, who knows he's going into crisis, and he will hear the voices.

Lecture Forty-Six
The Red Badge of Courage—Brave New World

Scope: Crane's central strategy in his war novel is to juxtapose the inner, private world view with the external world of others and nature. Henry Fleming is subjected to this dynamic, and he thinks of his acts as a performance, a public spectacle that must be validated. But we see that the natural scene is utterly out of phase with the so-called heroics of battle. We see this because Crane has invented a staggering new kind of prose to force upon us: a welter of disorienting colors, a figurative language that sees animality and metamorphosis everywhere it looks, an expressionistic genius that twists the familiar world of forms and concepts into something grotesque and new, a discourse of energy that locates power in things rather than people, and an all-out critique of the possibility of human control, especially in a war setting. Crane's book has been read in various ways, including as a rites-of-passage account and as a mythic presentation of war. It is perhaps best seen as a collision course with death, and as such, the central scenes of rendezvous with death seem to prophesy Crane's own premature death.

Objectives—Upon completion of this lecture, you should be able to:

1. Summarize Crane's method of "inside/outside" narration;

2. Give examples of two types of critical interpretations *of The Red Badge of Courage*; and

3. Explain how Crane's depiction of death differs from the Romantic vision.

Outline

I. Crane's basic strategy consists of narrating from both "inside" and "outside." Being a soldier is portrayed as a theatrical event in terms of how you see yourself and how others see you.

    A. For the most part, Henry Fleming is alone with his senses, but he is periodically shocked by other views.

1. At the very beginning, Henry's mother articulates the corrective view: He is a small part of a large event.
2. At key junctures, Henry overhears the officers speaking of his regiment's behavior and character; he is stunned by their pejorative view.
3. Henry utterly internalizes this dynamic of inside/outside; he obsesses about how others might see him. In the beginning of the story, he runs away, and this act haunts him. At the end, his bravery is understood as a performance, one that can now be validated.

B. Yet Crane makes us understand that the inside/outside dialectic is more radical than this; the entire war comes across as absurdity, as senseless noise and killing in a nature that has no connection with it.

II. Crane's brilliance as a writer is most on show in his rendition of war as a kind of perceptual and experiential chaos. His artistic mission is to show us what war *really* looks like and feels like.

A. We first note the staggering use of vivid, stunning, disorienting colors in Crane's descriptions.
1. Crane is justly thought of as a great "Impressionist" writer, and his rendition of the visual world parallels the Impressionist painters' works.
2. A world that comes to us predominantly as colors is also a world that is losing some of its conceptual definitions.

B. We also see that Crane's world is a bestiary—not that there are so many literal animals in it, but that it is rendered through animal metaphors.

C. Looking forward to the Imagism school of poetry, Crane's most dazzling verbal touches suggest a style that is best termed *expressionistic*. Comparable perhaps to Emily Dickinson, Crane reconfigures the world we think we know by clothing it in shocking images and metaphors.

D. One of Crane's favorite games here is to underscore the frightening slippage between things and animals, between machines and people.
1. In many striking passages, "things" are invested with a kind of furious in-dwelling power in animate form. It is as if power itself had been displaced from humans to their "instruments."

2. The corollary to such passages is found in the numerous notations of humans as mechanized, "thingified." We see this as a strangely urban phenomenon, as if the "crowd" psychology were found to be operative in war as well. But battle itself might be understood as an "infernal machine." In his best passages, Crane evidences a genius for unpacking these images, as if their explosive formal power—to reconfigure our world—led to an equally explosive conceptual revolution.

E. There is no easy or agreed-on way to assess the vision and significance of *The Red Badge of Courage*.

1. Many critics have seen in Henry Fleming's experience an exemplary case of rites of passage, consisting of the classic phases of this paradigm: separation, initiation, and incorporation. There is much truth here.

2. Other critics, attending to Crane's metaphors, have seen in his story a mythic presentation of war, replete with primitive images of sacrifice and savage new gods. This reading completes the rites-of-passage presentation as an interpretation of what Henry Fleming becomes: a barbarian.

3. One unmistakable result of Crane's work here is that the traditional view of war as a "great Game," as an exercise in strategy and design, is utterly cashiered. The only cogency at hand here is that of death.

4. Death would seem to be the ultimate truth and quarry of Crane's novel; many scenes actually choreograph the movements of the dying. Death is repeatedly imaged as the story's inevitable rendezvous, not only for the dying, but also for Henry, who encounters it in a remarkable passage early in the text.

5. It is hard not to see this book's repeated staging of an encounter with death as a prophetic dress rehearsal for Crane's own doomed, brief life.

Lecture Forty-Six—Transcript
The Red Badge of Courage—Brave New World

This is Lecture Forty-Six, and it's the second lecture on *The Red Badge of Courage*. In this one I want to focus more on the actual depiction of the war. I spoke in my last lecture about the scientism of Crane's endeavor, the way in which human behavior really is understood to be a question mark. In crisis, in the heat of battle, no one really knows how he is going to behave, and that that's part of the sort of rigorous scrutiny of the text. I closed that lecture with this reference to the "many tongues of fear" that speak inside of you and the ears that we have to hear that. I want, with that reference, to move into the depiction that Crane gives us as well, of what it feels like on the inside to be in situations like this.

Crane's text really defies any kind of confident markings as to what school it belongs to. You've noticed I've already talked about Realism, Naturalism and Impressionism. Now I'm going to talk about Expressionism too. It simply runs in and out of all of these models, and there's something very heterogeneous about the way Crane has tried to tell it. It's not like he's interested in literary schools. He's interested in a series of strategies to get across what he wants to get across. I've already talked about the scientism. What I want in this lecture to talk about is the kind of dramatic perspectives that are going to be used; and in particular, the way in which the response of others is so central to this text, the way in which really being a soldier in a war is a kind of theatrical event.

It's a series of spectators watching your behavior, and of course, even that doesn't say it all, because that becomes a psychological truth. You then internalize that. How do I look? How am I doing? What do they think? This is what fear, what remorse, and what one's self- expectations have to do with. How do you see yourself? How do others see you? You remember early on when he tells mom that he's going to war. "You're just one little feller amongst a whole lot of others," she tells him. That's one of those notations where the outside world is brought in, and it cuts you down to size. It makes you realize that your private fantasies of things are just that, private fantasies.

Outside perspective frequently breaks into the text. In one nice passage Henry hears officers talking. One officer asks another one,

> "What troops can you spare?"

> [And the officer answers] "Well, I had to order in the 12th to help the 76th; haven't really got any. Ah, but there's the 304th. They fight like a lot of mule drivers. I can spare them best of any."

That's his unit, the 304th: "Mule drivers!" This blows him away.

> He and his friend exchange glances of astonishment. The general explains, "Get 'em ready. I'll watch developments from here. Send 'em in." [Then as he's leaving, the officer says to the other one] "I don't believe many of your mule drivers will get back."

> With scared faces, the youth and his companion hurried back to the line. … New eyes were given to him. And the most startling thing was to learn suddenly that he was very insignificant. The officer spoke of the regiment as if he referred to a broom. Some part of the woods needed sweeping, perhaps, and he merely indicated a broom in a tone properly indifferent to its fate.

It's an interesting image, that notion of the broom. The woods needed sweeping. It picks up an earlier reference as well, when they see a lot of dead bodies and someone says, "Lost a pile of men, they did. If an old woman swept up the woods she'd get a dustpan full." And the bodies are really just so much debris, dirt, left in the wake of conflict. You just have to sweep them up and get them out. But when the living soldiers see themselves as just potential debris—they're waiting to be swept up, and that that's how their officers regard them—that leads to a kind of different view, and it's a hard one.

At one point later, there is a kind of revenge feeling. "As he noted the vicious wolf-like temper of his comrades, he had a sweet thought that, if the enemy was about to swallow the regimental broom as a large prisoner, it could at least have the consolation of going down with bristles forward." Even if they're just going to be swept away or are going to be part of the broom that the others swallow, at least they can cause some damage. That sense of being jolted out of his own ease by hearing the officers refer to his group as mule drivers is the kind of contrapuntal technique of the story, how others see you. As I said, there's a consistent focus on performance, on spectacle. As you probably know, Henry Fleming, when the first encounter comes, bolts and runs. This dogs him throughout the story, that he is a coward. He has shown himself, and he must prove himself.

As the story goes on, he will prove himself; but of course, he's convinced throughout that others are looking, others are checking out what he's going to do. He sees people—whether he's running or whether he's fighting bravely—he's constantly aware of being sort of under the gaze of other people. "They had all become spectators," the text will write. At the end of the story, you never get past that notion that this is a kind of histrionic event.

> Regarding his procession of memory he felt gleeful and unregretting, for in it his public deeds were paraded in great and shining prominence. Those performances which had been witnessed by his fellows marched now in wide purple and gold, having various deflections. They went gayly with music. It was a pleasure to watch these things.

This trumped up, really, kind of carnival; it's a kind of spectacle, as something that is a scene, and on stage, for other people. One piece of this is a persistent need for approval. This story flirts with sentimentalism frequently when you have these soldiers very dependent on whether their officers approve of them—think that they're gallant and brave. When they do, the story becomes rather soft. That's a part of it.

What I'm trying to sketch is a kind of inside-outside dialectic. On the one hand, Crane is going to render what it feels like to be in these situations of crisis and violence. On the other hand, he's going to show us, he's going to punctuate this with commentary responses. The viewpoint of other people, already, as I say, deflates. But that's not all. The outside inside can be thought of in a much simpler way too, which is human beings in a physical setting. That's also outside inside. The human subject placed on a stage once again, but a stage that seems to be so strange. The stage itself is rendered. It's rendered in its alterity. It's rendered in its difference in this text.

> As he gazed around him the youth felt a flash of astonishment at the blue, pure sky and the sun gleanings on the trees and fields. It was surprising that Nature had gone on tranquilly with her golden process in the midst of so much devilment.

Here's nothing but carnage, fire, smoke, guns, noise, and killing. You look around and the sun hasn't stopped shining. Things still seem to be resplendent with the beauty of nature. How is that possible, given all the bloody business at hand? Crane's text is strongest in its efforts to render something of the vividness and the ferocity of these events in terms of the natural setting that they take place in. Crane defined the artist as a person who really is a kind of moving camera and not acting on the scene, just depicting it, rendering it. This is a rather wonderful definition. "The artist I think is nothing but a powerful memory that can move itself at will through certain experiences sideways, and every artist must be in some things powerless as a dead snake." You're not in there to change anything, to sculpt it, to scope it, or anything like that. You're just there to be utterly attuned to it, sensitive to it, to be the lens that it comes through, the place where its trace is left. A dead snake. You're not supposed to alter it.

I think that there is a kind of code there, a kind of stoic code of "seeing in through to the end" and not trying to change it, being the vehicle for it to come through to others. This leads to some of the vivid Impressionism of this work. There's an explosion of color in this story; that places are given to us as sort of just resplendent with color. "He was aware that these battalions with their commotions were woven red and startling into the gentle fabric of softened greens and browns. It looked to be the wrong place for a battlefield." It looks like a quilt; it looks like a painting. How can this be a battlefield?

There's a real aesthetic fantasia going on in the text where you get this overwhelming presence of color itself.

> The level sheets of flame developed great clouds of smoke that tumbled and tossed in the mild wind near the ground for a moment, and then rolled through the ranks as through a gate. The clouds were tinged in earthlike yellow in the sunrays and in the shadow were a sorry blue. The flag was sometimes eaten and lost in this mass of vapor, but more often it projected, sun-touched, resplendent.

You get the makings here of a real stylist who really wants to get across the light effects, the gleanings.

That's why I say, "Here's the Impressionist Crane." Just like the great paintings of impressionism, what you get is this explosion of luminosity and of the way light recasts and remakes the world. What you lose is a sense of firm contours and lines. Its color is everything. That's going to be a kind of corrosive device as such that color sculpts this scene, in which case you can no longer see the contours of events in the way you've been educated to look for them. Of course, there's a wonderful irony in this text as well. Colors, we know in military terms, represent the flag. There are many sequences here where people are trying to battle for the flag. You get the sense that this is a kind of outlandish color symbolic parade, the color of the smoke, of the sun, of the trees, of the leaves, the color of the flags. All of these are doing battle with each other. People are losing their lives. The moral vocabulary is going out of business and what you're getting instead is a kind of aesthetic, a fantasia, a carnival, a kind of explosion, and a riotous sense of just sensory perceptions. Of course, it can look a bit mad. As I said, the human moral conceptual lines tend to disappear.

I've talked about color. A device that's very prominent in this story is also transformation, metamorphosis. There are lots of very powerful metaphors placed in the story, and one of the most prominent ones is that of bestiality. The people are turning into animals throughout, or to monsters. "A moment later the regiment went swinging off into the darkness. It was like one of those moving monsters wending with many feet." Or, "There was an occasional flash and glimmer of steel from the backs of all those huge, crawling reptiles." This thing is turning into a menagerie. There is sense here that again the human scale, human contours, are being transformed, are altering into something quite different. This is what leads to the possibility of seeing Crane as an expressionist writer, the kind of go-for-broke stylist, who in some of his metaphors reminds one of Emily Dickinson, who looks forward to imagism as a poetic movement. Things get reconfigured.

Some of the metaphors are really quite stunning. "In the eastern sky, there was a yellow patch like a rug laid for the feet of the coming sun." I mean that's an astounding sort of figure of speech there, a rug for the sun. "And against it, black and patterned-like, loomed the gigantic figure of the colonel on a gigantic horse." There's the war god, the divinity, who presides over this slaughterhouse. There are remarkable passages where things get reconfigured in terms that are really quite dazzling. "The shells, which had ceased to trouble the regiment for a time, came swirling again and exploded in the grass, or among the leaves of the trees. They looked to be strange war flowers, bursting into fierce bloom."

Sometimes you move from the violence of war into pastoral imagery that works in a very weird way. The shells explode like flowers. "The insects were making rhythmical noises. They seemed to be grinding their teeth in unison." These is a constant barrage of these new metaphors that transform this natural and human scene into new colors, new creatures. The battle itself will be described in remarkable kinds of ways. "Bullets began to whistle among the branches and nip at the trees. Twigs and leaves came sailing down. It was as if a thousand axes, wee and invisible, were being wielded. Many of the men were constantly dodging and ducking their heads." An image of a thousand axes out there, cutting things, going after us. Or this one:

> There was a rustling and muttering among the men. They displayed a feverish desire to have every possible cartridge ready to their hands. The boxes were pulled around into various positions, and adjusted with great care. (And here comes the simile) It was as if seven hundred new bonnets were being tried on.

What a remarkable domestic image to throw into the war here; seven hundred new bonnets being tried on. This is making it new. I mean this is what the modernist is going to say 20 years after Crane. Make it new. This is the sort of thing that Ezra Pound's going to talk about and Crane's already doing it. He's taking this scene, and he's totally baptizing it in a new way. He's giving us a totally different kind of vocabulary for understanding these events.

I said that there is a lot of animality, that the war becomes a menagerie, that the soldiers are described as reptiles. It gets even more insidious than that, though. What you have in this text—and this is a prophetic move because it's going to be repeated in later texts as well in the 20th century—is things that are inert, that are inanimate made animate, made into animals, animated. You begin to realize that power's being displaced. The machines that are supposed to serve the people become the animals, the living creatures of the war, and that the humans of course are going to become the machines. There's an awful kind of inversion, a kind of capsizing, an upheaval, catechism, and it works throughout the text. The guns seem to have a kind of autonomy of their own. "The guns squatted in a row like savage chiefs. They argued with abrupt violence." Do you hear how these guns are animate, how they are authoritative, they don't require people to do anything?

> It was a grim pow-wow. Their busy servants (That is us, the soldiers) ran hither and thither. (That's the guns; then the shells will be described in the same way) …As he, leading, went across a little field, he found himself in a region of shells. They hurtled over his head with long wild screams. (They're the ones making the noise) As he listened he imagined them to have rows of cruel teeth that grinned at him. (The guns are described in still another strong

passage) …The guns in the rear, aroused and enraged by shells that had been thrown burlike at them, suddenly involved themselves in a hideous altercation with another band of guns.

This is war between guns. We are just their servants. We are simply hustling back and forth as they conduct the primary business at hand.

This is not just metaphor now. This is displacement. This is usurpation. This is a re-conception of what the scene of battle is like—another device that he uses—which I think he must have gotten from his efforts in *Maggie* and describing the bowery and understanding the brutal machinery of city life—the urban setting as itself an industrial machine—all of that is put to good use as well in the war; because in the war, much of the psychology that writers like Whitman and Baudelaire understand about city crowds becomes very much present again as you are with a squadron of people and rushing into battle. Henry Fleming becomes aware that he is bonded, welded, not by choice but by the design of the war, with his own cohort of soldiers, and that there's a sense that he has no maneuvering room, no freedom of action in any of this.

The battle itself is often depicted in mechanical terms. I've told you about the way the machines are depicted in animalistic terms; well, the battle is often mechanical. "The battle was like the grinding of an immense and terrible machine to him. Its complexities and powers, its grim processes fascinated him. He must go close and see it produce corpses." What a great notion here. It's a corpse-making machine. It's a machine that grinds, and it turns out—like on an assembly line—human cadavers. "The youth joined this crowd and marched along with it. The torn bodies expressed the awful machinery in which the men had been entangled." Another passage that has some of the same power in it, "Men ran hither and thither, seeking with their eyes, roads of escape. With serene regularity as if controlled by a schedule, bullets buffed into men." It's just astounding. Bullets buffed into men. They're running into this systemic death and that that's the way it's now being depicted here. It's an awful kind of machinery that's gone awry.

We've heard of armies called killing machines, but it strikes me that you really begin to get a systemic picture of it. You begin to get a sense of some organizational chaos that's at work here. Crane is on the outside *and* the inside. Henry Fleming gives us a sense of what it feels like to be in this. I used my preposition intentionally: in it, inside of it, trapped in it, unable to get clear of it.

He felt carried along by a mob. (That could have been a city notation) The sun spread disclosing rays, and, one by one, regiments burst into view like armed men just born of the earth. The youth perceived that the time had come. He was about to be measured.

There's that scientism. Now it will be found out. "For a moment he felt in the face of his great trial like a babe, and the flesh over his heart seemed very thin." This is a beautiful notation, very, very fragile and precarious here. "He seized time to look about him calculatingly;" an interesting adverb there. This is what he's going to calculate. "But he instantly saw that it would be impossible for him to escape from the regiment. It enclosed him, and there were iron laws of tradition and law on four sides. He was in a moving box." One of the most striking notations in the book: "He was in a moving box."

What does it feel like to be in a moving box; that your own autonomy, your hegemony, your maneuvering room, all of that is gone? The box moves, you're in it. Then, with a kind of real savvy, Crane moves from that into the kind of moral recognition that seems to be coming late, but now comes, "As he perceived this fact, it occurred to him that he had never wished to come to the war. He had not enlisted of his own free will." Of course he has. But it's in this moment that it begins to dawn on him what he's done. "He had been dragged by the merciless government, and now they were taking him out to be slaughtered." That follows the recognition that he was in a moving box.

There's something really wonderfully developmental in Crane here. You get the sort of chaotic representation of the violence, the tumult, the color, the crescendo, but then it gets translated into these astonishing metaphors, machinery that's gone awry, bullets buffing into men. Finally it gets translated back into conceptual terms. "What am I doing here? How has this happened? I didn't will this. The government is getting ready to slaughter me." There's a kind of wonderful educational process that's being chronicled and charted in this text. It moved from a kind of mob psychology to a scientific measuring. He's looking calculatingly to the moving box and then to the corrosive thought process. "What am I doing here?" People have not known how to measure this book with any kind of finality, partly because it says a lot of different things.

One measuring stick is that it's a story about rites of passage. It's about a young man growing up. It has the classic movements of rites of passage, which is that you are pulled out of your community, you are on a liminal threshold phase where you have your initiation, and then you are reincorporated into the community as an adult. That's what rites of passage means in tribal cultures. You could argue that's exactly Henry Fleming's experience. He's pulled out of his family, he has this initiation experience in the war, and he says, in his own words, that he was now a man at the end.

So that will cover what it covers; but that won't take the full measure of the story. What view of war is being put forth here? Many people have rightfully seen this as a kind of mythic representation of war, as a story really, a kind of religious story, about war as a kind of new, savage, primitive religion. "They were going to look at war, the red animal, war, the blood-swollen god, and they were deeply engrossed in this march." This continues the same notion that the people are all being indoctrinated or initiated into some horrible kind of ritual.

> Many of the men were making low-toned noises with their mouths, and these subdued cheers, snarls, imprecations, prayers, made a wild, barbaric song that went as an undercurrent of sound, strange and chantlike with the resounding chords of the war march. ... The brigade was hurrying briskly to be gulped into the infernal mouths of the war god.

Moloch, the war god, swallows up and devours the human beings. That's also a reading of the story; that introduction or initiation into a realm of savagery. One thing that's clear is that the older 19th century notions of war, the kind of things that were debated in military councils and among military strategists are totally cashiered—the sort of thing that you have in Kipling with war as the great game, as the set of strategic chessboard maneuvers, which is the way historians have written about war.

That's gone forever from a story like this. There's no sense of design, no sense of pattern, no sense of form and no sense of strategy in this text. It's instead bodies that are being fed into a machine. It's coming afoul of the bullets that buff into you. There's no rationale. Henry Fleming, in a moment of crisis, realizes he has no idea why he's there. Here is the other truth of war that's coming across. It has nothing to do with the drawing rooms, the strategic sessions and the accounts that the historians have given us. It is an experiential, chaotic, carnivalesque scene. The only cogency that is put forth here is a very different one. It's not the cogency of military strategy, of our aims that are going to be somehow promoted by dent of this war.

Listen to this passage. It really tells you the cogency and coherency of war. "Other men, punched by bullets, fell in grotesque agonies. The regiment left a coherent trail of bodies." That's the cogency; the coherency is the bodies. They are lined up. It's a death-making machine. Death is going to be the ultimate truth of this text. It choreographs death. It's a dance of death. This mesmerizes Crane; he's drawn over and over to what it looks like when people encounter violent death, when they are shot.

> The men dropped here and there like bundles. The captain of the youth's company had been killed in an early part of the action. His body lay stretched out in the position of a tired man resting, but upon his face there was an astonished and sorrowful look, as if he thought some friend had done him an ill turn. The babbling man was grazed by a shot that made the blood stream widely down his face. He clapped both hands to his head. 'Oh!' he said, and ran. Another grunted suddenly as if he had been struck by a club in the stomach. He sat down and gazed ruefully. In his eyes there was a mute, indefinite reproach. Further up the line a man, standing behind a tree, had had his knee joints splintered by a ball. Immediately he had dropped his rifle and gripped the tree with both arms. And there he remained, clinging desperately and crying for assistance that he might withdraw his hold upon the tree.

> Under foot there were a few ghastly forms motionless. They lay twisted in fantastic contortions. Arms were bent and heads were turned in incredible ways. It seemed that the dead men must have fallen from some great height to get into such positions. They looked to be dumped out upon the ground from the sky.

That's why I call it dance of death, choreography. Here is cogency. This is formal. This is hieratic, all of these remarkable figures that now dot the landscape and give it the strange new form. If you were flying over as a Martian, you would be able to make something aesthetic out of this. The text allows you to see war that way. There's not much human meaning in it at all.

Death is seen as the terminal surprise in this text, and Crane tracks it hypnotically. We have a sequence where Henry Fleming is surrounded by two figures, the tall man and the tattering man, and both of them are a kind of ballet of dying. They've been hit, both of them wounded, and the language is remarkable. One of them is described, "As if he were taking infinite care not to arouse the passion of his wounds." That's what happens when you get wounded badly enough. You know that any move at all will cause your death. Don't arouse that particular passion. So the stunned surprise of people, "'Lord, what a circus and by jiminy, I got shot. I got shot. Yes, by jiminy I got shot' He reiterated this fact in a bewildered way, as if he did not know how it came about." The book's great rendezvous is with death. In a very lovely sequence—I say lovely it's lovely from a literary point of view—Henry Fleming meets the specter of death. He walks into this place, "A place where the high arcing bows made a chapel." You can't miss the religious significance of it. "He softly pushed the green doors aside." Here is the liminal threshold experienced, open the doors and enter the truth, "and entered. Pine needles were a gentle brown carpet. There was a religious half-light. Near the threshold he stopped, horror-stricken at the sight of a thing. He was being looked at—mind you he's not looking—by a dead man who was seated with his back against a column like tree."

Here is the grisly core of the story: The death god, whom you encounter, he's got his eyes on you, "The dead man and the living man exchanged a long look." And, we have a terrible description here, "The mouth was open. Its red had changed to an appalling yellow. Over the gray skin of the face ran little ants. One was trundling some sort of a bundle along the upper lip. His last memory of this is seeing the ants swarming greedily upon the gray face and venturing horribly near to the eyes." One of the most terrible notations of the vulnerability of human life, that's what Henry Fleming encounters. He survives the story, but the story choreographs the encounter with death. In that light, it is terribly prophetic for the brief life of Crane, the way in which he will be drawn to war, to death, and, as I said, like a comet or a meteor, will burn out at the age of twenty-eight.

Lecture Forty-Seven
Stephen Crane—Scientist of Human Behavior

Scope: Although Crane is most celebrated for *The Red Badge of Courage*, some would argue that his greatest accomplishments lie in the realm of the short story. His two most famous forays in this genre are "The Open Boat" and "The Blue Hotel." In the former, he offers a sobering account of his own experience in surviving the sinking of a steamship off the coast of Florida, and we see here a far more disciplined and restrained form of writing than was true of his war novel. Yet Crane succeeds even more powerfully in evoking the contest between puny humans and a ferocious, impersonal environment, endowing this virtually mute battle with a kind of largeness of soul that is very moving. The second story comes to life in a fierce Nebraska winter setting, and it constitutes one of Crane's bravura pieces about the mission of art: to depict the violent vagaries of human behavior under intense stress. Crane is reflecting on his own medium as well: the explosive power of words. A Crane coda can be seen in his astonishing rendition of Americana in "The Monster," a grisly text that turns yesteryear into nightmare.

Objectives—Upon completion of this lecture, you should be able to:

1. Summarize why "The Open Boat" is considered by many critics to be Crane's most consummate work;

2. Explain how "The Blue Hotel" conveys a sense of language as not just descriptive but prescriptive; and

3. Describe how "The Monster" anticipates both the small-town and horror literature of the 20th century.

Outline

I. Many consider "The Open Boat" to be Crane's single most achieved work of art. It does not have the fireworks of *The Red Badge*, but it more than offsets the earlier text by the grandeur of its subject and the discipline of its treatment.

A. This story is based on Crane's real-life experience. On December 31, 1896, Crane set sail on the steamship *Commodore*, carrying arms to Cuban rebels. The boat sank off the coast of Florida, and Crane survived his experience in a tiny open boat with two crew members and the captain. Crane was so scrupulous about getting the story right that he asked the captain to check out his version before publishing it.

1. The pyrotechnics and "special effects" of *The Red Badge* are absent in this solemn account of a trial at sea.

2. Crane's depiction of the four humans in this tiny boat is simple and beautiful; they work together flawlessly. There is no emotional subplot, virtually no interest in character as psychology.

3. The great antagonist here is the sea itself, and Crane is able to depict the fate of puny humans in a fierce world with as much power as he did in the war novel. The tiny boat comes to us as a symbol of human torture, reminiscent of Poe's "Pit and Pendulum."

4. As usual, the integrity of this piece consists in the unflinching honesty and accuracy of Crane's perspective. What does it look like in this open boat? Crane's genius for one-liners is on show as well.

5. Crane is the reporter right to the end, telling it straight even as the little boat capsizes, and they go down.

6. This account of human endurance, so unrhetorical, so "cool" in its language, achieves great beauty in its final lines about "earning" the right to "interpret" nature.

II. "The Blue Hotel" differs radically in tone from "The Open Boat." It is filled with histrionics, and it is an ongoing meditation about the resources of art, as well as the ingredients of disaster.

A. Crane is again dealing with his favorite topic: How do humans act under great stress? In this brief text, he shows us how to choreograph such reactions, how a room with four people can produce astonishing fireworks.

1. We note, first, the Blue Hotel itself as a kind of strident metaphor, a human construct in a harsh setting, a piece of theatrical machinery.

2. Crane's experiment consists of putting together the right (i.e., explosive) mix of people within this peculiar container, with

freezing arctic conditions outside. His catalyst for the forthcoming violence is the Swede, a precarious figure who seems exaggerated, puffed up, and who spews omens. We see the group's resistance to the Swede's behavior.

3. Crane offers some explanations: the Swede is laboring under a clichéd picture of the "Wild West." Crane suggests—with diabolic irony—that those violent days are over.

4. The Swede proceeds to become demiurgic, monstrous, bidding to take over the entire text.

5. We start to realize that all of his exaggerations, all of his ridiculous claims about being murdered, are going to become true. This text is about prophecy—how its meaning can be literal, how it actualizes its own language and turns its words into deeds.

6. Crane is showing that "words" are not merely conventions, but that they can trigger real explosions. Empowered language peppers the text, language that breaks out of its normal frames and predicts events to come.

7. At the close, the Swede seems to carry the day by defeating Johnnie, but then, in a stunning "reversal," he is murdered. This is no reversal at all, but rather a fulfillment of the story's own premises.

8. Crane wraps up his piece with a stunning bit of magic: The "game" has been completed, and all the characters were "players" in ways they never suspected. All the parts have now fallen into place, according to a higher logic of both violence and art. Here is Crane's dark wisdom. In the final analysis, fate can be seen as an equation; Crane was the scientific observer of crisis.

III. We leave Crane by glancing at his weird text, "The Monster," in which he abandons the melodrama of war, sinking ships, and wild Westerners and Swedes, to come back "home" to small-town America, Whilomville.

A. Here is a version of the town where Tom Sawyer and Huck Finn grew up, a nostalgic place that is poised between gas lights and electric lights, on the threshold of modernity.

B. It is here that the jaunty, lovable, good-looking black handyman, Henry Johnson, performs a heroic act by saving Dr. Trescott's son

Jimmy from a burning house, a house that contains the doctor's laboratory.

1. Johnson is horrendously disfigured—"defigured"—in the process.
2. This faceless man, this "monster," does not know what horror he arouses in people; he starts to "haunt" the town, to become a threat to the community.
3. Crane has crafted a story of racial anxiety that bids to change our view of yesteryear forever. He takes the American small town beyond the neuroses of Anderson's *Winesburg, Ohio*, to offer a vision of horror that is close in spirit to Stephen King and David Lynch.

Essential Readings:

Crane, "The Blue Hotel" "The Monster," "The Open Boat," in *Prose and Poetry* (Library of America, 1984).

―――, *The Red Badge of Courage* (Norton Critical Edition, 1962).

Recommended Readings:

Kazin, *An American Procession* (Vintage, 1985).

Topics for Further Consideration:

1. Explain how Crane challenged received notions about war in The Red Badge of Courage.
2. Both "The Open Boat" and "The Blue Hotel" are made up of explosive contests in which human beings either confront or release great violence. Explain how the two stories differ.

Lecture Forty-Seven—Transcript
Stephen Crane—Scientist of Human Behavior

This is Lecture Forty-Seven, and it's the final lecture on Stephen Crane. Although *The Red Badge of Courage* is clearly the Crane text that is the canonical one—the one that everyone knows—it's also true that he's the author of a body of short stories and other fictions that are sometimes really amazing to read. Moreover, they don't resemble each other. I'm going to speak in this lecture on two of his most famous short stories, "The Open Boat" and "The Blue Hotel," which are totally different in character, and then close the lecture with some commentary on a very strange he wrote called "The Monster."

All three of these stories can be thought of as kind of anatomical in a way, as a kind of scientific scrutiny and critique, again. Of human valor, or the human nervous system under stress, in crisis. Many Crane critics regard the story I want to start with, "The Open Boat," as the finest thing that he wrote. It doesn't have any of the pyrotechnics and the kind of imagistic brilliance of *The Red Badge of Courage*. It doesn't seem to be written in the same impressionist vein. It's based on a real life experience that Crane was on the steamship *Commodore*, and it was headed to Cuba to bring arms to the Cuban rebels, and it went down off the coast of Florida. Crane survived in the water for 30 hours with three other people, a captain, an oiler, and a cook. The oiler, who comes across as the sort of stalwart of the group, did not survive this experience. When Crane had written his piece, he actually gave it to the captain to read before publishing it to make sure that he hadn't cheated, he hadn't somehow fudged on this story or turned it into literature. He wanted it to really have a kind of authentic ring to it.

Many people think that it's Crane's finest piece. It's much more disciplined, more sober, more restrained than anything that we have in the other piece. It signs off on one of the large components of *The Red Badge of Courage*, which is the inner world of Henry Fleming. Crane has focused there on this young man's responses to crisis and to war. In this story, there's virtually no characterization. There's almost nothing said about the psychology of these four people. In fact, these four people on this boat are utterly harmonious, working together. Crane has elected not to explore any kind of psychological inquiry as to what it feels like to be there. He's wanted to do something else instead, which is to deliver their actual situation. You remember that reference, when he was in an iron box in *The Red Badge of*

Courage, the discovery that one is trapped by circumstances and has no maneuvering room or maneuverability. I think that, that's very much what this piece is about. The grandeur of it comes partly from its rigor.

"Many a man ought to have a bathtub larger than the boat which here rode upon the sea. These waves were most wrongfully and barbarously abrupt and tall, and each froth top was a problem in small boat navigation." This text is going to, rigorously show you what it looks like from that bathtub boat, from that tiny little boat in which they spent 30 hours. "As each stately wall of water approached, it shut all else from view of the men in the boat, and it was not difficult to imagine that this particular wave was the final outburst of the ocean, the last effort of the grim water." You see what they see. You cannot see beyond it. He elects to tell you that. He said, "Viewed from a balcony, the whole thing would doubtlessly been weirdly picturesque; but, the men in the boat had no time to see it. If they had had leisure, there were other things to occupy their minds."

This situation of four men in a boat, that size of a bathtub, comes to us really with the same kind of sense of enclosure and torture that we have in Poe's story, "The Pit and the Pendulum." There's a kind of horror here in the total inequality between their own valor and their own craft and the monstrous power of the ocean and the elements. You could read it—he doesn't say this—but you could read it as a discreet metaphor of the human beings' position within that universe, that our lives are that. We are in a tiny, little, frail craft the size of a bathtub in some huge sea that is angry and stormy. We can see no more, each wave that comes over the edges.

Crane has a kind of brilliance for one-liners in this piece. The story's first line is really quite lovely. "None of them knew the color of the sky." That's how the story starts, "None of them knew the color of the sky." I think that you have to chew on that a little bit. It's not because they're colorblind. It's because they're all obviously totally engrossed—have to be—with maneuvering and steering that little bathtub boat that they're in. There's a sense here that you really are locked out as well as locked in, in this text, that this perspectival narrative gives you the sense of imprisonment of these people. There's a kind of integrity in this piece. As I said, it has soberness. It doesn't have the explosive picturesqueness of *The Red Badge of Courage*. Everything is told straight, as these things come to this group of four. He narrates in a kind of really relentless fashion. Even as the boat is ready to go down, you've got this sort of camera-type reporting that's going on. The captain has said:

> "Now, boys, the next one will do for us, sure," said the oiler. "Mind to jump clear of the boat." The third wave moved forward, huge, furious, implacable. It fairly swallowed the dingey, and almost simultaneously the men tumbled into the sea.

That is it. This wave comes, this is the one that will do them in, and then they are in the drink. Crane asks questions in this text as well, about the meaning of this type of experience. He's referring to nature here, and this is the nature again of the Naturalist worldview.

> She did not seem cruel to him, nor beneficent, nor treacherous, nor wise. But she was indifferent, flatly indifferent. It is, perhaps, plausible that a man in this situation, impressed with the unconcern with the universe, should see the innumerable flaws of his life and have them taste wickedly in his mind and wish for another chance. A distinction between right and wrong seems absurdly clear to him, then, in this new ignorance of the grave-edge, and he understands that if he were given another opportunity he would mend his conduct and his words, and be better and brighter during an introduction, or at tea.

That's kind of a sweet closing civilized phrase, given the sort of primitivism of where they are. In another reference that I have often wondered about— it's a garrulousness that's out of place in this story—he develops another analogy that takes the measure of what's happening in this story. I'm going to try this one out on you. This is again the Crane figure, who's the correspondent and who was in the boat. The correspondent had been made acquainted with the fact—now I want you to hear the dryness of this presentation—that a soldier of the Legion lay dying in Algiers. "But he had never regarded it as important. Myriads of his schoolfellows had informed him of the soldier's plight. But the dying had naturally ended by making him perfectly indifferent." You hear that reference, "indifferent," just like nature.

> He had never considered it his affair that a soldier of the Legion lay dying in Algiers, nor had it appeared to him as a matter for sorrow. It was less to him than the breaking of a pencil's point. Now, however, it quaintly came to him as a human, living thing.

There is no longer merely a picture of a few heroes, with the breast of a poet, meanwhile, drinking tea and warming his feet at the grate. It was an actuality; stern, mournful, and fine.

> The correspondent saw plainly the soldier. He lay on the sand with his feet out straight and still. While his pale left hand was upon his chest in an attempt to thwart the going of his life, the blood came between his fingers. In the far Algerian distance, a city of low square forms was set against the sky that was faint with the last sunset hues. The correspondent, plying the oars and dreaming of the slow and slower movements of the lips of the soldier, was moved by profound and perfectly impersonal comprehension. He was sorry for the soldier of the Legion who lay dying in Algiers.

It's just a little insert into this really rigorous text. It's about the sort of *threshold* of knowledge. Only in this critical juncture, mind you, he doesn't have the leisure to think at all. I mean, he's working, like they all are, constantly, relentlessly, to keep that craft afloat. This story, that he had heard as just a piece of data, the kind of stuff that clutters all our minds, all of a sudden is transformed from its informational-neutral status into something rich and strange. He now sees Algiers. He sees this soldier. He sees the hands trying to stanch the blood. It's as if that is the genesis of storytelling in a narrative. You have to be there. You have to be at the edge of death to understand death as something that happens to people, that changes them from being data, facts of life, into something that has pathos.

Mind you, this too has been told in a very sober fashion. He hasn't expatiated on the emotional plenitude of it. It's as if now he understood. That's how this story effectively comes to a close. At the end, they are saved, except that one of them will die. They are brought up to the beach, finally rescued. The last paragraph of the text:

> When it came night, the white waves paced to and fro in the moonlight, and the wind brought the sound of the great sea's voice to the men on shore, and they felt they could then be interpreters.

They felt they could then be interpreters. You have to pay your dues to be an interpreter. It's not a question of having imagination and fantasy. It's a kind of grueling initiation. You have to have been there. You have earned the right then to be a moralist, an interpreter, to say what things mean. There's a very severe code, it seems to me, that's coming into view here. That's "The Open Boat."

The other story—which you really sort of, depending on your taste, have to choose between these two stories—is the utter extravaganza called "The Blue Hotel." I like it a lot. It's a baroque story, even though it's very, very short. It has all of the excesses that you find in *The Red Badge of Courage*.

It doesn't have the sobriety and the kind of tautness and leanness of "The Open Boat." It's a great experiment as well, with behavior in crisis, except that, whereas, "The Open Boat" signs off of any kind of psychological investigation, this one will utterly zoom in on just those features. It's the epitome of the over-sensitized vision of Crane. Sometimes Crane makes you think that he was born with his insides on the outside, that he responds to things like a seismograph. There's a quivering dimension to Crane's work, which is not a necessarily easy piece of equipment to have when you're a journalist covering wars all over the globe. This story, I think, really conveys something of that sort of precariousness and that sense of being sort of constantly bombarded by stimuli.

There's something seismographic about this text, about human explosions that are happening around the clock, the way you might get a sense, if you look at your own EKG or an EEG—and you watch that, you know, that all you have to do is hiccup and the thing goes crazy—you realize that there is a roller coaster dimension to human feeling. That's what this text is going to try to bring out into the open. It's also very consciously artful. In fact, I think it's meta-textual, as they would say today. It's a kind of meditation about its own status as a literary text. It's about language in a way that nothing in *The Red Badge of Courage* or "The Open Boat" tells you. Those are really sort of reporting stories. This one is constantly thinking about its own status, about what it's doing, and about the peculiar role of words in the kinds of crises and explosions that Crane wants to render here.

One way you can tell that it's about language is the way the opening sentence goes: "The Palace Hotel at Fort Romper was painted a light blue, a shade that is on the legs of a kind of heron, causing the bird to declare its position against any background." You're quite aware of the painterly dimensions of this thing. The title of this story has to do with color. It's light blue, and it stands out against this background. The Palace Hotel then was always screaming and howling in a way that made the dazzling winter landscape of Nebraska seem only a gray swampish hush." That's what you've got here. You will see that these terms, screaming and howling, are going to be quite literalized in the text. It's as if the description here is going to generate the story. Here you've got this mildly garish hotel, painted light blue like the color of a certain kind of heron, in this wintry arctic landscape in Nebraska. It's as if this will be the source of some of the fury of the story itself.

The story, as I said, is about art, it's about form, and it's about structure it's about metaphors and it's about theatrical arrangements. This hotel, which seems garish thrown into this particular wintry setting, is what the story is going to measure. This piece is like a chemical experiment. If you put together, the right mix of players into this setting—which is the blue hotel—you can produce an explosion. You can catalyze something. You can make these things come to a boil. The blue hotel is going to be the peculiar container within this arctic freezing setting; it's a big snowstorm.

This blue hotel is run by a man, Scully, who comes to the train as it goes through this town and hopes that people will get off and stay in his hotel. They do. There are a bunch of players in this one. One of them, the most interesting one, is the Swede. One of them is also the correspondent—we know who that's going to be—or the Easterner, that's going to be the Crane figure. Then there's going to be a cowboy, who's a westerner. It's a very sort of interesting mix of people here. But the Swede is the most intriguing figure because he is the extravagant, exaggerated, melodramatic, histrionic figure. He's filled with omens. He comes in. The first description of him is that he resembles a "badly frightened man." He looks like something is the matter. "People have begun to look at him askance as if they wished to inquire what ailed him. He strode toward the men nervously, as if he expected to be assaulted."

A little bit later down, he starts conversation. He speaks to Johnnie, who's the son of the hotel owner.

> "I suppose there have been a good many men killed in this room." The jaws of the other men dropped, and they looked at him.
>
> "What in the hell you talking about?" said Johnnie.
>
> The Swede laughed again his blatant laugh, full of a kind of false courage and defiance. "Oh, you know what I mean all right."
>
> "I'm a liar if I do!" Johnnie protested. ... "What might you be driving at, mister?" The Swede winked at him again. It was a wink full of cunning. His finger shook on the edge of the board. "Well, maybe you think I have been to nowheres. Maybe you think I am a tenderfoot?"
>
> "I don't know nothing about you," answered Johnnie. "I don't give a damn where you been. All I got to say is I don't know what you're driving at. There hain't never been nobody killed in this room."

This sort of ominous talk continues.

"They say they don't know what I mean," he remarked mockingly to the Easterner. [The Easterner is the Crane figure.]

"I don't understand you," the Easterner says.

"Oh, I see, you are all against me."

They continue to get worried about him. Finally he jumps up and he says,

"I don't want to fight! I don't want to fight!"

You read this, and you wonder what's happening?

"I suppose I'm going to be killed here before I can leave this house!" [Then] "These men are going to kill me."

"Kill you?" [This is Scully, the owner] "What are you talking? What is this, Johnnie?"

"Damned if I know. I can't make no sense of it. He says a good many men have been killed in this room, or something like that. Says he's going to be killed here too. I don't know what ails him."

Well, one explanation that the Easterner gives is that this is a kind of cliché picture of the Wild West that the Swede has got in his mind.

"He's frightened!" said the Easterner.

"What of?"

"I don't know, but it seems to me this man's been reading dime-novels. He thinks he's right out in the middle of it—the shooting and the stabbing and all."

"But this ain't Wyoming," says the cowboy, "or none of them places. This Nebraska."

"Yeah," said Johnnie, "why don't he wait till gets out West."

The Easterner laughed. "It isn't any different out there in these days. But he thinks he's right in the middle of hell."

So this is Crane sort of saying he thinks he's got this sort of Hollywood sense of the Wild West. That's what is on his mind. Well, the Swede begins to take over the text, this sense of anxiety, this sense of sort of something bubbling up, fear, this sort of ominous certainty he's going to be killed, sort of wells up into a kind of weird form of behavior where he sorts to take over everything. He wants a chair. "'Scully's going to get it.' 'No,' says the

Swede. 'I'll get it for myself.' He rose and stalked with the air of the owner off into the executive parts of the hotel." We read that he talks; he talks arrogantly, profanely, and angrily. He becomes a sort of magnetic center of things. Scully, the owner, seems to go along with it.

> At six-o'clock supper, the Swede fizzed like a fire-wheel. He sometimes seemed on the point of bursting into riotous song, and in all his madness, he was encouraged by old Scully. ... The Swede cursed frightfully. When Scully returned, his entrance disturbed a cozy and friendly scene. The Swede again cursed. ... The Swede has picked up the fashion of board-whacking, and they begin a card game.

He plays cards with Johnnie and the cowboy and the Easterner. Well, what the story's going to do is take all of the Swede's sort of manic ominous notions and is going to literalize them. All the things that he's worried about are going to happen in the story. You can say this is a kind of big—sort of obvious—device. I want to argue it a peculiar way. I want to say that this story is about how language generates reality. I mean, that is prophecy. A prophecy is; you say something, then it happens. You can say, "Well, that's the gods who have acted on your words." But what if you view it the other way? That it's language itself that becomes so demiurgic, so much the source of reality, that the words generate the deeds. They move from being lingual, from being just words, and they move into plot and into action. I think that's what this text is about.

It has to be motivated. The motivation is one that we're familiar with, three words. "Then suddenly," (this is Scully,) "he heard three terrible words produced by the Swede," (which are,) "you are cheating." Such scenes often prove that there can be little of dramatic import in environment. Any room can present a tragic front, and any room can be comic. This little den was now as hideous as a torture chamber. With that remark, "you are cheating," we're back to "The Open Boat," we're back to this tiny little box that people are in, where pure destruction is getting ready to happen. So the explosions start to take place, and myth begins to take place in front of our eyes. It's as if Crane said, "What I have written about in war, and in people in critical circumstances, like in a bathtub boat in the sea, lives, is present in all human beings if the right circumstances catalyze it." This is the chemistry of Crane.

Under the right circumstances, the war will reappear. Slaughter will come back. That's what will happen in this story. All of these people are going to be transformed into this sort of primitive ritualistic battle. It's as if this is a layer of the psyche that is just waiting for the right kind of stimuli. They're going to fight. They're going to fight it out. The Swede is roaring, "Yes, fight!" He was like a demoniac. "I'll show you what kind of man I am. I'll show who you want to fight. Maybe you think I can't fight. Maybe you think I can't. I show you." The characters start to be transformed. You read about the Celtic visage of the old man who says, "All right, we'll let them fight. I can't put it up with it any longer. I've stood this damn Swede 'til I'm sick. We'll let them fight." And fight they do.

As they fight, each of the characters begins to take on historic dimensions. We've heard the word "Celtic" there. "Scully's face could be seen set in the austere impersonal lines that are pictured on the countenances of the Roman generals." You get a sense that the whole history of war is going to come back into this text.

Suddenly a holocaust of warlike desire caught the cowboy, and he bolted forward, as these two people were slugging it out, with the speed of a bronco.

> 'Go it, Johnnie, go it. Kill him, kill him.' The cowboy, Scully, and the Easterner burst into a cheer that was like a chorus of triumphant soldiery, but before its conclusion the Swede had scuffled agilely (They're all rooting obviously for Johnnie) to his feet and come in berserk abandon at his foe.

Then he destroys Johnnie. He hits him so hard that Johnnie

> ... fell, even as a bundle might fall from a roof. The Swede instantly staggered into a little wind-waved tree and leaned upon it, breathing like an engine, while his savage and flame-lit eyes roamed from face to face as the men bent over Johnnie.

Now, this fight takes place in the outside. They go out of the blue hotel, and they walk into the raging snowstorm. I really think that is the symbolic truth of the story, that the story is now entering into a kind of elemental level of things, where just raw force will be the atmosphere and the stage. This is the experiment he wants to show you, that this phase of things can be triggered or inaugurated by the wrong set of events, if someone calls someone else "a cheat."

I want also to say that this is remarkably connected with the functioning of language. You have a description of Scully's voice as "a voice of thunder." I want to suggest that voice is like thunder, that voice participates in the elements here. As they get angrier and angrier, there's something more and more primitive. The old man, Scully, watching his son take a beating here, burst into a sudden brogue. "I'd like to take that Swede and hold him down on a stone floor." That's how it's written—I'm reading it the way it's written. "And beat him 'til jelly with stick." The cowboy is going crazy the same way. "I'd like to get him by the neck and ha- hammer him." It's split like that, the verb, in the text. "Hammer that there Dutchman." Cowboy doesn't think he's a Swede. "Dutchman 'til he couldn't tell himself from a dead coyote." It's like chorale. "I'd bate him." It's meaning bite, but b-a-t-e is how he spells it. "I'd bate him until he—I'd show him some things."

You've got this sort of contrapuntal language of the cowboy and Scully both getting brought into the crescendo here. I want you to hear that it's a speech crescendo. It's a kind of verbal crescendo. The Swede defeats Johnnie. He defeats Johnnie, and he then goes out of the blue hotel, we can't figure out where this story's going. He goes into a bar. He's pretty proud of himself. He says he loves snowstorms. This is his element. He's drinking, he sees this other little gambler and asks this man to drink with him. The gambler doesn't want to [but he] insists that the gambler drink with him. "You won't drink with me, you little dude. I'll make you then, I'll make you." He grabs the gambler by the throat, and of course, the gambler has this long knife, which he puts right into the Swede. "A long blade in the hand of the gambler shot forward, and a human body, the citadel of virtue, wisdom, power, was pierced as easily as if it had been a melon."

So the story ends exactly with the way the Swede had forecast it. He will be murdered. Not quite in the framework that he anticipated, but in the barroom instead. In fact "he buys it," in our phrase, that's the way the story is written. "The corpse of the Swede, alone in the room, had its eyes fixed on the dreadful legend that dwelt atop of the cash machine, "This registers the amount of your purchase." It's like a kind of economic transaction.

At the end of the story, we learn, to our amazement, that Johnnie was cheating, that the Swede was right. The Easterner, the Crane figure, had seen it. The cowboy can't believe it. Then the Easterner gives him his theory of what happened here. "Johnnie was cheating. I saw him. I know it. I saw him. I refused to stand up to be a man. I let the Swede fight it out alone. And you, you were simply puffing around the place and wanting to fight." And then old Scully himself, "We're all in it." Watch how this becomes translated into a linguistic formulation. This poor gambler isn't even a noun, the man who actually put the knife in. He's not even a noun. He's a kind of an adverb. "Every sin is the result of a collaboration. We five of us have collaborated in the murder of this Swede." This is the infernal machine. This is the box he was in a box. This is the machinery of fate. We are all players. None of us choose it. We have no volition. These things are being played out. We are acted on. The last line, the cowboy, "Well, I didn't do anything, did I?" And the whole story says it doesn't make any difference what you thought you were doing. That was what was coming to pass here.

The last story—has a kind of coda that I'll just say a word about—is this weird piece called, "The Monster." In it, Crane goes to small town Americana, Whilomville. It's like Twain's Hannibal, Missouri. It's the place where Huck Finn and Tom Sawyer lived. It's a town going from gaslights to electric lights. He tells a story of a young man, Henry Johnson, who is black, likeable, and favored among the women, saves the life of this young boy from a fire—the boy's father is a doctor and this happens in the doctor's house, in the doctor's lab—as he saves this boy's life, he falls unconscious going out of this burning house and chemicals come into his face and destroy his face. He has no face. He haunts the town. He becomes the monster of the town.

It's a vicious story. It's about horror. It's Edgar Allan Poe with a racist character. He haunts this town, and we begin to see a kind of America that goes out of the 19th century, beyond Sherwood Anderson, but towards Stephen King and David Lynch, a bucolic world that has turned into a nightmare.

Lecture Forty-Eight
Charlotte Perkins Gilman—War Against Patriarchy

Scope: Charlotte Perkins Gilman is not a name that everyone will recognize, yet she is indisputably one of the exciting and provocative additions to the "canon." Moreover, there is nothing vogue or whimsical about her new status: She is going to stay, and when people read American literature a century from now, they will still be reading her masterpiece, "The Yellow Wallpaper." Although largely eclipsed through most of the 20th century, Gilman was a veritable powerhouse a century ago. She was known most of all for her ground-breaking feminist work, as seen in key publications such as *Women and Economics* (1898), in which she announced a bold prophetic program of social reform based on recognition of women's rights (as opposed to their ongoing "enslavement" by the institutions of marriage, home, and work). But "The Yellow Wallpaper" is more than feminist tract; in addition to being a companion piece to Chopin's *The Awakening*, it belongs, as well, in the Gothic and psychic tradition of American romance, as seen in the horror stories of Poe and the psychological probings of Hawthorne, Melville, and James. Gilman's fictional account of her skirmish with madness is a harrowing descent into a mind on the brink—indeed a mind that goes over the brink—and also a rich social portrait of the power relations between men and women in the 19th century. Like all great art, this brief story bears witness, and we have much to learn, even today, in our seemingly more egalitarian age, from its depiction of woman's key dilemma in culture: Work? Or family? Have we solved this in our time?

Gilman's name and work, familiar to readers a century ago, were largely eclipsed until the reissue of "The Yellow Wallpaper" by the Feminist Press in 1973, the decade of *Roe v. Wade* and a host of landmark decisions about the rights of women in America. Gilman comes from the distinguished Beecher family, leaders of American feminism in the 19th century, yet her life and work are also stamped by the vicissitudes of family, especially by the impossible demands placed on women. The author's problems with marriage and childbirth led to the (loaded) diagnosis of "hysteria," which, in turn, led Gilman to her fateful encounter with

America's ruling physician of hysteria, S. Weir Mitchell. Mitchell prescribed for Gilman his then-famous remedy, the Rest Cure, and from that experience of torture we have the hypnotic tale, "The Yellow Wallpaper," the harrowing account of a woman essentially going mad by doctor's orders.

Objectives—Upon completion of this lecture, you should be able to:

1. Summarize how some of Gilman's ideas prefigured the feminist movement of the late 20th century;

2. Explain the nature of Gilman's ambiguous depiction of madness in "The Yellow Wallpaper"; and

3. Compare Gilman's depiction of vision with that portrayed in other classic American writers like Melville.

Outline

I. Gilman's brief short story, "The Yellow Wallpaper," indisputably crashed the gates and entered the American canon in literature, taking many by surprise.

   A. "The Yellow Wallpaper" was first published in 1892, then anthologized by William Dean Howells in *Great American Short Stories* in 1920, and then largely forgotten.

   B. The Feminist Press reissued this text in 1973, and it is now among the most widely read and assigned American texts of the 19th century. Along with Kate Chopin's *The Awakening*, "The Yellow Wallpaper" has simply changed the way we understand gender arrangements in the 19th century. Although the general public may not be familiar with Gilman, her name was indeed a household term a century ago.

II. Gilman comes from one of the most influential intellectual families of the 19th century, the Beechers. Her great-aunts were Harriet Beecher Stowe (*Uncle Tom's Cabin*), Catherine Beecher (pioneering advocate for new roles for women in the household), and Isabella Beecher Hooker (women's suffragist).

   A. Yet, in ways that are specific and often tragic, *family* seems to be the greatest problem of Gilman's life and her art.

1. Her father, Frederick Beecher Perkins, was an intellectual who abandoned his wife and child and led to their continuous economic straits.
2. Her mother was a cold, repressed woman, and we know from Gilman herself just how love-starved she was as a child.
3. After much hesitation, Charlotte married Walter Stetson, a handsome Rhode Island artist, a free spirit in some areas but decidedly conservative in his views on marriage. We have a record of Charlotte's constant wrestling with the double demands of marriage versus work. It is here that she is an emblematic figure for women today.
4. In 1887 Charlotte gave birth to a daughter, Katherine, a somewhat sickly infant, and she experienced what—today— we would call *post-partum depression*.
5. She was then sent to the leading neurologist in America, S. Weir Mitchell, who was especially famous for his treatment of hysterical or neurasthenic women. Hysteria, a "condition" that has been discussed by (male) doctors ever since the Greeks, was rife in 19th-century America. Emotional instability, regressive behavior, nervous fits—the whole phenomenon usually related to some form of alleged sexual disorder. Mitchell's Rest Cure was the great 19th-century answer to this problem; Charlotte underwent it.
6. Charlotte almost lost her mind. Finally she bolted, left both Walter and Katherine, and moved to California to live with her friend Grace Channing. In 1891 she wrote "The Yellow Wallpaper"; in 1913, she wrote "Why I Wrote the Yellow Wallpaper," explaining her reasons for the text.
7. Charlotte later lived with both Grace and Walter (who were, by then, married to each other), and the three of them jointly brought up Katherine.

B. Readers a century ago would have known a different Charlotte Perkins Gilman, the author of explosive texts about the conditions of women in America. In particular, her *Women and Economics* (1898) was a landmark book; it is now a forgotten classic.
1. Gilman attacked the way female children were brought up in America, indicting the "sexuo-economic" relationship that enslaves women in marriage, and tracing its despotic hold in child rearing.

2. Gilman also indicted "home" as the locus of gender exploitation and other forms of imprisonment. She argued that children need not be raised by their blood mothers but can be reared in collectives, a view that points beyond even nurseries toward our contemporary day-care centers.

C. Other texts, such as *The Home: Its Work and Influence* and *Human Work* continue the attack against patriarchal arrangements. She consistently argued from a socialist position against the American worship of the ego, rather than valuing the importance of the collective. She proposed kitchenless houses, feminist apartments, new dress codes, and new spaces where new social relations might be fostered. Gilman was a friend and equal to Susan B. Anthony and Jane Addams of Hull House. Sigmund Freud knew and respected her work.

D. Nonetheless, if she is to be remembered tomorrow, it will doubtless be for "The Yellow Wallpaper," her only fictional effort that is unvitiated by didacticism.

III. "The Yellow Wallpaper" was seen, from the beginning, as a horror story, but the terms of that horror have changed over the years.

A. Gilman tried to get the piece published when she wrote it in 1891, but the *Atlantic Monthly* vehemently rejected it.

B. What happens in this strange story?
   1. A nameless female protagonist recounts her experience of Weir's Rest Cure in an ancestral house while on vacation with her child, sister-in-law/helper, and doctor/husband, who prescribes and supervises the cure.
   2. Essentially confined to the bedroom/nursery, the protagonist secretly writes about her experience in violation of the "rules" against writing.
   3. Her writing displays an increasing fascination with the strange yellow wallpaper in her room, and she begins to discern odd patterns in it, finally identifying with it, and ultimately "entering" into a realm that is hard to name—Fantasy? Madness? Freedom?

C. The Feminist Press reissued this text in 1973, a decade of achievements in American women's issues.

1. The story was initially thought to be a heroic tale of feminine resistance, an emblematic version of the well-known thesis of Gilbert and Gubar: "the madwoman in the attic."

2. As the feminist debate has become more complex, with many earlier gains now reconsidered, and as ideological criticism has focused ever more on the insidious forces that constitute subjectivity itself, this tale becomes less clear. Is it a victory? Can madness be a triumph? Is patriarchy altered by the outcome?

3. Given the vantage point of this course—our knowledge of complicated first-person narratives in Poe, Melville, and James—we can see the richness and ambiguities of Gilman's achievement. In particular, as in "Benito Cereno," we will be attentive to the cultural component of *seeing*, the use of metaphors, and the parallel between "our" reading experience and the protagonist's interpretation of the wallpaper. Finally, we will want to ask: What is madness? Escape? Freedom? And how does our interpretation parallel that of the narrator?

4. Let us consider the opening page of this story, to see the richness of tone that Gilman achieves at the outset. The writing exhibits a skepticism of conventional Victorian attitudes.

Lecture Forty-Eight—Transcript
Charlotte Perkins Gilman—War Against Patriarchy

This is Lecture Forty-Eight, and it's the first of two lectures on Charlotte Perkins Gilman's story, "The Yellow Wall-paper." One of the pleasures in doing this course on American Classics is to put in a few surprises. In fact, "The Yellow Wall-paper" is now firmly established as a sort of new conical text; but, for a lot of people in the general public, it's not a text that they've heard of; and, she's not an author that people know anything about. This is a must read and it's an easy read; it's all of 20 pages long. It's one of the great, new entries into the canon; and, it's probably one of the most taught texts we have today in American studies or in women's studies.

Charlotte Perkins Gilman, as I said, isn't a name that everybody recognizes. The story "The Yellow Wall-paper" was first published in 1892; and, William Dean Howells anthologized it in a collection of Great American Short Stories in 1920. Then, it essential disappeared after that. It was reprinted by the Feminist Press in 1973 and now it's among the most widely read American text of the 19th century in women's studies, in American literature courses and world literature courses. I think that anyone who reads it isn't likely to forget it. It ranks, essentially, with the texts like Kate Chopin's book, *The Awakening,* as a kind of explosive new voice that we've not paid attention to from the 19th century.

The irony in everything that I've just told you is that if we have American grandparents and great grandparents they'd have know exactly who she was. Charlotte Perkins Gilman was a household name at the beginning of the 20th century. She comes from one of the most distinguished 19th century American families, the Beechers. Her great aunts were Harriett Beecher Stow, author of *Uncle Tom's Cabin,* Catherine Beecher, who was one of the pioneering advocates of new roles for women in the household—of which is a very much a part of what Charlotte Perkins Gilman does—and then her other aunt was Isabella Beecher Hooker, who was one of the major promoters of Suffrage Rights and Women's suffrage. She comes from an extremely eminent family.

The double irony here is that family is the great problem in her work, and it's the great problem in her life. Her father, Frederick Beecher Perkins, was an intellectual who essential abandoned his family and led to their economic straights. They moved 18 times in 19 years. Her mother was a very cold, repressed woman who found it impossible to give Charlotte any affection, and there are memories that we have of Charlotte referring back to these days.

> She would not let me caress her, and would not caress me, unless I was asleep, this I discovered at last and did my best to keep awake until she came to bed. Even using pens to prevent dropping off and sometimes succeeding. Then how carefully I pretended to be asleep and how rapturously I enjoyed being gathered into her arms, held close and kissed.

It's a heart breaking confession. It's about a love-starved child written from the perspective of a woman who measures how much damage this has inflicted on her; and, we're going to see that this is a recurring pattern in her own life and her own role as mother.

After considerable hesitation she married a very, dashing, handsome Rhode Island artist named Walter Stetson. He was quite a bohemian in terms of the way he lived; but, he had very conservative views about gender and about the way she was supposed to live, which lead to great problems, un-resolvable problems, for her. One letter states that quite simply "as much as I love you, I love work better and I cannot make the two compatible." She's one of our strongest apologist for work as the basis for sanity and a sense of well-being; and, moreover, she states, with great clarity, the central conflict in the lives of many, many young women in this society today. So, a century before now we have someone articulating the irreconcilable tug of war, between work on the one hand, and marriage on the other. The text I think is really luminous from that point of view.

In 1887 she gave birth to a daughter, Katherine, who was a sickly child—not terribly sick but sickly, colicky this that and the other—and experienced what today we'd call—but they didn't have this language then—a postpartum depression. That's a very central notion for understanding what this story is about. With this depression, she was sent to the leading neurologist in America in the late 19th century, he was the immensely successful, S. Weir Mitchell, who was particularly famous for his treatment of hysteria—or *neurasthenic* as they then often said—women. If you looked at 19th century cultural studies you realize that America appears to be crawling with hysterical women.

Hysteria is a term that has been used usually by men to describe women's ailments. The etymology of hysteria goes back to the Greek term for uterus, and it's thought that any of these symptoms, or this disorder in general, is probably associated with some aspect of female reproduce or sexual or menstrual problems. At least, that's how it was thought then. As you know, right on into Freud and others this tradition continues, of dealing with hysteria. Hysterical patients were emotionally unstable. They were thought to be regressive. They had nervous fits that looked a great deal like epileptic seizures. People argued about the etiology of hysteria. As I said, people thought it went back to some sort of a sexual disorder. Sometimes people thought, however, it could go back to other kinds of mistakes in life, like masturbation. If a woman masturbated this might, in fact, provoke this hysteria. Some thought it was a metabolic disorder. Some people thought that these women were over sexed. Some thought that they were frigid; and, in general, we have case studies of women who thought of themselves as nymphomaniacs and others who thought of themselves as frigid. All of this, a kind of cluster of symptoms, had to do with hysteria.

I'm going to read you—you may think I'm being sensationalist, but this is the way a New York physician in the 1840s described one of his hysterical patients.

> The patient writhing like a serpent upon the floor rending her garments to tatters, plucking out handfuls of hair and striking her person with violence with contorted and swollen countenance and fixed eyes resisting every effort of bystanders to control her.

I mean it really is a spectacle. Well, Weir Mitchell had developed this famous "rest cure," which was the way that you could effectively treat this disorder. I'm going to read you Mitchell's own language for what's involved in the rest cure. This is Mitchell.

> I have, of course, made use of every grade of rest for my patients: from insisting upon repose on a lounge for some hours a day, up to entire rest in bed. In carrying out my general plan of treating in extreme cases it is my habit to ask the patient to remain in bed from six weeks to two months at first and, in some cases, for four or five weeks. I do not permit the patient to sit up or to sew or write or read or to use the hands in any active way except to clean the teeth. Where at first the most absolute rest is desirable, I arrange to have the bowels and water passed while laying down, and the patient is lifted onto a lounge for an hour in the morning and again at bed time and then lifted back again into the newly made bed.

This is how one feminist has described, very distinctively, how she understands Mitchell's procedure. "The aggressive sexual content of the classic rescuer, with its assault on almost every orifice of the passive adult female body, is obvious." If you think about what's happening in this particular cure, apart from the infantizing of the woman as well, no activity; above all, no reading.

That's what Charlotte Perkins Gilman had; she took the rest cure. She almost lost her mind, and she bolts, she leaves. She left her daughter, Katherine, with her husband, which was quite a thing to do in those days, went to California to live with a woman friend who was an old friend of hers, and eventually wrote "The Yellow Wall-paper" in 1891. Years later, in 1913, she also wrote a little piece called "Why I wrote The Yellow Wall-paper" which need to hear. She says "Many a many reader has asked that, why I wrote it." She says that one Boston physician protested the story and said it ought not to be written,

> ... it was enough to drive anyone mad. Another physician, in Kansas I think, wrote to say it was the best description of incipient insanity he had ever seen, and—begging my pardon—had I been there? Now the story goes like this: For many years I suffered from a severe and continuous nervous breakdown tending to melancholia—and beyond. During about the third year of this trouble I went, in devout faith and some faint store of hope, to a noted specialist in nervous diseases, the best known in the country. This wise man put me to bed and applied the rest-cure, to which a still-good physique responded so promptly that he concluded there was nothing much the matter with me, and sent me home with solemn advice to 'live as a domestic a life as far as possible,' to 'have but two hours' intellectual life a day,' and 'never to touch pen, brush, or pencil again' as long as I lived. This was in 1887. I went home and obeyed those directions for some three months, and came so near the borderline of utter mental ruin that I could see over.

And she explains that she then worked her way out of this.

> Using the remnants of intelligence that remained, helped by a wise friend, I cast the specialist's advice to the winds and went to work again—work, the normal life of every human being; work, in which is joy and growth and service, without which one is a pauper and a parasite—ultimately recovering some measure of power. Being naturally moved to rejoicing by this narrow escape, I wrote "The Yellow Wall-paper," with its embellishments and additions,

to carry out the ideal (I never had hallucinations or objections to my mural decorations) and I sent a copy to the physician who so nearly drove me mad. He never acknowledged it. This little book is valued by alienist and as a good specimen of one kind of literature. It has, to my knowledge, saved one woman from a similar fate—so terrifying her family that they let her out into normal activity and she recovered. But the best result is this. Many years later I was told that the great specialist had admitted to friends of his that he had altered his treatment of neurasthenia since reading "The Yellow Wall-paper."

Well, this is an interesting piece of cultural history. Gilman's later life involved living in a ménage a tois with Walter and with Grace Channing—her friend, who then later became Walter's wife—and the three of them then brought up the daughter Katherine.

I said our grandparents and great grandparents would have recognized her name, but they wouldn't have recognized, "The Yellow Wall-paper," that's not what they would've thought. She was known as one of the leading intellectuals in the country and certainly—arguably—the leading female intellectual in the country at the end of the 19th century. She wrote a book that was a classic called *Women in Economics* published in 1898. In it there were a number of theories are worth referring to. One is her sustained charge that female children are brought up in such a way as to produce a servile personality. What she calls the "sexual economic relationship" that, essentially, is like being brought up in a harem, the way young girls are brought up. She challenges the gender differences in the way we treat young girls versus young boys. She talks about the way young girls are clothed, the dress modes and everything else. She indicts home itself as the locus of all of this kind of corruption and enslavement of women and the female children. She makes the argument their blood mothers shouldn't—needn't—raise children. Those are not necessarily the best people to raise children; they could be raised in collectives. So she looks, already it seems, to have moved past nurseries, to day-care centers or kibbutz's, to the way that other societies have thought about these matters.

She wants economic independences for woman. In other texts such as "The Home: Its Work and Influence"—you can imagine the argument that goes on there and another one called "Human Work"—she indicates over and over what we now would call "patriarchal arrangements." She also is a real socialist. She indicts as well, the individualist creed and ethos of American culture. The way that we're trained and brought up is to believe in our own personal sovereignty, our own individual freedom, our own sort of, "go at it alone/can do" physiology of life. She argues that the cultivation of the ego is a kind of a diseased phenomenon because we totally overlook and scant the importance of the group, the collective, the community, of the society of which we are a part. There's another important move as well in her work, she proposes new kind of buildings, she interested in architecture, she wants houses without kitchens, she wants feminist apartment houses, and she wants spaces where new kinds of social relations might be possible.

I can see in this the kind of thinking—that you'd get in the Le Corbusier in the 1920s—where he wants to re-imagine apartment buildings in which we could reconceive the relations between men and women and families. I see Gilman's ideas at the core of that. She was a friend of the people who were important in the feminist movement in the late 19th century, such as Susan B. Anthony or Jane Adams of Howell's house. As you probably could guess, people like Freud knew about her work, she courted them. She wanted to get women past the four K's: *kütchen, kinder, kierscher, klider*; those German K's, the kitchen, children, the church and clothes. That's how she would've been remembered if we could go back in time and ask people in 1900, "Who was Charlotte Perkins Gilman?" If we ask anybody today— and certainly if we ask anybody probably tomorrow—who she was, it will be "the person who wrote "The Yellow Wall-paper."

She wrote a lot of fiction, most of which is not considered very good, it's usually very didactic; but, this piece is a keeper. She hoped the story would be published in 1891; she had trouble getting it in print then. She sent it to Howells, who sent it to his own reader, Horace Scudder, who was the editor of the *Atlantic Monthly* who returned it with this message: "I could not forgive myself if I have made others as miserable as I have made myself." [He] didn't want this one to be published at all.

So what's the story about? It's told from the point of view of a nameless female protagonist who essential undergoes a version of Mitchell's rest cure in an ancestral home while on vacation with her husband—who happens to be a doctor and who prescribes the cure—and with her child whom we never see in the text and with her sister-in-law who was a helper. She spends all her time—because this is what is essentially decreed for her—in this bedroom in this ancestral house, which really is also a former nursery as she comes to understand but she, the child, isn't there. She sneaks her writing in because that's one of the things she's forbidden to do, but the writing is the story, it's for us to get her account. She writes about her increasing fascination with the strange yellow wallpaper in this room, and she begins to see odd patterns in it and she begins to identify with it, and she begins to enter in some sense into it and into a kind of fantasy world that it generates, and into visionary states.

This text, published in 1973 by the Feminist Press, is [in] the same decade as Rowe vs. Wade. It's a decade that marks, essentially, one of the great high points, and one of the most sort naive and positive moments of the American feminist movement in the 1970s. This text comes across as a kind of *heroic banner* text at that point. It's not an accident that is who published it. It was thought to be a great tale of female resistance. An emblematic version of a book that was also published in the late 1970s, that has changed literary circles and that I've alluded to earlier—Gilbert and Guber's book, *The Mad Woman in the Attic*—in which they write about the 19th century female imagination. They write about the sort of characterization of women in 19th century literature which is most perfectly figured in the *Mad Women in the Attic,* and which refers to Bertha Mason Rochester in *Jane Eyre.* That's the condition of the female in the 19th century culture; that she's locked up, she's imprisoned and she goes mad. You can see that a text of a women imprisoned in this room, undergoing this enforced rest cure, could be seen as a perfect sort of specimen as well of the mad women in the attic; and it's a dramatization of her escape.

Now the criticism on this text has changed over the past decades because the feminist debate itself has changed, and it's become more complicated, and a lot of the earlier gains are much more problematic now. It's not certain they can be kept under attack; and moreover, the notion of an empowered heroine sort of single-handily challenging the dictates of a patriarchal culture, that's a more naive view today than it would've been in the 1970s. Partly because of cultural studies and theological criticism, people are more and more attuned to the constraining environmental forces that condition or coerce you know behavior, and in fact, constitutes subjectivity. We're not as confident in determining what this story means. If she does go mad at the end, in what sense could we call that a victory? Is the encounter with the wallpaper to be understood as a kind of assertion? If so, what sort of assertion? Where is this woman at the close of the story? In what sense can we say that she's had a victory? Is patriarchy any the less dominant at the end of this story? Is anybody changed because of this story?

From our point of view in this course on American Literature, we can bring still other perspectives to bear on this. We should think about the breathless, first person narratives of Poe that we've looked at; stories like, "The Telltale Heart" and "The Black Cat." These are ghost stories as well; and, they're stories where the breathless first person is the target as well as the vehicle of the story. This person describes an experience; but we are taught to think about the psychology of that figure as well. We want to reflect, in that sense, about what this means for whom; for her, for us, and for Gilman. It's clear from what I've read to you that Gilman wrote this as a way of accounting for others, for what she'd done, and [for] hopefully helping people.

Those are all a bunch of pointers for we looking at, and let me add to them a few more and then we'll take a brief look at the story. Let's bear in mind a few other things; recall for example, the Melville story "Benito Cereno," where we see everything through the lens, through the prism of the American sea captain Delano, who is very naïve, who thinks that blacks are like Newfoundland dogs, and therefore is singularly ill-equipped to understand the story that he's telling us. Melville, in a kind of diabolic way, delights in having narrators who don't understand the events that they're recounting. You could argue that that to primes us for reading this story, sort of on a slant and at angle, having to decipher everything, having to realize that what one sees isn't just rectal but it's also culturally or ideologically constructed.

Moreover, another issue: What do we make in the pattern in the wallpaper—not just, what does she make of it? A still further issue, and we saw this in talking about "The Turn of the Screw," is how does our reading of this text, our interpretative adventure in some strange and disturbing way, mirror or replicate what she's doing? If she's reading that text and going mad, and we're reading her, what's it telling us about the processes of interpretation, about whether there are any guidelines or conventions that govern it? Finally, as I've already hinted, it makes us wonder about the status of madness. Can madness be thought of as another world; as an escape, as a triumph, or as an assertion? I think that's not an easy one for us to resolve. You know of theories like those of R.D. Lang, where in a kind of simplistic way—I'd rephrase it by saying that he's argued that anyone—that mad people are, in fact, actually responding to the world around them, but it's an appropriate response to the horror of the world and that most of us shut off certain kinds of perceptions or stimuli in order to maintain equilibrium. In some sense, I think Freud's model of the brain bears out that same knowledge; that there are constant stimuli and that homeostasis allows us to keep most of it out.

None of what I've said really tells you much about the tonality of the story, the beauty of the story; and therefore, for you to hear the voice and to realize what a delicious piece it is. What an economy, what a narrative economy Gilman has crafted here to tell this story. It goes like this. I'm going to read you the first page and a little bit more.

> It is very seldom that mere ordinary people like John and myself secure ancestral halls for the summer. A colonial mansion, a hereditary estate, I would say a haunted house, and reach the height of romantic felicity—but that would be asking too much of fate!

I want you to hear echoes of Poe again and of the gothic of haunted houses. She's aware that this will sound exaggerated to call it that, "height of romantic felicity."

> Still I will proudly declare that there is something queer about it. Else, why should it be let so cheaply? And why have stood so long untenanted? John laughs at me, of course, but one expects that in marriage.

That line is going to be uncommented—it's just like that. "John laughs at me of course, but one expects that in marriage." This is par for the course here and this is what marriage is thought to be. He's a doctor she's some sort of frivolous wife; of course her fantasies and her fancies are to be laughed at. Mind you, any critical perspective here then has to be ours. She's not going to say, "What kind of husband is it that laughs at what his wife says and is what kind of a normative definition the marriage is."

> John is practical in the extreme. He has no patience with faith, an intense horror of superstition, and he scoffs openly at any talk of things not to be felt and seen and put down in figures.

You begin to see the kind of collision course here, between the kind of scientific, empirical world view that the doctor/husband has on the one hand, and this woman's own realm, things that are now linked—to be with faith, superstition—things that can't be felt and seen and put down in figures. "John is a physician and *perhaps,* I would not say it to a living soul of course, but this is dead paper and a great relief to my mind. Perhaps that is one reason I do not get well faster."

We're beginning to realize that maybe he's part of the problem. Maybe his mindset is also what's driving me mad, making me sick. You see, he does not believe I'm sick, and what can one do?

If a physician of high standing, and one's own husband, assures friends and relatives that there is really nothing the matter with one but temporary nervous depression—a slight hysterical tendency—what is one to do? (And of course the ante is upped still further) My brother is also a physician, and also high standing, and he says the same thing. So I take phosphates or phosphites—whichever it is, and tonics, and journeys, and air, and exercise, and am absolutely forbidden to 'work' until I am well again. Personally, I disagree with their ideas. Personally, I believe that congenial work, with excitement and change, would do me good. But what is one to do?

I find it a remarkably seductive opening to a story. We come into that voice. We see this strange mixture of stereotypical Victorian notions about husbands and wives. "He laughs at me and that's what one expects in a marriage," and a healthy suspicion nonetheless that there's something, that maybe he's the root of my problem, that maybe all of these doctors, these males, these people with these scientific views and their suspicion or their sort of mockery of anything that would be imagination, that maybe that's what the problem is, and the marvelous sense that "I wouldn't tell this to a soul." I mean those lines in literature are always delicious because we're getting it; it's being told to us and it couldn't be more public than this. It allows us to begin to realize that writing is going to be liberating. It's going to be emancipatory. Where it's going to lead is less clear; but, it's going to be the one free access that she has, access to others, access to her own feelings, which can then be articulated [and] materialized through language. All of that, I think, is shown to us in the first page. We'll look at the rest of it in the next lecture.

Lecture Forty-Nine

"The Yellow Wallpaper"—
Descent into Hell or Free at Last?

Scope: This 20-page account of a young wife's ordeal while "convalescing" is one of the most harrowing and unforgettable pieces of prose in American literature, lodging itself in the minds of readers much the way Kafka's grisly fables do. Gilman achieves an astonishing richness and economy in her piece by using the husband, John, as the wife's doctor. This characterization illuminates both the crippling gender arrangements of the 19th century and gives us an all too recognizable portrait of doctor-patient bullying that resonates even today. Yet, the story's strongest claim on us involves the difficulty of final assessment: What can we make of the protagonist's increasing entry—and final exit—into fantasy? Is it indeed fantasy? What do readers see in this remarkable wallpaper? Is Gilman's text about a single, conceivably psychotic woman, or is it about the operation of an entire culture?

Objectives—Upon completion of this lecture, you should be able to:

1. Summarize the importance of the movement from description to pattern in Gilman's depiction of the wallpaper;

2. Explain the ways in which "The Yellow Wallpaper" can be viewed as a "triumph of imagination" and as a "social tragedy"; and

3. Describe how Gilman's story can be seen as a parable about women in general, not just one woman.

Outline

I. It is no accident that the bedroom where the protagonist is to have her Rest Cure is also a former nursery. Motherhood and babies are part of this story.

    A. Gilman offers us a number of details about this nursery that make us wonder where we are.

1. The room is also said to be a gymnasium, complete with barred windows and "rings and things in the walls." There are unsettling connotations here.
2. We hear repeatedly how heavy the bed is, even that it is "nailed down," and again, as readers of Poe, we wonder.
3. In a remarkable sequence, we learn that the entire floor is scratched and "gouged." With this description, it is hard not to think of torture chambers where people have suffered in the past, and where they are to suffer once again.

B. The central feature of the story is, of course, the astonishing wallpaper.
1. It is first described in terms that move from the aesthetic to the experiential. Gilman's terms are, once again, loaded.
2. Particular attention is given to the color of the paper. It is a yellow that is "unclean," that is "sickly sulphur." Here too the connotations are interesting: urine, feces, babies, semen?
3. The protagonist's project of deciphering the wallpaper is, of course, a violation of the husband's basic law: No writing. What does this tell us about writing? About women's options? About authority?
4. Above all, the protagonist is admonished not to give way to "fancy," and "fancy," or imagination, is, of course, the generative force not only of this story, but of literature itself.
5. The husband, John, is portrayed with a mix of horror and sympathy. He genuinely believes he is a perfect mate; we see his patronizing and bullying very differently. How might his behavior be viewed in the 19th century?
6. The descriptions of the wallpaper start to become more urgent and disturbing, especially in the depictions of uncontrollable organic and vegetable life. What do these descriptions connote?
7. The crucial move from description to pattern is enacted as the protagonist begins to make out a "story" and "figures" in the paper. She understandably fears what is now unfurling. The pattern seems to grow, to become virtually cancerous.
8. At this point, the wallpaper resembles the old polaroid film that comes into focus as you watch it. The contours that begin to appear tell a shocking story about entrapment. Whose?

9. As the narrator seems to move ever more fatefully and passionately into the realm of fantasy and vision, we note that she begins to take control of the story, even usurping the traditional prerogatives of the doctor himself: surveillance and diagnosis.

10. The final pages register the vertiginous "exit" of the protagonist into the "wallpaper," as the story of entrapment and liberation becomes more urgent and hallucinatory. The world of the wallpaper moves to the world outside the window. The protagonist becomes the "authority" of the text through fantasy.

II. The great challenge of Gilman's story is: What do we make of it?

A. As we watch the protagonist move further into the realm of imagination and fantasy, we are reminded of that "Negro country" that Babo was seeking in Melville's "Benito Cereno," a place where personal imagination becomes law and reality. Here is the realm of virtuality and of art.

B. We cannot escape, however, the awful recognition that this so-called triumph of imagination is a social tragedy. It "proves" that women are hysterics. It leaves the patriarchy stronger than ever. And it leaves us with questions about the possible efficacy of vision. Can madness ever be an answer?

C. Although the protagonist's own fate is ambiguous, there is nothing ambiguous at all about the gender and cultural arrangements that Gilman is able to illuminate through her extremist fable.

1. Gilman offers us, decades before Woolf's famous essay, a hallucinatory version of "A Room of One's Own."

2. Yet, Gilman also gives us a story about a group, not just one woman, that is entrapped and seeking emancipation. Art offers us a kind of script and illumination that could scarcely be conceived or actualized in other ways.

Essential Readings:

Gilman, *"The Yellow Wallpaper"* (Rutgers University Press, 1993).

Recommended Readings:

Essays in Erskine and Richards, eds., *"The Yellow Wallpaper"* (Rutgers University Press, 1993).

Topics for Further Consideration:

1. Can you place "The Yellow Wallpaper" in the horror story trajectory that we have seen in Poe and James?

2. What kind of moral or social valuation do you finally give to the close of "The Yellow Wallpaper"?

Lecture Forty-Nine—Transcript
"The Yellow Wallpaper"—
Descent into Hell or Free at Last?

This is Lecture Forty-Nine, and it's the last of the lectures on Charlotte Perkins Gilman. In this one, I would like to deal more frontally with the story itself, not just about Gilman, and to take a closer look at the actual mechanics of the story, the way it moves. It's really quite a dazzling performance. I don't know anything exactly like it. You'd have to reach out to writers like Kafka, perhaps, to find some sort of parallel.

As we noted, this narrator, this protagonist, this woman, the wife is sort of imprisoned in this room, more or less, which seems to have been some kind of a nursery. I say "some kind" because it's described in very sort of suggestive ways.

> It is a big, airy room, the whole floor nearly, with windows that look all ways, and air and sunshine galore. It was nursery first and then playroom and gymnasium, I should judge; for the windows are barred for little children, and there are rings and things in the walls.

You begin to get the hint that the barred windows, and the rings, and things in the walls, that she has earlier compared this place to a haunted house, and that this room is going to look more and more like a torture chamber. That the bed, we are told, is very heavy. The bed itself seems nailed down to the floor. We read that, "The floor is scratched and gouged and splintered. The plaster itself is dug out here and there, and this great, heavy bed which is all we found in the room, looks as if it had been through the wars." I say torture. You get the sense that creatures have tried to get out. They've gouged, they've scratched, and they've left their markings. This space that she's in bears a kind of history, a record, a series of traces that queue into the story that's coming, that make it more ominous and threatening. She will not say that. She will not interpret these things. She just describes them, and says, "This is what I see:" the bars, the rings, the things, the gouges, the scratches. But most readers begin to suspect punishment, torture, something very bizarre happening.

Needless to say, the primary ingredient here is the wallpaper itself, and it's described in fairly remarkable ways. Here's how she describes it:

One of those sprawling flamboyant patterns committing every artistic sin. It is dull enough to confuse the eye in following, pronounced enough to constantly irritate and provoke study, and when you follow the lame uncertain curves for a little distance they suddenly commit suicide—(That's an unusual description of a pattern in a wallpaper curves an then it offs itself, commits suicide) plunge off at outrageous angles, destroy themselves in unheard of contradictions.

So what kind of pattern could this thing be? She goes on to describe her sensory response to this paper:

The color is repellent, almost revolting; a smoldering unclean yellow, strangely faded by the slow-turning sunlight. It is a dull yet lurid orange in some places, a sickly sulpher tint in others. No wonder the children hated it! I should hate it myself if I had to live in this room long. There comes John, and I must put this away,— he hates to have me write a word.

A lot is on show here: that the writing is done on the sly, that he is the censor who will not allow the text to exist at all; but also, the characteristics of the paper that I've just cited for you. They "commit suicide," and they "destroy themselves in unheard of contradictions." These terms start to hum and echo and resonate in this story. You begin to realize that this is talking about her cultural status. It's talking about, perhaps, her own agenda— suicide—and the characteristics of the paper: repellant, revolting, smoldering, unclean, yellow, sulfur tint. It's a nursery.

This woman has just given birth to a child whom she's not really taking care of. People have argued that this yellowish texture, color, smell— sulfur—suggests feces, urine, diapers, the uncleanness, the odors of a baby's body; and, perhaps one could go further and suggest the odors of anybody. In any event, we begin to realize there's a whole cluster here, there's a certain amount of synesthesia in this story; things go together.

Of course, John is not very interested in any of this and he wants her to stop fantasizing about this story, about the paper. "John says, 'We will ask Cousin Henry and Julia down for a long visit,' but he says he would as soon put fireworks in my pillow-case as to let me have those stimulating people about now." It's a wonderful phrase "fireworks in my pillow-case." What a sort of image of insanity itself, or the bed, what happens when we are supine for six or eight hours a day, dreaming? That's the way having visits from other people are going to be characterized. That's not allowable.

We're going to see that there are going to be fireworks in her head anyway in this text. He patronizes her in ways that are familiar, "You know the place is doing you good," he said, "and really, dear, I don't care to renovate the house just for a three months' rental." She wants to remove the yellow paper. He's not going to do that. They're only there for three months. "'Then do let us go downstairs,' I said, 'there are such pretty rooms there.' Then he took me in his arms and called me a blessed little goose, and said he would go down to the cellar, if I wished, and have it whitewashed into the bargain." So he's obviously going to do nothing.

Well, the paper acts up throughout this text. "This paper looks to me as if it knew what a vicious influence it had! There is a recurrent spot where the pattern lolls like a broken neck and two bulbous eyes stare at you upside down." So now the pattern is beginning to come alive. "Two bulbous eyes stare at you, inverted, upside down." There, too, critics have said maybe this suggests the fetus for a little baby, an infant, staring at you. We don't know. The paper continues to exert its power and a pattern begins to emerge.

> This wall-paper has a kind of sub-pattern in a different shade, a particularly irritating one, for you can only see it in certain lights, and not clearly then. But in the places where it isn't faded and where the sun is just so—I can see a strange, provoking, formless sort of figure, that seems to skulk about behind that silly and conspicuous front design.

It's a very important description. It's the beginning of something that's going to be developed further. You've got the front design of the paper; but she begins to aspire, discern behind that, some figure that is skulking about, and I want you to think about what the ramifications of this are, and not just in terms of her imagination. I want you to think about this as a kind of structural setting. You've got a repeating pattern on the one hand, and then you've got this dim perception—or this sort of sporadic perception, depending on the light or whatever—of this figure trapped behind that, skulking about behind that silly and conspicuous front design. I'm going to develop the argument later, with other passages that emphasize this still further, that I think that there's a kind of spatial argument for our own situated-ness within society and within culture here and that there are laws—patterns designs—on the one hand, and we are born into this. We didn't choose it. We didn't construct it. We are the figure that makes our way behind this framework that law and culture have erected.

I'll talk more about that as I go. The pattern emerges more and more fully and she tries to describe it. She says:

> I know a little of the principle of design, and I know this thing was not arranged on any laws of radiation, or alternation, or repetition, or symmetry, or anything else that I ever heard of. It is repeated, of course, by the breadths, but not otherwise.

It keeps repeating but it doesn't follow any design that she's ever seen. Here's the way she describes it:

> Looked at in one way each breadth stands alone, the bloated curves and flourishes—a kind of 'debased Romanesque' with delirium tremens—go waddling up and down in isolated columns of fatuity.

It's really a striking notation: "Bloated curves and flourishes." One thinks again of the body, perhaps of the pregnant body. The story is written of a woman in postpartum depression.

> "Debased Romanesque" with delirium tremens—go waddling up and down in isolated columns of fatuity. But, on the other hand, they connect diagonally, and the sprawling outlines run off in great slanting waves of optic horror, like a lot of wallowing seaweeds in full chase.

There's something really sort of nausea provoking in that description: "Great slanting waves of optic horror," "Wallowing seaweeds." A sense of capsizing, a kind of rolling motion that's being, somehow, promoted and conveyed and actualized by this paper. There's a lot of creatural discomfort in this text. She continues to respond to the paper. She begins to see the figure ever more sharply in it. "Behind that outside pattern the dim shapes get clearer every day." It's always the same shape only very numerous. "And it is like a woman stooping down and creeping about behind that pattern. I don't like it a bit. I wonder—I begin to think—I wish John would take me away from here!" This woman begins to assert herself ever more strongly.

> John was asleep and I hated to waken him, so I kept still and watched the moonlight on that undulating wall-paper till I felt creepy. The faint figure behind seemed to shake the pattern, just as if she wanted to get out. I got up softly and went to feel and see if the paper DID move, and when I came back John was awake.

> "What is it, little girl?" he said. "Don't go walking about like that—you'll get cold."

I want you to see the parallel there. She sees this figure behind the paper trying to get out, shaking the paper. She gets up, walks over to the paper, and feels the paper. He watches her trying to get out. You can't miss the kind of parallelism between her plight, her own condition, and what she perceives in the paper; and, he continues to bully her. He's explaining that she's getting so much better. "Bless her little heart! She shall be as sick as she pleases! But now let's improve the shining hours by going to sleep..." She says, well, "can't we go away?" [He responds] "Only three weeks left. No problem. And you are better." "Better in body perhaps—"

Obviously, she's going to say, "but worse in mind" or "worse in spirit." He doesn't want to have any of this.

> "My darling," said he, "I beg of you, for my sake and for our child's sake, as well as for your own, that you will never for one instant let that idea [Like, I may be losing my mind] enter your mind! There is nothing so dangerous, so fascinating, to a temperament like yours. It is a false and foolish fancy. Can you not trust me as a physician when I tell you so?"

Well, we watch the pattern continue. It grows, and I would like to argue that's probably its strongest feature—is that it grows. It spawns itself. It is the generative principle and it's compared to other things that we know that spawn themselves. "The outside pattern is a florid arabesque, reminding one of a fungus. If you can imagine a toadstool in joints, an interminable string of toadstools, budding and sprouting in endless convolutions—why, that is something like it." I think that this imagery of the toadstools and the funguses—these things that just grow out of the earth, mould, rot, fungus— all of this expresses a kind of horror, it seems to me, of the life-principle— in the sense that it's running amuck. It's producing these terrible forms. It can't be stopped. This is also an appropriate, although disturbing, image for the human imagination, for human fancy. We can't just turn it off. The more we try to control it, in a sense, the more, sort of, activated it becomes; and so, this thing begins to move into kind of unchecked growth— cancerous, in some sense—unstoppable, and it takes over the story, and its image becomes more and more focused.

It reminds me of the Polaroid cameras that we don't use so much any more, where you watch this thing—it starts out black and it takes, you know, X number of seconds as all the contours and colors become a recognizable image. That's the way this 20-page story is moving. It takes on more clarity too, I think, in its ideological implications. "At night, in any kind of light: in twilight, candle light, lamplight, and worst of all by moonlight, it becomes bars!" Can't miss what she's saying here: the outside pattern and the woman behind it is as plain as can be. I didn't realize for a long time what the thing was that showed behind, that dim sub-pattern, but now I am quite sure it is a woman. By daylight she is subdued, quiet. I fancy it is the pattern that keeps her so still, that it is so puzzling. "It keeps me quiet by the hour."

So, you get this sort of sense that, at night, this woman starts to roam. At night, she tries to break out of prison; and once again, that's essentially what the story is about, about this woman trying to find an escape, trying to get through the wall, get through the bars, to make her way out. Now, as I said, for me, that is a kind of allegorical picture of the human subject's position within a culture, that we see the repeating pattern, the repetition, and we see that as a front design, the mesh, as I said, of social and cultural concepts and precepts and then the kind of fitfulness of the human being, sort of trapped behind that.

Two things begin to happen in the last pages of this story and I think it's interesting to think of them together. On the one hand, what everybody recognizes is that this character moves further and further into what we'd have to call a visionary state or madness. She begins to identify further and further with the figure she sees in the wall. A less remarked element of this, however, is that she also begins to take over the doctor's role in the story. She begins to be the person who diagnoses and observes and examines and interprets others. She moves from being the object of the medical gaze, the object of the male gaze, and starts to become the authorized subject, in a sense. And some of the passages go like this; they're really quite wonderful. "The fact is I am getting a little afraid of John." So he's the scary figure. "He seems very queer sometimes." So she's not queer, John is. "And even Jennie," (the maid) "has an inexplicable look." So there she is, the scientist, the doctor. It strikes me as a scientific hypothesis that this paper is making them all loony.

"I have watched John." She's the observer. That's what doctors do is they watch you, they watch your symptoms. That's what Weir Mitchell's job is. Now she's taking on that role, "I have watched John when he did not know I was looking, and come into the room suddenly on the most innocent excuses," and we're beginning to see that she's the strategist of the story, the tactician of the story, surprising others, making their behavior into her knowledge. "…come into the room suddenly on the most innocent excuses, and I've caught him several times *looking at the paper*! And Jennie too. I caught Jennie with her hand on it once." Well, this intrigues her. She grows into this role. "I don't want to leave now until I've found it out, there is a week more, and I think that will be enough." Like, my experiment will probably take exactly a week. "I'm feeling ever so much better! I don't sleep much at night, for it is so interesting to watch developments," Because it's at night that I'm doing my experiment. "... but I sleep a good deal in the daytime."

Well, I see this as a conferring of authority onto this figure. There's a kind of very interesting reversal of roles between her and that of her husband, who is the kind of characteristic sort of figure of power in the story and in her life. So she begins her exit from what we think of as the world of sanity, and it's really hypnotic. "The front pattern does move—and no wonder!" At first, remember, you've seen that as a series of bars, they can't move. Now it's beginning to move. You know why? The woman behind shakes it!

> Sometimes I think there are a great many women behind, and sometimes only one, and she crawls around fast, and her crawling shakes it all over. ... And she is all the time trying to climb through. But nobody could climb through that pattern—it strangles so. I think that is why it has so many heads. They get through, and then the pattern strangles them off and turns them upside down, and makes their eyes white! ... I think that woman gets out in the daytime! And I'll tell you why—privately—I've seen her!

And now the woman is no longer going to be located in the paper. She's moving. She's clearing out. She's outside as well; and what I want you to bear in mind here is that there's a kind of overflowing, there's a kind of lava-like effect here. The vision that has been located entirely in the wallpaper is now extending to the entire public world as well, the world outside the window. "I've seen her! I can see her out of every one of my windows!" She's really getting replicated now. "It is the same woman, I know, for she is always creeping, and most women do not creep by daylight." So these women are making their exit and you can't mistake this, there is a kind of symbolic emancipation here. This is women's liberation in a very peculiar key; these women are coming out from the bars, this is seen as a deranged mind, if you wish, and they're getting outside of that room and they're still creeping, though, all around.

> I see her on that long road under the trees, creeping along, and when a carriage comes she hides under the blackberry vines.

I don't blame her a bit. It must be very humiliating to be caught creeping by daylight! I always lock the door when I creep by daylight.

We're moving into Poe territory now.

I can't do it at night, for I know John would suspect something at once. And John is so queer now, that I don't want to irritate him. I wish he would take another room!

I think that's an important line, too. I don't even want him around anymore; that all of the activity I need—and I want you to hear intellectual, imaginative, but also erotic activity—I don't need this husband around. I lie on that bed and I look at that wallpaper and I am being exercised. There is an engagement here. "Besides, I don't want anybody to get that woman out at night but myself." She's going to be the person who opens the jail, lets out the women. Well, it goes still further.

Jennie wanted to sleep with me—the sly thing! but I told her I should undoubtedly rest better for a night all alone. That was clever, for really I wasn't alone a bit! As soon as it was moonlight and that poor thing began to crawl and shake the pattern, I got up and ran to help her. (And this wonderful notation,) I pulled and she shook, I shook and she pulled.

That's what I had in mind when I said that she's been exercised. To me, that's a very erotic description. These two women, working together, moving the paper away but now united in some kind of joint activity, some rhythmic activity. "I pulled and she shook, I shook and she pulled, and before morning we had peeled off yards of that paper." So we're moving, it seems to me, further and further, if you want, into madness but also out of the kinds of constraints, the kinds of bars, that have kept her; and I think the activity becomes more and more, in a sense, eroticized. It becomes more and more sort of active on her part. She's not just watching any more. She's physically engaged in this. She's the one who opens up the bars. She is the one who is responsible for this person to finally get out, that they become increasingly sistered, paired, inseparable—the figure in the wallpaper and herself—and they can't be kept *in* any longer.

The close of this story is really masterfully written. They're on the verge now of this stay in this haunted house or ancestral home being over. "We shall sleep downstairs to-night, and take the boat home to-morrow. I quite enjoy the room, now it is bare again. How those children did tear about here! This bedstead is fairly gnawed!" She looks at the bed. It's been eaten into. "But I must get to work. I have locked the door and thrown the key down into the front path." Notice now that she's keeping other people out. This is her space—thrown the key away.

> I don't want to go out, and I don't want to have anybody come in, till John comes. I want to astonish him. I've got a rope up here that even Jennie did not find. If that woman does get out, and tries to get away, I can tie her!

She senses, "This is my other self." There is the double role of jailer and inmate. She tries to move the bed. "I could not reach far without anything to stand on! This bed will not move! I tried to lift and push it until I was lame, and then I got so angry I bit off a little piece at one corner, but it hurt my teeth." Do you hear the circularity of this? "This bedstead is fairly gnawed" and then, 10 lines later, "I bit into it." This story is beginning to loop. Everything she saw when she walked into this house: bars on the windows, gouges on the floor, and markings on the bed. This story is producing. It's about what she is doing. It's a terrible story in the circular sense that it bites its own tail. It's about its own production.

> Then I peeled off all the paper I could reach standing on the floor. It sticks horribly and the pattern just enjoys it! All those strangled heads and bulbous eyes and waddling fungus growths just shriek with derision! I am getting angry enough to do something desperate. To jump out of the window would be admirable exercise, but the bars are too strong even to try. Besides I wouldn't do it. … I know well enough that a step like that is improper and might be misconstrued. I don't like to look out of the windows even—there are so many of those creeping women, and they creep so fast. I wonder if they all come out of that wall-paper as I did? … It is so pleasant to be out in this great room and creep around as I please! I don't want to go outside. I won't, even if Jennie asks me to. For outside you have to creep on the ground, and everything is green instead of yellow. But here I can creep smoothly on the floor, and my shoulder just fits in that long smooch around the wall, so I cannot lose my way.

And here, at this closing juncture, John makes his last appearance. He wants to get in and see what's going on.

Why there's John at the door! It is no use young man, you can't open it! How he does call and pound! Now he's crying for an axe. It would be a shame to break down that beautiful door!

"John dear!" said I in the gentlest voice, "the key is down by the front steps, under a plantain leaf!" That silenced him for a few moments.

Then he said—very quietly indeed, "Open the door, my darling!"

"I can't," said I. "The key is down by the front door under a plantain leaf!" And then I said it again, several times, very gently and slowly, and said it so often that he had to go and see, and he got it of course, and came in. He stopped short by the door.

"What is the matter?" he cried. "For God's sake, what are you doing!"

I kept on creeping just the same, but I looked at him over my shoulder.

You have to visualize this: she went like this, doing her creeping in this room.

'I've got out at last,' said I, 'in spite of you and Jane. And I've pulled off most of the paper, so you can't put me back!' Now why should that man have fainted? But he did, and right across my path by the wall, so that I had to creep over him every time!

And that's how it closes. You couldn't write a more compelling story. It is at once, exit and entry. You don't know which to emphasize. Freedom and enslavement, all of those things becomes totally, sort of collapse into each other here. By the end of the story her private view is the authority of the text. She's the speaker of the text. She's the one who causes him to faint. She can't be stopped. She has gotten out, [but] out into what? You know, one doesn't know how to assess that. She's moved into the world, it seems to me, of fantasy and imagination, perhaps. Maybe that's where freedom is. We saw this as far back as "Benito Cereno" again. Babbo, the black slave, organizes that elaborate masquerade—that theatrical sort of text on board this ship—because that's a form of mastery. There is no Negro country that they can go to in Melville's story and so the shaping power, of crafting your circumstances, is, in itself, a rare form of assertion. I think something like that's happening here. This woman's imagination has become activated. It can't be stopped, policed and censored. As I said at the beginning however, the social bottom line—if we believe in bottom lines—is very dicey. She doesn't get out. You can imagine that John, when he recovers from his faint, is just going to be confirmed in his view that she really was crazy. She'll be put away in an asylum.

There's certainly no imagination of a social solution to this here. All of these creative powers, which are on show in this text, find no kind of ideological form or format. And yet, this text is incredibly clear to us as whether or not the character succeeds in reforming the society. It certainly is an allegorical portrait of the entrapped condition of women, a women trapped behind this frame, these bars of custom and convention.

Here, then, is a story of a room of one's own—in a sense that Virginia Wolf did not have in mind—the entrapment within one's own mind; and yet, we sense that that may. Thoreau said, "I have traveled a great deal and conquered, in one's mind is a world" and she moves in that world. The last thing I want to say about this text is that, if you step further back from it, and stop asking whether she gets in or out, what you see is an incredible spectacle of female libido, of a woman's feelings moving from inside to outside and scripting events. This is going to one of the male plots that we're going to see, this is the plot that will concern Hemmingway, Faulkner, Elliott and others—this specter of this woman's own desire playing itself out.

Lecture Fifty
Robert Frost and the Spirit of New England

Scope: Robert Frost may be one of the most well-known and beloved
American poets of the 20th century. His poems, which are often
about the woods and farms of New England and are written in
rural, everyday language, constitute a body of writing that looks a
good deal like folk wisdom. We read Frost as if he were our
Breughel or our Currier and Ives, a portraitist of a bygone day that
we remember fondly. This image is misleading on two counts.
First, it has led to a certain amount of scorn for Frost's work
among literary critics and, second, it has lulled us into thinking
that his work is gentle and affirmative. It is important to recognize
that Frost belongs in the front ranks of modern poetry, because he
deals with the same crises of belief that Eliot, Pound, Yeats, and
Stevens do. The difference lies in Frost's approach to these issues,
which is by means of an idiom that is not erudite or "high brow"
and by dint of a vision that is shot through with sardonic wit and
wry pragmatism. The matter-of-fact outlook of Frost's poetry is,
however, entirely compatible with a rich vision of language and
passion, even of fantasy. Moreover, his perspective on nature,
although it harks back to Emerson, Whitman, and Dickinson in its
pursuit of spirit, has an ominous dark side with which we need to
come to terms. Finally, Frost stands virtually alone among modern
poets in celebrating the meaning of *work*, choreographing the
human dance with the soil, to take the measure of our simple yet
complex investment in the rhythms of life. Despite their homely
manner and materials, Frost's poems are large propositions,
bidding to reconfigure altogether our sense of who we are and
where we live.

The reputation of Robert Frost is by no means a settled matter, and
there are many scholars of American literature, even today, who
deny all seriousness in his work. Born in 1874, Frost predated the
great modernist writers—Eliot, Pound, Joyce, Stevens,
Hemingway, Faulkner—even though his first book of poems, *A
Boy's Will*, appeared in 1913. Frost's rural idiom, his selection of
New England as the sufficient base and prism for examining life,
is in some ways parallel to Faulkner's choice of Mississippi, but

the ease and facility of Frost's verse stand in stark contrast to the portentous difficulties of modernism. Frost's work was not congenial to the ideological critics of the 1930s and 1940s, nor to the East Coast intelligentsia that often shaped the reputations of writers. But, if we look more carefully at the Frost corpus, especially at some of his most well-known poems, we shall see that they are considerably more open-ended and less settled than is usually thought.

Objectives—Upon completion of this lecture, you should be able to:

1. Summarize the ways in which Frost's work diverges from the modernist movement of his time;

2. Give examples of Frost's dark and violent treatment of nature; and

3. Explain the duality in some of Frost's work that contrasts the outside and the inside worlds.

Outline

I. Robert Frost's position in the canon of classic American literature is fiercely contested, despite the undeniable popularity that his poetry has always enjoyed.

    A. Frost's reception by critics has been vexed, ever since his first book of poems was published in 1913.

        1. Frost was born in 1874 and actually published work as early as 1894, before Crane's *Red Badge of Courage*; before the careers of Lawrence, Joyce, Eliot, and Pound; before Fitzgerald, Hemingway, and Faulkner were even born.

        2. Frost's major collections appeared during the early decades of the 20th century, putting him under fire by two distinct groups. His apparently easygoing poems differed radically from those of the great modernists T. S. Eliot and Ezra Pound. Their work was learned, difficult, and highly wrought: It alluded to earlier cultures, took a pessimistic view of modern life, and was overtly international. On the other hand, Frost also fared poorly at the hands of a critical establishment that, from the 1930s on, was interested in issues of Marxism and ideology.

        3. For the purposes of illustration, compare Frost's lead-off poem in *A Boy's Will* (1913), "The Pasture," with Eliot's

vastly more complex "invitation" in "The Love Song of J. Alfred Prufrock." Any reader can see the radical differences in manner and language. In contrast to the international bent of modernism, Frost seemed a committed New Englander, even to the point of being a closet Republican, critical of Roosevelt and the New Deal.

4. The seeming ease and accessibility of Frost's poems not only damaged his reputation in the eyes of many critics, but led to the conclusion that folks who liked Frost didn't really like poetry or modern literature in general. He was accused of being both facile and philistine, and there is a "cutesy" streak in his work.

5. The more serious criticism is that Frost neither delves inward very far (as, say, Dickinson does), nor offers a panoramic view of his nation (as, say, Whitman does).

6. Finally, in 1959, Lionel Trilling paid homage to Frost on his 85th birthday. Trilling more or less declared that the war between Robert Frost and New York was over, that Frost indeed belonged in the great iconoclastic tradition of American literature.

B. Trilling was right. When we reconsider some of Frost's most famous poems, we discover how bristling and unsettling they actually are. "Stopping by Woods on a Snowy Evening" epitomizes this feature of Frost's genius.

1. Like generations of schoolchildren, we are lulled by the sing-song rhythms of this sweet poem.

2. The setting seems idyllic and soothing at first glance.

3. Yet, in the end, the piece announces a tug-of-war between the ethical and the natural realms of life.

4. Just as the first line hints, the poem is about ownership: not who owns the woods, but whether the woods own the speaker, whether the human subject can maintain self-ownership. There is a distinct threat of dissolution, of letting go, that we shall see much of in Frost.

5. Most of all, the poem is disturbing in its evocation of the woods themselves as seductive and alluring. We recall Hawthorne's "Young Goodman Brown" and the Puritan fear of nature.

C. Frost is capable of ringing changes on this theme of nature as enticement. Consider "Come In" in this light.

    1. Significantly, the poem terms the woods "dark," and we see that "song" is allied to darkness as well, as if all poetry had its source in darkness.

    2. Dying light is shown to be the bird's message. This equation is suggestive: Light produces song, and song produces light.

    3. Nature is "pillared," as if it were a cathedral; yet it is also a temptation for losing oneself.

    4. The speaker rejects the dark woods because he is "out for stars." How do we assess this? Is he looking for safety, retreat, a divine plan?

    5. The laconic closing remark about not being asked is signature Frost. Humans are outsiders, whatever natural reveries they have. This admission that we are not "of" the woods gives closure to the piece.

D. Frost can present encounters with the dark woods in ways that are still stranger, sometimes bordering on horrifying, as in "The Draft Horse."

    1. These dark woods match anything that Hawthorne could produce in the way of horror.

    2. The encounter with violence seems to be in keeping with the design and directives (two Frost concepts) of a higher authority. We don't seem that far from Kafka's totalitarian world.

II. Frost definitely has a black side: apocalyptic, drawn to cataclysm, focusing on the theme of human abandonment and alienation.

A. Well-known poems, such as "Bereft," spell out the virulence of nature and its seemingly personal attack on the human subject. This piece demonstrates the loss of support in a human life.

B. Other pieces, such as "Acquainted with the Night," are still more stark in their existential portrait of abandonment and alienation. Here we see a world in which humans have no "home" whatsoever. Again, echoes of Kafka can be heard in some of Frost's work.

C. Perhaps the most disturbing feature of Frost's vision comes with his awareness that the most devastated and desolate sites are *on the inside*. Consider "Desert Places" in this regard.

1. The mobility, the acceleration, of the piece is initially striking. There is no stability here.
2. Moreover, the woods seem to have taken over entirely. In this poem, they own everything, showing us how far we are from "Stopping by Woods."
3. Frost's depiction of emptiness as whiteness recalls Melville's famous chapter in *Moby-Dick* on "The Whiteness of the Whale."
4. Frost's closing tone is splendid, like a child with his back against the wall: "They cannot scare me."
5. The worst is yet to come: True emptiness and devastation are on the inside. Here is a view of the human soul that is supremely inhospitable.
6. Yet, the piece has a strange kind of pride, as if the human condition could match the horrors of nature any day of the year.

III. Can you go past the "nothingness" on the inside of people? At his best, Frost is willing to jettison the story of human constructs and set his sights heroically, resolutely, on the natural scene. To face the phenomenal world without any imaginative window dressing is a challenge to poetry. Consider, as a closing poem, "The Wood-Pile," in this light.

A. The poem begins in laconic fashion. The speaker has no direction, no plan.

B. We understand early that this is a story of humans lost in a hostile world.

C. Frost's evocation of the bird's "vanity," its error in thinking the natural world is self-related, underscores the issue of romantic projection.

D. We then move on to the woodpile itself.
   1. Here is the finite, unsymbolic world; it is the world of things, resistant to metaphor.
   2. Yet, the woodpile unmistakably signals an abandoned human project.
   3. Nature seems to have taken over, to have proven the futility of human doing.

4. The speaker then muses about motivation. Why would one abandon this woodpile and go on to "fresh tasks"? Is this a reference to poetry?
5. The brilliant but enigmatic final notation causes us to reconsider our notions of utility. Is this a triumph of human achievement after all? Does all human labor have unforeseen real consequences?

Lecture Fifty—Transcript
Robert Frost and the Spirit of New England

This is Lecture Fifty, and it's the first of three lectures on Robert Frost's poetry. I think one could say that Frost is the most popular poet in America in the 20th century, or at least that Frost was [back] then. However, it's also the case that one's image of Frost is often a simplistic image. He looks like a kind of cozy, genial New England sage, reminding one of Courier and Ives prints. It's also the case—and not everyone knows this—that Frost's stock, as it were, in terms of the literary marketplace, varies a great deal depending on whether you're talking to general readers or whether you're talking to professors of poetry. The critics have often given Frost a very hard time; and I'll want to look at that. In this first lecture, I'm going to try to talk about the New England-ness of Frost's work, looking at some fairly familiar pieces and then moving on in subsequent lectures to other themes.

The first thing to say about Frost is he started very, very early. He's born in 1874. He publishes a poem in 1894. This predates a story like *The Red Badge of Courage*. His first work is written before the careers of Lawrence, Joyce, Elliot and Pound—the great modernists—come into play; in fact, his first works are published before Fitzgerald, Faulkner and Hemingway are even born. So we think of him as a 20th century figure, but he really does go further back. Now, one reason we think of him as a 20th century figure, is that his books and collections of poems didn't start appearing until 1913. So, this puts him in the wave of American modernism. It's also the case that, in terms of this critical debate that I've alluded to, he was really under fire from two distinct groups.

On the one hand, the great literary modernists that I've already mentioned—in particular, people like T. S. Elliot, Ezra Pound, D. H. Lawrence, or others of that stamp—represent a new kind of poetry for American literature. It's very frequently learned that it's difficult to access and it's allusive to the echoes and refrains of earlier poetic texts. It laments, usually, the fall of civilization—particularly Elliot and Pound. In that vein, it's highly wrought and it's very complex. It's difficult literature. Frost looks like [the] odd man out against this particular company. Therefore, he has been charged with being facile, simplistic, a bumpkin. On the other hand, there's still another strain that is politically correct—that's really an unfair way to characterize it—it could "politically engage" former criticism. That is very important in the late '20s and early '30s in the United States, and with pretty recognizable leftist leanings having to do with the fascination with Russian, with communism.

Critics who expected art and literature to have a kind of political thrust to it—to have at least some oblique relation to the plight of the proletariat or somehow the distribution of resources, or rethinking the social model of American democracy—those people also found that Frost had nothing to offer them. They found there wasn't the expected indictment of capitalism that they were yearning for. So, he disappoints on a lot of those fronts. I'm going to read to you the first poem that appears in his first published collection, *A Boy's Will*, and you will hear how simple some of this poetry can be. It's called, "The Pasture."

> I'm going out to clean the pasture spring;
> I'll only stop to rake the leaves away
> (And wait to watch the water clear, I may):
> I sha'n't be gone long.—You come, too.
> I'm going out to fetch the little calf
> That's standing by the mother. It's so young,
> It totters when she licks it with her tongue.
> I sha'n't be gone long.—You come too.

It closes with that refrain, the inviting of the reader into this bucolic, folksy Wadsworthian framework. We'll think about another poem that appears at about the same time by T. S. Elliot, "The Love Song of J. Alfred Prufrock,"

> Let us go then, you and I,
> While the evening is spread out against the sky
> Like a patient etherized upon a table.

That doesn't sound like Frost at all. I think that helps you gauge the kind of country, rural, bucolic dimension to Frost that particularly irks people who favor sophisticated, complex, elegant poetic forms.

As I said, there's no ideological agenda either. There is a kind of delight in a bucolic New England that some of Frost's nastiest critics claimed didn't even exist when he wrote the poems; it was a reconstruction, it was a kind of canny, sly and dishonest construct of New England. In fact, Frost was very politically conservative. He was critical of Roosevelt. He was critical of the New Deal in the 1930s. He was pretty much a closet Republican of sorts; and this too, as you can imagine, got on people's nerves. One critic called him "a crackle barrel versifier speaking with a New England accent."

Now a third problem that one runs into is that the people who liked Frost often were people who didn't like poetry, in general. They liked Frost, "He's the only poet I like to read," and that sort of thing. These people are then usually very contemptuous of modernism and its arduousness in the first place; so, this doesn't help. His best friends are not giving him a lot of help. He's got this kind of folksy tone, a kind of directness in his verse that people really went after. "He can be cutesy," I don't think that's really totally false as a critique. I'll read you a few lines from a very long poem called, appropriately, "New Hampshire."

It's lines like this where you can feel his petulance, "How are we to write the Russian novel in America as long as life goes so unterribly?" This is during the kind of infatuation of the American intelligencia with what's happening in Russia and the communist experiment. We don't have anything to reform over here, as far as Frost is concerned. You can see him taking a few cracks at the New York intellegencia, "Lately in converse with a New York alec / About the new school of the pseudo-phallic," et cetera. This doesn't make great poetry but it certainly says, "Get these guys off my back; there is a pretentiousness in that outfit that I don't particularly care about." He closes this long piece about New Hampshire—about the granite virtues of the state, etc—if New Hampshire falls, New England is out of the picture.

New Hampshire has got to be in. This is how he closes the poem:

> Well, if I have to choose one or the other,
> I choose to be a plain New Hampshire farmer
> With an income in cash of, say, a thousand
> (From, say, a publisher in New York City).
> It's restful to arrive at a decision,
> And restful just to think about New Hampshire.
> At present I am living in Vermont.

I think there's a kind of laconic, tongue-in-cheek-ness to Frost's poetry that he hasn't been fully credited for. Another criticism of him is that the poetry is too superficial. Malcolm Caley, a very distinguished American critic, said that, "He doesn't strike inward like the great poets," and one thinks of Dickinson here, "Nor does he have the great large panoramic view," and one thinks of Whitman there. But rather, I quote now, "The diminished but prosperous and self-respecting New England of the tourist home and the antique shop in the abandoned gristmill." There's another little jab at him.

This internecine warfare with the critics has really taken its toll on Frost's reputation. I've had arguments with critics and teachers of American literature, particularly in Europe, who wouldn't be caught dead working with Frost, who just think Frost is a joke. "How could you possibly have been fooled by that?" There was a famous event on Frost's 85th birthday, where Lionel Trilling, who was the great Dean of American Critics at Columbia, finally paid homage to Frost and acknowledged his pedigree as an American rebel. I'm going to quote Trilling:

> I conceive that Robert Frost is doing in his poems what Lawrence [D.H. Lawrence] says the great writers of the classic American tradition did. That enterprise of theirs was of an ultimate radicalism. It consisted, Lawrence says of two things: a disintegration and sloughing off of the old consciousness... and the forming of a new consciousness underneath. So radical a work, I need to scarcely say, is not carried out by reassurance, nor by the affirmation of old virtues and pieties. It is carried out by the representation of the terrible actualities of life in a new way. I think of Robert Frost as a terrifying poet.

I think Trilling is right on the money. He can be a terrifying poet. This was the moment where, in a sense, peace was declared between New York and Robert Frost. He is a disturber of the peace. Even in the poems that seem most hypnotic and lull us to sleep with their beauty and their rhyme scheme, there's something more going on in them. I'm going to read you one that you probably all know—when I was in school we had to memorize this one. It has this iambic tetrameter scheme of it. You can't get it out of your head much less, you know, lose it.

> Whose woods these are I think I know,
> His house is in the village though.
> He will not see me stopping here,
> To watch his woods fill up with snow.
> My little horse must think it queer,
> To stop without a farmhouse near,
> Between the woods and frozen lake,
> The darkest evening of the year.
> He gives his harness bells a shake,
> To ask if there is some mistake.
> The only other sound's the sweep,
> Of easy wind and downy flake.

> The woods are lovely, dark and deep,
> But I have promises to keep,
> And miles to go before I sleep,
> And miles to go before I sleep.

Well, as I say, "The woods are I think I know," you can't miss the rhyme scheme of it. It's too perfect. It seems like a kind of dollhouse poem of sorts. It has a certain kind of lyrical beauty in it, about the natural setting in the beauty of the woods, the obvious contrast between the kind of pragmatic practical gender, like, "Why are you stopping here?" The horse wants to carry out the pragmatism, gives his head a shake, "the harness bells a shake." But the man is hypnotized by the beautiful woods and wants to stay there. In a sense, this articulates the tug of war between the natural world on the one hand and the ethical or social obligations and responsibilities on the other hand. "I have promises to keep, and miles to go before I sleep." I think those things are obvious. Some of the other things that are maybe a little bit less obvious is that first line, "Whose woods these are, I think I know," is an interesting line. Who do the woods belong to? Does anybody own the woods? "Whose woods these are, I think I know. His house is in the village, though." Should there be a villager who possesses these woods?

I don't think that the poem is a leftist critique of owning woods. I do think that the poem is asking about ownership; and, finally, it's asking about ownership in a still more interesting way, which is that the woods threaten to own the poet. That's what the worry here is, "The only other sounds the sweep of easy wind and downy flake. The woods are lovely, dark and deep." That's a beautiful line, "The woods are lovely." That's the woods as threatening. That's the woods all the way back to Hawthorne's "Young Goodman Brown," where the woods are the dark place where Satan hangs out, where you could never come back from those woods, you feel the hypnotic appeal, the seductive appeal, of the woods because they could possess you, they could take you over, you could lose your ownership of yourself because of this demonic appeal of the woods, the siren like appeal, "Lovely, dark and deep."

I think that the appeal, the almost swooning appeal of dissolution—of coming apart and dissolving in nature—persists in Frost's work; and, I think that represents a kind of desire for extinction as well, a fascination with throwing over all kind of social or responsible thought. Frost brings a number of changes on this theme as well, "of coming into the woods." That's the most famous poem on it.

You remember that poem I started with, "The Pasture?" Here is another one; it's called, "Come In." You come, too.

> As I came to the edge of the woods,
> Thrush music—hark!
> Now, if it was dusk outside,
> Inside it was dark. (The woods are lovely, dark and deep.)
> Too dark in the woods for a bird
> By sleight of wing
> To better its perch for the night
> Though it still could sing.
> The last of the light of the sun
> That had died in the west
> Still lived for one song more
> In a thrush's breast.
> Far in the pillared dark
> Thrush music went—
> Almost like a call to come in
> To the dark and lament.
> But, no, I was out for stars
> I would not come in.
> I meant not even if asked,
> And I haven't been.

Very different, tonality, from "The Pasture" piece where, "I'm going out to the pasture. You come, too." This is a much more complicated sense of access. I come not into the woods, to the edge of the woods. It was dusk outside. It's dark in there. Something of the threat of the woods is contained here. "The darkness where the bird lives," and notice the way the bird's song is somehow tied up with the residual light that's left. The last light of the sun that had died in the west still lived for one song more in the thrush's breast, as if the song of the birds is, in some sense, the light that is dying. We are supposed to see that in two ways: the light produces the song but the song produces the light too—and the evanescence and fragility of both of those, also the alterity of both of them. I'm on the outside; they're there.

"Far in the pillared dark," he writes. That whole stanza could really be Emily Dickinson's. She wouldn't have written it so simply; but these are her notions. You remember "Further in Summer Than Birds" and some of those oblique poems about the natural language that speaks to us of mortality and death. "far in the pillared darks." The woods become pillars that are in a church. "Thrush music went, almost like the call to come in to the dark and lament." Darkness here is the darkness of death, the end of life. All of that is packed into those lines, the cathedral of the woods. Then that brilliant final stanza, "But, no, I was out for stars," so that the sights of this poet are not, in this poem, going to be on the woods and the darkness—the kind of seductive darkness, the deathlike darkness there—but beyond and above the stars themselves.

"I would not come in," and then that beautiful twist at the end, "I meant not even if asked, and I haven't been." This poem acknowledges we are not of the woods. We may write about them, but we have no privileged access. We are not insiders to the world of nature. We are working on it. We are processing it. We are turning it into our song, just as the light is turned into the bird's song. These are modern issues. These are things that you don't see as sharply, it seems to me, in romantic 19th century poetry. Frost is encountering them. Now sometimes, a representation of the woods can be darker still. I'm going to quote you a poem that's not usually talked about in Frost. It goes like this:

> With a lantern that wouldn't burn
> In too frail a buggy we drove
> Behind two heavy a horse
> Through a pitch-dark limitless grove.
> A man came out of the trees
> And took our horse by the head
> And reaching back to his ribs
> Deliberately stabbed him dead.
> The ponderous beast went down
> With a crack of a broken shaft.
> And the night drew through the trees
> In one long invidious draft.
> The most unquestioning pair
> That ever accepted fate
> And the least disposed to ascribe
> Any more than we had to hate.
> We assumed that the man himself
> Or someone he had to obey
> Wanted us to get down
> And walk the rest of the way.

What an ominous poem, like nature has a contract out for you. At a certain moment, a figure appears out of the woods, out of the dark woods, slices your horse up and you figure, "I think it's time to walk the rest of the way."

So, there's a threatening, menacing dimension to much of Frost. This is the Frost that Trilling had in mind when he says he's a terrifying poet. Some of the most, I think, beautiful poems are about the threat that nature has for us, the fact that we live in a place that is a natural disaster in some ways, and that we have no privileged spot in it, no particular wisdom; and above all, no fit. Heidegger uses the term *Geworfenheit*. We're thrust into the world, a world not of our own making or choosing. Frost gives you that same sense of alienation [and] of being not at home in the woods or on the earth.

One of his well-known poems is called, "Bereft;" and it's a poem where the natural world essentially scalps the figure of the poem. It's the wind that is blowing at this man,

> Where I heard wind like this before.

He comments on the seasons.

> Summer was past and day was past
> Sombre clouds in the west were massed.

The place he's standing on is beginning to come apart.

> Out in the porch's sagging floor
> Leaves got up in a coil and hissed
> Blindly struck at my knee and missed.

Then this will be translated into a statement of his own isolation and abandonment.

> Something sinister in the tone
> Told me my secret must be known
> Word I was in the house alone
> Somehow must have gotten abroad,
> Word I was in my life alone,
> Word I had no one left but God.

Not a very happy close. "I had no one left but God…and I'm not very sure about him, either," is what the implication of this line is.

This is a kind of systematic loss of support, an increasing sense of being, as the title says, bereft. Another very well known one called "Acquainted with the Night," is the most Kafkaesque of all of his poems. "I've been one acquainted with the night. I've walked out in rain and back in rain. I have outwalked the furthest city light." This is about a figure leaving the dark city, leaving the lights; and language repeatedly fails in this poem. That he sees the watchman on his beat, "and drop my eyes unwilling to explain." He hears a sound and it's an interrupted cry that came over houses from another street, "but not to call me back or say goodbye." Finally, he looks—not at the stars as in some of the poems—but he looks up at the clock, the church tower clock, and the Kafka line goes like this: "One luminary clock against the sky proclaimed the time was neither wrong nor right. I have been one acquainted with the night." We were out of phase, out of sync, out of time; that there is no correlation between your calendar, your watch, your motions, your life and the official public schema.

These natural scenes in some of Frost's most interesting poems, or in this case, this urban scene, can also be transformed metaphorically into versions of the human condition, versions of how it feels to be alive. Here is another one where he describes a natural setting, [it's] called, "Desert Places."

> Snow falling and night falling fast, oh, fast
> In a field I looked into going past,

There is the sense that he's really on the move here. Snow is coming down. Falling is repeated several times there.

> And the ground almost covered smooth in snow,
> But a few weeds and stubble showing last.

The whole world is disappearing under the snow. Nature is going to take it all over.

> The woods around it have it—it is theirs.

A real sense of usurpation here.

> All animals are smothered in their lairs.
> I am too absent—spirited to count;
> The loneliness includes me unawares.

And then, a stanza about the snow, the white blank snow that's as blank as anything in Melville:

> A blanker whiteness of benighted snow

> With no expression, nothing to express.

Then the last stanza, which reclaims all of this isolation—desolation—this whiteout landscape.

You think that's something? Listen to what he can match it with, "They cannot scare me with their empty spaces." A belligerent child here:

> They cannot scare me with their empty spaces
> Between stars—on stars where no human race is.
> I have it in me so much nearer home
> To scare myself with my own desert places.

So all of this that you've seen, is just the prologue to the ultimate desolate scene, which is inward, the inside landscape that has been ultimately configured by all of these references. There's a kind of pride in that, "They can't scare me." There's a sense in which the real horrors are our own and we take a certain kind of pride. This sense of desert spaces leads to a Frost who is scrupulously honest about window dressing, about noble ideals. In other words, the notion of a cozy Frost is just utterly inappropriate. "So much nearer home. I have it in me so much nearer home." But there is no home. It's just, "on the inside I'm even more kicked out, more marginalized, more lost than I am in this natural setting."

The last poem that I want to refer to is a strange poem, and it's a poem where the poet faces head-on the material phenomenal world and asks the question, "Is there anything that sustains us in terms of human values?" Is there anything among things that retains some human significance or is the world a purely alien material place in which we are more or less castaways? We have no fit. Nothing sustains or promotes our purposes. This poem is called "The Woodpile" and it's kind of laconic. It's *asking*, as Wallace Stevens would have said, trying to find out what will suffice.

Frost reminds one of Stevens a great deal except that we've always known that Stevens is looking at a de-sacrilized world, where God has exited, and trying to find out what meanings are left, and invoking poetry is one of them. Frost is not going to be that literary. He's not willing to do that. But, he is looking for what will suffice. This is, "The Woodpile:"

> Out walking in the frozen swamp one grey day (That's the place where Frost likes to hang out, a gray day and a frozen swamp)
>
> I paused and said, "I will turn back from here.
>
> No, I will go on farther—and we shall see." [And a real sense of wishy-washiness, doesn't know where he's going, doesn't have a game plan, no pattern]
>
> The hard snow held me, save where now and then

One foot went through. [An ominous sense, too, that there's no security there, either] The view was all in lines

Straight up and down of tall slim trees

Too much alike to mark or name a place by

So as to say for certain I was here

Or somewhere else: I was just far from home. [That's Frost territory. This place is not me. I can't name this place. I can't call it this and I can't call it that. I'm not sure if I'm going here or if I'm going there. I am far from home]

A small bird flew before me. He was careful
To put a tree between us when he lighted,

Frost is, like Dickinson, a wonderful zoom-shot poet of the behavior of animals.

And say no word to tell me who he was
Who was so foolish as to think what he thought.
He thought that I was after him for a feather—
The white one in his tail; like one who takes
Everything said as personal to himself.

There's a little conceit there that the bird thinks that I want to get his feather. The bird is the victim of the same egocentrism that governs our lives. We think the world responds to our picture, our safety, and our human condition; whereas, in fact, the world is indifferent.

One flight out sideways would have undeceived him.
And then there was a pile of wood for which
I forgot him and let his little fear
Carry him off the way I might have gone,
Without so much as wishing him good-night.

The poem changes directions: first the woods, then the bird, and now the wood-stand, a pile of wood.

It was a cord of maple, cut and split
And piled—and measured, four by four by eight.

Hear that language. It's the language of a person who's lived in the woods. It's the language of a carpenter. It's the language of a person who works with his hands. There is the material certainty of the world packaged, solid; it's real.

> And not another like it could I see.
> No runner tracks in this year's snow looped near it.
> And it was older sure than this year's cutting,
> Or even last year's or the year's before.

We see this as a kind of relic, as a ruin, as a woodpile that has been cut several years back and still exists here. That's going to be the subject of the meditation.

> The wood was grey and the bark warping off it
> And the pile somewhat sunken. Clematis
> Had wound strings round and round it like a bundle.

Delicate imagery here that the natural plants themselves are tying it up the way human beings would. You watch this. This woodpile is being turned into a bundle for us.

> What held it, though on one side was a tree
> Still growing, and on one a stake and prop,
> These latter about to fall. I thought that only
> Someone who lived in turning to fresh tasks
> Could so forget his handiwork on which
> He spent himself, the labour of his axe,
> And leave it there far from a useful fireplace

So here you've got this woodpile that's an abandoned woodpile. What's it doing? It's the kind of the thing that Frost likes to think about. This was done. This is the fruit of human labor. This wood was cut in order to produce heat for human beings. Here it is, in the middle of the woods, in the winter. What's it doing? He said, "Someone who left this must have had urgent things to turn to. I thought that only someone who lived in turning to fresh tasks could so forget his handiwork on which he spent himself, the labor of his acts, and leave it there far from a useful fireplace," and listen to what this woodpile is doing in the last two lines of this poem. "Leave it there, far from a useful fireplace, to warm the frozen swamp as best it could with the slow, smokeless burning of decay." "With the slow, smokeless burning of decay," those last lines are really quite wonderful I think. First, there's a reference to the person who constructs things and then leaves them, turns to fresh tasks. Perhaps he's thinking about his own life. Maybe it's a personal inflection. I don't know.

Then there's this final, mellow reflection that this woodpile, which to all extents and purposes is a ruin—it's abandoned—and it is kind of positive proof of our lack of purposiveness. We can't get things done. It's what nature does. It takes its way. It has its way. The last line says, "no." This woodpile is warming this frozen swamp. It is, in fact, creating the heat of decay itself, the slow, smokeless burning of decay. With that image, you get a sense that perhaps our views are always short sighted, that the labor that this man—whom we don't see—gave to produce this woodpile has extended life that goes on year after year after year. One of the lectures I'm going to give is on labor. Do we know when things are dead? Do we know when they're over? Do we know when they stop serving? That's the way the close of this poem finishes. It still serves.

Lecture Fifty-One
Robert Frost—"At Home in the Metaphor"

Scope: Because metaphor is the central vehicle for going beyond the literal or the phenomenal surface of things into figurative or spiritual realms, all poets, at all times, have a vital stake in its significance. Metaphor allows the poet to yoke together diverse areas of experience and thought. Yet, metaphor may also be suspected of falsely domesticating the world by substituting the poet's own projections and fantasies for the "hard facts." Among modern poets, Wallace Stevens is credited with exploring the ramifications of this issue, especially insofar as the imagination comes to stand as sustaining article of belief in a desacralized world. Yet, Frost rivals Stevens in this area, and his concern with metaphor is all the more engaging when we realize his scrupulous desire to give the material world its due. His most interesting poems along these lines are at once playful and inquisitive, indulging in metaphoric flights while remaining lucid about metaphor.

Objectives—Upon completion of this lecture, you should be able to:

1. Summarize the dilemma inherent in Frost's use of metaphor;

2. Give examples of Frost's acknowledgment of the human need for fictions; and

3. Explain Frost's notion of the purpose and consequence of song.

Outline

I. Frost's most succinct statement about the centrality and risks of metaphor is found in his talk "Education by Poetry."

   A. Metaphor is the indispensable vehicle, the passport, as it were, for poetry, because it enables a kind of "translation," or even transcendence, that crosses from one realm to another. Hence, the journey from the literal to the figurative is an elemental journey in poetry, but it is worth asking what the "cost" of the journey is.

   B. A central issue in the status of metaphor is its subjectivity, its flaunting of a personal vision that transforms the givens of the objective world into the new dispensation of the poet. Part of the integrity of poetry consists in remaining aware of this transaction, this poetic operation, that bids to alter the phenomenal world.

C. One fascinating example of the stakes of this argument can be found in Kafka's famous parable about metaphor, in which he points to both the strengths and weaknesses of figurative utterances.

D. Wallace Stevens is the modern poet most known for his concern with the status of metaphor. His post-romantic celebration of metaphor as the demiurgic triumph of the imagination in a desacralized world marks a key moment for 20th-century poetry.

II. Frost is as drawn to the dilemma of metaphor as Stevens is, even though he is less given to extravagant pronouncements on the subject. He will not speak of "supreme fictions" or "Thirteen Ways of Looking at a Blackbird," but he is deeply concerned with conceptual honesty, with the need to distinguish between the physical world that will not budge and the mobile projections we foist upon it.

A. One of Frost's most moving poems on this subject is "The Need of Being Versed in Country Things."

1. As in "The Wood-Pile," we see here a *ruin*, the remains of human shelter, the failure of human enterprise, in a hostile natural setting.

2. The poem suggests that human will is powerless to sustain human projects.

3. At a key moment, however, the murmur of the birds becomes a human "sigh," and metaphor—or, in this case, personification—takes over.

4. The poet's diverse figures and similes create a human drama that is doubly compelling, in that the poem restores a human presence that has been driven precisely from the scene.

5. Frost closes the poem with a clear reference to his own fictive procedures, the endowing of a natural scene with human significance. We are to understand that this is the inevitable task of art itself, but we must recognize our artifice.

B. "Birches," one of Frost's most famous poems, is a lively, even playful, romp through the same conceptual arena.

1. At the outset, the speaker acknowledges two distinct interpretations of the shape of birch trees, one of them scientifically likely, the other frankly fanciful.

2. Frost takes pleasure in developing the rational scenario, even though he will announce that he chooses not to believe in it.

3. The more interesting course of action for the poem is to offer a compelling fiction about birches, a fiction that centralizes a boy's will (and remember that the title of Frost's first collection was *A Boy's Will*).

4. The boy's game with the birches symbolizes rites of passage, and it is loaded also with sexual innuendo.

5. The climbing of birches is understood to be a kind of practice in ascending "toward" heaven, moving toward flight and release. We can see in this ascent an ideal education for the poet.

6. The beauty of this piece resides in the poet's fine attempt to possess both heaven and earth, to rise and fall. He tells us that the poem is also about love, about process. Frost's special economy consists of it being "good both going and coming back."

C. "Directive" is a late, rich metaphoric piece about going to heaven or, rather, going back to paradise. This quest poem is clearly Frost's playful version of Eliot's "The Waste Land."

1. The poem begins with our condition of confusion and sense of being lost. We need markers.

2. The poem rambles through a series of sardonic phases as it makes it way—both temporally and spatially—toward truth, which starts to appear as a form of salvation entailing death.

3. The poem closes with humorous references to the Grail and the Gospel—once again referring to Eliot's poem—but they are now transformed into the humble, imagined possessions of children. That, the poem suggests, can save us. Can it? How far can we ride the metaphor?

D. Frost's strongest, most uncompromising poem about the tension between our need for fiction and the "hard facts" of life is to be found in "The Most of It."

1. He begins here with the basic human condition. We are alone and unsponsored.

2. The only noise we hear is echo, a repetition of our own noise; whereas we seek response. Frost is working here with motifs that go back to Ovid, Milton, and Wordsworth.

3. Part of the grandeur of this poem is related to the powerful natural setting that the human subject interrogates.

4. The last half of the poem evokes a great vision, but far from being merely the "counter-love" sought by the speaker, it is fabulous beyond any domestication. Is this the appearance of the God? Is there something grand and noble about being in a world without human form?

E. The perfect sequel to Frost's primitive poem is the haunting piece "Never Again Would Birds' Song Be the Same." Here Frost is directly tackling a theme dear to Wallace Stevens, especially as expressed in "The Idea of Order at Key West."

1. The poem is delicately stamped by the matter-of-factness of a male speaker trying to evoke a vision of love and beauty.

2. Frost makes the remarkable assertion that human song—composed of both love and laughter—enters nature and becomes bird song.

3. We note the drama of "rising," of going "aloft"; this is not just about human noise.

4. Taking a step that is atypical, Frost harks back to Adam and Eve, and we realize he is retelling the story of family, of the enduring nature of love.

5. We note that the mythic "garden" of the beginning becomes the familiar "woods" of the end, as the piece carries out its temporal task.

6. Ultimately we realize that the notion of Eve's voice as part of the birds' song is a two-way street, asking us to hear Eve in the birds.

7. Frost's larger gambit here is to suggest that song changes the world, that human love and human poetry become part of phenomenal reality, endure over time, and are appreciated by later poets, readers, and lovers. Here is a view seen in Whitman. It is close to modern notions of textuality, as if the private view of "echo" seen in "The Most of It" had now become a view of tradition itself, of the labor of the community throughout history.

Lecture Fifty-One—Transcript
Robert Frost—"At Home in the Metaphor"

This is Lecture Fifty-One, and it's the second lecture of three on Robert Frost. In this lecture I want to focus most on the use of metaphor in Frost. Metaphor is the quintessential figure or *trope* in all of poetry. Metaphor is the trope that allows us to move from one realm to another, to compare things from one realm to another. Even in the apparently most guileless poetry—or in fact, for that matter, conversation—we are always using metaphor. We are always shifting fields. That's the only way we can make sense of things. Some people have argued that even language itself is essentially a metaphor since words are not the same as the things that they name. All poets use it. Modern poets become very suspicious of it, or very concern with it.

Wallace Stevens is well known as a poet who really ruminated about the status of metaphor, about what it means to metaphor-ize things, what it means to yoke things into some figurative schema and to call them by other names. Stevens distinguished a lot between dead metaphors and live metaphors; that a dead metaphor prevents vision, whereas a fresh, vital metaphor allows us to discover something new and exciting and un-thought of about something. On the other hand, time has its way, and so, fresh metaphors today can be dead ones tomorrow. We don't really know. In any event, Frost, like all poets, has thought about this. Frost, like Stevens, has written more about this and made it a kind of speculative component of his own poems in a way that's not usually recognized, that he's concerned about the crisis in metaphor. He's concerned about the metal operation, the kind of colonizing operation of which metaphor consists.

That is to say, to yoke something into another sphere is, in some sense, to master it, to gain control of it—but at what cost? I'm going to quote you a very funny sequence. This is an essay—or talk—that Frost gave called, "Education By Poetry." This is what he says about metaphor:

> Unless you are at home in the metaphor, (and of course that in itself is a metaphor, to be at home in it) unless you have had your proper poetical education in the metaphor, you are not safe anywhere. Because you are not at ease with figurative values: you don't know the metaphor in its strength and weakness. You don't know how far you may expect to ride it (another metaphor) and

when it may break down with you. You are not safe in science; you are not safe in history.

It's a wonderful, wonderful last phrase. You expect him to say, "and as a poet, I need this for my verse." He says, "You're not safe in science. You're not safe in history." He's saying that these apparently objective, neutral, non-tricks playing discourses, science and history, are just as larded with metaphor as poetry is and literature is, and he's right. People have done studies about legal discourse and how saturated it is with metaphor. People have also done studies about scientific language as being chuck-full of metaphoric devices as well. It seems to be a kind of indispensable aid to thinking. We can't get clean of it, clear of it. I think that when he says the strength and the weakness, part of what he must mean by the weakness is that you stop seeing that it's a metaphor. You believe that it's the truth. You believe that it is factual, literal; whereas, it's not literal, it's figurative. It's only a kind of way of thinking about something.

Therefore, Frost's work often reminds, it gently wraps on us on our knuckles. It lets us know that this is the game we're playing. The poems I going to talk about in this lecture have a game dimension to them, even though some of them are very moving, and some of them have a kind of pathos as well. Stevens went the full routes. Stevens said that we remake the world, and he called it a supreme fiction. You may remember poems like "Thirteen Ways of Looking at a Blackbird," which is only about metaphoric extensions of the real thing. Frost will never go that far. He is drawn to the moves of metaphor, moves that can be thought of as dodges, moves that can also be thought of as ways of harnessing and domesticating the world. One of the poems that I'm going to read to you now is called "The Need Of Being Versed In Country Things." It's a complex title, "The Need Of Being Versed In Country Things."

I think "versed" is a nice term there because it evokes the notion of poetry as well as being experienced in. I think you could probably argue that for Frost, poetry is a form of garnering experience. It's a way of learning about the world. They're neither being versed in country things. You get the familiar Frost situation of a ruin.

> The house had gone to bring again
> To the moonlight sky a sunset glow.
> Now the chimney was all of the house that stood,
> Like a pistil after the petals go.

So you get this evocation of a house that only has a chimney left, it's been destroyed, and it's compared to a pistil after the petals go. People have tried to argue, "Maybe there's a kind of phallic dimension to this pistil and the petals have left it, and will it stand." We'll see how that works.

> The barn opposed across the way,
> That would have join the house in flame
> Had it been the will of the wind, was left
> To bear forsaken the place's name.

So now we know it was a fire that destroyed the house. Just by the pure chance—that the wind was not blowing in a certain direction—the barn survived; otherwise, it would be gone too. Now the barn is an intact relic that bears the name of what used to be the house. You can see that this theme is once again abandonment, ruin, the haphazardness of life, the way in which things that look like they're permanent are simply erased, removed. He's going to evoke the past life of this house, the way that life flowed through it in contrast to its current state.

> No more it opened with all one end
> For teams that came by the stony road
> To drum on the floor with scurrying hoofs
> And brush the mow with the summer load.

That's the way the barn and the house used to function.

> The birds that came to it through the air
> At broken windows flew out and in,
> Their murmur more like the sigh we sigh
> From too much dwelling on what has been.

That last stanza begins to translate things. The bird's sigh is more like we sigh; it becomes humanized. It becomes at least compared to a human meditation, the sigh that we would express in thinking about the evanescence of human life or the tragedy of this burned barn, burnt house. They fly in through broken windows. Their murmur more like the sigh we sigh from too much dwelling on what has been; again, very cunning language. Too much dwelling, dwelling as a verb, but also it evokes the notion of dwelling as a noun, which of course is what's been removed here. That's what's gone. So this poem is—if you'll allow me—polysomus. It works multiple meanings out of its own terms. You're supposed to think about the kind of humming or residence of these words—he returns to the birds:

> Yet for them the lilac renewed its leaf,
> And the aged elm, though touched with fire;

So that the natural world continues to live, this hasn't killed it, even though the elm has been touch by fire.

> And the dry pump flung up an awkward arm;
> And the fence post carried a strand of wire.

You're hearing metaphor, the dry pump flung up an awkward arm. He wants that pump to be enlisted, but consciously as a support here, it wants to help out with this house that's been destroyed.

"Flung up and it's not easily done." It's an awkward arm, "the fence post carried," fence posts don't carry things. That's what humans do.

> For them (this is the bird) there was really nothing sad.

Because, after all, the trees are still growing and you've got this wonderful assistance. We got the fence post that's doing its thing. It makes it still a living site for the birds. The dry pump is putting up its arm.

> Though they rejoiced in the nest they kept, (because they're
>   still living here)
> One had to be versed in country things
> Not to believe the phoebes wept.

You had to be versed in country things not to believe the phoebes wept, which is to say, you had to know that these are just birds, that they are expressing no human feelings or emotions or reflections on this.

Their song and their sigh had to do with the constructing of their own nest. For all the world, that's not what you think. You'd look at it and you'd hear them, and you'd look at that house and see it burn down, and you would think that there is something awful here, that the sigh has to do with human wreckage. So it's a very, I think, moving poem about the recognition that the animal world, the mineral world, the vegetable world has no human dimensions to it, but that our world consists of always yoking them in, essentially displacing unto them, projecting unto them the human drama of our lives, which is the drama of life and death—even though nature knows no death.

The trees and the plants still live, and metaphor gets enlisted that way. It's one of the ways in which we bring the inanimate and the inhuman into our human sphere. But we have to know we're doing it. We become Walt

Disney when we don't. We really think that mice are called Mickey and that they, you know, live human lives etc? This is an awareness of that operation, of what it means to do things like this.

One of Frost's most famous and most playful poems in this area is called "Birches," and it's a little bit long, but I think you'll like it. It's characteristically "Frostian" in the way that it's going to go in two directions at once. It's going to play out a might have been—or a might—be interpretation, and then it's going to reject it.

> When I see birches bend to left and right
> Across the lines of straighter darker trees,
> I like to think some boy's been swinging them.
> But swinging doesn't bend them down to stay
> Ice-storms do [that]…

So figure what you've got here, birches that are bent like this against the other straight trees. I like to think that boys have been swinging on them but we know that it's ice storms that make this happen. He's going to talk about ice storms here.

> Often you must have seen them
> Loaded with ice a sunny winter morning
> After a rain. They click upon themselves
> As the breeze rises, and turn many-coloured
> As the stir cracks and crazes their enamel.

It's a beautiful description of what trees look like coated by ice, and then as it melts and cracks.

> Soon the sun's warmth makes them shed crystal shells
> Shattering and avalanching on the snow-crust
> Such heaps of broken glass to sweep away
> You'd think the inner dome [of heaven] had fallen.

And you would think, by having read this, that this poem is going to be about ice storm, but it's not.

> They are dragged to the withered bracken by the load,
> And they seem not to break; though once they are bowed
> So low for long, they never right themselves:
> You may see their trunks arching in the woods
> Years afterwards, trailing their leaves on the ground,

And this is really a surprising description of what the trunks look like as they're like this [he demonstrates] and trailing their leaves on the ground. You have to visualize this.

> Like girls on hands and knees that throw their hair
> Before them over their heads to dry in the sun.

Very playful description of what the trees look like bent like that, and then this wonderful line,

> But I was going to say when Truth broke in
> With all her matter-of-fact about the ice-storm,
> I should prefer to have some boy bend them

We're back to the beginning of the poem, "I like to think some boy's been swinging them." That's really what he wants to talk about. Here is the scientific explanation. I'll give it to you. I'll play it out, but now lets get down to the heart of the matter. We're in the reel of metaphor, human projection, human desire, and human fantasy. "I should prefer to have some boy bend them," and then you're going to get the evocation of this boy,

> As he went out and in to fetch the cows—
> Some boy too far from town to learn baseball,
> Whose only play was what he found himself,
> Summer or winter, and could play alone.

Now I don't want to get lewd here, but people have argued—and I think, suggestively—that there are kind of sexual energies in this poem.

Think about that reference again to the tree that's bent down with the leaves on the ground—looks like some girl bending over with her hair over her head like that. It's a posture that you might want to think about for somebody to be bent like that, because you'll see how these images get picked up again as the poem continues. Then, "a boy playing alone," let's think about some of the games that boys play when they might be alone, because the poem may be about that too.

> One by one he subdued his father's trees

Just think about some of the possibilities here.

> By riding them over and over again.

There are the trees. He rides them down

> Until he took the stiffness out of them,

137

And there you have again, a possible sexual reference.

> And not one but hung limp, (really does go that direction) not one
> was left
> For him to conquer. He learned all there was
> To learn about not launching out too soon
> And so not carrying the tree away
> Clear to the ground…

When you let go, when you get to the edge of things, when you get to the
limit, all of my terms can work in several different directions here.

> …He always kept his poise
> To the top branches, climbing carefully
> With the same pains you use to fill a cup
> Up to the brim, and even above the brim.
> Then he flung outward, feet first, with a swish,
> Kicking his way down through the air to the ground.

That's a wonderful suggestive play of the boy who rides the birch all the
way out as the birch begins to bend under him and then swishes down to the
ground, moment of release.

> So was I once myself a swinger of birches.
> And so I dream of going back to be.
> It's when I'm weary of considerations,
> And life is too much like a pathless wood
> Where your face burns and tickles with the cobwebs
> Broken across it, and one eye is weeping
> From the twig's having lashed across it open.
> I'd like to get away from earth awhile
> And then come back to it and begin over.
> May no fate willfully misunderstand me
> And half grant what I wish and snatch me away
> Not to return. Earth's the right place for love:
> I don't know where it's likely to go better.
> I'd like to go by climbing a birch tree~
> And climb black branches up a snow-white trunk
> Toward heaven, till the tree could bear no more,
> But dipped its top and set me down again.
> That would be good both going and coming back.

There's a wonderful economy here. You don't lose on any one of these particular trajectories.

> One could do worse than to be a swinger of birches.

It's a beautiful poem. It's written again in the laconic matter of fact, you know, plain style Frost. There are no $50 words in this poem at all. It takes something that none of us has ever thought about, about what it means to ride these trees going up towards heaven but still coming down. It represents really the kind of rhythmic, pulsing life as Frost sees it.

I may quote you another passage from Frost in one of his essays, because I think it carries some of the same feeling here about the rhythmic dimensions of things. It's the most exciting movement in nature; he's writing about the poetry of Amy Lowell here.

> ... is not progress, advance, but expansion and contraction, the opening and shutting of the eye, the hand, the heard, the mind. We throw our arms wide with a gesture of religion to the universe; we close them around a person.

That the instinct is to possess the world. We close them around a person. That Frost has a very weird optic on things. He's coming at the world from an angle that reminds of Dickinson. There is something surprising about the vantage point of Frost in this whole poem about birches. It seems to suggest that he makes this poem speak to us of sexual education, the maturation of pleasure, of release, but also of pure play, of moving up and coming down of a life being played out between aspirations towards the heavens etc., and life on the earth.

Now, the next poem that I'm going to very briefly talk about is one of Frost's most famous poems. I don't think it's one of his best. It's called "Directive." It's a very late poem. It's a very playful poem also. It's a poem, as the title "Directive" suggests, about going to heaven, about being saved. I think it's clearly Frost trying to write the poem that T.S. Eliot wrote in "The Waste Land," a poem about salvation, a poem about finding your way to the source, a way back to wholeness, a way to healing. It's a poem that is filled with lots of checks and balances. It starts with recognizing of how confused our state is.

> Back out of all this now too much for us,
> Back in a time made simple by the loss
> Of detail, burned, dissolved, and broken off
> Like a graveyard marble sculpture in the weather,

So we are getting clear of all of that. Back behind all of those things,

> There is a house that is no more a house
> Upon a farm that is no more a farm
> And in a town that is no more a town.
> The road there, if you'll let a guided direct you
> Who only has at heart your getting lost,

That's what the poem is about, [going] to this never-never land, this origin, origin of wholeness, purity, truth that would somehow be behind or beyond all of the messy complications of the lives that we lead. In the end of the poem he talks about how you get to this place, this source.

> And if you're lost enough to find yourself
> By now, pulling your ladder road behind you
> And put up a sign CLOSED to all but me.
> Then make yourself at home. The only field
> Now left's no bigger than a harness gall.
> First there's the children's house of make-believe,
> Some shattered dished underneath a pine,
> The playthings in the playhouse of children.
> Weep for what little things could make them glad.

The place you're going to is being characterized as a dollhouse, a playhouse, or a construct.

> Then for the house that is no more a house,
> But only a belilaced cellar hole,
> Now slowly closing like a dent in dough.

That notation to me is mind-boggling. What you're going to do first is compare it to a playhouse. Then it's a house that's no more a house, and then it's belilaced. I've never heard that adjective before, "a belilaced cellar hole." You're going into the pit. Then it is disappearing as you watch because it's like closing like a dent in dough. You put your hand in dough, and you watch the dough just get rid of the space that you've just made. All of this is the illusiveness of your salvation, of finding the source, of getting back to God. It closes with the difficulty of ever getting there.

> I have kept hidden in the instep arch
> Of an old cedar at the waterside
> A broken drinking goblet like the Grail

That's a clear reference to Eliot's poem, "The Waste Land," the story about the Grail and the Fisher King and all of that.

> Under a spell so the wrong ones can't find it,
> So it can't get saved, at St. Marks says they mustn't.
> (I stole the goblet from the children's playhouse.)
> Here are your waters and your watering place.
> Drink and be whole again beyond confusion.

Well as I said, I don't think this is one of Frost's greatest performances. It is one that is frequently cited. It is certainly the nostalgia for wholeness, for finding the source. It's his, I think, mocking references to the erudite poetry of Eliot. It transforms it into childlike ventures and it's very open to question whether any salvation is going to be possible here.

The more provocative pieces in Frost, about finding some vision of God or wholeness or truth, are really located in the poems that stay with the natural world, that don't truck and grails and sources of this sort. I'm going to look at a poem called "The Most of It," which is one of his greater performances. "He thought he kept the universe alone," is the first line. It's a line that Wallace Stevens could've written.

> He thought he kept the universe alone; (the hubris of that)
> For all the voice and answer he could wake
> Was but the mocking echo of his own
> From some tree-hidden cliff across the lake.

"Echo" as you probably know is one of the oldest motifs in poetry. It goes back to Ovid. You see it in Milton. You have in Wordsworth. It's the narcissist view of the world; that all we can hear is a projection of our own voice, that in the world we live alone, surrounded by our own echoes, that there can be no contact with other, no apprehension of others. So this person is seeking an answer. All he hears is his own echo.

> Some morning from the boulder-broken beach
> He would cry out for life, that what it wants
> Is not its own love back in copy speech, (echo)
> But counter-love, original response.
> And nothing ever came of what he cried

There's the lost individual crying for response, for the universe to respond, for there to be some final encounter. Nothing ever came of what he cried. And here comes the great conclusion.

> Unless it was the embodiment that crashed
> In the cliff's talus on the other side,
> And then in the far distant water splashed,
> But after a time allowed for it to swim,
> Instead of proving human when it neared
> And someone else additional to him,
> As a great buck it powerfully appeared,
> Pushing the crumpled water [up ahead,]

Just listen to this language. This is a scene of great power, but it's not a human figure that we can cotton up to, some father God that can accept us.

> And landed pouring like a waterfall,
> And stumbled through the rocks with horny tread,
> And forced the underbrush—and that was all.

It's one of Frost's remarkable poems because it gives us this apprehension of some extraordinary force, this animal god, I suppose, this great buck that essentially forces the elements into his own path. The crumpled water becomes the waterfall, horny thread, and that was all. It's as if Frost is saying the natural world is the world of great power. The natural world has a kind of fabulousness because this is a story of fable, and of fabulousness that we can never domesticate. Our little anthropological schemes of God, who has a mustache or has a beard and has white hair and who loves us and takes us to his bosom, what a cheap trick that is. The world has a kind of raw, imperial power that we can see all the time in waterfalls, and in the animals in the woods. If we want to try to imagine godhead and divinity, why don't we thing along those terms? I think that this poem, for me, has a kind of authority and a kind of integrity that the piece about the grail doesn't quite have.

The last piece that I'm going to read you is a follow up to this poem. It has a wonderful title, "Never Again Would Birds' Song Be The Same." We've had that motif in a lot of the poems that I've read you, about the song of the bird, the song of the thrush, the dying light of the sun becoming the birdsong. Now we're going to see how it works here. It's going to be a rather strange piece for Frost. "He would declare and could himself believe..." You have, like you did in the last one, this male speaker who's being treated a bit ironically, who doesn't have the full picture.

> He would declare and could himself believe
> That the birds there in all of the garden round
> From having heard the daylong voice of Eve
> Had added to their own an oversound,
> Her tone of meaning but without the words.

This is unusual for Frost because he's referred us all the way back to Adam and Eve and the Garden. That's the Garden. It's Eden that's being talked about. Eve's own voice has somehow conferred onto the birdsong its music,

> Had added to their own an oversound,
> Her tone of meaning but without the words.
> Admittedly an eloquence so soft
> Could only have had an influence on birds
> When call or laughter carried it aloft.

So it's not just Eve saying close the door, Adam or anything like that. It's laughter. I think joy is invoked—perhaps in a sexual connection—has invoked love between them.

> That produces the sound that moves up aloft.

That's the sound that becomes part of the bird's own song.

> Be that as it may be, she was in their song,
> Moreover her voice upon their voices crossed
> Had now persisted in the woods so long

Mind you you're not in the garden anymore. You're not back in Eden. You're in the woods today. The huge leap here had now persisted in the woods so long

> That probably it never would be lost.
> Never again would birds' song be the same.
> And to do that to birds was why she came.

It's just a haunting piece that the birdsong comes from Eve having come and communicated to the heavens her laughter and her joy, her call. Not the words, the sound. Now it's in the voices of the birds, and now we hear it. Now, through this, we move all the way back to the story of Adam and Eve. We hear the human voice. I'm still talking about metaphor, how we domesticate the world. How a world of inanimate things or of animals somehow gets yoked into a human story, a human fable. That's what this whole piece is about. We now hear Eve's voice, make out Eve's voice in the song of the birds. We have to work to do that perhaps. That is the labor that makes the world a fluid place. It's the labor, the metaphor that allows us to hear a song, the chirping of the birds, and to imagine this lovely fable of this being originally the joy and call of Eve.

I'd like to suggest to you in closing that that is a lovely image, perhaps, of the continuity of poetry itself, that poetry is not simply what I write today. It is birdsong. It is echo. It is a voice that's made up of other voices. It's Frost signaling the historicity, the melodious tradition of his own medium. There's a sense here in which literature is being thought about itself, that the song we hear is a song that has been going on forever. Its echo, once again, as it was in the other piece; and, there is a kind of labor, a critical labor, a reading labor, an imaginative labor involved in that. There is also a very great sense of vision and recall and recapture when we do that.

Lecture Fifty-Two
Robert Frost and the Fruits of the Earth

Scope: Although countless poets have waxed lyrical about nature and the "good life," very few have ever written about work. Perhaps taking his cues from Thoreau's example in *Walden*, Frost has left us with some unforgettable poems about man's interaction with the earth. This interaction becomes spiritual in that it inscribes the human being in the eternal cycle of life. It would seem that Frost is implicitly celebrating a kind of male fertility in such poems, but it is crucial to grasp the richness and boldness of Frost's view of labor itself: It is a process that only appears to be over when the product or the task is completed. Frost is committed here to a view of human gesture that is wonderfully open-ended and future-bound in ways that no one can plan or anticipate. Here, too, Frost is reflecting on diverse kinds of labor—tilling the soil and picking apples, making love, writing poems—and he makes us understand the unsuspected reach and grandeur of such activities.

Objectives—Upon completion of this lecture, you should be able to:

1. Give examples of how Frost uses rural life to embody the human condition;

2. Explain how Frost is a descendant of Whitman and Dickinson in his perception of everyday life; and

3. Summarize Frost's view of the relationship between poetry and science.

Outline

I. Frost is inimitable in his complex interweaving of agriculture, love, and poetry in his poems about working the soil.

A. "Mowing," one of Frost's earliest poems, establishes the crucial nexus that reigns in his work: facts as precious, labor as voice, labor as future-bound.

1. We note, at the outset, that the elements themselves do not speak, but that human implements become "lingual," have a

strange speech of their own, which the poem seeks to interpret.

2. Frost boldly reconceives our notion of "dream" in this poem. He retrieves the notion from the realm of fancy or unreality and suggests that it has elements in common with facts and work.

3. The poem never loses sight of the particulars involved in mowing.

4. "The fact is the sweetest dream that labor knows" remains one of Frost's most sibylline phrases, a haunting suggestion that the separation of these categories has been wrong all the time. *Things* can exist in a love relationship to us, and that relationship is labor; moreover, labor *knows*, is a form of knowing. Knowledge is dissociated here from all bookish notions and becomes something vigorous, even visceral. Work/life becomes poetry here.

5. The piece ends with a reference to the "long scythe," a classic symbol of death and time, yet it whispers "life" here. The closing terms, "left the hay to make," open on to a vista of ongoing growth and development, of a kind of continuous "production" beyond our finite efforts.

B. "Putting in the Seed" focuses entirely on the conflation of planting crops, making love, and creating poetry. The poem also displays Frost's technical genius in its rigorous form as Shakespearean sonnet.

1. The first notation spells out the man-wife connection. This piece is going to be a strange love poem.

2. We note how the speaker merges death and birth, plants the petals along with the seeds, insists on their togetherness.

3. At a key moment, the poem becomes incandescent, as if its speaker realized that a powerful allegory is being enacted here. This is the moment that Emerson prescribed for poetry: to make the facts luminous with spirit.

4. The poem closes with a dignified, slow-motion, five-line account of the miracle of creation, the palpable trajectory from seed to plant. We cannot miss the human dimensions of Frost's seedling here or how this event also speaks for the processes of making love and poetry.

C. "After Apple-Picking" is arguably Frost's strangest performance in this area. Using the most common New England activity of apple-picking, he offers us a surreal, hallucinatory evocation of the human condition, going back to the Fall.

   1. The description of the "two-headed ladder" that sticks "through" the trees emphasizes, once again, Frost's interest in metaphor. The ladder is a conduit to other realms, a set of parallel points and tracks.

   2. This poem is grounded in the speaker's fatigue and drowsiness, which sets the stage for dreaming and slipping.

   3. Frost's language is dense here. "Essence" applies to apples and to the underlying core of meaning; this labor will be appropriately followed by a sleep that is like hibernation.

   4. Frost is working in the same territory that Whitman did in "The Sleepers," but he does so in an idiom all his own.

   5. The strange reference to the vision through the glass picks up the famous Pauline notation of "through a glass darkly," with its desire for final knowledge and recognition.

   6. The poem moves into dream material as we survey a world of apples. We see a drama of loss and salvation enacted in that strange code.

   7. Ultimately the poem speaks to us about man's covenant with the earth, a kind of stewardship that mandates making good on our labor, on the fruits of the earth.

II. Frost's range makes him a metaphysician of the earth, the successor to both Whitman and Dickinson in his capacity to see spiritual events in everyday life. His zaniest effort in this area may well be "A Star in a Stone-boat," a piece that can be read as the poet's *ars poetica*.

   A. This poem seems petulant right from the beginning: "Never tell me." It is going to propose some odd theories.

   B. Frost sets upon the stage his opposite number, a laborer who is entirely unperceptive.

   C. The phrase "the air in which we roll" nicely signals the insistent notion of mobility in this piece, the view that the world is a far more puzzling and changing place than we know, with a gravitational pull that is also conceptual.

   D. The stone at the center of the poem goes through a number of avatars, including wing, tail, and heat. We note that it is allied to beauty, producing flowers not grain. Frost is offering us a parable about the beauty that is inherent in our "meanest" things, if we could open our eyes.

   E. This piece is shot through with a kind of interstellar energy. For Frost, science and poetry can be bedfellows.

   F. Frost leaves us with a sense of synthesis and magic that we saw in Thoreau's *Walden*, as if the measure of a pond, like the character of a stone, were "star-shot," or filled with magic. Looking at walls can be a visionary activity.

III. Frost emerges as celebrator of our internship on earth, our involvement with the processes of life and labor. But his whimsical and sardonic eye give his work a tonality that is unmistakable, differing sharply from the performances of Whitman and Dickinson.

   A. "Gathering Leaves" maps out a seasonal ritual that we all know. Frost handles it with deftness and wit, and pathos, too.

   1. Dead leaves epitomize futility. We all know their weightlessness and how awkward they are to handle.

   2. Frost emphasizes the negatives: No weight, no color, just—we might say—the dead skins of life.

   3. But labor is labor. We realize that the future may come into play here, that this work may lead to more than we thought.

   4. And it does, once we consider the unstated referent of the poem: human memory. Now we see all the traffic here, between death and life, absence and presence, language and reality.

   B. To end this discussion, we will examine one of Frost's briefest, most laconic, and unsublime pieces, "The Span of Life."

   1. The conditions of writing this lecture are in play here: My 13-year-old golden retriever, Nappie, lies on the floor and barks.

   2. Here is the pulse of poetry: to make *us* perform the labor that turns language into meaning, old age into memory of youth, death into life.

Essential Readings:

Frost, *Selected Poems of Robert Frost* (Holt, Rinehart and Winston, 1963).

Recommended Readings:

Cox, *Robert Frost: A Collection of Critical Essays* (Prentice Hall, 1962).

Topics for Further Consideration:

1. Explain whether you regard the "New England-ness" of Frost's poetry as a weakness or a strength.
2. Summarize Frost's vision of the nature and significance of labor.

Lecture Fifty-Two—Transcript
Robert Frost and the Fruits of the Earth

This is Lecture Fifty-Two, and it's the final lecture on Robert Frost. I want to talk about the theme and forms of labor, work. It's an unusual theme. You don't find a lot of poetry written about labor or about work; and for Frost it's doubly applicable because his poetry is a lot about living in the country. It's about humble but real forms of labor and activity that people in rural communities experience: chopping wood, building houses, and doing gardens. It's also the case that Frost, as we know—since that's why we're working with him—is a poet. So much of his labor has got to be language, words; and that's the kind of connection that you'd expect. The notion of work is going to move in both directions.

I'll refer you to one more notion of labor, which is that, when Adam was expulsed from the Garden of Eden, in a sense, work is born. That's when sweat appears and things like that. Labor is also thought to be pain. Women experience great pain in giving birth, etc., and there are fables that say that there was a time, an Edenic time, when none of these things hurt, when labor didn't exist. Frost is not going to take that tack at all. He's going to celebrate labor and work, and he's going to do it in a bunch of poems that are really quite splendid. They surprise us again and again. This man has a way of coming at things from angles, or saying things about apparently familiar subjects that just blow us away.

The first poem is a very early poem of Frost's called "Mowing." It's written in the sonnet form. He has this gift for writing you know. Sonnets are among the most formally rigid forms. You've got a very tight metrical scheme and rhyme scheme and Frost just uses his own very, very plain style—his very low vocabulary in the sense that there's nothing sort of over-literary about his language—and works in this genre.

> There was never a sound beside the wood but one,
> And that was my long scythe whispering to the ground.
> What was it, it whispered? I knew not well myself;
> Perhaps it was something about the heat of the sun,
> Something, perhaps, about the lack of sound—
> And that was why it whispered and did not speak.

So your instruments speak, the instruments with which you work the earth. They have their own voice. Human tools speak their language, perhaps speak our language, and perhaps speak us. "It was no dream of the gift of idle hours, or easy gold at the hand of fey or elth." So the language of the scythe, the whispering of the scythe is not some fairyland, fey, elth, it's not some never-never fantasy escape, that's not what this is talking about. It's talking about the heat of the sun. It's talking about the ground itself.

> Anything more than truth would have seemed too weak
> To the earnest love that laid the swale in rows,
> Not without feeble-pointed spikes of flowers,
> (Pale orchises), and scared a bright green snake.

There he describes the actual work in the garden, the mowing itself, no escape involved here. Then these last two lines that are just quite beautiful,

> The fact is the sweetest dream that labor knows.

It re-conceives our whole notion of dreams. Dreams are not some sort of perfect cloud where we could live on after death, dreams are not even some sort of perfect ease that we could have, dreams have to do with our contact with the elements. Work and fact go together for Frost, that our encounter— I want to push this—our intercourse with the land, with the soil, with the processes of life is what sowing and harvesting have to do. These are the facts of our life, and these are also the dreams of our life; these are the highest things we can know, not the things that we want to get done so that then pleasure can come.

> The fact is the sweetest dream that labor knows.
> My long scythe whispered and left the hay to make.

"My long scythe whispered and left the hay to make," a very strange ending. First of all, what is the obvious sort of expected reference for a scythe? It's the implement of death. It's the grim reaper with his scythe that cuts you down. This scythe whispers life, this scythe produces labor that then produces something else, and it cuts the grass. You say. "Well it's over, but the grass will then make hay." This is frost once again simply telling us that the lines that we think mark the endings of things don't; that things continue. Therefore, when you want to take the measure of what you have accomplished, what work you have wrought, what you have done, it isn't easy to do it. You can't tell it after life; that was the poem about the woodpile. It's been abandoned for several years, it's still heating up a frozen swamp, and so too cutting the grass is only the first stage in a continuous sort of production cycle, a continuous sense of life and alteration and change and result. That's the way the line is written, "My long scythe whispered and left the hay to make." It's like the hay is going to spawn. It's going to be spawned, and it's going to be reproduced.

I think that labor in Frost's view has a kind of futurity. It extends beyond anything that we can easily gauge. We don't know the final consequences of what we have worked to do; and again, you can link this back to language, poetry. The poet dies but the poem lives; the poem continues to speak. Eve is dead—if Eve ever was—but the birdsong continues to speak her. There is a constant sense here that, what looks over, is not over, what looks fixed is not fixed, and labor is one of the ways that frost moves into this material.

The next poem I want to read is called "Putting In The Seed" and, as you can tell by the title, it's going to be similar. It too is a sonnet.

> You come to fetch me from my work to-night
> When supper's on the table, and we'll see
> If I can leave off burying the white
> Soft petals fallen from the apple tree.
> (Soft petals, yes, but not so barren quite,
> Mingled with these, smooth bean and wrinkled pea;)

What is he doing? It's a directive to his wife, "You come and fetch me from my work tonight," what's he going to be doing? "Come and get me when the supper's on the table and I'll have to leave off burying the white soft petals from the apple tree." That would seem to be a notation of death, the end of the flower, the petal that falls off. What does he do? He buries it with the pea and the bean as part of its own cultivation and rebirth, that the apple flower petal will help this germination process. And then that sentence finishes, "And go along with you." That's what you're supposed to do, bring me back because I'm entrenched in this process of sowing, putting in the seed.

> And go along with you 'ere you lose sight
> Of what you came for and become like me,
> Slave to a springtime passion for the earth.

This is going to be the rituals of spring; they're entrancing, and they're hypnotic. We may forget to eat, we may not go into that table if we both watch it carefully enough, and you'll see that this poem is about watching for the miracle of spring, which is the miracle of creation. It's the miracle when the earth is renewed, when life starts again. You've heard this language, this utterly down-to-earth language about the earth, nothing high-faulting in it. All of a sudden, this poem becomes allegorical and spiritual.

> How Love burns through the Putting in the Seed
> On through the watching for that early birth
> When, just as the soil tarnishes with weed,

Nice verb there: "tarnishes." The soil is now sort of rusting and tarnishing, weeds are growing up, this is the end of the growing season, the soil is tarnishing, and it's getting overgrown.

> The sturdy seedling with arched body comes
> Shouldering its way and shedding the earth crumbs.

So the last five sentences of this poem—or lines—are about the creation of life, about the seed, which is described really as a human infant. "The sturdy seedling with arched body." Have you watched when beans first come up, the way they come up bent and then they finally open themselves like that?

"With arched body come shouldering its way and shedding the earth crumbs. How love burns through the putting in the see." Emerson said that nature is spiritual, that facts are a sign of spiritual realities, and that was the advice that Whitman took in writing his poetry, to talk about the world as we see it but to understand that it is shot through with spirit and soul and divinity. "The grass is the handkerchief of the lord," Whitman said. I think that in his own way Frost is absolutely in this tradition here. He realizes that sowing seeds is the mandate that God has given us, it is the continuation of love, and it is constantly paralleled here to the love between this man and his wife.

The poem starts by saying "When supper's on the table you come to get me." I'm busy putting in the seed here, but it's about their own entente, their own understanding with each other, and "pull me away" because otherwise you too will stay here and watch what happens, "then you watch through the seasons." It turns out, "How love burns through the putting in the seed on through the watching for that early birth when," and it's like this is the grand event, this is the main event. This is the greatest show on earth when the seed comes up, "just as the soil tarnishes with week the sturdy seedling with arched body comes shouldering its way and shedding the earth crumbs."

It's a very warm poem. It has that kind of dignified, slow motion, epochal sense because time is too slow; we can't stand there and wait for our seeds to finally produce. But in this poem, it's all telescoped within those last five lines, as we see time become invisible and the production of life appears. I think then that it's fair to say that the poem, in a sense, echoes human lovemaking, human production. That's why the seed is described as shouldering an arched body. It's clearly personified. The last reference, which is equally obvious, is a reference about making poems. It's a reference about seeding and producing art. It's about language too. It's about his process, or his own procedures.

The next piece that I want to look at is called "After Apple Picking," which, of course, couldn't have a more New England-ly title to it than that. Yet once again it's Emersonian, or it could be Thoreau-like in the sense that it takes the events of a natural setting—whether it's Walden Pond or whether it's walking in the woods—it shows you that this is an allegory about the spirit. The first line tells you that, "My long two-pointed ladder sticking through a tree toward heaven still." You couldn't have a more perfect notation of a symbol, a ladder going up towards heaven and going through the tree, prongs going beyond, that pointing towards heaven. You climb the tree, and you harvest the apples, but you're on a trajectory that goes further than that, and it's pushing you towards the heavens themselves.

> My long two-pointed ladder's sticking through a tree
> Toward heaven still,
> And there's the barrel I didn't fill
> Beside it, and there may be two or three
> Apples I didn't pick upon some bough.
> But I am done with apple-picking now.

"I'm done with apple picking now," the work is over, the labor is over. Now I've just finished pointing out in the other poems like "Mowing," you don't ever know when the labor's over, but you know when you get down off the ladder, you know when you put the apples in the barrel, it is finished.

> Essence of winter sleep is on the night,

The fatigue of the work is going to cause him to sleep. It's almost a surrealist poem; it's also what the word "essence" suggests, the essence of the apples too, it's the scent.

> Essence of winter sleep is on the night,
> The scent of apples: I am drowsing off.
> I cannot rub the strangeness from my sight
> I got from looking through a pane of glass
> I skimmed this morning from the drinking trough
> And held against the world of hoary grass.

When you first read it, you assume he's talking about a pane of glass. He's not. He's talking about a sheet of ice on the trough where they're drinking from, and he held it up and looked through it. It's almost a Pauline meditation through a glass darkly, where you look through this sheet of ice and the world looks strange.

> It melted, the ice and I let it fall and break.
> But I was well
> Upon my way to sleep before it fell,

Dream comes right here into the poem; you don't know if he's talking about what he really did or about a dream that he had.

> I was well
> Upon my way to sleep before it fell,
> And I could tell

That maybe dreaming is the last stage of work. Maybe work then produces our dreams. We'll see that he's going to dream about his work.

> What form my dreaming was about to take.

Well, what do you think his dream was going to be? It's going to be apples obviously.

> Magnified apples appear and disappear,
> Stem end and blossom end,
> And every fleck of russet showing clear.
> My instep arch not only keeps the ache,
> It keeps the pressure of a ladder-round.
> I feel the ladder sway as the boughs bend.
> And I keep hearing from the cellar bin
> The rumbling sound
> Of load on load of apples coming in.

So he dreams of more and more apples, of huge magnified apples.

> And I keep hearing from the cellar bin
> The rumbling sound
> Of load on load of apples coming in.
> For I have had too much
> Of apple-picking: I am overtired
> Of the great harvest I myself desired.
> There were ten thousand thousand fruit to touch,
> Cherish in hand, lift down, and not let fall.

This word "fall" has been used several times, and he's beginning to hint that the stewardship of these apples is a religious gesture. Every one has to be removed from the tree. If one falls it will be ruined.

> There were ten thousand thousand fruit to touch,
> Cherish in hand, lift down, and not let fall.
> For all
> That struck the earth,
> No matter if not bruised or spiked with stubble,
> Went surely to the cider-apple heap
> As of no worth.
> One can see what will trouble
> This sleep of mine, whatever sleep it is.
> Were he not gone,
> The woodchuck could say whether it's like his
> Long sleep, as I describe its coming on,
> Or just some human sleep.

One thing, of course, that labor produces is sleep. Enough labor will produce a permanent sleep. The woodchuck hibernates, he performs his efforts, his gestures, and his seasonal tasks and then he is out, entirely, for a period. The poem with its dream—those magnified apples that are just sort of spinning, russet-flecked etc—there's something filmic about this, to pick the character of dream that comes from over-fatigue, and there's a kind of wonderful sort of riddling, enigmatic kind of development here; that the apple picking, then the dream, and then the final meditation about sleep, could be the final stage of a life.

It suggested there's a covenant—I use the word stewardship—which one must make. One has a role to play, vis-à-vis the fruits of the earth. They don't just grow, you also have to harvest them—and harvest them religiously, spiritually—not letting one fall and hit the earth because it would be ruined. He is a metaphysician of the earth; he is the successor to both Whitman and Dickinson in seeing spiritual event in everyday life.

I'm going to read you a relatively unknown poem—that last one was known—I think, in a sense, it speaks for his career as a poet. It's called "A Star In A Stone Boat." Most of us, unless we live in New Hampshire, don't know what stone boats are. That's the rig that the farmers have built for moving heavy stones when they're clearing the very stony New England soil. It's a very whimsical poem in its own way, but it's a poem that I would like to call an *ars poetica* in the sense that it is about the way one writes poems. It's about what Frost's life is like. I won't read it all to you.

> Never tell me that not one star of all
> That slip from heaven at night and softly fall
> Has been picked up with stones to build a wall.

There's the given premise. You think that walls are made of rocks and stones, and usually they are. How can you be sure that the stars that fall didn't get in there as well, by mistake, by accident?

> Some laborer found one (This is a star that fell) faded and stone cold,
> And saving that it's weight suggested gold,
> And tugged it from his first too certain hold,
> He noticed nothing in it to remark.
> He was not used to handling stars thrown dark
> And lifeless from an interrupted arc.

So the laborer, who's the opposite of Frost, is picking up stones to build his wall, and he picks up one of these; he thinks it's a stone. He doesn't know it's a star; it's in the dark.

> He did not recognize in that smooth coal
> The one thing palpable than the soul
> To penetrate the air in which we roll.

This whole poem is unusual with these triple rhymes for each stanza. "The one thing palpable beside the soul / To penetrate the air in which we roll." Frost is really cosmic here, that we live in a kind of swirling galaxy, and there are only two things in it that are palpable, the stars and the human soul, everything else is weightless and immaterial. He had this man picking it up. This laborer had no idea what he had.

> Nor know he might move it from the spot,
> The harm was done; from having been star-shot
> The very nature of the soil was hot.

That should've been a clue; he picks up the stone and it's hot under. It isn't a regular stone. There is something special here.

> And burning to yield flowers instead of grain,
> Flowers fanned and not put out by all the rain
> Poured on them by his prayers prayed in vain.

This star stone produces flowers, this star stone is very special. Well not for this guy. He's going to stick it into his stone boat and move it; that's all.

> He dragged it through the plowed ground at a pace
> But faintly reminiscent of the race
> Of jostling rock in interstellar space.

This guy is sluggishly moving along; and for Frost, it reminds him of the race out there in the heavens, in the Milky War, in the interstellar space. Again this poem takes this extraordinarily distant look at our small human creeping activities.

> It (the star) went for building stone, and I, as though
> Commanded in a dream, forever go
> To right the wrong that this should've been so.
> Yet ask where else it could've gone as well,
> I do not know—I cannot stop to tell;
> He might have left it lying where it fell.

They put this star into a wall, into a fence.

> From following walls I never lift my eye
> Except at night to places in the sky
> Where showers of chartered meteors let fly.

Here's the poet. I walk around. I look at walls. That's my job. That's my profession. I'm looking at walls. I don't look in the sky except occasionally to see the meteors. What am I looking for? What do all of us look for?

> Some may know what they seek in school and church
> And why they seek it there; for what I search
> I must go measuring stone wall, perch on perch;

We're going to see what kind of star this is—and stone this is.

> Sure that though not a star of death and birth, (So not the kind of
> star that has to do with the birth of Jesus or anything like that.)
> So not to be compared, perhaps, in worth
> To such resorts of life as Mars and Earth, (Not that kind of star.)
> Though not, I say, a star of death and sin (don't enlist my star in
> any kind of religious system.)
> It yet has poles, and only needs a spin
> To show its worldly nature and begin
> To chafe and shuffle in my calloused palm (And now we realize
> this thing is actually in the poet's hand.)

> And run off in strange tangents with my arm
> As fish do with the line in first alarm.

This is an interesting notation. This thing moves, it lives, it comes from another world, and it gives me the same sense of quickness and resistance as when a fish is on the line, that magic moment we realize something that is living is tugging against us and that we have it.

> Such as it is, it promises the prize
> Of the one world complete in any size
> That I am like to compass, fool or wise.

That's the end of the poem. This is the metaphysician of the earth; the stone walls that he looks at. Poems like "Good Fences Make Good Neighbors" those are poems that are all about the world being star-shot, absolutely luminous if we knew how to see it. It's these heavenly bodies that are in the natural bodies, the inanimate things that we see and work with.

The next piece that I want to look at is a piece that, when I prepared this lecture a couple of months ago—or at least a month ago—was right when the leaves were beginning to fall. The poem is called "Gathering Leaves" which is of course a topic that is something that is quite prosaic and pedestrian for most of us in the autumn. He captures again the awkwardness, the frustration that all of us feel when we are gathering leaves, and he tells you why.

> Spades take up leaves
> No better than spoons,
> And bags full of leaves
> Are light as balloons.
> I make great noise
> Of rustling all day
> Like rabbit and dear
> Running away.
> But the mountains I raise
> Elude my embrace, (Have you ever tried to carry a lot of dead leaves in your hands?)
> Flowing over my arms
> And into my face.
> I may load and unload
> Again and again
> Till I fill the whole shed,
> And what have I then?

A shed full of dead leaves, sacks and sacks, you can still see the providence, they're all over the place. What is it, what have you got?

> Next to nothing for weight,
> And since they grew duller
> From contact on earth
> Next to nothing for color.

It really is not measuring up, and again, I think if you were a human being who lived in a place where leaves didn't exist, you wouldn't know what this poem is about. You have to have gone through the experience of gathering leaves, and knowing the strange sense of volume, that is weightless and impossible to get hold of, and to do anything with.

"Next to nothing for weight, / And since they grew duller / From contact with earth / Next to nothing for color." This looks like a distinctly losing enterprise, but remember Frost always is telling us you don't know how to take the full measure of your labor, you just think it's worthless. Here's how the poem closes.

> Next to nothing for use.
> But a crop is a crop,
> And who's to say where
> The harvest shall stop?

"A crop is a crop / And who's to say where / The harvest shall stop?" One way of making sense of this whimsical poem really is to think of the dead leaves as human memories, as the shape of our past, of everything that's over, the dead skins of our lives. It's hard to embrace them, it's hard to hold them, it's hard to weigh them, and yet the ritual activity of collecting them up metaphorically senses on a trip like that. There is a wonderful sense of repossession in this poem, and this is the same stewardship that goes into plucking the apples, or putting in the seed. You owe it also to collect the dead leaves. It's all part of that same wonderful cycle.

I think it has a certain humor here—and irony—because it's a particular work ritual that many of us have experienced. Frost then lets us get a sense of the play here, the unstated reverent of things. As I say, once you factor the notion of memory and of human past into this poem, all of this activity begins to hum, has a different kind of significance, different sets of possibilities.

The last poem that I'll read you of Frost's in this course is a poem that has a very ambitious title. It's called, "The Span Of Life." We expect a kind of epic statement here about the scale of a human life; and you're in for a surprise. It's very brief—it's only two lines long—and it's not about a human life at all. It goes like this:

> The old dog barks backward without getting up.
> I can remember when he was a pup.

Hope on. "The old dog barks backward without getting up. / I can remember, when he was a pup." I have a 13-year-old golden retriever—and I swear to you I'm not manufacturing this—if you've ever had really old dogs, they can't move around much, they lie there, and this sort of mechanical bark comes out of them periodically, "brp, brp," like that. He [my dog] was doing it as I was reading this poem and putting it into this course, and I've had him since he was only eight weeks old. I performed exactly the labor the Frost poem is about; however, it made me think of this adorable little—because goldens are really quite irresistible when they're puppies—little puppy.

I could see that puppy only in my mind's eye and I could see it through this old dog lying there, barking, that can hardly walk anymore. And I said to you, that "The Span Of Life" sounds like a kind of grandiose title about the scale and scope of human life, and in fact, it's not. It's about the dog's life—but of course I'm not telling the truth. The dog doesn't remember its life, I don't think; but I do. It's about, once again, metaphor. It's about a kind of imaginative reach into the world. It's us thinking about the span of life even of our dogs, or of the dead leaves or putting in the seed. It's that human labor that makes the world, which intrinsically probably has no human meaning. It makes it into something significant.

This little piece, I think, is a nice one to close; it takes the issues of memory and death and life and puts them into I think a kind of warm and wonderful and brief New Hampshire-like style.

Lecture Fifty-Three
T. S. Eliot—Unloved Modern Classic

Scope: If Robert Frost is America's most beloved poet, the author of unforgettable lines about "mending walls" and woods that are "lovely, dark and deep," T. S. Eliot is his opposite number in virtually every respect. Eliot is cosmopolitan, international, urban, polyglot, elitist, and literary throughout. Eliot speaks to us of high culture, of the canonical works of the European past, and his poetry is a tribute to the great tradition that reaches back to classical antiquity. But Eliot is unmistakably modern as well, because his themes are the crisis of belief and the breakdown in culture. His complex, demanding poems inevitably contrast the brutal and impoverished state of modern life as he saw it with the richness and coherence of earlier eras. Eliot's reputation has taken a considerable beating in the latter decades of the 20th century, because his work is openly elitist and, therefore, inhospitable to criticism that champions the causes of any marginalized group, including women, workers, and people of color. Because Eliot is synonymous with the recognized canon of "classic" literature, he came under attack during the Culture Wars. There is a suspicion, as well, that his concern with order and form—stemming in part from his anxiety about contemporary disorder—conceals a bias towards fascism and intolerance. Yet, Eliot is simply a dominant presence in English-speaking poetry of the first half of the 20th century, and no amount of dislike will remove him from this seminal position. Finally, the status of Eliot as our "classic," as a poet whose great motif is *ruins* ("fragments shored up against my ruins"), is an issue we cannot duck, for it is inseparable from the goals of this program on American classics: Can these fragments be read? Are they dead or alive? Can they make us whole?

Eliot came from a prominent New England family and benefited from familiar advantages, including education at Harvard, the Sorbonne, and Oxford. His background led to a prestigious career as a poet and critic and the award of the Nobel Prize for Literature in 1947. Eliot's importance was immediately recognized. He set the terms for the poetry (and prose) of high modernism. He single-handedly consigned some writers to oblivion while bringing others to the fore. His tastes and his crises (emotional and religious) were the guiding light for an era, even though he claimed that poetry is inherently impersonal. Eliot's view of history and the "tradition" has come under fire, but it is a complex theory, warranting our consideration in an age that is still obsessed with "making it new." "The Waste Land" is Eliot's *magnum opus*, but we can see, even in the early "Love Song of J. Alfred Prufrock," the makings of a poetry that introduces a new note in American literature.

Objectives—Upon completion of this lecture, you should be able to:

1. Summarize Eliot's role in arguing the importance of tradition and the individual talent;

2. Explain how "The Love Song of J. Alfred Prufrock" is a modernist poem; and

3. Summarize the "mythical method" employed by Eliot and other modernists.

Outline

I. The veritable opposite of Frost, T. S. Eliot must be seen as the "ruler" of high modernism, Eliot shared the stage with Pound, Auden, the aging Yeats, Joyce, and others, but his poems and his essays acquired paradigm status even as they appeared.

A. Thomas Stearns Eliot was born in St. Louis in 1888 to a prominent New England family that first arrived from England in the 17th century. The family was committed to public service and religious leadership. Eliot's grandfather went to St. Louis in 1834, established the first Unitarian Church there, and founded Washington University.

B. The young Eliot went to Harvard in 1906, finished college in three years, did graduate work in philosophy, studied at the Sorbonne, returned to Harvard, and joined the faculty. He was on a traveling fellowship in Germany when the war broke out. He then went to Oxford to read Greek philosophy and more or less stayed in England the rest of his life (becoming a British subject in 1927), except for prestigious academic appointments in the United States.

C. "The Love Song of J. Alfred Prufrock" appeared in 1915, and Eliot continued to publish poetry, plays, and essays for the rest of his life. He worked for a time with Lloyd's Bank, but then became active in publishing, was editor of *The Criterion* until the late 1930s, and became a director of the London house Faber and Faber. Eliot won the Nobel Prize for Literature in 1947.

D. Eliot's most famous and influential poem, "The Waste Land," was published in 1922, and it, along with James Joyce's *Ulysses* (of the same year), are key texts for literary modernism.

E. Eliot's later important poems are "The Hollow Men" (1925), "Ash Wednesday" (1930), and *Four Quartets* (1943). He also made notable efforts to revive poetic drama in the modern era; *Murder in the Cathedral* is his most memorable achievement in this endeavor.

F. In addition to his creative work, Eliot also published a number of landmark essays on literature that turned out to be as influential as the poems themselves, especially in the academic world.

G. Eliot is important, even today, because "The Waste Land" changed the face of modern literature. Its themes addressed cultural despair, but its form was shockingly new. The poem consisted of a mix of references, allusions, and quotations from earlier texts, cohabiting with Eliot's own brand of truncated lyricism. Eliot's essays were no less ground-breaking.

  1. His likes and dislikes worked their way into English departments throughout the world. Hence, his rejection of romanticism, his enthusiasm for the metaphysical poets of the 17th century, his championing of Dante and Baudelaire as great spiritual visionaries brought new views to the study of literature. It was again possible to fuse the sublime and the conversational, the religious and the secular, by dint of associative logic and jarring discords.

  2. Eliot's essays on prose were no less significant, especially his assessment of the "mythical method" that stamps Joyce's *Ulysses*. In articulating what he takes to be Joyce's strategy, Eliot spells out much of the forthcoming program of modernism to be seen in works by Yeats, Pound, Mann, Faulkner, and O'Neill.

  3. An earlier essay, "Tradition and the Individual Talent," published in 1919, remains provocative even today. Invoking "tradition" as the "mind of Europe," Eliot offers a remarkable vision of culture as something that lives, evolves, and is altered by the creation of new works. The view of impersonality put forth here was equally influential—and misleading—as a theory of poetry.

4. Critics interested in uncovering voices that have been either unheard or silenced—women writers, writers of color, writers from the margins—do not find much to like in Eliot's view of tradition.

5. The remarkable mobility in Eliot's conception, however, suggests a suppleness with which we should come to terms. The tradition is not something monolithic, but something that lives.

H. Eliot's ability to re-imagine the relations between the individual and the tradition—to create a poetry that uses individual utterance as a prism, a lens for seeing history and culture—is central to a host of writers who follow. The fierce visions of Eliot's fellow St. Louis writer, William Burroughs, and the virulent confessions of Eliot's poetic successor, Robert Lowell, testify to the enduring legacy of Eliot's views.

II. To see what is new in Eliot, we have only to examine his poems, even the very early ones that already strike a different chord.

A. "The Love Song of J. Alfred Prufrock" begins with a (now famous) invitation to the reader. Bear in mind Frost's special invitation to *his* reader in "The Pasture."

1. The opening lines usher in imagery of disease, urban anomie, alienation. We recognize the influence of Baudelaire and Laforgue, especially in their city poems.

2. Eliot shows himself already as the unrivaled master of ditties and refrains that we will remember all our lives. He has a gift for epigram. He is also giving us an anatomy of culture: sterile, superficial, vain, pointless.

3. Eliot also sounds a signature note about fear and insecurity: Prufrock is hounded by doubts and anxiety, about the impossibility of passion or direct utterance.

4. Life is presented here, as Frost has also said, as "a diminished thing," but Eliot adds a new kind of protagonist: the second-rater, the man in the margins, the onlooker who cannot act.

5. Part of Eliot's economy and charm lie in the languid lyricism that remains, throttled though it is; Prufrock cannot act, but he can indeed yearn.

B. If, however, we are to grasp Eliot's stature and accomplishment—and understand why he is so "unloved" today— "The Waste Land" must compel our most serious attention.

   1. This poem is arguably the most elitist ever written. It is woven out of references to other texts, many of them arcane to today's readers. To top things off, Eliot also published several pages of notes to his poem, explaining his allusions, telling us where to look. Many felt then, and many feel today, that this kind of bibliographic research and erudition has nothing whatsoever to do with poetry.

   2. We will deal in detail with "The Waste Land" in the following lecture, but consider now the closing lines. Listen to their strangeness.

   3. How is one to assess these shards, these fragments? Are these dead letters? Is the "tradition" essentially fragments, ruins? What about our own American classics? Eliot's project is on our plate in this program.

Lecture Fifty-Three—Transcript
T. S. Eliot—Unloved Modern Classic

This is Lecture Fifty-Three, and it's the first of two lectures on T.S. Eliot. Given the framework of this course, I'd like to present Eliot essentially as the opposite number to Robert Frost. Whereas Frost has a kind of New England, folksy reputation, if not reality; Eliot comes across to us as a very, very sophisticated, cosmopolitan, international, and distinctly elitist kind of figure. On the other hand, Eliot is enormously more influential in English and American literature than is Frost. As I said, I think Frost suffered in many ways from the neglect of critics—or the dislike of critics—which I think was misfounded, but the nonetheless happened.

Eliot, on the contrary, during the time that he wrote his major poems and essays, was a figure who was almost religiously attended to. It's the case now that for the last two decades Eliot's fortunes have been very much under attack. Eliot is not taught very much in major universities today—I'll talk more about that as I go on—for reasons both good and bad, some of which are really intrinsic to the work. He's not easy to teach. He's increasingly hard to teach. We're going to see that some of those reasons also have to do with ideological issues, and with the way the canon and American studies have changed. In this first lecture, I want to talk about the Eliot corpus, about the Eliot reputation. I want to refer in some detail to some of Eliot's extremely seminal essays of literary criticism that have really shaped the way literary studies in this country have been conducted, and then to look at the very wonderful early poem, "Prufrock," and close the lecture, essentially, with a kind of coming towards, "The Waste Land," which will be the bulk of what I want to talk about in the second lecture on Eliot.

First: The life and career. He comes from an interesting, terribly distinguished family. He was born in St. Louis in 1888, to a very prominent New England family that had come to America from England in the 17th century, and which had a long tradition of men in public service and religious leadership. It was his grandfather who had gone to St. Louis, in 1834, and had established the first Unitarian Church there. He was a very powerful man in terms of the anti-slavery movement. He helped keep Missouri in the Union during the war. He founded Washington University—it would have been called Eliot University, except that this man said, "No, you can't do that." So that's the background that T.S. Eliot is born into: Thomas Sterns Eliot.

He went to Harvard in 1906. He finished it in three years. He did graduate work in philosophy. He studied at the Sorbonne in Paris. He returned to Harvard. He was appointed an assistant in philosophy from 1913 to 1914, the time of the First World War. He was on a traveling fellowship in Germany when it broke out. He then began to read Greek philosophy. He stayed in London. He went to Oxford and he began to publish articles and poems. "The Love Song of J. Alfred Prufrock," appeared in 1915, which is the beginning of modernism—of literary modernism, which I'll be talking about. He went from teaching to banking with Lloyd's of London. He combined those careers, as a writer and as a banker. He was an editor and a writer for journals, in particular *The Criterion*, which he edited until the late 1930s. In 1927, however, he became a British subject and stayed away from the United States for really a large number of years, returning to Harvard in 1932 and 1933 as the Charles Norton Professor of Poetry.

He lived his life mostly in London. He became one of the directors of the publishing house of Faber and Faber. He won the Nobel Prize in Literature in 1947; and he died in 1965. So that's, in a nutshell, some of the dates. His most famous and influential poem is "The Waste Land." It was published in 1922, which has been called the *anno mirabilis*. It's the same year that Joyce's *Ulysses* was published. This is the great moment for high modernism. A number of major poems were published after that, frequently having to do with Eliot's own religious crises: "The Hollow Man" in 1925, "Ash Wednesday" in 1930, "Four Quartets" in 1943. He also made a notable effort to revive poetic drama for our 20th century audience. His most famous, and I think most successful play in this area is, *Murder in the Cathedral*, the story of Thomas á Beckett. He also wrote more contemporary materials like, *The Cocktail Party* and *The Confidential Clerk*.

As I said earlier, he published landmark, crucial essays on literature throughout his life. Now why does he matter so much? Well, "The Waste Land" changes the face of modern literature. That's why it has to be in a course like this, whether or not people like it, or whether or not people can read it. It changes the face of modern literature, both formally and I think thematically. It's poetry of cultural despair, of yearning; but a yearning that's completely different from the immediate 19th century predecessors of both romanticism and Victorian poetry. Moreover, he becomes the great arbiter of literary taste and judgment. His likes and dislikes influence an entire generation, perhaps two generations of poets, novelists, and particularly professors, who help to mold opinion in any society.

Eliot rejected, out of personal temperament, romanticism. He helped English departments throughout the United States rediscover the great metaphysical poets of the 17th century whom he liked—John Donne most particularly, but also Crashaw, Andrew Marvell—and his interest in the metaphysical poets of the 17th century helps to account for the very marked qualities of his own work. He fuses the religious and the secular in his poems, the sensuous and the intellectual. He fuses them at the same time he makes you aware of their disjointedness. He has a remarkably conversational voice in his poems. He delights in associative logic, but also jarring discords; and, there is the kind of wit that runs through this work.

There are lots of jokes in his work as well. He's drawn to poets who themselves are very religious. Dante is probably the figure that he most revered. But he's also drawn—I say, he dislikes the romantics. He has not much use for Wordsworth and Keats and people like that. He probably would have had contempt for Shelley and Byron; but in the 19th century, he likes Baudelaire. He thinks that the French poet, Baudelaire, is a poet who harks back to the Dante tradition, a poet of sordidness and pain, self disgust—that's a theme that Eliot easily identifies with—but also a poet who focuses on the modern scene and his own soul and focuses, therefore, on poetry of Paris on the one hand—living in 19th century Paris—but also a kind of tortured search for salvation, for something finer.

I'm going to read you a brief comment from an essay on Baudelaire, because I think he makes Baudelaire a central figure in the development of modern poetry. Eliot is the clearinghouse. All roads go through Eliot. This is from the essay on Baudelaire.

> It is not merely in the use of imagery of common life, not merely in the use of the imagery of the sordid life of a great metropolis, but in the elevation of such imagery to the first intensity—presenting it as it is, and yet making it represent something much more than itself—(It's in all of this, he says) that Baudelaire has created a mode of release and expression for other men.

You know, you can hear Emerson there too; although Eliot washes his hands of the Americans. In fact, I think the Emersonian view, that facts are shot through with spirit, is totally congenial to this same view of poetry that you seen in Baudelaire. All of Eliot's published essays become gospel in the academy. He was as influential on the development of prose as he was on poetry.

One of his most famous essays, and one of his most on-target essays, is an essay written on Joyce's *Ulysses*. It's where he talks about Joyce's mythical method. It's a luminous statement, really, for the cultural strategies of modernism. He says, "It is here that Mr. Joyce's parallel use of *The Odyssey*." As you know, *Ulysses* is framed on *The Odyssey*. Hugh Kenner once pointed out that if you actually open up Joyce's book and read it, and don't look at the title, you're not going to see Homer. It's an exceptionally erudite, indirect, oblique set of correspondences. Nonetheless Eliot knew it. Eliot, of course, saw the title.

> ... the parallel use of the *Odyssey* has great importance. It has the importance of a scientific discovery. No one else has built a novel upon such a foundation before: it has never before been necessary.
> ... In using the myth, in manipulating a continuous parallel between contemporaneity and antiquity, Mr. Joyce is pursuing a method which others must pursue after him. They will not be imitators, any more than the scientist who uses the discoveries of an Einstein in pursuing his own, independent further investigations. (And listen carefully this is what he likes about the use of the myth and the use of the past.) It is simply a way of controlling, of ordering, of giving a shape and significance to the immense panorama of futility and anarchy which is contemporary history.

We live in a world that is utter murk, anarchic, chaotic; and, we can frame it, order it, assess it, make it presentable, and make it useable by aligning it in a kind of systematic way, whether ironic, critical, whatever, with the past. Now he's wrong about Joyce in some ways. Joyce's book is not a critique of contemporary life. Joyce is a much broader figure than Eliot. Eliot read Joyce this way, and I think that a lot of other writers are going to go in with this. I'll close the last sentence I've closed there with this, "It is, I think, Joyce's mythical method. I seriously believe a step toward making the modern world possible for art," because otherwise, how could you write when you look around you? This is written in 1923, at a time, you know, in the wake of the First World War, with the growing interest in Marxism and communism, with a whole series developments in modern society that Eliot is very, very unhappy with, and doesn't know how to make sense of.

I want you to think about that esthetic, because it applies to Yeats, to Pound, to Thomas Mann, Faulkner, Eugene O'Neill; and in our day, John Gardner, Tom Stoppard, that the whole model of writing a modern text, I'm thinking of Gardner's book *Grendel* or Stoppard's *Rosencrantz and Guildenstern*. You rewrite the old text in terms of modern views, or you rewrite the modern life in terms of the older text, but you work the parallel. So, it's an extremely fertile formula that Eliot is really giving us here.

No less seminal is his essay—written even earlier in 1919—called, "Tradition and the Individual Talent." That's where Eliot really gives us a view of literature, where he articulates the importance of the tradition. Mind you, "Tradition and the Individual Talent" is not a title that is going to endear Eliot to people who like romanticism. Romanticism usually takes the view that what we look for is genius and originality. This whole essay says genius and originality are not the attributes of great literature. Instead, what counts is what we look for in a great poet. What makes a great poet is the way in which that poet works the tradition. Eliot goes on to say that, the historical sense, or what the tradition is, he says, can't be inherited. "If you want it, you must obtain it by great labor. It involves the historical sense, and that involves a perception not only of the pastness of the past, but of its presence." That's an interesting line on the present-ness of the past. Here's how he articulates that:

> ... the historical sense compels a man to write not merely with his own generation in his bones, but with a feeling that the whole of literature of Europe from Homer and within it the whole of the literature of his own country has a simultaneous existence and composes a simultaneous order.

So that all of literature flows through the blood of a great poet. Now mind you too, his purview is entirely Euro centric. It's entirely Western. You notice that he uses that phrase, "a simultaneous order." He says the existing monuments of the great texts—Dante, Shakespeare, and Chaucer—form an "ideal order among them," (And listen,) "which is modified by the introduction of the new, the really new work of art among them." This is one of the most interesting features of the theory; that every new important work of literature changes the past. It's not just that the past changes us; we change the past. We create the past. That is to say, when Eliot writes, we don't think of Dunn or Dante in the same way. We see that they lead to him. We see a different kind of picture here. It's almost a cubistic view of history, that every new important work enters into the whole, the mosaic, and it changes the mosaic. There's something very mobile about this, it all can be altered and recomposed.

> Whoever has approved this idea of order, of the form of European, of English literature, will not find it preposterous that the past should be altered by the present as much as the present is altered by the past.

He goes on to say that this creates great responsibilities for the poet. Because, if you are serious, you are entering into a conversation—and the conversation's not the wrong word—in which you are talking to the past and shaping the way we will then see the past as well. This isn't as antiquarian as it may sound. You can imagine; this view has been under great attack in the last 20 or 30 years. As people attack the canon, as people realize that the canon itself is composed of privileged voices—usually white male voices—[they realize] that there are lots and lots of people who have been systematically either not heard from or muted; voices of women, voices of people of color, voices of people at the margins, voices of the proletariat, whatever—maybe you could be—and so, people have been very uneasy with Eliot's so-called, "mind of Europe."

That's the mind he wants, which is an elitist view of what literature is. It's by definition, totally Euro centric with its dead white males. However, this view still is not without interest. It looks towards Borges, who wrote a very wonderful essay called, "Kafka and his Precursors," making the same argument that Eliot does, that every time a great writer comes along, and we can then see that this writer is picking up on something that somebody may have written two or three hundred years earlier, it changes the early figure as well, which is really Eliot's point too. There's something really very self-evident in a lot of this; that we do create the past; that, as we determine what it looks like, we reshape it in every generation, and each different school of history gives us a new version of what the past looks like.

This is inevitable. Eliot's ability to imagine the relation between the individual in tradition, or to see an individual utterance—an individual work of art as somehow refracting the entire tradition and altering it—this is a terribly important contribution, it seems to me, to literature. Eliot's impact on writers, as I said, is enormous. The most obvious examples would be modern poets, but modern novelists as well. I think of a person like William Burrows, who comes from St. Louis as well. *Naked Lunch* has lots and lots of "The Waste Land" in it. Among poets, one thinks of someone like Robert

Lowell, who could not have written *Life Studies*, confessional poetry, had it not been for Eliot.

Now I said the word confessional. Eliot himself argues that literature is not meant to be confessional. It's not meant to be private. It is, instead, our way of hooking up with the tradition. He says the progress of an artist is a continual self-sacrifice, a continual extinction of personality. He calls it a process of depersonalization. He says the poet has not a personality to express, but a particular medium, which is only a medium and not a personality, in which impressions and experiences combine in peculiar and unexpected ways. This doctrine of impersonality became terribly influential for really many, many decades. Then later in life, people realized that Eliot's own work was coming entirely out of his personality, that his poetry was much more confessional than anybody had anticipated.

I'd like now to pass into the poetry itself, and to start with, "Prufrock," which, as I said, is his first major poem. And you'll remember, I contrasted it in my Frost lecture with, "The Pasture," and with that little refrain, "You come too," that easy invitation. In contrast, this one:

> Let us go then, you and I,
> When the evening is spread out against the sky
> Like a patient etherized upon a table;
> Let us go, through certain half-deserted streets,
> The muttering retreats
> Of restless nights in one-night cheap hotels
> And sawdust restaurants with oyster-shells:

This is a very new note in modern poetry, this extraordinary simile. "Like a patient etherized upon a table." This is Baudelairean, in some sense. He is thinking of Baudelaire and LaForge, a number of late-19th century French poets. It brings a kind of imagery of sickness and disease, decay and deterioration; but also, modern problems of hygiene, modern problems of institutions, into poetic language.

No one would have ever thought of using a word like "etherized" in a poem. Or to describe the sky, "the evening is spread out against the sky like a patient etherized upon a table." It's an utterly stunning line. This is the kind of wit, the kind of intellectual, cerebral wit that Eliot has been looking for in the metaphysical poets and that he essentially introduces into English language poetry: disease, urban, virtually surreal, some of these analogies. Then in the same first part of this poem, a ditty that Eliot has the genius for being able to give us, and just stays in the language and in human brains,

"In the room the women come and go, talking of Michelangelo." How much is packed into that? The kind of fatigue of chitchat, of polite conversation, of cocktail parties and all of that. The status, the degraded status, the ditty-like status of high art, that's what Michelangelo has come to.

> In the room the women come and go
> Talking of Michelangelo.

Those lines I think are immortal. They're going to stay with us forever. They tell us again about the recycling of culture. They tell us about the present-ness of the past. It is not a very happy story about the present-ness of the past, but it's there. Maybe this is the fate of great art that it turns into these kinds of little jingles. This poem also is a poem that is striking for the sense of fear, that it has the sense that one of Eliot's great themes is sterility, fear in the sense that modern life is overwhelming. His heroic figure—rather his protagonist—is usually a second-rater. It's someone who is unable to move or unable to act.

> Do I dare
> Disturb the universe?
> In a minute there is time
> For decisions and revisions which a minute will reverse.
> For I have known them all already, known them all:—
> Have known the evenings, mornings, afternoons,

And here comes another one, "I have measured out my life with coffee spoons." That line too is with us forever. "I have measured out my life with coffee spoons. The mass of men lead lives of quiet desperation at the row road." My view is that this one is just as good a candidate. How many of us read a line like that and say, "That's right, I have measured out my life with coffee spoons," those little rituals, those little secular, mundane rituals are in fact the units by which we could measure a life?

I love "Prufrock." This poem also has a sense—partly because it's readable in a way that I'm not sure "The Waste Land" is—it has a pathos to it that is very upfront. As I said, the figure of Prufrock is a kind of second-rater. "No I am not Prince Hamlet, nor was meant to be." That's the line that I can see leading to Stoppard's *Rosencrantz and Guildenstern*, that the heroic figures of the past are not usable anymore. We only can use them, in a sense, if we either spoof on them, or we signify on them, or we in some sense alter them, or we take the minor figures of their story—Rosencrantz and Guildenstern—and approach them that way. There is a kind of lyricism that's possible here, which is very beautifully expressed in the last lines of the poem.

> I grow old ... I grow old ...
> I shall wear the bottoms of my trousers rolled.
>
> Shall I part my hair behind? Do I dare to eat a peach?
> I shall wear white flannel trousers, and walk upon the beach.
> I have heard the mermaids singing, each to each.
> I do not think that they will sing to me.
> I have seen them riding seaward on the waves
> Combing the white hair of the waves blown back
> When the wind blows the water white and black.

Eliot has the makings of a lyric poet; he's just strangling himself. He won't let himself write that. This lyricism is constantly being checked and choked, but also, in some strange way, enriched by this ironic cutting voice as well. He can talk about the mermaids as long as he can say, "I do not think they will sing to me." "We have lingered in the chambers of the sea by sea-girls wreathed with seaweed red and brown, till human voices wake us and we drown." That's how the poem ends.

It's a poem that expresses a kind of moment of despair at the right time, and in the early years of the century. It's a very lyrical piece as well, as a kind of ice water piece. It's about the residue of romantic longing.

The main event nonetheless, if we are thinking about Eliot's status as a classic, is "The Waste Land." That's the magnum opus of 1922. We have to try to figure out what it means, why it's important, what one is to make of it. It is the elitist text of all time. It uses six—*six* foreign languages. It refers to countless famous and countless not so famous other European texts: *The Tradition, The Mind of Europe* and texts not from Europe as well. It—and here is the most anomalous thing of all—is published with notes. This marks a change in poetry. Some people have never gotten over this. It's the cruelest blow of all: poetry as research. He actually pens four pages of notes. We've learned since that he said it's because the poem wasn't long enough for the kind of format of the book, that they said you've got to make it four pages longer and, instead of writing more poetry, he wrote notes. It was halfway a spoof, but nonetheless the notes came in and they are with us forever.

In the notes he has given us obscure references. It changes the notion of poetry. Is poetry researched? Is poetry a puzzle? Is poetry something that sends us to the library? I mean, what's the point of this? So he gives us explanations. He tells us that he wrote this poem after he had read Jessie Weston's book on the grail legend, *From Ritual to Romance*. He also refers to Fraser's book *The Golden Bow*. We know that he is interested in anthropology. He's interested in these various legends, references to vegetation ceremonies and things like that. He tells us at the end of the notes, for example, that he has been reading the *Upanishads*, the great Indian epics, and in those he has found particular references as well that mean something to him.

For example, the words, datta, dayadhvam, and damyata—you may not know this—mean, give, sympathize, control. That's what they mean. He says the fable of the meaning of the Thunder, which is part of "The Waste Land," is to be found in this Upanishad. That's what those words mean. The word shantih is the formal ending of the Upanishad, and it means "the piece which passeth understanding." That's what those words mean. Here's how they sound. I'm going to read you the last lines of "The Waste Land" before, in the next lecture, getting into the whole "Waste Land." I want you to ponder what this medley of languages is doing, of how you could use these fragments. "I sat upon the shore fishing." This is the Fisher King. This is the figure of the grail legend that is wounded, sterile. He's been emasculated. He is waiting for wholeness. That's the idea that the grail is perhaps going to make this possible.

> I sat upon the shore
> Fishing, with the arid plain behind me
> Shall I at least set my lands in order?
> London Bridge is falling down falling down falling down
> *Poi s'ascose nel foco che gli affina*
> *Quando fiam uti chelidon*—O swallow swallow
> *Le Prince d'Aquitaine à la tour abolie*
> Those are all pieces of poetry.
> These fragments I have shored against my ruins
> Why then Ile fit you. Hieronymo's mad againe.
> Datta. Dayadhvam. Damyata.
>   Shantih shantih shantih

That's the end of "The Waste Land." There you have an astounding conflation of materials. The Fisher King, which is the only part most of us can figure out there, and when someone says that they "sat upon a shore fishing" we know what that's talking about. "Shall I at least set my lands in order?" There's the cultural remark. Is it possible to create some form of cogency, coherence among these fragments? The wonderful use of London Bridge is falling down, falling down, falling down. How many of us have ever thought what that says? That's apocalypse. "London Bridge is falling down." It's the end of the world. Children sing it all the time and have a good time with it. And then, *poi s'ascose nel foco che gli affina*, that's from Dante in the Italian, and it's the reference to the Provencal poet, Arnaud. It's about purification. It's about leaping into the fire in order to purify, which has references to Augustine as well. Then, *quando fiam ceu chelidon*, that is, "when will I be like the swallow," in Latin.

Then, "o, swallow, swallow." He refers to myths of the nightingale, to creatures of legend that have had their tongues cut off and transformed into birds because they've been raped. All of these things are going to be part of "The Waste Land," it's being alluded to at the end. And then, *La Prince d'Aquitaine à la tour abolie*, it means "the Prince of Aquitania and the abolished tower." It's a beautiful line from the very lovely French poem of the late to mid-19th century by Gerard De Nerval.

Those fragments are all fragments, in some sense, of apocalypse, of purification, of purgative moments, and somehow of the restoration of wholeness. "These fragments," which is exactly what they are, "I have shored against my ruins. Then I'll fit you," that comes from the Spanish tragedy by Tomas Kidd in the 17th century. Then the Indian terms, datta, dayadhvam, damyata, and shantih, shantih, shantih, the piece of understanding. All of that is given to us in its original form. These are the fragments. So the challenge is what can be made of this, which we will look at in the next lecture.

Lecture Fifty-Four

T. S. Eliot—"The Waste Land" and Beyond

Scope: Despite Eliot's claim of impersonality, we know that this poem was written during a time of intense personal anguish, and much of the poem's pathos and power derives from this state. Still, the grand challenge is to domesticate the poem's fierce strangeness, its formidable array of artifice and allusion. Eliot has told us of his debt to the anthropological work of Frazer and others, and we see that the "waste land" is a metaphor of spiritual sterility. Eliot explores and expresses this sterility by means of old myths and rituals, involving sacrificial legends, the story of the Grail, and vegetation rites, all intended to provide a choral view of culture's need for vitality and rebirth. Beyond the myths, however, we crash into Eliot's central technique of allusion and citation, usually of older literary or religious texts, enlisted in a powerful series of contrasts with the impoverished conditions of modern life (as Eliot saw it). What we make, or do not make, of these fragments, these allusions, is the heart of the matter. But interpretation is not simple, because the poem takes the form in which the past always remains for us: as residual texts that we either can or cannot read. Our analysis of Eliot's famous poem will be followed by a brief look at his haunting final poetic work, *Four Quartets*.

Objectives—Upon completion of this lecture, you should be able to:

1. Give examples of how "The Waste Land" projects the sterility of the modern age;

2. Describe the use of fragment and allusion in Eliot's poetry; and

3. Summarize how Eliot's Christian beliefs are expressed in "The Waste Land."

Outline

I. "The Waste Land," we now know, is an intensely personal poem, despite Eliot's theory of impersonality. The text is larded with references to the poet's own anguish, and it is a more "human" document for just this reason.

A. We see evidence of the poet's convalescence at both Margate and Lausanne.

B. The theme of nervous breakdown is central to both the poem and the poet.

C. Even here, in these notations of anomie, we come across Eliot's favorite technique: embedded quotations. What are we prepared to make of this?

D. Pound's editing of the poem turned it into a more fragmented, modernist document.

II. "The Waste Land" is understood to be a metaphor of cultural pessimism and sterility. It depicts a culture that is dying and longs for vitality or rebirth.

A. Eliot has signaled his debt to Jessie Weston's *From Ritual to Romance* and Frazer's *The Golden Bough*. Are we expected to follow suit? Must we read anthropologists to understand the poem?

B. We do need to see how the legend of the Fisher King is interwoven with other myths and legends of wound, sterility, and rebirth. The story of the Grail relates, therefore, to other sacrificial myths. Eliot's brilliance is to present this situation as a landscape, a landscape of drought and ruin, a heap of stones. We see here the very iconography of broken belief systems; the recurring question is: Can they be made whole?

  1. Early and late in the poem, Eliot offers us direct references to the Fisher King, and we recall Eliot's earlier concern with failure of passion in "Prufrock."

  2. The references to sacrificial myths include the Hanged Man, as well as deaths by fire or drowning that might be restorative.

  3. Christ himself is evoked in this series, first at Gethsemane, then at Emmaus.

  4. Eliot also includes images from the modern world in his purview. He borrows explicitly from Baudelaire's rendition of 19th-century Paris as both infernal and the place where modern redemption must be sought. Using Baudelaire, Eliot depicts modern London as a place of the living dead, with specific reference to London Bridge, finally cited in its nursery rhyme version as "falling down." This reference to falling cities is symbolic of Eliot's pessimism and apocalyptic sense of modern culture, with revolution and anarchy everywhere.

5. Eliot's cultural pessimism has been sharply criticized along ideological lines, because he appears to be a defender of the Old Guard. Some of the most intriguing criticism suggests a kinship between Eliot's yearning for order and form and the appeal of fascism itself. The example of Pound, a spokesman for fascism, is instructive here. Today, Eliot's politics tend to be resented in the academic world.

C. The central technique of "The Waste Land" is its use of fragment and allusion. These matters bear scrutiny.

1. What is a fragment? Because all fragments come from "wholes," how much of the "whole" must we know to understand the fragment?

2. E. D. Hirsch, in his book *Cultural Literacy*, presents a view that is strikingly analogous to Eliot's: Culture exists in the form of texts, and education consists in becoming acquainted, if not with the texts themselves, at least with their titles or key quotations. What is to be made of this theory?

3. Can we not also say that culture itself, the past itself, invariably exists in this textualized form? Inside our own minds there exists a series of fragments, of ruins, consisting of titles or one-liners that we have retained (or that we have never gone beyond): To be or not to be. Mine eyes have seen the glory. London Bridge is falling down. Chaos is come again. The promised land. Call me Ishmael. To be great is to be misunderstood.

4. These are the nuggets of many texts. What meaning do they have by themselves?

D. Eliot's strategy is to boldly allude, but also to contrast, to refer to these charged references to the past, while commenting precisely on our degraded, "unredeemed" present. This is the "mythical method" Eliot celebrated in Joyce.

1. We can consider Eliot's treatment of the "departing nymphs" in "The Waste Land" as representative of this strategy. Eliot achieves a great economy and a strange music by conflating Spenser, Sydney, Day, and Marvell and a contemporary description of sexual abuse and indulgence on the banks of the Thames.

2. A second example can be found in the depiction of lovemaking as it now happens in London (in 1922) by Tiresias (the central consciousness of the poem, according to Eliot's original design). We remember the poem's earlier references to sexual passion, as well as Shakespeare's depiction of Cleopatra.

III. Eliot continued to evolve as a poet, and his rich sequence of four long poems, *Four Quartets*, written during the early years of World War II, explores issues of religious crisis and belief as seen in "The Waste Land," but in a much less extravagant or allusive manner. A look at "East Coker" will illuminate what is continuous and what is altered in Eliot's poetry. These lines are haunting in their fine awareness of life as both linear and circular. They suggest, as well, the makings of a new kind of art, composed of everyday terms that could still, somehow, bring to life the past and the future.

Essential Readings:

Eliot, "Tradition and the Individual Talent," "The Love Song of J. Alfred Prufrock," "The Waste Land," *The Four Quartets* in *The Complete Poems and Plays* (Harcourt, Brace & World, 1952).

Recommended Readings:

Cox and Hinchliffe, eds., *The Waste Land: A Collection of Critical Essays*, essays by Kenner and Kermode (MacMillan, 1968).

Topics for Further Consideration:

1. Discuss Eliot's view of the relationship between "the tradition and the individual talent."

2. Explain the significance of the "fragment" in *The Waste Land: A Collection of Critical Essays*.

Lecture Fifty-Four—Transcript
T. S. Eliot—"The Waste Land" and Beyond

This is Lecture Fifty-Four, and it's the last of the Eliot lectures. It's the one where I'm going to try—I don't know if one can ever succeed in this—to look more carefully at "The Waste Land" and to try to give us a fuller sense of what it portends—what kind of story—because there is a narrative element to it that it's telling. Above all, to focus more closely on what this technique of fragment and allusion entails, what kinds of questions it raises, what kind of challenges it presents, how risky a method it might be in terms of the historical sequences; whether this poem remains readable or not. We'll finish the lecture with reference—I hope—to some of the later poetry of Eliot after "The Waste Land."

Despite Eliot's claim that the great poets are never confessional and they're never writing about themselves; and that personality is not the proper subject of poetry, instead it's the extinction of personality; and that the poet is something of a lens or a conduit, but not towards himself—it's through which the tradition speaks and through which the age speaks—despite all of that we know now—we didn't know then—that "The Waste Land" was written during a period of really intense personally crisis for Eliot. His marriage with Vivian was tumultuous, was filled with problems, some of them sexual in nature. He had a series of what we would probably call nervous breakdowns, where he was convalescing at both Margate and at Lausanne in the autumn of 1921 when he drafted the poem. There are references in the poem to being at this "edge of a nervous breakdown" or of "convalescing," and in particular, both Margate and Lausanne—where he was a patient—are referred to. We can see them in the poem.

We know that the poem is larded with personal references, "On Margate sands. I can connect nothing with nothing." There's the sense of the kind of chaotic feeling of life, where everything is loose ends, nothing comes together. While the reference to Lausanne is not very polite, "In this decayed hole among the mountains," we now know that's the place he's referring to. The general issue of bad nerves, of impending breakdown is much more memorably expressed in one of the conversations within "The Waste Land" that goes like this, and it's all in quotation marks:

> 'My nerves are bad tonight. Yes, bad. Stay with me.
> 'Speak to me. Why do you never speak? Speak.
> 'What are you thinking of? What thinking? What?

Can you hear how each sentence just gets pared down further and further?)

> 'I never know what you are thinking. Think.'
> I think we are in rats' alley
> Where the dead men lost their bones.
> 'What is that noise?'
> The wind under the door.
> 'What is that noise now? What is the wind doing?'
> Nothing again nothing.
> 'Do
> 'You know nothing? Do you see nothing? Do you remember
> 'Nothing?'
> I remember
> Those are pearls that were his eyes.
> 'Are you alive, or not? Is there nothing in your head?'

This is just a brief snippet, but it certainly conveys a conversation between two people of anomy, a sense of boredom [that] is so intense I believe that something is coming apart. There's a sense of frustration, of failure of marriage perhaps, of a conversation between a man and a woman. I think the term that Eliot used was *abulia*, which is a kind of despair that is both psychological and metaphysical; which, I think, is how he came to understand his own position. This passage I read, on the one hand, is very conversational; but pared down, in the way that Samuel Beckett's work is pared down, where the words just get simpler and simpler and more and more resonant, "What are you thinking of? What thinking? What?" You can see a kind of attrition process here, a sense of diminution going on.

That's not all. That answer, "I remember those are pearls that were his eyes." Do you remember? Does anybody remember? I'm wondering whether that is a fragment from one of the most beautiful passages in Shakespeare? It comes from *The Tempest*, and it goes like this, this is what Eliot is alluding to:

> Of his bones are coral made;
> Those are pearls that were his eyes:
> Nothing of him that doth fade
> But doth suffer a sea-change
> Into something rich and strange.

It's a very mysterious evocation of, in some sense, the search for the father. The father has drowned, the search for the origin principle. Also there is the extraordinary sense that death is transforming, death by drowning. "Those are pearls that were his eyes. Nothing of him that doth fade but doth suffer a sea-change," our term sea-change comes from this line of Shakespeare, "a sea-change into something rich and strange." We are transformed, altered through death into something finer, not something worse. It's not rot and decay. This would be the kind of poetic vision that would be counter to the theme of decays to realty and despair or abulia that Eliot alludes to in his own life.

What is one to make of what I just read you, the six lines from Shakespeare from which one is taken and put into the poem? Needless to say, Eliot wants you—if not to literally recognize—to somehow quiver to the subliminal sense that this you know, you've heard this. Of course this is an enormous claim, an enormous dependency on his part. When he originally wrote this poem it was much easier followed than it is now. He wrote it as much more of a narrative sequence, where there was a story, and then the central figure—he called him a figure—was Tiresius, the person from the Sophoclean plays about Oedipus, the blind seer. There are many legends about Tiresius and why he was punished, because he was witness to scenes that he shouldn't have seen, of snakes coupling and things like that, or he answered the goddess Hera the wrong way or Juno. I can't remember. He was punished for that.

The version we have is much more difficult to follow, partly that's thanks to Ezra Pound. When Eliot wrote the poem and showed it to Pound, Pound, in his own language, "put it through the sieve three times" and made it into the cubist document that we have. Eliot would have written a much more cogent 19th century piece of poetry. Pound, who was much more aggressively modernist even than Eliot, turned it into something discontinuous; into the kind of snapshots, jarring pieces of things that are evident in some of the passages that I've read to you.

Then we need to be able to somehow bring to that, conversation between the man and his wife. "What do you remember? I remember those are pearls that were his eyes," it's about what is said. What do you remember? What in the past still lives in your mind, in your thinking, in your language? All we have, of course, is a piece of it. As I indicated, the poem itself, as Eliot has told us in his notes, comes from his reading of Jesse Westin, the book on the Grail legend, *From Ritual to Romance*, and from Fraser's influential book, *The Golden Bow*. You can think of them both as antecedents of Joseph Campbell and his work on myth, his more recent work. Eliot signals this in the notes.

Do you have to read Jesse Westin and Frazier in order to understand "The Waste Land" in order to understand these passages? Pound said no. He said, "I have not read Ms. Westin's *Ritual to Romance* and do not at present intend to." Pound is wonderful.

> As to the citations, I do not think it matters a damn, which is from Day, Milton, Middleton, Webster, or Augustan. I mean so far as the functioning of the poem is concerned. One's in cult pleasure in reading "The Waste Land" would be the same if Webster had written *Women before Woman* and Marvell, *The Metamorphosis*.

He added this, which is a splendid line as well:

> This demand for clarity in every particular of a work, whether essential or not, reminds me of the pre-Raphaelite painter who was doing a twilight scene but rowed across the river in daytime to see the shape of the leaves on the further bank, which he then drew in with full detail.

Just think about the implications of that little story. Do you have to know? Do you have to take the poem in one hand and run into the library and pull out the references in the other hand? Do you have to read the notes, in other words? It's not easy to answer that because if you don't know enough, you know nothing. To know everything would be paralyzing. It would take you a lifetime. You do have to know what the story of the Grail is—it's this urn thing, more or less, that had the blood of Christ, it is thought. It's part of the medieval legends about Percival, knights that were seeking the Holy Grail. Then it gets used as a kind of possibility for synthesis, for healing, and for wholeness again.

The Fisher King legend, which comes again from the story of Percival and the quest for the Grail, has to do with vegetation myths. That's what the anthropologists told us. This is what one critic has said Eliot learned from Westin, "The basic resemblance between the vegetation myths of the rebirth of the year. The fertility myths of the rebirth of the potency of man." From sterility to potency. "The Christian story of the Resurrection and the Grail legend of purification," all of these become figures of each other.

> The common source of all these myths lay in the fundamental rhythm of nature; that of the death and rebirth of the year and of their varying symbolism was an effort to explain the origin of life. Such knowledge, along with the researchers of psychology, pointed to the close union in all these myths of the physical and the

spiritual, to the fact that their symbolism was basically sexual, the cup and lance of the Grail legend as well as in the Orpheus cults.

So that's a kind of learned commentary about how Eliot has really got a big stew there. He's working with a lot of different notations, and notions that are coming from different disciplines, and they're all forming the subtext of this poem, from which he will pick and chose these pieces.

Now, again, the question is how much sleuthing do you have to do to be able to make sense of this? As I said, the legend of the Fisher King seems to be important. In the old stories the land is sterile, and the pursuit of the Grail is an effort to restore vigor, potency, life, and to make whole. This poem is peppered with images of broken belief systems, of dead relics, of sterility, "a heap of broken images" is what Eliot says in the first page, "Where the sun beats a heap of broken images." You can easily see that too is definition of culture. That's what we're left with, those fragments. "Fragments I have shored against my ruins," is what he writes at the end of the poem.

There are references as well to "Prufrock" with that sense of "do I dare, do I just dare disturb the universe, sense of failure or fear?" Here there are references also to fear and failure. There are references to sacrificed cults, the hanged man that might produce the kind of potency that we're looking for. "Rituals that might restore life—"Death by Drowning"—and there's the reference from *The Tempest*, "Full fathom five thy father lies. Of his bones are coral made. Those are pearls that were his eyes."

These subchapters within "The Waste Land," "Death by Drowning," "Death by Fire," all of these deaths may lead to transformation, may lead to life. Christ can be, therefore, invoked as a paradigmatic figure whose death may or may not heal, depending on whether you are a believer. So Gethsemane will be invoked in the poem, and it will be involved traumatically [so] that you will have a reference.

> After the torchlight red on sweaty faces
> After the frosty silence in the gardens
> After the agony in stony places
> The shouting and the crying

This is a reference to Gethsemane; this is the scene, this is the garden, and these are all the references to the suffering of Christ. We see Christ also at Emmaus in this poem, again a kind of a cult reference, "Who is the third who walks always beside you?" Christ figures in with other figures from anthropology in this text as well. It's not antiquarian; it's not just a kind of learned use of older figures. Eliot wants it to be modern. He wants it to be talking about his world. This is why Baudelaire is such a major figure in Eliot's mindset. Baudelaire managed to convert modern Paris, the Paris of his moment, into a kind of spiritual landscape without prettying it up, looking directly at the sordidness and the horror and the poverty and the brutality of the modern city. Because Baudelaire writes about prostitutes, he writes about misery, and yet he manages to see this as a kind of spiritual quest as well, as a religious quest. Baudelaire, as I say, that's why we have London Bridge. That's why we have London in this poem, because of the way Baudelaire has put Paris in.

London is a dying city. London is the "Unreal city," he writes, and that's a reference to Baudelaire.

> Unreal City
> Under the brown fog of a winter dawn,
> A crowd flowed over London Bridge, so many,
> I had not thought death had undone so many.

He looks at the teaming crowds that go across the bridge, and they're the living dead. Death has undone them. You remember the closing reference, "London Bridge is falling down, falling down, falling down?" There are other references to cities too. These are more disturbing references towards the end of the poem.

> Who are those hooded hordes swarming
> Over endless plains, stumbling in cracked earth
> Ringed by the flat horizon only
> What is the city over the mountains
> Cracks and reforms and bursts in the violet air
> Falling towers
> Jerusalem Athens Alexandria
> Vienna London
> Unreal

What I just read you is a reference to the political turmoil of the time, of the 1920s and late teens. This is the socialist nightmare, as far as he's concerned, the communist nightmare, the anarchist nightmare, that's what it means. "Those hooded hordes swarming over endless plains," this is the threat from Russia. All of the cities are cracked and crumbling, "Falling towers, Jerusalem, Athens, Alexandria, Vienna, London." So the Baudelairean reference to London Bridge, "And I had not thought death had undone so many," becomes widened. This is *tradition* in the individual talent. It becomes widened into a larger commentary about the mind of Europe, which is what he said he wanted to write about, the larger status of Europe today, at least as he saw it from his particular conservative position.

Eliot was a banker at Lloyds of London. He was not much amused by what was happening in Russia. Therefore, Eliot is a huge target from any criticism from the left. Eliot is out of phase, many people think—thought then—with what is most vital and happening on the political stage. Eliot, in 1928, made this utterance, which you can imagine lost him many, many friends, "I am Anglo-Catholic in religion, Royalist in politics, and Classicist in literature." You can imagine liberals all over the world have a big party about this. Eliot was upfront about it. He is anti-Semitic; there's not question about it. There's probably a lot of racism as well in his work. There are leanings with fascism. I want to just for a moment make that point even more clear. Eliot's own yearning for form, his sense in which the chaos that is modern life—which is how he saw it—can only become art by that mythical method that Joyce used, of somehow paralleling it with earlier cultures where there was cogency, where life made sense, where there was form, and probably where there's a certain kind of hierarchy as well, socially. Where you didn't have the hordes and the crowds and the mobs and things that you see both in the modern city, and that are, essentially, threatening to come over through the Russian Revolution.

Eliot stands for high culture, he stands for high modernism, he stands for elite art, and you can say this is only one step away from the kind of worshipping of form and order that fascism itself presented to a Europe that was very threatened. Fascism was the response to exactly what was happening in the wake of the Russian Revolution.

Fascism is a returned order. Fascism is a clear sense of discipline and form. It's therefore, not accidental that Ezra Pound, who mid-wifed "The Waste Land" as one of the great high modernist poets, becomes a spokesperson for Nazism, and is tried later after the war. There is a very credible, logical link between the kinds of "formalism" of Eliot's views, including his religious views: "Anglo-Catholic in religion, Royalist in politics, Classicist in literature," that can lead to terrible kinds of things.

Mind you, too, Eliot being identified with all of these fields has made Eliot all the more unteachable today. Eliot is profoundly, politically incorrect. He's absolutely on the wrong side of all the issues. He's not taught for a lot of reasons. As I said, you could argue that the poems aren't readable, that's a good reason not to teach them. It's also that his politics are just despicable to many, many people in the American academy today. There are cases, and I can document them, of people who've lost their jobs because they wrote on Eliot. If you're in an English Department that believes that we have a liberal mission here, or that there are not enough either authors of color or authors of minorities, women authors, etc., and we can't afford to have our young faculty people working on this material, you could lose your job. It has happened.

So these are not issues that are quaint and behind us, they're still going on. The technique of "The Waste Land," "These fragments I have shored against my ruins," raises the whole question of, "What is a fragment?" Think about this: A fragment is something that has come from a whole. That's the only thing; you've got to define it that way. Do you have to understand the whole thing to understand the fragment? How much of the whole do you have to understand to be able—I mean, after all, we can't call something a fragment if we don't see it as having come out of some larger nexus, some larger containing structure. Therefore, what do you remember?

"I remember those are pearls that were his eyes." That's the fragment that won't mean anything if you can't somehow annex or access *The Tempest*, or at least that line in Shakespeare. There was a book that was much talked about a decade or so ago by E.D. Hirsh, called *Cultural Literacy*. What Hirsh argued is that this society—Hirsh reminds me a lot of Eliot here—is so heterogeneous, and has so little common ground, verbally, linguistically, and intellectually that there should be a basic number of texts that people are familiar with partly for social reasons, [for] this kind of bonding, common ground, the "materials of conversation," the materials, really, of a culture. So therefore, what Hirsh does is he lists the things; a finite list of what you should be familiar with. Therefore, you should know who Hamlet is. Did you hear what I said? You should know who Hamlet is—you could spend a lifetime trying to understand the Shakespeare play called *Hamlet*, that's not the same thing as to know who he is—you've got to know he is the hero of Shakespeare's most canonical text. You can know a little bit more; he is the Prince of Denmark. You could know a little more, he said, "To be or not to be." I mean—you can just keep going as to how much you need to know. That's the question: How much do you need to know before knowing who Hamlet is means anything? That's point one.

Point two. This is a statement about what culture becomes. What is the status of history? The status of history is a series of fragments that are in our minds. "In the room the women come and go, talking of Michelangelo." So what's in our minds? Well, think about it. "To be or not to be." "London Bridge is falling down." "Ring around the rosy." "Full fathom five they father lies." "Mine eyes have seen the glory." "The promised land." "Nothing will get you nothing." "It is a wise man that knows its own child." "Chaos has come again." "All right, I'll go to hell." "Call me Ishmael." "To be great is to be misunderstood." At least a third or half of those you've heard in this course. It is the form in which the past lives or dies. You can see it both ways. The fragments are the state in which life continues. The challenge is can we access the whole?

That's Eliot's diagnosis of his culture. We are living in a world of ruins and fragments. We somehow need—like a blood transfusion—to bring back the fuller culture, to somehow access it, and get it to our bloodstream. These are the nuggets of our text, the ones that I just read you. What meaning do they have by themselves? Eliot's procedure is very allusive and it's contrastive, and I will just allude to one or two segments to give you a little more of the feel of the poem than I have up to now. For example, he refers to a poem by Spencer about the nymphs at the Thames, "The nymphs are departed. Sweet Thames, run softly, till I end my song." Then a few lines later, "The nymphs are departed. And their friends, the loitering heirs of city directors departed, have left no addresses." Now the nymphs are the women who were being exploited by the bankers and businessmen in London, who fornicate on the banks of the Thames and have left, the men have not left any addresses. This is Spencer being reworked into a modern context.

Or you have a line like this, "But at my back in a cold blast I hear the rattle of bones," or a little bit later, "But at my back from time to time I hear," the reader of English poetry who has read Andrew Marvell's "To His Coy Mistress" knows "I hear time's winged chariot drawing near." That's the line that's supposed to follow, "I hear time's winged chariot drawing near;" it's all of us being pursued by time. Marvell's poem "To His Coy Mistress," is about living for the moment, having love, having sex, because time's winged chariot is drawing near. Eliot knows that course, but this is what he writes, "But at my back from time to time I hear the sound of horns and motors, which shall bring Sweeney to Mrs. Porter in the spring." He starts with the Marvell reference; the second line is the sound of horns and motors—that's London, that's Baudelaire's Paris—that's the modern city.

Yet the sound of horns and motors, he explains to us, is also a reference to another poet, Day, which goes like this,

> When of the sudden, listening, you shall hear,
> A sound of horns and hunting, which shall bring
> Actaeon to Diana in the spring,
> Where all shall see her naked skin...

It's one of the classic transgressions in Greek mythology. Actaeon ends up in the wrong place at the wrong time, sees Diana naked, and will be punished for it, much as Tiresius is punished for having seeing things he was not supposed to. So you've got Marvell, you've got Day, and then it closes, "which shall bring Sweeney," who is Eliot's archetypal modern figure—degraded figure, apelike Sweeney is what he's called in one of the earlier poems—"to Mrs. Porter in the spring." Sweeney is going to a whorehouse in the spring. So this is what has happened to the earlier culture of coherence, beauty, love, et cetera. He will rework Shakespeare's *Anthony and Cleopatra*, as well, and then will contrast it with a modern scene of sexual intercourse that is very degraded, that has absolutely no romance. It's not degraded in any sense of violence; it's utterly mechanized. It's about when the carbuncular clerk comes to visit the female typist. You can just feel the contempt.

Eliot writes this scene against the background of Cleopatra, against the tradition of rich, sensual romantic love, et cetera. This is the allusive way of writing, but it's also contrapuntal in a way that it contrasts what Eliot sees as a degraded modern culture against a richer past. I told you I wanted to close with a reference to a later Eliot. The final poem I want to glance at is the really quite remarkable, "Four Quartets." The one segment—it's in four different long pieces—are about Eliot's own religious quest. They're written during World War II. They're much more sober [and] less extravagant than "The Waste Land." It's not that same kind of allusive model. I think the allusive model is doomed. Eliot is now one of the fragments, as well. It's hard for us to process him. This poetry, I think, is different.

> In my beginning is my end. In succession
> Houses rise and fall, crumble, are extended,
> Are removed, destroyed, restored, or in their place
> Is an open field, or a factory, or a by-pass.

Old stone to new building, old timber to new fires,
Old fires to ashes, and ashes to the earth,
Which is already flesh, fur and faeces,
Bone of man and beast, cornstalk and leaf.
Houses live and die: there is a time for building
And a time for living and for generation
And a time for the wind to break the loosened pane
And to shake the wainscot where the field-mouse trots
And to shake the tattered arras woven with a silent motto.

It's a beautiful sense of the linearity of history. "In my beginning is my end," of the way in which things moved from birth to death and continually get recycled. The last part of this same segment goes like this:

Home is where one starts from. As we grow older
The world becomes stranger, the pattern more complicated
Of dead and living. Not the intense moment
Isolated, with no before and after,
But a lifetime burning in every moment
And not the lifetime of one man only
But of old stones that cannot be deciphered.
There is a time for the evening under starlight,
A time for the evening under lamplight
(The evening with the photograph album).
Love is most nearly itself
When here and now cease to matter.

Everything in this poem says the moment sends us backwards and forwards, it's not linear. This poem closes then, "In my end is my beginning." And that's Eliot's project, to make all things somehow luminous in the single notation of the moment.

Lecture Fifty-Five

F. Scott Fitzgerald's *The Great Gatsby*— American Romance

Scope: Fitzgerald has long been thought of as the darling of American literature, the glamorous yet doomed chronicler of the Jazz Age. Precocious, witty, devilishly handsome and gifted, a remarkable stylist and observer, Fitzgerald produced two of the most memorable novels of the century—*The Great Gatsby* (1925) and *Tender Is the Night* (1934). These succeed in delineating his own personal romance and travails against an echoing backdrop of American manners and aspirations. His fascination with the revels and excesses of the Roaring Twenties, as well as his acute sense of social rituals, hierarchies, and jargons, make him at once a historian of his moment and a figure much neglected in today's English departments. Yet, *Gatsby* is certain to remain a key American document, perhaps our finest presentation of the lure of money and fortune in the early years of the 20th century. Beyond that it stands as a nearly perfect embodiment of what we know as the American dream: the possibility of constructing your own life, of becoming truly a self-made man, a feat of volition and freedom that is at the core of American democratic ideology. In this sense, too, Fitzgerald may appear prehistoric to many cultural critics, because his belief in self-making seems naive given contemporary views of ideology's stranglehold on the human subject. For all these reasons, we need to look hard at *The Great Gatsby* to see our myths writ large. We may also discern in Fitzgerald's lyrical monument a mirror that can still disturb.

Fitzgerald is our great chronicler of the giddy 1920s. In his masterpiece, *The Great Gatsby*, we see an evocation of the boisterous excesses of the period, its manic rejection of a more prim Victorian past, and a keen understanding of the real energies at play. Gatsby himself is the hero of the American Dream, our 20th-century inheritor of Benjamin Franklin's legacy of self-making, of moving from humble origins to exalted deeds; yet, the tonality of this book is radically different from the prudent discipline practiced and preached by Franklin. On the contrary, Fitzgerald delivers the music of a madcap era and he shows us what ultimately "finances" great fortunes: not simply money or brains or luck, but burning *desire*, the driving force that harnesses our power and moves worlds. Fitzgerald is to be understood as the lyric poet of capitalism, the man who best understood (perhaps because he could least resist) the magic of riches and glamour. To present this phenomenon fundamentally as a love story, a story of desire so strong that it seeks to reverse time and recapture the past, is to fuse the personal and the cultural in striking fashion.

Objectives—Upon completion of this lecture, you should be able to:

1. Summarize how Fitzgerald's fiction offers a window onto the Jazz Age of the 1920s;

2. Give examples of how Jay Gatsby is a 20th-century incarnation of Benjamin Franklin; and

3. Explain why Fitzgerald's reputation has suffered in recent years.

Outline

I. We begin with an overview of Fitzgerald's career and reputation.

    A. Fitzgerald's position in American literature is that of chronicler of the Jazz Age, the giddy 1920s, when America frenetically rejected its prim Victorian 19th-century past in pursuit of pleasure.

        1. Born in 1896 in St. Paul, Minnesota, Fitzgerald went to Princeton as a precocious writer and a wild party boy. While there, he began what would later become his first novel, but left the university in 1917 to join the Army.

        2. At an Army post near Montgomery, Alabama, Fitzgerald met the beautiful, talented, well-born, and unstable Zelda Sayre, whom he courted and later married. This core experience is replayed variously in the plots of both *Gatsby* and *Tender Is the Night.*

        3. Fitzgerald became a literary success with his first novel, *This Side of Paradise* (1920), and his second, *The Beautiful and the Damned* (1922). Each work is replete with the Fitzgerald staples: wealth, glamour, narcissism, a tinge of horror, brooding, and death. *The Great Gatsby* (1925) is his masterpiece, but his wild life with Zelda, saturated with excess, alcoholism, and impending madness on her part, leads

inexorably toward "crackup." *Tender Is the Night* (1934) testifies eloquently to this evolution.

4. *Gatsby* is Fitzgerald's most accomplished book, but *Tender* is his most complex and heartbreaking, and his last unfinished novel, *The Last Tycoon* (1940), dealing with Hollywood, makes us wonder what he might have done had he not succumbed to his demons. "There are no second acts in American literature," Fitzgerald is famous for saying, and he understood *failure* in a way that few others did.

B. Fitzgerald is not in great demand today in the academic world.

1. There is doubtless more critical interest, along feminist lines, in his doomed but brilliant wife, Zelda.

2. Fitzgerald and Zelda were among the "beautiful people." They attended never-ending parties and went on binges; they drank themselves into stupor; they were breathtakingly handsome, smart, savvy, and spoiled. This attachment to the rich and famous, this fascination with the way the beautiful people lived, does not endear him to critics interested in ideological arrangements. Fitzgerald is usually dealt with as a target rather than as a subject in fashionable work today.

II. *The Great Gatsby* presents all the major themes of the 1920s: wealth, parties, and dreams.

A. Gatsby appears to us, and to his fellows, as a legendary figure of wealth and mystery.

1. Like the ancient gods, for whom there are multiple myths of birth, there are multiple legends of "origins" for Gatsby. He may be a nephew or cousin to Kaiser Wilhelm, a German spy during the war, an Oxford man, a bootlegger, or a killer. Mysterious and elusive, he fits Tom Buchanan's scathing judgment: "Mr Nobody from Nowhere."

2. Gatsby's origins may be unknown, but his parties are indisputable. Owner of a huge mansion on the water in "West Egg," Long Island, he regularly hosts gala events to which people come for pleasure, revelry, and mayhem. In the party scenes, Fitzgerald delivers the flavor of the Jazz Age. There is an air of madcap evanescence, conveyed by language that is often stunning in its freshness and wit. Nick Carraway offers

us an unforgettable retrospective of the folks who came to Gatsby's parties.

B. At the center of all this, of course, is the mysterious Gatsby himself.

    1. Fitzgerald enlists his narrator, the commonsense Nick Carraway, to "deliver" the mysterious title figure.

    2. Gatsby can be understood as the 1920s (manic) version of Benjamin Franklin, the boy without resources who *made himself* into a tycoon. Gatsby's is the "rags-to-riches" American story, but without Franklin's prudence and civic-mindedness. Gatsby is also—as we shall see—more sinister and far more romantic than his 18th-century forebear.

    3. Gatsby, we learn, bought this mansion and gives these parties in hopes of one day re-encountering his lost love, Daisy. Daisy is now married to Tom Buchanan and lives in a mansion across the bay in "East Egg," the more traditionally wealthy part of Long Island. Gatsby can see the green light on her dock, which comes to represent all his desire and longing.

    4. Gatsby tells Nick (his neighbor) of falling in love with Daisy when he was stationed in the South, five years earlier, an officer with infinite dreams but no real claims. This love affair was the spiritual high point of his life, and Fitzgerald offers us an exquisite evocation of love and sexual desire as the prime forces that move the world.

    5. Our discussion thus far is relatively chronological, but narratively backwards. We begin this text with Nick, then Daisy (Nick's cousin) and Tom, then Gatsby's fabulous parties, and then the request that Nick invite Daisy to tea, so that Gatsby can at long last see her again and make good on his dream.

    6. This long-awaited rendezvous is handled with Fitzgerald's characteristic charm and wit and pathos. It moves from near-disaster to tearful reunion to stunning triumph of love, glamour, and even wealth.

    7. Gatsby's character is elusive and full of pathos. His aura is reflected in the enormous parties he throws, a wild pursuit of the American dream that is deeply romantic.

    8. At this point, interpretation of Fitzgerald becomes uncomfortable. These passages echo with an extraordinary lyricism, as in the scene with the shirts. Fitzgerald is the poet of capitalism; yet, the reader must wonder: Can this dream be truly gratified? Is the American project saddled with a flawed design? This book is about the beauty of the dream and the imperfection of the dreamer.

Lecture Fifty-Five—Transcript
F. Scott Fitzgerald's *The Great Gatsby*— American Romance

This is Lecture Fifty-Five, and it's the first of three lectures that I'm going to give on Fitzgerald's *The Great Gatsby*. In this first lecture I want to talk about the life and career of Fitzgerald, and then I want to begin talking about *Gatsby* in terms of its romance; in terms of its existence as a kind of portrait of the glittery 1920s, of the great parties, and of the kind of aura that surrounds Gatsby himself.

Fitzgerald is our great chronicler of the Jazz Age, of the giddy '20s at a time when American seems to reject its earlier more austere prim Victorian past, its 19th century heritage. There's a kind of sense of hedonism, of pleasure, and of recklessness—of taking chances—a sense of risk taking in Fitzgerald's work that has to be understood against the backdrop of sobriety and prudence and decorum. Fitzgerald is the great party boy of American literature, as he was in his own life. He is a Midwesterner. He comes from St. Paul, Minnesota, but he goes to Princeton where he is a party boy. He's part of the Triangle Club. He's part of Cottage Club. When I was an undergraduate at Princeton, people still talked about Fitzgerald's escapades; diving into fountains, all night orgies, and this, that, and the other. He had great literary ambitions even then, as an undergraduate.

He began writing his first book at that point. He leaves in his senior year, in 1917, to join the army; and he meets, in an army post near Montgomery, Alabama, the very beautiful, mesmerizing, talented, wellborn, Zelda Sayre, whom he courts and later marries. This episode, this fateful event in his life, it's the core experience of his best books. It's what gets replayed in *Gatsby,* and it gets replayed in a different way in *Tender is the Night.* Fitzgerald has early success. He becomes a kind of overnight literary figure with his first novels, *This Side of Paradise*, which is published in 1920, and *The Beautiful and the Damned* in 1922; and his themes are the recognizable themes of wealth, glamour, narcissism, but with an undercurrent of horror and of brooding and of death.

One senses, even in the early work, this kind of insidious move towards what he later himself calls "crack-up," and *Tender is the Night,* of course, is the novel that takes the measure of that. *Gatsby* is his most achieved, perfect book. *Tender*, arguably is a more heartbreaking book; and his last unfinished novel about the film industry in Hollywood, *The Last Tycoon* makes you wonder what Fitzgerald might have gone on to do had he lived. He dies in 1940. He succumbed, however, to alcohol, despondency, depression, disillusion, and despair. As I indicated at the very begin of this course, he died thinking that his own name would be forgotten in American literature. He's the one who said there are "no second acts" in American literature. He understood failure. Some very fine essays [have been] written about Fitzgerald's grasp of failure, in a way that his obvious perfect counterpart, Hemingway, never understood. Hemingway was a kind of robust, winning figure throughout.

Fitzgerald is riddled with doubts as well, as having a kind of extraordinary natural gift. Fitzgerald is not in great demand in the academy today. You have to look for courses that teach Fitzgerald at the major universities in the English departments. There is more critical interest, in fact, in his doomed, fascinating, brilliant wife Zelda than there is in his work. Much feminist inquiry has been devoted to Zelda's work, Fitzgerald's attachment to the rich and to the famous, his fascination with the way the beautiful people lived—and he was one of the beautiful people. I want to get that across. He and Zelda were dazzling. They were hypnotic. They had never-ending parties. They'd drink themselves into stupor but they were breathtakingly beautiful; smart, savvy, elegant, trendsetters, vain, ambitious; and all of this consorts very, very poorly with contemporary critical theory.

Our interest today in the academy and sorting out the ideological arrangements behind an author's work, that's not the kind of thing that Fitzgerald really invites. So much work on Fitzgerald that does exist uses him as a target rather than as a subject. You all remember—everybody knows—the famous exchange between Hemingway and Fitzgerald. Fitzgerald: "The rich are not as we are." Hemingway: "No, they have more money." Everybody has assumed that that is the realist deflation, Hemingway having the last line and the last laugh. Fitzgerald is right; the rich are not as we are. There is romance and glamour that he knew something about, that he succumbed to; but that he also chronicled for us in a way that others have not. *The Great Gatsby* gives us a kind of wonderful portrait of wealth, of parties, and of dreams. Early in this novel Gatsby appears to us as a kind of legendary figure of mystery, of wealth.

They're legends; in fact, they are the ancient gods of multiple origins. No one knows where he comes from. They keep talking about, "Who is this man Gatsby?" One person says that he is a nephew or cousin to Kaiser Wilhelm. Another says I think he was a German spy during the war. Still another person says he's an Oxford man. Someone else says he's a bootlegger. Someone else says he's a person who killed a man. How can one person be all of these different origins? He's illusive. He's mysterious. Tom Buchanan calls him "Mr. Nobody from Nowhere" and we're going to see how much that phrase means. Wherever he comes from, he certainly knows how to give a mean party and much of the most wonderful writing in *Gatsby* has to do with these parties.

He is the owner of a huge mansion on the water in West Egg, Long Island—which is the way Fitzgerald calls it—and he regularly hosts these gala events to which people come for revelry, for pleasure, for mayhem; and then as I say, you get the flavor of the Jazz Age itself. I'm going to just quote you a few snippets from it just to give you something of the sense of these wonderful parties. You hear about a machine in the kitchen that could extract the juice, I think Fitzgerald says of over 200 oranges in half an hour if you just press a little button. You have these great descriptions of the hams and the various wonderful foods that are brought in by the caterers: the pastry pigs and the turkeys et cetera, the orchestra playing yellow cocktail music. Here's Fitzgerald's language, "Laughter is easier minute-by-minute spilled with prodigality, tipped out at a cheerful world." You can just get the sense of the *swell* of this and of the sort of evanescence of it as well. The people come to these parties to sort of try to get "their fix" in them. He notes Englishmen who are there well dressed, sort of sidling up to these Americas who are fabulously rich and having fun. Nick writes, "I was sure they were selling something, bonds or insurance or automobiles."

He writes that they were terribly aware [of] how much easy money was within their grasp if they just knew how to place the right word for it. There's a sense of evanescence, of madcap, of mayhem, of mobility, and of transformation. "A tray of cocktails floated at us through the twilight." You don't see someone handing it. The cocktails just float right up at you. We sat down at a table with two girls in yellow and three men, each one introduced to us as Mr. Mumble. It captures the feeling of chitchat at a party, like everything is sort of almost dreamy and on the move. Part of the pleasures in this book comes from that. We hear of the singing that goes on at these parties, the stunts.

"The moon had risen higher." It's all very lyrical too. "The moon had risen higher and floating in the sound was a triangle of silver scales." It's all being turned into music in front of our eyes, "trembling a little to the stiff, tinny drip of the banjoes on the lawn." Some of the language can be also more than just mood evocative. Some of the metaphors that Fitzgerald uses are quite brilliant. We have a conversation here about a man talking with intensity to a young actress, and the man's wife, who is trying to get him to leave after attempting to laugh at the situation—in a dignified and indifferent way—broke down entirely and resorted to flank attacks. At intervals she appeared suddenly at his side, "like an angry diamond."

No one has ever written a phrase like that, "like an angry diamond" and "hissed, 'you promised' into his ear." So part of it is just the mood that comes out of these parties. There are also the wonderful names. Nobody can outdo Fitzgerald for creating a kind of roster of figures that are wonderfully crafted by him. The people who came to the party at a key point in this book—Nick Caraway, the narrator is referring to a schedule, a timetable from July 5, 1922 on which he had written the names of the people who came to Gatsby's wonderful parties, and some of these names are really quite wonderful. "Clarence Endive from East Egg who came... the O.R.P. Schraeders, and the Stonewall Jackson Abrams of Georgia, and the Fishguards and the Ripley Snells." And then these sort of exotic names are going to be sort of beefed up with the kind of inside information that Fitzgerald packs into the book. "Snell was there three days before he went to the penitentiary, so drunk out on the gravel drive that Mrs. Ulysses Swett's automobile ran over his right hand." Of course, you read about his, didn't you, in the papers that year? You know what happened to Snell. This is before he went into the pen.

So, you've got three pages just of these remarkable names of the people. "Benny McClenahan arrived always with four girls." And he says never the same girls, but they were sort of identical. They could—you know—each one could become the other. He says:

> I have forgotten their names—Jaqueline, I think, or else Consuela, or Gloria or Judy or June, and their last names were the melodious names of flowers and months or the sterner ones of the great American capitalists whose cousins, if pressed, they would confess themselves to be.

All of this to give you that party atmosphere; and as I say, if you just read the book as a kind of document of the period you get a lot of that but, of course, the splendor of it is Gatsby himself, this elusive figure behind the scenes. Nick is the commonsensical narrator from the Midwest who's there to frame, to take the measure of the Gatsby phenomenon. At the beginning of the text, even though we don't see Gatsby, Nick tells us what is remarkable about this man.

He says there was something gorgeous about him, some heightened sensitivity to the promises of life. At another point he says it was an extraordinary gift for hope, a romantic readiness such as I've never found in any other person. I want you to think about those terms, romantic readiness, gift for hope, heightened sensitivity to the promises of life. Gatsby is going to be the 1920s version of Benjamin Franklin. It's not going to be the prudent Franklin, the circumspect Franklin, the workaholic Franklin, but it's going to be the self-made man. It's going to be the man who makes of his life a grand success, who crafts and sculpts his life. It's a quintessential American story. It is the "rags to riches" story. Gatsby is a bit more sinister than Franklin—a lot more sinister—and he's far more romantic because, unlike Franklin, Gatsby did it all for love. This is one of the great love stories of our century. We know that Gatsby bought this mansion because from it he can look across the bay to the green light where Daisy lives. Daisy, his lost love, now Daisy Buchanan, married now to wealthy Tom Buchanan who lives in a fine house in East Egg, which is where the more traditionally wealthy people live in Long Island.

Gatsby tells Nick about his falling in love with Daisy when he was stationed in the south where we see a replay, I think, of Fitzgerald's encounter with Zelda. Five years before the events of the story start, Gatsby, stationed as an officer in the south, had met Daisy; an officer with great dreams but no cash, no standing, nothing really that will stand for him. Yet, when he meets this woman, he knows that this is the great pinnacle of his life and there's a very beautiful evocation of it, which I think is really the romantic heart of this book, "He talked about the past," Nick says, "and I gathered he wanted to recover something, some idea of himself that had gone into loving Daisy." He keeps the reference of trying to return to this particular moment, and it's a moment five years ago where he and Daisy were walking. He was courting her, and the leaves were falling, and he said they came to a place where the sidewalk was "white with moonlight," and they stopped and they turned toward each other, and the language is quite beautiful.

> Out of the corner of his eye Gatsby saw that the blocks of the sidewalks really formed a ladder and mounted to a secret place above the trees—he could climb to it, if he climbed alone, and once there he could suck on the pap of life, gulp down the incomparable milk of wonder. His heart beat faster and faster as Daisy's white face came up to his own. He knew that when he kissed this girl, and forever wed his unutterable visions to her perishable breath, his mind would never romp again like the mind

of God. So he waited, listening for a moment longer to the tuning-fork that had been struck upon a star. Then he kissed her. At his lips' touch she blossomed for him like a flower and the incarnation was complete.

I think it's one of the most perfect romantic notations in American literature. It comes to us in the middle of the novel, after we've seen Gatsby's extravagant sumptuous parties and wealth, and we're coming to the origins of it here. We know that this is what it's all about. He has built this—or bought this palace—and had these wonderful parties and made the money in order to recapture the moment that I just read to you, that moment where he gulps, gulps the incomparable milk of wonder, where he sucks on the pap of life. It's like an initiation into the godhead that is identified with love for this woman, when kissing her and she opens like a flower at this point.

Now, as I say, this is in the middle of the novel. I told it chronologically forward; but it is narratively backwards. We begin the novel with Nick, then Daisy, Nick's cousin, and Tom her husband. Then Gatsby's fabulous parties and then the request—which is still mysterious for the reader—that Nick should invite Daisy to tea—Nick is Gatsby's neighbor, he's living in a very modest house, unlike Gatsby—and only then do we realize why Gatsby wants Nick to invite Daisy to tea. It's because of the passage I read. All of his life has been to come to this moment where he could finally encounter this woman again, from five years back where he had this aesthetic sense of plenitude and promise met, the long awaited rendezvous then on his part. Daisy, of course, doesn't know anything about this.

She comes because Nick invites her. She has no idea; and it's beautifully done when, in fact, she does come because obviously Gatsby wants this encounter to be perfect. He's invested a very great deal into it and Fitzgerald handles it with very considerable charm and humor. At first it's important that the place be fixed up properly. Nick has no money. Nick lives in a very modest, thread bare kind of place, and Daisy arrives, and she comes to the door or comes in with it, and then Gatsby, all of a sudden, knocks at the door. Fitzgerald writes that he is as "pale as death, with his hands plunged like weights in his coat pockets." It's raining. He's "standing in a puddle of water glaring tragically into my eyes" like this is going to be a disastrous fiasco. You can't rekindle or reencounter this moment of magic. You listen to it. Nick, of course, tries to discreetly stay in the background.

Daisy, of course, has no idea that this is coming.

> ... I heard a sort of choking murmur and part of a laugh, followed by Daisy's voice on a clear artificial note: 'I certainly am awfully glad to see you again.' A pause; it endured horribly, I had nothing to do in the hall, so I went into the room.

And there is Gatsby standing there and these two stiff figures who don't know how to get it going again and Daisy is "sitting, frightened but graceful, on the edge of a stiff chair." How is this going to be somehow saved? Well, of course, that is what's going to happen. It's raining. Nick absents himself as he's supposed to, goes outside, stands under a tree because it's raining so long, and then he figures, after 30 minutes, he's got to go back in there and it would just be improper to stay out that long. He goes in trying to make all the noise he can. He says "making every possible noise in the kitchen, short of pushing over the stove—but I don't believe they heard a sound."

We see them sitting there, at either end of the couch, looking at each other as if some question had been asked. Everything is changed now. "Daisy's face was smeared with tears, and" then he says "when I came in she jumped and began wiping it with her handkerchief," but the change really is in Gatsby. "He literally glowed; without a word or a gesture of exultation a new well-being radiated from him and filled the room. 'Hello old sport,' he says, as if he hadn't seen me for years." He [Nick] said, "For a moment I thought he was going to shake hands." I mean he's just been outside for a little while but there's that real sense of magic here, that you're coming into a new realm here.

Gatsby says, "'What do you think of that? It's stopped raining.' 'I'm glad, Jay.' Her throat, full of aching, grieving beauty, told only of her unexpected joy." Now we're going to have the moment where Gatsby is going to be able to share his riches with Daisy, to show her what he has built in homage to her. "'I want you and Daisy to come over to my house,'" he said, 'I'd like to show her around.'" Nick, of course, wants to back off. The show is between him and Daisy. No, Gatsby wants them all there.

> "My house looks well, doesn't it?" he demanded. "See how the whole front of it catches the light."
>
> I agreed it was splendid.

"It took me just over three years to earn the money that bought it."
[I mean you can really hear the work that's gone into this, and the lies, the mixed stories.]

"I thought you inherited your money," Nick says.

"I did, old sport, but I lost most of it in the big panic—the panic of the war."

You really get a sense early on that Gatsby is not just elusive and mysterious but there's something phony. There's something bogus. There's something constructed about his man, and there's a lot of pathos in the way in which this man speaks of what he has done for Daisy. "I keep it always full of interesting people, night and day. People who do interesting things. Celebrated people." And one feels that he's straining, wants her to see what he has done for her.

Well, Gatsby is described as a person who is completely overwhelmed here—and that is literally the image that Fitzgerald is going to use—that he hadn't stopped looking at her. Fitzgerald says he is revaluing everything in his mansion now in terms of her response to it, whether she also values it; and sometimes he stared around his possessions in a dazed way as though, in her actual and astounding presence, he says none of it was real. Once he nearly toppled down a flight of stairs. He's just sort of giddy, dazed, tumbling. He was running down like an overwhelmed clock.

I'm trying in this lecture to get across something of the aura of Gatsby. This book is dependent on that. It starts with all those references, as I said, to his own origins, bootlegger, nephew of the Kaiser, German spy, Oxford man, somebody who killed a man. All of this suggests a kind of mysterious figure, and that aura is also what the parties are meant to give us; the fabulous wealth, ease, the zaniness of these parties, all of the celebrities sort of coming in and dancing and singing, Mr. Mumble, the various little voices you hear, the people that you meet at these crazy parties, all of that is the sort of creation of Gatsby; and, when we finally get—in the middle of the book—to the encounter between Gatsby and Daisy, it's as if we're coming back to the origins of this, about why, what makes a man produce this kind of wealth.

What is it that drives the American dream, because that's what we're talking about in this text. That's why I compared it to Benjamin Franklin. It's not just smarts. It's not just ambition. There has to be something that finances the ambition itself; and in this case it's clear, it's a deep, romantic view of things, that it's out of his boundless love for this woman that all of his desire is unleashed, and it's a desire that now is actualized in the form of his wonderful accomplishments, his possessions, his grand house.

This is the book that really has something of the poetry of capitalism in it—which is a term, you know, that would get me fired if I didn't have tenure, to say something like that because it's so un-politically correct. The poetry of having material possessions; of things, the beautiful things that you could have, that a love like this has sort of driven him to have; and so, in a crazy passage that has no narrative purpose at all, we have a description of his shirts. There's no other passage that I know of in American literature like this.

> He took out a pile of shirts and began throwing them, one by one, before us, shirts of sheer linen and thick silk and fine flannel, which lost their folds as they fell and covered the table in many-colored disarray. While we admired he brought more and the soft rich heap mounted higher—shirts with stripes and scrolls and plaids in coral and apple-green and lavender and faint orange, with monograms of Indian blue. (You have to visualize this sort of richness of color here.) Suddenly, with a strained sound, Daisy bent her head into the shirts and began to cry stormily. 'They're such beautiful shirts,' she sobbed, her voice muffled in the thick folds. 'It makes me sad because I've never seen such—such beautiful shirts before.'

To me, this is what poetry is about that these shirts become the kind of *objective correlative* of all of the pent up desire and longing that is now. She flowered when he kissed her. She opened like a flower. It's all blooming and blossoming in this sequence here, and those rich shirts, that wonderful profusion of fabric of many colors, which is really like the horn of plenty. It's like the bounty of life in material form, then she weeps into them, and you just have to imagine. To me, the sensuousness of the scene, of this woman plunging her head into this group of shirts and weeping, well, the text, it seems to me, wants us to be sensitive to the beauty of these things. We may say that these are ephemeral things. We may view that these are just material possessions. As I've said, Fitzgerald clearly is the odd man out in English departments today, that if you're interested in a Marxist criticism, or even any kind of an ideological reading, then no one is going to quite persuade you that a whole group of shirts on a bed has a whole lot of bottom line value.

Fitzgerald's book hinges on your being willing to see the romance of the shirts, to see the romance of material possessions, to see the driving force of desire and appetite and beauty that go into all of that. That's why I say he's the poet to capitalism. There's a kind of lyricism of things. This will not stand up, as I said, to a tough minded analysis along Marxist or even other kinds of lines; but, you'd have to be tone deaf and a bit masochistic, I think, not to enjoy something of the sort of shimmering beauty of these passages, that these are things and the things themselves can be imbued with beauty and feeling and richness. Now, the text wants us to take the measure of those things.

If this text is taught, it is usually taught as a kind of warning. It's taught as a kind of fable about the excesses of capitalism, or about the tawdriness of dreaming, or about the wrong-headed nature of the American project. It's about the flawed design of thinking, that your life would reach its apotheosis in beautiful shirts and in a great mansion where you could finally encounter the woman of your dreams and share all of this with her.

So, Fitzgerald is about the dream. At the same time, it seems to me that the book takes the measure of this materialist ethos. It wants us to see the beauty of it but it also takes its measure. One of the most marvelous passages is at the end of the sequence between when Daisy and Gatsby are together again and Fitzgerald writes there must have been moments even that afternoon when Daisy tumbles short of his dreams, not through her own fault but because of the colossal vitality of his illusion. It had gone beyond her, beyond everything. "He had thrown himself into it with a creative passion, adding to it all the time, decking it out with every bright feather that drifted his way. No amount of fire or freshness can challenge what a man will store up in his ghostly heart." It's a very, very lovely notation.

What is happening here is an equation; between the endless infinite dream itself and the moment of gratification. Can that ever measure up? Does Daisy have to fall short? Even if she's perfect, can she possibly be commensurate with the energies that have been fueling his life for the past five years? People have said the worst thing you could ever do about a dream is to actualize it, or to realize it, that it can't be done, that it's in desire itself that you have the great driving forces of life, but that the gratifications never measure up. The people themselves never measure up, and that's what Fitzgerald is writing about. He's writing about that green light on the dock that Gatsby has looked at that symbolizes Daisy and for which he has done the things he's done, bought and built the things that he's bought and built. How could you write a book that would somehow do justice to the beauty of the dream and yet be wise about the ways in which the dream can never be fully gratified, or that the person who gratifies it may not be as perfect as the dream?

Lecture Fifty-Six

The Great Gatsby—A Story of Lost Illusions?

Scope: *Lost Illusions*, one of Balzac's great novels, and Dickens's *Great Expectations* both chronicle the trajectory from delusion and dream to a chastened sense of reality. Realism can be thought of as a mode of thinking and writing that routinely deflates "large" appearances, brings them back to their small causes, educates us about the snares of the world. There is a comparable critical bent to *The Great Gatsby*: We come to understand that all people are flawed. Tom Buchanan is arrogant, brutal, and racist; Daisy is ultimately "careless"; Jordan Baker is dishonest; Nick himself is also labeled "careless"; and, above all, Gatsby is revealed to be knee-deep in crime and shady business. In a flourish of deflating "explanation," we encounter, at the end of the novel, the schedule of self-improvement aids of James Gatz (which is Gatsby's real name), bringing this high-flying hero to a mean point of origin indeed. All of this leads to the even more serious concern: Is the dream itself flawed? Can desire, the superhuman desire that has animated Gatsby, be sustained even after it is gratified? Is this also to be a "lost illusion"?

Objectives—Upon completion of this lecture, you should be able to:

1. Summarize how *The Great Gatsby* can be situated in the tradition of the realist novel;

2. Describe how Gatsby is a heroic protagonist; and

3. Give examples of how *The Great Gatsby* is a "narrative of disenchantment."

Outline

I. Literary realism may be thought of as the narrative of disenchantment.

   A. Nick informs us at the very outset that his experience in the East with Gatsby has been a lesson in corruption and decay.

       1. Like Conrad's Marlow in *The Heart of Darkness*, Nick takes the measure of events.

       2. We will learn just how flawed these characters actually are.

3. Tom Buchanan comes across as rich, arrogant, brutal, and comically racist.

4. Daisy, the great love interest, will not bear up. Not only will she finally abandon Gatsby when the heat is on, but in a key description, her magic voice is "explained" as the voice of *money*. Here too we see the deflations of realism: Look behind the glamour and you find the purse.

5. Jordan Baker, Daisy's friend and Nick's potential love interest, is also exposed as a professional golfer who cheats, who is incurably dishonest. Dishonesty seems to be an occupational hazard in this novel.

6. Jordan later implies that Nick too has been dishonest with her. He is labeled "careless," the exact term that Nick uses to indict Tom and Daisy for their heartlessness.

7. Above all, Gatsby himself will be examined and found wanting. We will see that he is implicated in countless shady deals and sleazy operations, that he is mixed up with criminals, and that he is Daisy's social inferior. In short, he seems discredited.

8. In the end, Nick likens his stay with Gatsby and company to a descent into hell, and he plans to return to the Midwest, a place where virtue and principle still exist.

B. All these actions are quintessential features of realism, the critical genre par excellence.

1. Balzac's *Père Goriot* and *Illusions Perdues* are chronicles of rot and corruption in mid-19th-century Paris, focusing on the loss of innocence brought on by trying to succeed in the modern city.

2. Dickens's *Great Expectations* follows essentially the same formula as Pip learns how corrupt and corrupting his "pursuit of success" has been.

3. Flaubert (whom Fitzgerald admired) tells this story over and over, especially in Emma Bovary's loss of belief and romantic expectations in *Madame Bovary*. This is the generic collapse of ideals, representing the saga of an entire generation's disenchantment after the failure of 1848 that Flaubert represents in *L'Education Sentimentale*.

4. Fitzgerald gives us the list of the partygoers on the flyleaf of July 5, which perfectly symbolizes the book's project: to tell

the story of July 4, the great party, on July 5, the day of the hangover. In this light, grand celebrations and revelries look much poorer. Large things shrink, are exposed in their underpinnings.

5. We may think of this process of deflation in terms of *thinning*, which is how Nick puts it. In other words, think of the 1920s leading to the 1930s; this is not only Nick's thinning but America's.

6. This gambit of realism moves from illusory appearances to mean truths. Legendary figures are exposed and deflated. We need merely to consider our own age of journalistic exposés to know how badly heroism fares in our time.

7. The final "deflating" document of the text is the schedule of James Gatz found in the flyleaf of his book, exhorting the young future Gatsby to perform a number of self-help tricks to guarantee *success*.

II. Behind all the reduction and criticism, the key question remains: Can the dream resist this realist exposure or is it illusory as well?

A. What, then, is left in this story? Is Gatsby really great? Is the novel great? Is anything great? What survives realism?

B. The core of the novel is desire, the generative force of Gatsby's dream and his life. He did what he did out of desire. What will happen when he re-encounters the lost love? Can she measure up?

1. Early in the book, Fitzgerald warns us that no flesh-and-blood creature can compare with our dreams.

2. Gatsby seeks—madly, heroically, splendidly—to reverse time, to recreate the past.

3. He insists that Daisy *erase* the past five years with Tom.

4. Yet Fitzgerald knows that time cannot be erased. After the moment of truth, we see a quiet scene of Tom and Daisy eating chicken together: They are married folks.

5. Gatsby dies as a man shorn of his dream.

6. Here is a text of unflinching realism. Is it true?

Lecture Fifty-Six—Transcript
The Great Gatsby—A Story of Lost Illusions?

This is Lecture Fifty-Six, and it's the second of my three lectures on *Gatsby*. You may remember in the last lecture I tried to talk about the aura of the dream and its material properties, the way in which the text has invested in constructing for us something of the glamour and beauty and impact of the dream, and of desire. I closed that lecture with a cautionary note: "Can desire ever be actualized?" In this lecture I wanted to attack that from the other side, and to think about Gatsby as a critical performance, by which I really want to suggest that it falls into the very tradition of realism as a kind of deflating genre, as a genre that traditionally sees through illusions, sees through facades. The project of such books is precisely to enlighten the reader—or to chasten the protagonist.

Realism is then the narrative of disenchantment. Starting with enchantment and then our gradual understanding that enchantment is an illusion. It's bogus. There's something behind it we need to understand. That's the way this book is built. Gatsby is not the narrator, Nick Carraway is, the straight man from the Middle West. The sane, common sensical, thoughtful, analytic figure whose job it is to sort of take the measure of Gatsby; take it doubly, be aware of Gatsby's aura, his readiness, and his capacity for belief and hope. All the things we saw on the first page of the book; and, at the same time, to be the man who's able to see through things.

Nick tells us at the beginning of the book, not only that Gatsby was special but also that he's leaving the East. He's got to get back to the Midwest. You get the sense that the East is a place of corruption and inequity. "Conduct may be founded on the hard rock, or the wet marshes, but after a certain point, I don't care what it's founded on." There's got to be some foundation. There's got to be some basis for behavior. "I felt that I wanted the world to be in uniform, and at a sort of moral attention forever." This is the alternative to the laxity, to the speciousness, to the corruption that he's encountered.

I would like to compare him in some ways to Conrad's Marlow. We know that Fitzgerald really loved Conrad, and I think that that's sort of the role that Nick plays. It's very similar to Marlow, as he tries to take the measure of Jim, in *Lord Jim*; or as Marlow makes his way after and through Kurtz in *Heart of Darkness*. I see the same kind of sort of function for Nick. So we'll learn how flawed these characters are. All of them are going to ultimately show us their warts and their wrinkles and their vices. One of the most conspicuous targets here, of course, is Tom Buchanan. Early on we know that he is a sort of confused and dangerous person. Fitzgerald or Nick tells us that life after college was anticlimactic. He was a great football star. "One of those men who reached such an acute limited excellence at 21, that everything afterwards savors of anticlimax." That's a devastating remark it seems to me.

We know that this is a man who's confused by the world he's living in. This is a man who is threatened by certain changes. He has a certain racist view of the world. He's telling everybody about a new book that he's reading. "The idea is if we don't look out, the white race will be utterly submerged! It's all scientific stuff. It's been proved." So we can easily position Tom Buchanan. He can be a very cruel figure as well. Nick describes him as having a football player's body, "a hard cruel body." In one very unforgettable scene where Tom has brought Nick with him to meet Tom's mistress, Myrtle Wilson, and they have this drunken party, at one point in the party Myrtle, who's very jealous of Tom's wife, Daisy, is sitting there yelling—this is after midnight. Nick is sort of coming in and out of consciousness there—and Tom and Mrs. Wilson are standing face-to-face discussing whether she has "any right to mention Daisy's name. 'Daisy! Daisy! Daisy!' shouted Mrs. Wilson. 'I'll say it whenever I want to! Daisy, Dai—'" She can't get any further than that. "Making a short deft movement, Tom Buchanan broke her nose with his open hand." You know, football player "Move of the Year" here. The book is pretty swift and brutal at exposing these kinds of flaws in its characters.

Even Daisy, who is identified with the green light—the endless desire that Gatsby feels for her, that's fueled his own project and riches and wealth— Daisy herself is going to be discredited over the course of the book. We're going to see that she will stick with her rich husband, Tom Buchanan, and she will abandon Gatsby. She won't even attend his funeral. There's a very famous line—a key line in the book—about Daisy's own flaw. Fitzgerald very carefully presents Daisy as having a mysterious, seductive, hypnotic unforgettable voice. Men who've met her have not been able to forget that voice. The book always plays with that voice. She has this husky voice; it's thrilling, etc. They're trying to figure out what it is, and Nick says to Gatsby:

> "She has an indiscreet voice. It's full of—"

> "Her voice is full of money," he said suddenly. That was it. I'd never understood before. It was full of money—that was the inexhaustible charm that rose and fell in it, the jingle of it, the

cymbals' song of it...high in a white palace the king's daughter, the golden girl.

Now, again, an ideological criticism of this book is going to focus on that passage, "It's full of money," as to say, "Here's the expose." All of her so-called beauty and seductiveness and charm have only to do with money. That's all. What I want to say is, "That's *all?*" What is money after all? If you look at a dollar bill, or a thousand dollar bill, in its materiality, in its thingness, no one would ever mistake it for a diamond, or a painting. It's not an interesting object in itself. Yet people cut for money. They salivate for money because it is a kind of symbiotic launching pad. That is to say, money is the possibility of endless desire. We see money, and we see all the things that we might be able to buy with it. So, "a voice full of money" is actually a statement about desire. It's a statement about possibility. It's a statement about projection and fantasy. I think that, nonetheless, it's presented—at least on one reading—as a kind of critique.

In line with the argument I'm making now, many of the figures of the text come off badly. Jordan Baker, who is the romantic attachment for Nick in the book, is a professional golfer. We learn early on that she is a kind of inveterate cheater and liar. She cheats when she plays golf, and she lies about small, unimportant things. It's as if it's part of her nature, she can't *not* do it. Nick calls her "careless." In fact, careless becomes a key term in this text, at a very crucial passage later in the book, Tom and Daisy, when the book is almost over, are going to be called careless as well.

"They were careless people. They smashed up things and creatures, and then retreated back into their money, or their vast carelessness, or whatever it was that kept them together, and let other people clean up the mess they'd made." Nick has sort of been making love to Jordan. He has sort of been courting her, and wooing her. At the end, he backs off from her, and she says to him that, he too, is careless. It's a word that begins to get a lot of usage in this text. It suggests a kind of moral laxity, a kind of sloppiness, and a kind of bad faith.

Well, of course, the central figure that is most scrutinized and found wanting and flawed, is Gatsby. Gatsby, we learn, is up to his neck in shady deals. Tom Buchanan has been suspecting this all along. He is not socially fit even to kiss Daisy's feet. He is a prized associate of the criminal-like Meyer Wolfsheim, who we meet in the book. Meyer Wolfsheim comes to us as the man who fixed the World Series back in 1919. Gatsby is part of that kind of cohort. He's been Gatsby's great mentor, or at least one of them. Dan Cody was the first one. Meyer Wolfsheim has interesting cufflinks. Nick is staring at these cufflinks, and Wolfsheim says, "They're human molars." That gives you a sense of what this guy traffics in.

The phone rings throughout the book, with these very, shady suspicious calls to Gatsby about some illicit, criminal deals he's making. He is a bootlegger. He's up to his neck in prohibition. He's up to his neck in shady deals. In fact, he's been a kind of an attractive front man for Wolfsheim. We have plenty of evidence of that as the book goes on. There's a criminal story behind these grand parties, and all of the aura of Gatsby's wealth, et cetera, all of that's part of the realistic thrust of the book. You make your way through these grand, seductive appearances, and you get to a layer of criminality. Or, you hear a voice that sounds wonderful and you're told, "That's just money." Money is the prime force behind this, and this comes out further and further as the book goes on. That's why Nick wants out of the East and back to the Midwest.

As a matter of fact, he thinks that his stint in the East, his stay with Gatsby and company has been essentially a decent into hell. He compares it to a painting by El Greco. It's an interesting passage. He says, It's like a night scene in El Greco:

> … a hundred houses, at once conventional and grotesque, crouching under a sullen, overhanging sky and a lusterless moon. In the foreground, four solemn men in dress suits are walking along the sidewalk with a stretcher on which lies a drunken woman in a white evening dress. Her hand, which dangles over the side, sparkles cold with jewels. Gravely the men turn in at a house—the wrong house. But no one knows the woman's name, and no one cares.

It's a kind of eerie, ghastly, funereal scene of death, of corruption, and of excess. That's what he wants to withdraw from the book. It comes on page 178 of a book that only has 182 pages. It's like that's one of the final realist touches. This is the dirt that I have been in. This is the decent that I have completed. He wants to go back to the Midwest. He says, "This has been story all along of the West. Tom and Gatsby, Daisy and Jordan and I were all Westerners. Perhaps we possess some deficiency in common which made us subtlety inadaptable to Eastern life." You're supposed to see that as a moral statement. Go back to where "conduct is founded on something," not what you have in the East.

All of that then is the story of lost illusions, or exposed illusions, or of becoming unillusioned; seeing through the façade, seeing through the mist. That is the realist premise. I want to do a digression here and talk about some famous realist text from which I think Fitzgerald is taking his cues. The first and most obvious is Balzac, and one of his books is called *Illusions Perdues*, "Lost Illusions." Or *Paragorial* would be another example of it. These are chronicles of rot and corruption in mid-19th century Paris and the loss of innocence when a young person tries to succeed in such an environment. Needless to say, Dickens rewrites the same story in London for Pip, or for David Copperfield. You see the same story of the lure of the city, the "great expectations," the grand things that you're looking for; and then, by the end of the book, Pip too, is chastened, he's lost everything. He's lost Biddy; he's lost his innocence. Or Flaubert, whom Fitzgerald read with great care and attention, tells this story of lost illusions over and over. But it's closer to Fitzgerald because he tells it as a romance. *Madame Bovary* is the French version of this book, of *The Great Gatsby*.

There's no Gatsby in Flaubert. Flaubert would never have created a character like Gatsby; but the dream of love, the dream of the green light, the dream of creating a whole life out of your desire, that's what Emma Bovary languishes for and dreams about, her romantic expectations. Life does not measure up. Flaubert is much more surgical and brutal than Fitzgerald. There is Flaubert's equally great novel which follows *Madame Bovary*, which is *L'Éducation sentimentale* which is about the failed revolution of 1848, which is even more corrosive in the sense that it looks at the failure of an entire political project in terms of romantic aspirations and dashed hopes, the project of a more equitable social order that was dashed in 1848.

I think that Fitzgerald is in line with the same realist energy system, which is to say that you build these things up and then you deflate them. You collapse them. You expose them. You expose them as fraudulent. That's why that little fly-piece—that timetable that Nick wrote down all the names of all the people who came to Gatsby's parties on—was significantly dated July 5th. Fitzgerald doesn't pay much attention that, but I'm going to pay some attention to that. I want to think about what July 5th is within the cultural economy of this country. We all know what July 4th is; July 4th is the day of the great party, the great celebration. It's the great binge in some sense. July 4th is Gatsby. It's the grand parties, it's the drinking, it's the orgies, and it's the aura, the glamour and the romance. But what is July 5th? That's the day of the hangover. That's the day when you clean up the mess.

That's the day where you take a second look at all the grand things and they don't look so grand anymore; that's where you may have the broken glasses, you may have the vomit. July 5th is when you take the tally—if you have the courage to—of July 4th. July 5th is realism. July 4th is romance.

I think that this book is a July 5th document of sorts. It's taking the tally. It's taking the assessment. It's taking the measure of its apparently grand themes, and they come up short; they're revealed as small and as exposed in their underpinnings. That's why these characters are exposed in the way that they are. The novel is about the assessment given to the romantic scheme. It's in that sense that it is a proto-realist text. It's not going too far to see the novel as our great document of the '20s—which is July 4th—with already a view towards the '30s, the Depression, which would be July 5th. We're headed in that direction in this book. I don't think that's a great liberty for me to take to say that, because the text itself has a passage that really sums it up.

It's a remarkable passage, because this is written in 1925. Fitzgerald could not, without a crystal ball, have seen what effectively was coming; but, this is what he writes, "All of a sudden Nick says, 'I remembered that today is my birthday. I was 30.'" When you read this you've got to be thinking about the country's '30s, and '20s. It's what this book is about. "'Before me stretched the portentous, menacing road of a new decade.'" I think of the new decade for this country. "30," he says a little bit later, "'The promise of a decade of loneliness, a thinning list of single men to know, a thinning briefcase of enthusiasm, thinning hair.'" It's a remarkable passage. "Thinning list of single men to know, a thinning briefcase of enthusiasm, thinning hair." The '30s is thinning. The '30s is taking the fat out of all of the grandeur and the parties. The '30s is shrinkage. The '30s is finally taking the measure of the excess.

As I say, it's prophetic. It looks towards the history of this country, depression being in the wings there. This is precisely how realism operates. Great appearances are brought back to meager origins and truths—that the inebriation is over—legendary events and figures are dismantled. Don't for a minute think that anything is different today. We live in a world of thinning, not of fattening. It's not just people wishing that you couldn't be thin enough; but it's also the rhythm of expose is our journalistic ethos today. We dismantle and deconstruct all great figures. You couldn't go further in the deconstruction of Kennedy than [what] has happened in the last 15 years. All figures that may have appeared to be legendary, larger than life, heroic figures, the culture can't allow it. That's the critical, realist impulse. It cuts them down to size. It tells us about their warts. It shows us how unworthy they were. What small people they were, instead of the kind of larger puffed up people we took them to be.

All that, in other words—this zeal for deflation which is part of a critical investigation, part of the critical project—this is what our universities are about it seems to me. We have trouble believing in greatness. We think that belief itself is a dicey thing. If we believe in it, tomorrow we're going to read in the papers just how discredited whatever we believed in really is. We're going to see the fraud involved. I think that we live in an era of suspicion. I think I alluded in one of my earlier lectures to Freud's remark when he gave his lectures at Clark University, where he said, "I have brought the plague with me."

The plague is the era of suspicion. We don't take surface comments for what they claim to be. We look for ugly sources, ugly rationales behind them. This exposed notion of shrinking things into small origins, bringing things back, grand illusions. That's the title of Renoir's film: *Grand Illusion*, "Great Expectation." Can you hear this language? All the things that later turn out to be fraudulent, we have thought were great, we learn that they're small. They're not great at all. To see through appearances, back to causes. It's like exposing the magician's trick. You have thought it was magic. The realist impulse is at the end you see the gimmick. You see what made you deceived.

Sure enough, then, Jay Gatsby, the creature who was the creature of legend, will be brought back to his puny origins. He isn't Jay Gatsby at all. His real name was Jimmy Gatz. We're going to find out he changed his name, he changed his life, and he invented himself. At the end of the book, we're going to even see a document that is one of his source texts for self-invention. It is his schedule. Fitzgerald actually gives it to us in the text. We see it there. It's a schedule from 1906, and it's a "how-to" schedule. It's a self-help book that Gatsby had about how to become Gatsby. This is when he's still Jay Gatz.

> Rise from bed at 6:00.
>
> Dumbbell exercise and wall scaling, 6:15-6:30.
>
> Study electricity, 7:15-8:15.
>
> Work, 8:30-4:30.
>
> Baseball and sports, 4:30-5:00.

Practice elocution, poise, and how to attain it, 5:00-6:00.

Study needed inventions, 7:00-9:00.

It's a heartbreaking document. This is how this man got to his great castle, his palace there where he has these great parties. He carefully worked over this document. It's like an exercise regime. His general resolves, "No more wasting time at Shafter's. No more smokeing." Smoking is misspelled. "No more smokeing or chewing. Bath every other day. Read one improving book or magazine per week. Save $5." (And it's crossed out,) "$3 per week. Be better to parents." If you want, you can say this makes a human being out of Gatsby. It also is a kind of realist document. The man who is such a mysterious, illusive figure that we saw at the beginning of the book, is revealed at the end to be nothing more than someone who studiously worked out that particular set of rules and regulations. He has built himself, made himself, his tricks and his exercises.

I'm talking about whether the dream can resist the realist exposure. That's what this whole lecture is about. That's the question. What's left in this story? When you finish, and you've seen through everything, is Gatsby still "great?" Is this title now an ironic title? It makes a difference. Is the novel great? Could you have a great novel that really deflated the very notion of "greatness?" Is anything great? Will realism ever—will criticism—because I'm really talking about my own job—will criticism ever allow anything to remain great or are we always rolling up our sleeves, and analyzing, and saying, "Oh, wait a minute! We're not fooled by this!" That's why I said it's the plague that Freud brought. We are constantly showing how things work. We're not going to be fooled, tricked, or deceived into believing in them.

The core of the book is about desire: Gatsby's dream. It's not just for wealth. It's a dream for love. That's really quite fascinating I think. Fitzgerald has his dream, to reencounter his lost love. This is interesting, because most texts that are romance texts are about a love that's in front of you. This is about a love that's behind him. Five years in the past he encountered Daisy and had that wonderful, magic embrace. Therefore, the question is, "Can it be recaptured? And if recaptured, can it be maintained? Can she measure up?" I read you the passage earlier in the text where Gatsby himself is wondering. He's not so sure. There must have been moments even that afternoon when Daisy tumbled short of his dreams. Fitzgerald writes, "...not because of her own fault, but because of the colossal vitality of his illusion. (Then the closing line) ... No amount of fire or freshness can challenge what a man will store up in his ghostly heart."

The kind of production of desire, and the huge scope of his dream, no human being, flesh and blood, could possibly fill it up. Could possibly be commensurate with it. That's what he seeks. He seeks to recapture all he seeks to move from July 5th to July 4th. He wants to go back to the dream, to recapture her with all of her beauty, to recreate the past. Nick warns him— after all, this is five years back when he first wooed her—"'I wouldn't ask too much of her,' I ventured. 'You can't repeat the past.'" And you have one of the great lines in this novel, in all of American literature. "'Can't repeat the past?' he cried incredulously. 'Why of course you can!'"

What is the American dream if not that? You could repeat the past. You can reverse time. The past has no weight. It can be simply reversed. You can go back to it. Cancel out everything that has intervened since then. This what Gatsby wants; that's what he's going to try to make happen. The project of this book is to reverse the past. Reverse time. Recreate it. It's a godlike power. People usually can't do that. He's going to insist that Daisy erase her marriage to Tom Buchanan. Erase the very fact of living together with this man for five years. There's much pathos in these lives because Daisy is in love with Gatsby again when she sees him. So Gatsby tells Tom:

> "Your wife doesn't love you! She's never loved you. She loves me!"

> "You must be crazy! exclaimed Tom. [And it goes on this way.]

> "She never loved you, do you hear? She only married you because I was poor and she was tired of waiting for me. It was a terrible mistake, but in her heart she never loved anyone but me!"

That's the erasing of time. Daisy, of course, is called upon to validate this. She has to back this up.

> "... tell him the truth—that you never loved him—and it's all wiped out forever."

> Daisy looked at him. "Why—how could I love him—possibly?"

> "You never loved him."

> And she hesitated. "I never loved him," she said with perceptible reluctance.

[Tom says] "Not at Kapiolani?"

"No."

"Not the day that I carried you down from the Punch Bowl to keep your shoes dry? Daisy?"

"Please don't," she said. "You want too much!" she said to Gatsby. "I love you now—isn't that enough? I can't help what's past." (And she begins to cry.) "I did love him once—but I loved you, too, Gatsby.

"You love me, *too?*"

It's very, very beautiful, this sequence. He wants to erase the intervening five years. He wants to be—there's something godlike in this. To say that all of this data, this experiential data in the human heart, we can change it. We can go back to the moment that we met; all of these intervening chapters can be taken and simply rejected, put away. The text closes, as I said, with Daisy not quite living up to his expectations. At the end of this text, she will abandon Gatsby. She won't even come to his funeral. He will be murdered for something she did. They all know it. He waits for her to come. He's certain that she's going to come. No reader agrees with him. You know that she's going to stay with Tom Buchanan.

You have this really wonderful scene, picture, of her eating cold fried chicken with Tom Buchanan, her husband. You see it as a married couple, married for five years. So what if they have tiffs and fights? So what if right now she might even find that she loves Jay Gatsby again? They are married. They've been married. They're eating chicken. Fitzgerald writes that they were with each other like "conspirators." They in fact are. They're going to plan their exit. They're not going to stay for the trouble. They're going to leave. They're careless people. That's what he's already written. They leave other people to clean up the mess that they have left.

So Gatsby dies, essentially, waiting for Daisy to come. Fitzgerald, in a very haunting passage, tells us how Gatsby is bereft, how terrible it is to remove a man's dreams from him.

> ... he must have felt he had lost the old warm world, paid a high price for living too long with a single dream. He must have looked up at an unfamiliar sky through frightening leaves and shivered as he found what a grotesque thing a rose is and how raw the sunlight was upon the scarcely created grass. A new world, material

without being real, where poor ghosts, breathing dreams like air, drifted fortuitously about… like that ashen, fantastic figure gliding toward him through the amorphous trees.

And that's Tom Wilson. That's the husband of Myrtle Wilson, who is Tom's mistress. He is going to kill Gatsby, because Myrtle has been run over in a car by Daisy. He thinks that it was Gatsby who did it. I love that description itself. "What a grotesque thing a rose is. How raw the sunlight…a new world material without being real." The world becomes real to us because we coat it with our dreams. We invest it with our own projects. We remake it by debt of human desire. That's what has gone bankrupt here. The dream itself has been exposed. All of a sudden the frightening alterity, the inhumanity of the world crashes in upon him. This would be the ultimate move in a realist text. But it's not my last lecture; and so, I may have some surprises for you.

Lecture Fifty-Seven
Fitzgerald's Triumph—Writing the American Dream

Scope: Even though Fitzgerald's novel is relentless in its drive toward exposure, and even though it ultimately discredits virtually all its characters, it nonetheless never ceases to revere the dream itself. Moreover, Fitzgerald is less invested in a *thinning* exercise than in a *fattening* one. America is the land of the dream, because it is the only country in which people believe in self-making, believe that they are free agents, unconstrained by origin or class or birth. Fitzgerald's book is more committed to creation than it is to criticism: the creations of desire and self and language. We remember the fixation with Daisy's voice. Not only is it allied with money, but also with genesis, with naming the world into being. Words, too, can be free of referent. Fitzgerald struts his stuff verbally, offers us a splendidly "independent" language, shows word creations to be real. One of the most charming episodes of the novel is the "saga" of "Blocks" Biloxi, weird word-creature who seems a ghostly cousin of the other self-made man, Jay Gatsby. Fitzgerald is writing about the power of belief: our belief in words (the miracle of literature) and our belief in others (the miracle of desire). This belief—called "credit" in financial circles—is our covenant with reality, and it has nothing to do with realism.

Objectives—Upon completion of this lecture, you should be able to:

1. Explain the ambiguous origins of Gatsby and the commentary they offer on the American dream;

2. Describe in what ways Fitzgerald links America with paradise; and

3. Summarize Daisy's role as a creative force in the novel.

Outline

I. *The Great Gatsby* is ultimately more concerned with the processes of creation than with those of criticism.

A. Yes, the realist impulse is to deflate, to return large appearances to small origins, to see July 5 as the "truth" of July 4. But Fitzgerald is also poking fun at this procedure.

B. Tom Buchanan has been doing some research on this fellow Gatsby, and we end up with our plate full of ugly disclosures. But we need to remember how Nick first characterized Gatsby.

1. Gatsby represents promise, romantic readiness.
2. All those fictive "origins" for Gatsby, those guesses about where he comes from, tell us that he is simply not "explainable." He cannot be reduced to a single origin.
3. In one of the book's great speeches, Gatsby tells Nick precisely about his origins. He shows Nick the medal and the photograph. Still, we cannot miss the elements of parody and the absurd here. What is going on?
4. Gatsby is the elemental self-made man. He has spawned himself. Here is the 1920s version of Benjamin Franklin's legacy.
5. Gatsby is emblematic of the American dream: to be free of origin; not to be determined by the accidents of birth or class or color or race; not to be bound by the past. This is a dream of freedom and self-creation. The dream is called on to make the world.

II. This American dream is strangely and powerfully allied to the phenomenon of language.

A. For most of us, freedom of speech connotes political freedom, the right to speak our opinions. Could it be more elemental still?

B. Remember Daisy's voice, the voice that is full of money. It is also characterized precisely as a voice, as human speech.

1. Fitzgerald repeatedly refers to it as a voice of promise, of possibility. It is "thrilling," "breathless," an "exhilarating ripple."
2. The voice is what held Gatsby most of all; it was a "deathless song."
3. Daisy's voice is presented as a form of genesis, as the creation of the world, giving things a meaning they never had before and never will again. This is an artistic strategy of great ambition for a writer.

C. Fitzgerald's novel, although not formally experimental, is nonetheless committed to semiotic energy.

    1. Consider Fitzgerald's madcap style in this regard: his zany, absurdist metaphors and similes, his gratuitous excesses, and flights of fantasy. The book has a ludic "musical chairs" dimension to it. The order of the artist predominates: That is America.

    2. We are treated many times to Edenic passages, to America as a land of promise, of utter novelty, of new beginnings. Consider the passage on the Queensboro Bridge.

    3. The highlight of the book's ludic activity is the astonishing sequence revolving around the odd figure "Blocks" Biloxi, brought into the text at a moment of maximum seriousness: The "shootout" in a hot hotel room where the two males will fight it out for the golden girl. Fitzgerald gives us the magic performance of this word-figure. His name consists of both family and place; he comes from a writer's wonderland (Biloxi, *Tennessee*); he triggers the strangest actions, including death; he seems to be an impostor (thereby resembling Gatsby), claiming to know Daisy and to be from Louisville; and he grandly claims to have been "president of your class at Yale." It is here that Tom Buchanan rightly links Biloxi-at-Yale to Gatsby-at-Oxford. Here are the exploits of word-men.

    4. Have we not had actor-presidents? Could literature out-trump life by getting its man elected? The pure artifice and antics of Blocks Biloxi speak to us of the magic of Jay Gatsby: his aura, his career, his dream.

D. Yet Gatsby, unlike Biloxi, is flesh and blood. He is the tragic hero of belief as much as dream and desire.

    1. Gatsby gives himself to the dream. He also possesses a special smile that guarantees belief, belief in others. Here is a peculiar but real form of social contract.

    2. Fitzgerald saw the story of Gatsby as the story of those dreams and illusions that give glory to life, whether or not they are true.

    3. That "magical glory" is no less than the capacity to dream, to be free, to make yourself, and to make your life. The novel discredits the dreamer and the woman he dreamed of, but the dream is incorruptible.

4. This is America's first and truest article of belief. It is what the Dutch sailors saw when they first came to the New World.

5. The fact that we can never realize the dream changes nothing.

Essential Readings:

Fitzgerald, *The Great Gatsby* (Scribner's, 1960).

Recommended Readings:

Fitzgerald, *Tender Is the Night*.

Kazin, *An American Procession* (Vintage, 1985).

Kenner, *A Homemade World* (William Morrow, 1975).

Weinstein, *Nobody's Home* (Oxford University Press, 1993).

Topics for Further Consideration:

1. Summarize how *The Great Gatsby* continues the notion of the American dream first articulated in Franklin's *Autobiography*.

2. Describe the tug-of-war between the critical, deflating tendencies of *The Great Gatsby* and the counterforces of creation and romance.

Lecture Fifty-Seven—Transcript
Fitzgerald's Triumph—Writing the American Dream

This is Lecture Fifty-Seven, and it's the last of my lectures on *Gatsby*. We're going to have some fun in the lecture. You may remember in my last lecture I tried to build the critical argument that *Gatsby* is a realist text that wants to deflate grand illusions; that, essentially, it is a kind of corrosive treatment of greatness itself; it's a thinning text; it's a text that takes large appearances and reduces them down to small origins; that takes the magic and shows you the gimmick. I want to argue that that's a half-truth; or, to change the metaphor, that that's the short end of the stick.

What is wonderful about this book, in my opinion, is that it will not abide by those rules, despite I think, the ideological critics who want to see this book as a kind of critique of certain American accesses. The book is about creation and not about criticism. It's about magic and it's not about expose. Yes, the realist impulse is to deflate, to return to small causes and to chronicle July 5th as the truth of July 4th. It's like saying the hangover is the truth of the drunkenness. Well, it doesn't have to be seen that way at all. The book is consistently, I think, playful about the notion of foundation. You'll recall Nick saying that, "I don't know what moral behavior is founded on. It's got to be founded on something." Yet, the book suggests that won't quite wash. One of the people we meet is a friend of Myrtle Wilson, Mrs. Eberheart; and the book says she goes around to people's apartments to look at their feet. I love that little notation because it makes no sense except that it sort of makes thought of the idea of looking at foundations, at what people are actually standing on.

Tom Buchanan has been researching Gatsby. You know, at one point, Jordan Baker says to him, "You must've gone to a medium," which is a wonderful answer. Like, "Where are you going to get your information on this guy?" Tom gives him the great name, "Mr. Nobody from Nowhere." He says, "You're Mr. Nobody from Nowhere." And I'm going to return to that. What does that mean to be Mr. Nobody from Nowhere? Remember what Nick saw in Gatsby? He saw promise, romantic readiness, the gift for hope, and potential. Not fact, but projection. So in that sense, are all of those origins that are thrown out to us: cousin to the Kaiser, German spy, person who killed a man, and bootlegger. As I said, he's like the gods for whom there are multiple legends of origins, of how they were born, who produced them. In the book, Gatsby's always on the move. He's never where you expect him to be and he comes in by surprise. When we see him, he's always either tapping on a table, or he is in some ways sort of kinetic. He, in one beautiful sequence, tells Nick the story of his life. I want you to think about this. I want you to think about it in terms of realism versus what I'd have to call, "fabulation."

This is Gatsby telling Nick where he comes from, "I'm going to tell you something about my life. Don't want you to get a wrong idea of me, from all the stories you hear.

> "I'll tell you God's truth." (And his right hand goes up.) His right hand suddenly ordered divine retribution to stand by. "I am the son of some wealthy people in the Middle West—all dead now. I was brought up in America but educated at Oxford, because all of my ancestors have been educated there for many years. It's a family tradition." He looked at me sideways.

Nick's, you know, "What kind of game is this?"

> … I wondered if there wasn't something a little sinister about him.

> "What part of the Middle West?" I inquired casually.

> "San Francisco."

> "I see."

I don't know what to admire most there, San Francisco, or I see.

> "My family all died and I came into a good deal of money." His voice was solemn, as if the memory of that sudden extinction of a clan still haunted him. For a moment I suspected he was pulling my leg, (And this is the sort of thing Gatsby then goes into) … "After that I lived like a young rajah in all the capitals of Europe—Paris, Venice, Rome—collecting jewels, chiefly rubies, hunting big game, painting a little, things for myself only, and trying to forget something very sad that had happened to me, long ago."

Nick says it's very hard not to laugh, when he hears this. He says, "These phrases are so threadbare." Here's the image they evoke in his mind, "of a turbaned character, leaking sawdust at every pore, as he pursued a tiger through the Wade Boulange." That's how completely specious and constructed Gatsby comes across. Then Gatsby tells him about his military background. "Then came the war, old sport; it's a great relief. I tried very hard to die, but I seem to have an enchanted life." He talks about the commission that he got. He talks about his own heroism, about the awards that he received then.

> "I was promoted to be a major, and every Allied government gave me a decoration—even Montenegro, little Montenegro down on the Adriatic Sea!"

> (Nick says,) Little Montenegro! … My incredulity was submerged in fascination now; it was like skimming hastily through a dozen magazines.

It's just this series of quotations here. All of a sudden, Gatsby reaches into a pocket, and pulls out a medal. "That's the one from Montenegro," he says. And it looks authentic and it says, "*Orderi di Danilo, Montenegro, Nicholas Rex.*" Turn it over. "Major Jay Gatsby, For Valor Extraordinary." And Nick is stunned. "Here's another thing I always carry. A souvenir of the Oxford days. It was taken in Trinity Quad—the man on my left," he says, "is the Earl of Dorcaster." In that, we see a photograph of a dozen young men in blazers, in an archway, with spires behind them. There's Gatsby, with them. Nick writes, "Then it was all true. I saw the skins of tigers flaming in his palace on the Grand Canal; I saw him opening a chest of rubies to ease, with their crimson-lighted depths, the gnawings of his broken heart."

This is very beautiful writing. This is absolutely at the edge of tongue in cheek. It's floating on the surface. This is the game that they're playing together. We won't sort it out with how much truth, how much flim-flam, how much imagination, how much substance there is here. There is a medal, there is a photograph; and yet, there are these incredulous stories of this great romantic background and everything. What I want you to think about is the way in which Nick goes along with this. It takes two people to construct a web of beliefs, not just one. Belief is always a social concept. I want you to think about the literary coloration of it, too. Nick says, "like skimming through a dozen magazines."

And I want you to think about the geography of it. How does San Francisco get to be in the Middle West? This is a book that is about its own ontology, its own geography. It's a writerly wonderland and it's a place where the words can create the deed. That's what the dream is about. Fitzgerald is ultimately committed to that. It's a new space/time arrangement, a new cosmos. Gatsby is the archetypal self-made man. He has produced spawn, birthed himself. He doesn't want to be Jimmy Gatz. He doesn't want to be that, at all. His parents were shiftless and unsuccessful farm people. His imagination had never really accepted them—as his parents—at all. The truth was that Jay Gatsby of West Egg Long Island sprang from his platonic conception of himself. He was "a son of god." A phrase, which if it means anything, means just that: he must be about his father's business, self-conception, and autogenesis.

What do you think the self-made man means? It means to produce yourself, to be free of your origins. I want you to mull that over a little bit—to be free of origins—because we are dead center in American culture, in American myth, and in American dream. That's what America is: The place where you are free of origin. What do our terms like "upward mobility" mean, if they don't mean that? Why do people come to this country? Why have they come to this country? It's because they are leaving societies where they are determined by class, by birth, by race, and by all kinds of things. This is the democratic ideology that says you can make your life; you are not to be constrained or governed or coerced, or formed or deformed, by the accidents of your birth, or your gender, the color of your skin, or how much money your parents had. The old world works like that, but not the new world. The American dream is precisely a dream of self-invention. It's where you could create, craft yourself, construct your own life, and deny entirely the grip or the hold or the reality of the past.

So, Jimmy Gatz becomes Jay Gatsby. He sprang from his own platonic conception of self. I can't over emphasize the importance of that—as a piece of American belief, as a credo within this culture—and however much we may discredit it, however much we may learn later in life; we are, in fact, formed by race, class, parents, all the works, all that stuff that the realists show us. The great dream is that one would be free of those things. One would live in a world of freedom, and self-shaping; that willpower would be possible as the driving force to make your life. That's the dream that we try to inculcate in our young people and I think that this is the American democratic premise as well, a society of equality in which you are not precisely measured by your parents' money or by the class rank that you have.

So, the American dream is absolutely at the core of this book. It's not to be found so much in Gatsby's mansion, or Gatsby's money; it's to be found in Gatsby's own self-making. That's why I compared it to Benjamin Franklin, because it's one of the first records we have of a man who creates his own identity in front of our eyes and becomes a kind of living legend. I want to connect that now to language. "Freedom of Speech" is a term that we all know what it means. Freedom of speech has a kind of clear, political meaning. It means that all of us are enabled by the Constitution to express our views on any matters; that we live in a free society in which we can do that. I want to argue that speech and language have a kind of freedom, have a kind of dizzying independence in this book that is really quite wonderful and special. It's connected with the American dream; it's about the American dream. It is not so much freedom of speech as a political proposition, but freedom of speech as a writerly proposition, as what every writer deals with all the time, when he or she writes a book.

What is Daisy's voice? We are told its full of money, but it's more than that. It is a voice full of money; it's speech. It's a voice of promise; it's a voice of future; it's a voice of possibility. Fitzgerald describes it as breathless, as thrilling, as an exhilarating ripple; a voice that men found hard to forget, we hear. It's the voice that most held Gatsby, more than anything else. Fitzgerald writes, "I think that voice held him the most, with its fluctuating, feverish warmth, because it couldn't be over-dreamed. And voice was a deathless song." A deathless song, and I think he's trying to say, "Songs can be deathless. People can't be. Songs can be. The voice can be an endless set of possibilities." This is the voice that is described to us as a voice that makes the world anew.

"Daisy began to sing with the music in a husky, rhythmic whisper, brining out a meaning in each word that it never had before, and would never have again." I love that language. "She makes the world." This is genesis. When she sings, things mean things they've never meant before, that they'll never mean again. "Each change tipped out a little of her warm, human magic upon the air. An incessant spawning of new meanings." This is semiotic principle that's the production of meaning; it's a writerly formula. Language makes its own indigenous world in this book. That's why I said we're going to have some fun with this. This book is an incredibly playful, ludic, clowning book. It has irrepressible, metaphoric excursions in it. Things that have no narrative seriousness to them, they're just there in the book. You see people in the strangest kinds of descriptions. For example, a description like this: "We backed up to a gray old man, who bore an absurd resemblance to John D. Rockefeller." It's not Rockefeller. That's not going to be tested, but the world is constantly being yoked into analogies and similes.

Or you have, all of a sudden, a weird sense of Fifth Avenue. "It's so warm and soft, it's so pastoral, I wouldn't have been surprised to see a great flock of white sheep turn the corner." That's likely not to happen. Or, you meet a person selling dogs, and Myrtle wants to get a dog. They ask what kind of a dog is it.

"That dog, is it a boy or a girl?" She asked delicately.

"That dog? That dog's a boy."

"It's a bitch," said Tom decisively. "Here's your money."

Well, the dog is both a boy and a bitch. Verbally, you can have it both ways. He's not going to tell us which it is. This is a text that is filled with claims that only words make. They're reading a book that is titled *Simon called Peter*. Is he Simon, or is he Peter? The language says Simon called Peter. Myrtle's sister Katherine is quote, "Said to be very beautiful." Our sense of the truths of the world comes from the things that are said about it. Stories produce our realities. We don't have scientific tangible evidence for most of the things we believe. This is a book about generating belief. It's not about proving things, or disproving things. So, words have an extraordinary potency in this regime. We have, at one moment, someone singing, "I'm the Sheik of Araby." Oh, are you? I'm sure they're really not. You couldn't produce the paper that says, "I'm the Sheik of Araby," and yet, many, many people sang that song.

We sing songs like that. My children used to sit in the car and they would play games like, "My name is—" We grow up that way. We try on identities. We craft new ones for ourselves. Songs allow us that particular fantasy, as well. We are the Sheik of Araby. We are some other fantasy figure. We live fantasy lives. Words are usually the currency of those investments, of those voyages and trips. This book has some extraordinary zany notations in it. You have a passage like this. Daisy says, "You go, we'll ride around and meet you later. We'll meet you on some corner. I'll be the man smoking two cigarettes." Certainly, she's not going to be there with two cigarettes in her mouth. But that's the kind of clowning around, horsing around that has its own metaphoric potency in a text like this. I'll be the man smoking two cigarettes.

I said the book is ludic. The book is ludic in the sense that it's like musical chairs. People get confused with one another in this book, and sometimes they're tragic confusions. We will see that it is Gatsby who has killed Myrtle Wilson, whereas, in fact, it was Daisy who was driving when the car runs [her] over; or, Myrtle will look out the window as the cars go by, and she will see Jordan, and she will think that it's Daisy. Gatsby, as I said, will be slain for the wrong purposes. The cars themselves will be confused. It's a book where, in a very interesting way, the World Series can be fixed. Think about that. You think of the World Series as an event that happens. This book says no. It's an event that's arranged. Someone can fix it. The art world precedes anything in this text. It's a world of craft, a world of convention, and a world of the order of the artist. This is America. It's a new world. It's a world that is made in front of your eyes, and that's its fabulous promise. Just like the lives of Americans are not fixed in advance. You fix them. You make them. You reinvent them. Next year, you're going to' be somebody different. That's America.

One of the perfect emblems of that is when they're driving over the Queensboro Bridge, and the Queensboro Bridge is invested with all of that sense of shimmering possibility. "The city seemed from the Queensboro Bridge as always the city seen for the first time in its first wild promise of all the mystery and the beauty in the world." As they're going over that bridge, you see various kinds of people crossing it. Nick says, "Anything can happen, now that we've slid over this bridge. Anything at all." Even Gatsby could happen.

I would like to regard that bridge as precisely the bridge into a word world; a bridge that functions like the mirror does in *Alice in Wonderland.* You go in, or down the hole, and you enter the regime of the world of fantasy, of construct. Where you make the world instead encounter it already made. The scene that I'm going to allude to now, with some detail, is one of the weirdest, and to me, most delightful, zany, delicious scenes in all of American literature. It's one of the most improbable. It's a scene that strangely enough has not received any critical attention. It's the scene that takes place in the Plaza Hotel, on a hot, hot day—which is the showdown scene. Tom has been doing his homework, his detective work. He has proven that Gatsby is up to his neck in criminal activity. Gatsby is not worthy of Daisy. Gatsby, on the other hand, is now expecting Daisy to tell off Tom, to say that she's never loved him. It's like a shoot-out. It's high noon. It's the two guys duking it out for the golden girl. It's a very predictable scene, except what happens in it, is not predictable at all.

What happens in it is the weird appearance of the strangest character in the novel, who's name is "Blocks" Biloxi. They're in this hot, sweltering room—the heat's terrible in the hotel. Daisy remembers that she was married on hot, hot day like this. "Louisville in June. Somebody fainted. Who was it fainted, Tom? Biloxi, a man named Biloxi. Blocks Biloxi, and he made boxes. That's a fact." Every word here is loaded. "That's a fact and he was from Biloxi, Tennessee." Do you hear what I just said, "He was from Biloxi, Tennessee." I don't know how much geography you know, but Biloxi isn't in Tennessee. "He was from Biloxi, Tennessee." Well, what is this guy, Biloxi? What in the world is he doing in this high noon scene, where the two guys are supposed to fight it out for the girl? This is the figure of pure imagination, pure semiotic principle. His name Blocks Biloxi, and he makes boxes. His name is the same place that he comes from, Biloxi, Tennessee. It's as if you only had one kind of block, you had to use it for the name and for the place. It's like a child's game here.

Listen to the career of this weird figure. He's like being spawned by the enzymes of this text. The juices of the book are producing him. Comes out of nowhere into the key, climax scene of the book. "They carried him indoors into my house. He stayed three weeks until Daddy told him he had to get out. The day after he left, Daddy died." She thinks about it. There wasn't any connection, though. You read it, and you wonder, "Wait a minute. Who is this Biloxi guy?" He comes in and Daddy goes out. But he comes in drunk, and Daddy goes out dead. Then you hear more about his family. "There was a Bill Biloxi, from Memphis. Oh, that's his cousin." We're told. "He left me an aluminum putter, that I still use today." Biloxi, Biloxi.

> "Where'd you know him from, Tom?"
>
> "Biloxi? I didn't know him. He was a friend of Daisy's."
>
> "He was not," she denied. "I'd never seen him before. He came down in the private car."

Weirder and weirder this Biloxi guy; he's there, and yet, he's not anybody's friend. Nobody seems to know where he comes from. But he tells stories about himself. "He said he knew you. He said he was raised in Louisville." He's not through with his stories, Biloxi has still another one, "He was probably bumming his way home. He told me he was President of your class at Yale." I don't know how to properly state the importance of this statement in Fitzgerald Scott Fitzgerald. President of your class at Yale, that's like being the general of the universe. I mean, you don't get a higher rank than President of your class at Yale. Now, how does Biloxi get there? We're not even sure the guy's for real. He seems to be invented in front of our eyes, in the text. He's the kind of unbidden, irrepressible, ghost who comes in. He's a construct of words, as I said, same place name he's got. It's like a writerly wonderland, again, and San Francisco is in the Middle West, in the same way that Biloxi's in Tennessee. It can be done with words, but it doesn't happen on the map.

It can be done in this text and it's what's happening. It's by writerly fiat. He performs in the text. He enters the house supine, and three weeks later,

Daddy exits dead. He's a potent figure. He's making things happen. He spreads, as it were, so that then you have a cousin. So, there's a kind of family history being generated in front of our eyes. You're supposed to be thinking of Gatsby, Gatsby's constructed life, Gatsby making up his own story. This is an American story here, about Blocks Biloxi. He's the put together amalgam of person and place, and he spews out putters and cousins, death, and he looks more and more like Gatsby. No one knew him. He came to the wedding in the private car. That too is an allusion to Gatsby. He made his own story. He claimed that he knew Daisy. She says she didn't know who he was, and he claimed that he was raised in Louisville, but nobody can document that. As I say, his final apotheosis is that "he was President of your class at Yale."

Tom and Nick just stare at each other. But we didn't even have a president in our class at Yale. There weren't any presidents. Doesn't make any difference, Biloxi got there. Tom then makes the most fabulous connection to this. He turns around and looks at Gatsby, and says:

> "Mr. Gatsby, I understand you're an Oxford man."

> "Not exactly."

> "Oh, yes, I understand, you went to Oxford."

> "Yes—I went there."

> "You must have gone there about the time Biloxi went to New Haven."

This book has now generated its own world. You must've gone there about the time Biloxi went to New Haven. How do you take the measure of this? Is this true? Is this false? It's being produced in front of our eyes. We have a fabulous sense here, of language out-trumping reality. Language getting its own man elected to the president of your class at Yale. This is a country that has had actor presidents. People who play roles end up in certain positions. The line between construct, act, artist, performance and the political nitty-gritty world is a line that's being erased in this text. That's what this book is about, is erasing that line. It's about the potency of the imagination. It's about the potency of words; words spawning deeds, producing their own reality.

When our kids were growing up, we used to watch the "Electric Company." You'd have this character called Letter Man; it's like Letter Man ends up as president. Letter Man triumphs here. Well, as I say, all of this, in my opinion, is a kind of beautiful tribute to the hero of the book. Who is Gatsby? Gatsby is a creature of flesh and blood. He's the hero of dream and of promise and of belief. He's "gorgeous," is the term that Nick uses for him. Belief, belief, belief, belief is what makes things happen. Belief is behind Trumps, and Vanderbilts. It's behind all great fortunes. It's not just inheritance. It's belief, and it's desire.

Credit, our term that is so central a term in the banking world, the etymology of credit is belief. It's to believe that you will either get your money back, etc. This is the belief system that is at the core of this book. It seemed to be a kind of social contract in the most beautiful instance of it, is Gatsby's smile. It's one of those rare smiles with a quality of eternal reassurance in it; that you may come across four or five times in life. It faced, or seemed to face the whole external world for an instant, and then concentrated on you with an irresistible prejudice in your favor. It understood you just as far as you wanted to be understood, believed in you as you would like to believe in yourself, and assured you that it had precisely the impression of you that, at your best, you hoped to convey.

I can't think of a better example of the social contract. Rousseau's term is "the social contract." Rousseau would never have written this passage, but it is a social phrase. It's what a smile means when you smile to people to start the day off. It's the way in which we enable people through belief to carry out their own performances, their own lives. I look at you—as I give this lecture—and I read in your faces either denials or support, all the time. That's how we work in life, in conversations. Gatsby's smile is an act of generosity. It's an act of creativity; the thing that's being constructed is you. Your smile at *me,* that confirms *me,* is what energizes *me* to get through this day and to make it until tomorrow. That's the way life works. That's the kind of elemental social contract; it's like a blood transfusion that goes through life.

Everyday we depend on these kinds of exchanges. Gatsby is the hero of belief. That's what he does. This is inseparable from his great mansion and from his other achievements, as well. This book is about dream and glamour, and belief. It's about moving worlds in order to make it happen. There's a quote at the beginning of this text, "Then wear the gold hat, if that will move her. If you can bounce high, bounce for her, too, 'til she cry, lover, gold-hated, high bouncing lover, I must have you." That's the performance of the imagination. That's the performance of flight, the bouncing. This book, Fitzgerald said, was about, I quote, "The loss of those illusions that give such color to the world, that you don't care whether things are true or false, so long as they partake of the magical glory." That magical glory is the capacity to dream. That remains even if the dreamer and the actual things of the dreams are discredited. Dreaming—the capacity to believe in the future, to believe in that kind of freedom—that's not going to be discredited. That's incorruptible. That's essentially what America is in this book.

The book closes with an evocation of what the Dutch sailors saw when they first came to the New World. What we think of as Long Island and New York.

> And as the moon rose higher the inessential houses began to melt away until gradually I became aware of the old island here that flowered once for Dutch sailors' eyes—a fresh, green breast of the new world. Its vanished trees, the trees that had made way for Gatsby's house, had once pandered in whispers to the last and greatest of all human dreams; for a transitory enchanted moment man must have held its breath in the presence of this continent, compelled into an aesthetic contemplation he neither understood nor desired, face to face for the last time in history with something commensurate to his capacity for wonder.

Finally a place that is commensurate to dream. Yet, the dream is in the past. It's five years earlier. He believed in the green light. "It eluded us then; it's no matter. Tomorrow we'll run faster. And one fine morning, so we beat on, boats against the current, borne back ceaselessly into the past." You can't close the book more perfectly than that, the past that determines us all and the dream for the future that gives scope and grandeur to our lives.

Lecture Fifty-Eight

Ernest Hemingway's *The Sun Also Rises*—
Novel of the Lost Generation

Scope: As the 20th century comes to an end, Ernest Hemingway's reputation is among the most disputed in the American canon. There is much irony in this state of affairs, given Hemingway's unarguable status as the most influential American prose writer of the century. The Hemingway style can be found from the journalism of our newspapers and magazines to the minimalist writings of figures like Raymond Carver. The style is brisk, terse, cleansed of adjectives, seemingly objective, and aimed at rendering the precise moment and feeling of experience. Of course, it is the Hemingway legend—a legend that the writer cultivated all too assiduously, even tragically—that most offends today: Hemingway as Mister Macho, Hemingway as maniacal man of war, hunting, fishing, boxing, boozing, fornicating, slugging it out in one fashion or another. He was indeed larger than life. His biography spans the magic years in Paris in the 1920s, when he was the acknowledged leader of the Lost Generation of American expatriate writers; his exploits in the Spanish Civil War, "liberating" the Ritz in 1945; and, finally, his suicide in 1961, when the body could hold up no longer and the writing would not come. We will take a two-sided look at Hemingway, beginning with his first—and perhaps best—novel, *The Sun Also Rises* (1926), an unforgettable account of Americans encountering the mysteries of Paris and Pamplona. We will close with the haunting, posthumously published *Garden of Eden* (1986), which brings all the skeletons out of the Hemingway closet to offer the fullest picture of Hemingway's sexuality and writing.

We will begin with a brief account of Hemingway's career— including his publications, life, and legend—to begin taking the measure of this phenomenon. What did Hemingway's work do that was new? What is it still doing today? We will also look at the debate concerning his importance in today's critical climate. Our central text, *The Sun Also Rises* (1926), is often regarded as Hemingway's strongest effort. We know that it is partly based on real people and real events, but the story is always seen through the prism of the author's imagination. This novel introduced Americans to Paris of the 1920s, its streets and bars and restaurants and customs; you could do worse than to read it as a guidebook. Yet, the book is insistently concerned with values, with finding something to believe in, in the aftermath of the Great War. Through the story of Jake Barnes, the tight-lipped hero who is war-wounded and impotent, Hemingway rivals Eliot's "The Waste Land" in his meditation on sickness and health.

Objectives—Upon completion of this lecture, you should be able to:

1. Explain the reasons for Hemingway's fall from grace in American literary criticism;

2. Compare Hemingway's depiction of Europe with that of earlier writers, such as James; and

3. Summarize the ways in which *The Sun Also Rises* is an auto-biographical novel.

Outline

I. Arguably the most influential writer of our century, Ernest Hemingway is a giant figure in both America and Europe. Hemingway's career spans four decades and marks our century.

   A. Although the value of Hemingway "stock" is currently being debated, his status as a pioneer in shaping American prose in the 20th century is indisputable.

   B. There is a clear Hemingway "curve" that moves from the fresh, spare, tight-lipped early prose of the 1920s—focusing on hunting, fishing, boxing, bullfighting, war, love, and death—to an increasingly soft, unwittingly parodic prose that seeks to recapture the old greatness.

      1. *In Our Time* (1925) offers an unparalleled new style of writing. It contains brief stories of Nick Adams growing up and becoming a man, spliced with still briefer vignettes of war and violence.

      2. *The Sun Also Rises* (1926) is Hemingway's portrayal of the Lost Generation of American expatriates seeking their way in Paris and Pamplona. Here is the lean, taut style at its finest. Or is it?

3. *A Farewell to Arms* (1929) represents Hemingway's fateful experience on the Italian front in 1918, including his war injury and his failed love affair with Agnes von Kurowsky. All this is recast in the tragic love story of Frederick Henry and Catherine Barkley, who are caught in a world not of their making.

4. In the 1930s Hemingway produced no great novel, but wrote his great treatises on bullfighting and game hunting, *Death in the Afternoon* (1932) and *Green Hills of Africa* (1935).

5. Further successes include his epic account of the Spanish Civil War, *For Whom the Bell Tolls* (1940), and his enormously popular *Old Man and the Sea* (1952). Hemingway won the Nobel Prize in 1954.

6. Since his death in 1961, a number of works have been published, including the lyrical yet malicious *Moveable Feast* (1964), Hemingway's account of the early years in Paris from 1921 to 1926; *Islands in the Stream* (1970); and the remarkable *Garden of Eden* (1986) in which much that was repressed earlier is finally brought into the open. Watch out!

C. These titles do not take the measure of what Hemingway wrought. Swollen, pretentious, often cruel, he was a tragic personality who stamped our age.

1. Hemingway taught America about war. He felt that Stephen Crane was too literary, whereas he himself was *there*, telling us how it was and what it felt like. Hemingway's great theme is trauma: the pain and damage meted to the body, as well as the occasional dignity and courage of men in crisis.

2. He also taught us about sports: hunting, fishing, skiing, bull-fighting, boxing. Here too was a confrontation with pain, even with death, and an opportunity for "grace under pressure." Such situations came to stand for the condition of modern man; they are a rigorous measure of who and what he was.

3. These stories also took American readers to places they had never been, such as Paris, San Sebastian, Pamplona, and the Alps. Hemingway is part of the great tradition of tour guides beginning with Twain and passing through James.

4. Inherent in all this is Hemingway's stature as the macho figure of our century, incessantly measuring himself against all situations and against all comers and rivals. Hemingway is the

artist as hero, a dreadfully public figure. Yet, Hemingway resembles Whitman in the sense of having extraordinary charisma. He was a difficult man, petty when dealing with his rivals, yet exacting when it came to himself. He seems to have been singled out for physical disaster.

D. In many of the most prestigious English departments in American universities, Hemingway is virtually unread. There are some good reasons for this: How viable is his work at the end of the 20th century? How universal is the bullfight as an image of the human condition? Who do women or minorities find for themselves in these books? How significant—or ridiculous—is machismo today?

1. Hemingway can be his own most severe critic in these areas.
2. In the posthumous *Garden of Eden*, these issues are presented in dazzling and astonishing ways.
3. Like or hate his image, one must acknowledge the legacy of Hemingway's prose. The war on the adjective, the war on complex and articulated British syntax, the value ascribed to terseness and spareness, the understanding of silences that punctuate conversation: These are Hemingway's gifts to us, and modern journalism and prose are stamped with his imprint.

II. *The Sun Also Rises* presents us with much of the Hemingway legacy: a new language, expatriate Americans in Europe, the search for a new code.

A. Initially, the novel was read as a *roman à clef.*
1. Jake Barnes was Hemingway.
2. Brett was Duff Twysden.
3. Brett's "fiancé," Mike, was Pat Guthrie, Duff's cousin/lover/banker.
4. Robert Cohn was Harold Loeb, Hemingway's early supporter in getting work published.
5. Bill Gorton was Don Stewart, Hemingway's old buddy.

B. These events actually happened "in some fashion." Hemingway may have had an affair with Duff, who did go to San Sebastian with Loeb; there was a fishing party at Burguete and a visit to Pamplona for the San Fermin.

C. Other features of the novel are more indirect, but no less drawn from life. Hemingway's relationship to Scott and Zelda Fitzgerald is replayed in this novel.

    1. Hemingway's suspicion and dislike of Zelda is reflected in the shrew-like Frances Clyne who berates Robert Cohn (a writer) in classic fashion.

    2. Zelda's famous love for all-night parties, her capacity for drink, her obsession with taking baths are all part of Brett's makeup.

D. The novel delivers Paris of the 1920s. The fuller tourist picture provided in *A Moveable Feast*—including Sylvia Beach, Gertrude Stein, Ezra Pound, James Joyce, and Scott and Zelda Fitzgerald (along with the hilarious/malicious account of Scott's hypochondria and his "measurements")—is left out of the earlier text.

    1. The first novel is outfitted with Gertrude Stein's infamous pronouncement: "You are a lost generation." Hemingway has told us what this phrase actually meant.

    2. The phrase has remained in the culture as a description of an entire slate of gifted writers finding their way in Europe after the war.

    3. Hemingway confided to Fitzgerald that he had other titles in mind for *The Sun Also Rises*. He also gave Fitzgerald a sneak preview of the plot.

    4. We must not forget that the book is equipped with a second quotation, this time from Ecclesiastes, about what endures.

E. Hemingway is our tour guide to Europe. He takes pride in his knowledge.

    1. Do you know what pernod is? Most Americans didn't.

    2. Sightseeing in Paris looms large here, although it adds little to the plot.

    3. Above all, Jake Barnes is the consummate *insider*, savvy about Paris, Pamplona, and the bullfights. He is a true aficionado.

F. Despite the book's exotica, the story retains a sense of anxiety and despair just under the surface. We sense that we are in the aftermath of the war.

    1. The funny scene with the Count is precisely about finding the right *values*.

2. There is to be no joking about these matters, Hemingway reminds us.
3. Hemingway is as severe as Thoreau in suggesting that we pay for our lives with the only currency we have: our lives.
4. Hemingway's emasculated hero, Jake Barnes, is to be understood as a version of Eliot's maimed Fisher King, and the novel is about the search for healing and wholeness.

Lecture Fifty-Eight—Transcript
Ernest Hemingway's *The Sun Also Rises*— Novel of the Lost Generation

This is Lecture Fifty-Eight, and it's the first of five lectures on Hemingway. I'm taking a little bit of a chance here giving five lectures on Hemingway, partly because Hemingway's work is so much out of favor in so many English departments, and that's an issue that I'll want to address. I think Hemingway's significance is not really disputable. He is a major figure in American fiction and in European fiction. He is the most influential writer, I think, of our century. I didn't say, the greatest, but I think the most influential. Even people who like Hemingway take the view, I believe, that his earliest work is his most successful work. So, the first three lectures are going to be on what is arguably his best book, *The Sun Also Rises*. Then I will give two concluding lectures on a posthumous text called, *The Garden of Eden*, which Hemingway never quite finished. He couldn't finish it. It was edited, nonetheless, and published in 1986. I think it's an utterly remarkable text and I think it will be fun to bring that into this course.

In this first lecture, what I want to do is talk about the Hemingway career, the Hemingway reputation, the Hemingway legend, and the kinds of things that he did for American literature—and that no one else has quite matched, it seems to me. They are lasting contributions. There's a curve in his work, and it goes from the kind of tight lipped, spare, early fiction—that focuses on war, trauma, boxing, bullfighting, fishing, love, death—to a kind of writing that becomes more and more unintentionally parodic, unintentionally soft, trying to recapture the old greatness. He knew this. His first major text is *In Our Time*, published in 1925 when he was 27 years old. It's an unparalleled new kind of writing. It's a new style for talking about war reporting; brief vignettes of courage and punishment, in political but also in sporting situations; and it has some of the greatest stories: "Indian Camp," "Big Two Hearted River." It also has these remarkable little vignettes about the war in Europe. Then, in 1926, he publishes the book that I want to talk about, *The Sun Also Rises,* which is the great story about the lost generation, about the American expatriates in Europe. It's lean, it's mean—it's really mean—and it's a book, I think, that doesn't charm everyone; but in it, I think we can see Hemingway perhaps at his best.

That's followed, in 1929, by the great love story he wrote, *A Farewell to Arms*, which is a kind of fictional account of his own experience on the

Italian front where he was wounded—young, the age of 19—and his failed love affair with Agnes Von Korowsky, the nurse who tended him. These two figures, of course, become recast as Frederick Henry and Catherine Barclay, lovers who are caught in a world beyond their making. It ends, of course, with Catherine's death in childbirth; which is, I think, a kind of recurring phenomenon in Hemingway's work. Nothing quite matches the glory of those three texts, *In Our Time*, *The Sun Also Rises* and *A Farewell to Arms*. There, too, I can't help but think that Hemingway knew it.

In the '30s, he writes a variety of things. Some novels that are not much regarded, like *To Have and To Have Not*, but also some classic treatises on bullfighting and hunting, *Death in the Afternoon* and *The Green Hills of Africa*. He gives us his epic account of the Spanish Civil War in 1940, *For Whom the Bell Tolls*, a rich, but flawed book in my opinion, about the idealistic love between the American who is in the Spanish Civil War volunteering and the Spanish woman, Maria. His other last breakthrough—during his lifetime, of course—is *The Old Man and the Sea*, 1952. He won the Nobel Prize in the 1950s. He died in 1961—suicide. The body just wouldn't hold up anymore. Then a spate of posthumous work, some of which are quite fabulous: *Movable Feast*, published in 1964—that Hemingway had written in the 1950 about his early years in Paris in the 1920s. So it's a series of removes. We get it after his death. It's a very, very cunning but fascinating text—*Islands in the Stream*, published posthumously in 1970 and then the one that I alluded to, *Garden of Eden*, published in 1986. *Garden of Eden*, by the way, exists as some 1500 pages of manuscript at the Kennedy Library, which Hemingway wrote in the 1940s and '50s and couldn't finish. It has multiple endings and things like that. Tom Jenks, at Scribner's, edited this into a very sleek book of only some 250 pages. We will want to look at it because it really changes the shape of the Hemingway curve and helps us better to understand what the early books have for us.

Now, that list that I just gave you of titles and dates doesn't really tell us who Hemingway was and what he was. He was a path-breaking figure. He was a legend. He was an impossibly conflicted and pretentious person. He was a tragic personality, but he stamped this century. He did a lot more than that. He taught the American public about wars. He himself said that he thought he'd outdone what Steven Crane did in *The Red Badge of Courage* because he knew that Crane had never seen a war, whereas he had been there. He felt that the stamp of authenticity was in his books. He was a firsthand witness to the carnage and also to the strange dignity of war, including its indignities to human life and values. We have the Italian front, and we have the Spanish Civil War in kind of unforgettable form because of, *A Farewell to Arms* and *For Whom the Bell Tolls*. He told us that he personally liberated the Ritz in 1945 in Paris, and maybe he did. We did not have him in Korea or Vietnam or the Gulf, and perhaps we should have.

He taught us about the beauty and terror of certain sports: hunting, boxing, and bullfighting. How each one is a confrontation with death, a kind of unparallel opportunity for what he called grace under pressure, a rigorous, unforgiving and never cheating measure of courage and, indeed, of our philosophy. He taught us about places that most of us had never been to, at least not much: Paris, San Sebastian; places some of us had never heard of, like Pamplona and the San Fermin—the Running of the Bulls. Even this doesn't really take the measure of what he did. He was the great macho figure of this century, for better or for worse, measuring himself, his courage, his muscles, and his endurance against any and all comers. He was the artist as he wrote, as witness, as performer. His life was public record. His hunting, his fishing, his drinking, his fornicating, his breakdowns and his suicide; everything was on camera at all times. He was physically, as you may know, a colossus, a huge, strong specimen of a man. He brings to our literature something of the physical and sexual aura that I think one sees in Walt Whitman's work. Like Whitman, his toughness and bravado can easily turn fluid.

His maleness is counter-pointed by the woman that he is also. He reminds me of Whitman. He reminds of Strindberg. There's something androgynous in him. His misogyny comes exactly out of that just as Strindberg's does because he knows that women can take over. He knows it about himself. He fought everyone he knew, sometimes physically, always verbally. He was very ungenerous towards his peers—those that he feared might last longer than him.

This is most conspicuous in his relationship to Fitzgerald and the write-up about Fitzgerald in *A Movable Feast* is really unfair and in some sense, tragic, because Fitzgerald had been dead for many years. Of course, Hemingway didn't publish it in his lifetime. He was singled out for all kinds of physical horrors and accidents. I'll read you what one writer said about him:

> As a boy, he fell and had a stick driven into the back of his throat, gouging out part of both tonsils. In 1918, when he was a Red Cross worker in Italy distributing supplies to soldiers, a mortar shell

exploded more than 20 fragments into his legs. He was then hit twice by machine gun bullets while carrying a more seriously injured man to the rear. As a young writer in Paris during the '20s, he was clipped on the forehead by pieces of a skylight that fell just as he was standing under it.

That's the kind of luck he had. He is standing under a skylight; it falls on him. Fortunately, that doesn't happen to everybody. "In Wyoming, in 1930, his car turned over and his right arm was pinned back by the top of the windshield and badly fractured, the bone sticking through the muscle." At another time, his brother Lester reports, Hemingway shot a shark with a rifle, but the bullet split into several small pieces of hot lead that ricocheted into the calves of both his legs. In 1949, while duck hunting in the marshes near Venice, he got a piece of shell wadding blown into his eye and a serious infection developed. In 1953, he crash-landed in Africa and the rescue plane that picked him up crashed and burned. "When he reached medical aid at Nairobi, just in time to read his obituaries, his internal organs had been wrenched out of place, his spine was injured and he was bleeding from every orifice." It's not really surprising that he writes about the damage that can be done to the body, what it can give out and what it can take.

One is hard put to find Hemingway in courses at our most prestigious universities today. Old farts like me enjoy working with him; but today's interest in ideological arrangements, in hearing the voices that have been kept out of the canon—particularly women writers, but others too, ethnic groups, people of color—all of this creates a kind of environment that has very little curiosity and even less patience for Hemingway. I don't want to be misunderstood here; there are lots of good reasons—also, who goes to bullfights—I mean, what is the universality of Hemingway's work? How many people go to the woods for trout fishing to find their metaphor of what life portends? How many people go to Africa for big game; and, of course, what's the status of that macho code today? But he's his own most severe critic at his best. He takes the measure of his own code. He doesn't let himself off easily.

This is going to be particularly evident in *The Garden of Eden*. There we're going to see for the first and only time, I think, in his work a stunning female character, a female character who makes the miraculous, heroic transformation from object to subject, no longer the object of male hunger and need, the nurturing figure like Catherine Barclay, or Maria in *For Whom the Bell Tolls*, but a woman who is a continuation of Lady Brett—

from *The Sun Also Rises*—with ideas and with desires that take over the text and take over the male protagonist as well. One can see why he couldn't finish this book. Hemingway's writing has changed the way we think of writing. He never does it openly, but his writing declares a war on adjectives and adverbs, at least more complicated adjectives than "good" and "nice." Those you can still use. The kind of British-type articulated prose that's what you find certainly in Melville, but also Hawthorne, the whole 19th century, Henry James absolutely, that kind of complex prose, that syntactically rich prose, that simply vanished because of Hemingway.

Hemingway's pared down minimalist style stripped bare prose, a prose that aims to render with precision the feel of the moment, the authenticity of the moment; a style that is made up of silences, of terseness, of spaces in between. Hemingway is a master at dialogue where very little is said. All of that seems to me is absolutely seminal in the following literature of this century. I think playwrights like Harold Pinter make sense as coming out of Hemingway. Certainly, prose writers, like Raymond Carver, make sense because of Hemingway; also, journalism, *Time* magazine writing. All of this is, I think, the Hemingway legacy: a language of simple words, simple things, trying to deliver the texture of things and a kind of freshness in this, a new economy, a kind of writing that is only apparently simple because it obliges us to negotiate it, fill in what's been left out. Hemingway said that. He often would write things and then remove something so that the reader would feel that there was something else that was there.

The Sun Also Rises is Hemingway's first and, as I said, perhaps his greatest novel. It does many of the things that I've claimed his work did. It brings to us Paris and Pamplona. It's about the expatriate writers and artists and it's about new worlds in a new language for American readers. The novel in the '20s when it came out was read as a kind of *roman à clef*, that is to say, it was a story with very recognizable people. Everybody knew that Jake Barnes was Hemingway, the hero of it. Brett—Lady Brett—was the British woman whom Hemingway knew very well. Dot Weisman and her fiancé, Mike, was Pat Guthrie who was, in reality, Dot's own cousin, lover, and who was bankrupt. All of that is in the book. Robert Cohn, who was the foil to Jake Barnes, is based on Harold Lobe, who was a person—a Jewish person whom Hemingway knew—who was an early supporter of Hemingway's and later whose life was, in some ways, ruined by this book because he's recast as Robert Cone.

The events of the book, in some sense, happened. We don't know the exact details. Hemingway probably himself had an affair with Dot, or the equivalent of Lady Brett. Now, of course, in the novel, Jake Barnes has been emasculated. Jake Barnes cannot make love. He's been wounded in the war. So, there's an interesting "turn of the screw" there as it were. We know that Dot did, in fact, go to San Sebastian with Harold Lobe. In the book, Brett goes with Robert Cohn. There was a fishing expedition. But in fact, in reality at this time, it was apparently a disaster. The stream that Hemingway loved—and took his buddies to—had been ruined by logging, it was filled with trash. You don't get that version of it in the novel. Other echoes are there as well. They are less direct; but perhaps they're more important. The figure of Brett and also the figure of a more minor female character, Frances Kline, who's Robert Cohn's woman, has a lot to do with Hemingway's sense of Zelda Fitzgerald, Hemingway's relationship with Scott and Zelda.

In one key scene in this book, Frances goes after Robert, who's a writer, in a kind of dreadful fashion, really taking him apart. That is very much parallel to what Hemingway saw in Zelda. Hemingway has a nightmarish sense of the shrew woman who bankrolls her husband writer and who essentially takes him apart. Moreover, Zelda—her famous love for all night parties, her capacity for drink, her mania for taking baths, her beauty and her desire to be desired, all of this—is part of the evocation of Brett. It's also Paris in the 1920s.

The Paris that is depicted in *A Movable Feast*, which Hemingway wrote 25 years later—or 20 years later anyway—gives us more information about the lost generation. It gives us more information about Sylvia Beach, Shakespeare and Company, Ezra Pound, Gertrude Stein and the Fitzgeralds. We don't see them in any direct curtain call way in this text. But still, this is the text about the lost generation and written at the time of the lost generation, unlike *A Movable Feast*. Of course, it has the famous quotation from Gertrude Stein, "You are all a lost generation." What you may know, if you've read *A Movable Feast* is that that phrase, "You are all a lost generation," which has become a cultural tag, is a phrase that Stein herself was told by a French car mechanic, a *garagiste*, who was complaining about a certain group of younger mechanics who couldn't work well at all. What he said to Gertrude Stein is that it's "a lost generation." All of a sudden, this extremely pedestrian remark becomes a kind of vivid symbol for an entire generation of American expatriate writers: Hemingway, Stein—Fitzgerald was posthumous—Elliott, Pound; disenchantment with

America, reaction against 19th century American morals and the loss of American innocence.

Hemingway had proposed to Fitzgerald another title for *The Sun Also Rises*. It goes like this: *The Sun Also Rises (Like Your Cock, If You Have One) A greater Gatsby (Written with the friendship of F. Scott Fitzgerald, Prophet of the Jazz Age).* That's not the one he used. He also described the plot of the novel to Fitzgerald, and he describes it this way:

> I've tried to follow the outline and spirit of *The Great Gatsby*, but feel I have failed somewhat because of never having been on Long Island. The action all takes place in Newport, Rhode Island and the heroine is a girl named Sophie Irene Lobe who kills her mother. The scene in which Sophie gives birth to twins at the death house in Sing-Sing where she's waiting to be electrocuted for the murder of the father and sister of her, as then, unborn children, I got from Dreiser. But practically everything else in the book is either my own or yours. I know you'll be glad to see it. *The Sun Also Rises* comes from Sophie's statement as she's strapped into the chair as the current mounts.

It has another subtitle which doesn't come from Fitzgerald and which, of course, is where the title is: "One generation passeth away, and another generation cometh: but the earth abideth for ever. / The sun also ariseth, and the sun goeth down, and hasteth to the place where he arose." It's about what lives and what dies, what abides. It's about the earth. That's from Ecclesiastes, the passage that he took it from.

Hemingway is our great guide to Europe. He's the great tour guide in American literature, more so than James, more so than Twain. There is a knowingness in his work, and this has got to have been very, I think, noticeable, very much felt by the readers in the '20s and '30s who were reading Hemingway. This is before everybody went on junior years abroad and things like that, and tourism wasn't the industry that it is now. Hemingway's books are larded with information, information that the Hemingway protagonist knows inside out. There's savvy, knowingness. This is all part of the posture of the Hemingway character, and Jake Barnes fills it perfectly.

For example, many Americans reading this book in 1926 would not have known what the drink called P-e-r-n-o-d, they probably would have said "*pernod.*" It's called Pernod. They wouldn't have known what it was. Hemingway tells you. "Pernod is greenish, imitation absinthe. When you add water, it turns milky. It tastes like licorice and has a good uplift, but it drops you just as far." You realize there's no narrative business being conducted by that phrase; no plot is being promoted. That's just Hemingway giving a little preview there. I've been there, I know, this is what Pernod is like. This is what it does to you.

Hemingway has a fabulous economy at showing you all the things he knows about Paris, but also putting the knife into all of the other bumbling Americans who don't know as much as he does. Robert Cohn, again, comes in for a lot of that. There are passages that just give us people walking the streets, Jake Barnes walking the streets of Paris. Again, there's no plot involved here. "Every morning I walk down the boulevard to the cafe for coffee and brioche." Just think how that one reads in 1926.

> It was a fine morning. The horse chestnut trees in the Luxemburg gardens were in bloom. There was the pleasant early-morning feeling of a hot day. I read the papers with the coffee and then smoked a cigarette. The flower-women were coming up from the market and arranging their daily stock. Students went by going up to the law school, or down to the Sorbonne. The Boulevard was busy with trams and people were going to work. I got on an S bus and rode down to the Madeleine, standing on the back platform. From the Madeleine I walked along the Boulevard des Capucines to the Opera and up to my office.

It's a panning shot. It's a walk shot. It's a shot that lets—lots of street names and avenues in Paris, the Madeleine, the Opera, and having a little brioche. This must have made readers salivate. This is how life should be lived. Hemingway doesn't stumble into this. This is cunning. This is savvy stuff. Jake Barnes is the consummate insider in this text. He knows the city. He knows the right restaurants. He knows the right bars. He knows the rituals. He knows the codes. When they later go to Pamplona for the San Fermin, he will stay at the right place with the man, Montoya, who runs the hotel there. Jake is well known there. Jake is the only American who was initiated into the bullfighting code. He is an aficionado. Montoya has this almost religious sense that others don't realize what bullfighting portends. Jake does.

So, the book has a sense of a kind of cultural initiation for us. Yet, underneath this guide view of the book, there's also an undercurrent of despair, there's an undercurrent of unrest. It is in the wake of the war. We know that. I think that's what Hemingway has consciously removed from his text. These are people skating on thin ice. These are expatriate Americans trying to find their way, trying to find a new set of values in a world that's essentially been blown apart. Many people have argued that the First World War was a far more culturally damaging event than the Second World War. It really destroyed the old world of Europe, as it was then known. It initiates a lot of other political movements as well. There's a persistent search for values in this book. You see it in funny ways and in less funny ways. One of the scenes, between Brett and Jake and this Greek Count, Mippipopolous, has to do with values.

Hear how this comes across. The Count says, "I've been in seven wars and four revolutions." And later, Brett asks him, "What were you doing? Were you in the army?" "I was on a business trip, my dear." And then, later, they're talking about values again:

> "I know," said the Count. "That's the secret. You must get to know the values."
>
> "Doesn't anything ever happen to your values?" Brett asked.
>
> "No, not anymore."
>
> "Never fall in love?"
>
> "Always," said the Count. "I'm always in love."
>
> "What does that do to your values?"
>
> "That, too, has got a place in my values."
>
> "You haven't any values. You're dead, that's all."
>
> "No, my dear. You're not right. I'm not dead at all."

That's Hemingway conversation. That's the kind of banter that goes on here. That quest for values is not really a laughing matter, even though they laugh at it. There is a kind of real seriousness here, that Jake himself measures his life in terms of values. He frequently talks about, "I thought I paid for everything." You had to work for things. You had to pay for them. You cannot cheat. The authenticity code has to always giving your money's worth so that you get your money's worth. The world was a good place to buy in. It seemed like a fine philosophy. As I say, there is no playing around with that. There's a wonderful conversation with the Count, and of course, we know that Jake is sexually wounded. You've got to understand this conversation in that way. We also know that Brett and Jake love each other, but they can't actualize it. So, the Count says:

> "You don't joke him."
>
> "That's it."
>
> "Do you now?" said the Count. "Do you joke him?"
>
> Brett looked at me and wrinkled up the corners of her eyes. "No," she said. "I wouldn't joke him."
>
> "See?" said the Count. "You don't joke him."

Can you think of another four-letter verb that sounds a little bit like joke that is obviously being played out in this particular speech here? But it's also about joking. It's like these things are not laughing matters, either. You've got to be serious. I used the word "economy," all of that's coming through in this tight-lipped prose, that there's a resonance, that there's an echoing here. It has rigor. Your currency is your life.

This is what Thoreau said. "The value of things is the amount of life that you have to put in to have them." Hemingway subscribes entirely to that. Hemingway never much talked about Thoreau. He saluted Twain. But he should have talked, it seems to me, about Thoreau as well. This is a text about people learning what is the cost of things. Brett, for example, who has toyed with men all her life, now is paying that particular price. We know that she is in love with Jake. We know that she says, "I simply turn all to jelly when you touch me." They ask, "Is there anything we can do about this?" And, finally, she says, "Don't we pay for all the things we do, though?" And then she says, "When I think of the hell I have put chaps through, I am paying for it all now." So that she has been a tease forever. She is a come-on for men. She turns them away when she feels like it and takes them on when she feels like it. Now the price is being paid. She's in love with a man who cannot act sexually with her. She's toyed with men and now she has a man who is emasculated.

All of that is part of the rigor of this text. It's part of its complex equations, its kind of honesty. For Hemingway, moreover, to have chosen as his own surrogate figure—his protagonist—this canny, knowing, savvy insider, a man who was sexually wounded, is a rather remarkable gesture on Hemingway's part, particularly given the macho dimensions of Hemingway's own personality.

I'm going to want to talk a lot about that in terms of sexuality itself when I get into more detail with this book and even when I talk later about *The Garden of Eden*. What I'd like to just signal now is the text that we just finished talking about, the text of "The Waste Land," because Hemingway has Eliot in mind, too. Eliot's hero is a Fisher King who has been sexually wounded, a Fisher King who represents his entire civilization looking for wholeness once again. Jake Barnes is Hemingway's effort to ask the same questions and look for the same answers.

Lecture Fifty-Nine
The Sun Also Rises—Spiritual Quest

Scope: Although Hemingway's novel seems realistic enough on the surface, we soon realize that the plight of his Americans in Europe has symbolic overtones. The hero of the story, Jake Barnes, is a classic Hemingway protagonist: tight-lipped, wounded (sexually) in the war, vulnerable but brave. His counterpart, Robert Cohn, shows us how the Hemingway code can be breached: by not behaving well. Paris is all drinking and partying, but the book changes course midway through as Jake and his cohort head to Spain for some fishing and the famous San Fermin Festival in Pamplona, the running of the bulls and the bullfights. In these scenes, "another country" is glimpsed, beyond the apparent hedonism and excesses of Paris. The hero of this realm is Pedro Romero, the gallant young bullfighter, who is targeted by the novel's femme fatale, Lady Brett. Unlike Twain's "innocents abroad," Hemingway's Americans bring corruption to an old and pure way of life.

Objectives—Upon completion of this lecture, you should be able to:

1. Outline the ways in which Jake Barnes stands as the classic Hemingway narrator;

2. Describe how *The Sun Also Rises* is built around a motif of pilgrimage; and

3. Explain how Hemingway reveals bullfighting to be a spiritual event.

Outline

I. Hemingway's Americans in Paris do a lot of wild partying, but they are all "sick" in some fashion.

    A. Jake Barnes is the classic Hemingway protagonist and narrator.

        1. Jake is tight-lipped, stoic, in control of things, savvy about the European world in which he lives.

        2. Jake is also wounded, rendered impotent by an injury from the war. He tries to be flippant about his injury, but his

relationship with the text's female interest, Lady Brett, makes this difficult. Love without sex is a problem.

3. Jake is hard-boiled in the daytime, but not at night, when he is vulnerable. Here is a central feature of Hemingway.

4. A careful reading of Jake's scenes with Brett raises the question: Just how impotent is he? This text is tricky in suggesting more than meets the eye. There are important, suggestive silences between the words.

B. Robert Cohn is presented as Jake's friend, but also as his foil.

1. Hemingway's inimitable gift for "doing in" people in a few well-placed jabs is evident in the presentation of Cohn.

2. Cohn is faulted most of all for not being "one of us"; he is Jewish. There is a clubby dimension to this book, and Cohn will pay for it as the "racial" outsider.

3. At key moments of crisis, Cohn does what we expect him to do: He "behaves badly." He sleeps with Brett; he wants to go fishing with "the boys." The Hemingway code is on show.

C. The fishing episode at Burguete is idyllic.

1. Hemingway, great admirer of *Huckleberry Finn*, depicts a landscape of camaraderie that Twain would have enjoyed.

2. There is a religious ritual in the description of catching and cleaning the fish.

3. Joined by an Englishman, Harris, Jake and Bill enjoy their moment of great happiness. We sense there are terrors underneath (the shadow of World War I). We can compare this scene with "Big Two-Hearted River"; there are parallels between Jake Barnes and Nick Adams.

4. Hemingway's sentimentality is on show when the male buddies part.

II. We understand the voyage of the Americans to Spain to be something of a pilgrimage. Spain is a place where the "values" are unlike those in France. There is more of "community" there, particularly in the Basque region.

A. Even the fishing trip can now be seen as a spiritual event, better, in its way, than the famous monastery of Roncesvalles, scene of *The Song of Roland*.

B. The notion of pilgrimage dominates the landscape, and we sense that spiritual values are now in play.

1. Hemingway's presentation of the Basques, even on the trip from Bayonne to Pamplona, is rich in suggestions of "community." There is a sacramental overtone in the sharing of bread and wine with the Basques.
2. Jake, always the initiated, is close to Montoya, the hotel owner in Pamplona. Here we come to understand the concept of *aficion*, the spiritual passion that unites lovers of bullfighting. Jake is the only American to be part of this.
3. Hence, bullfighting is not a sport: It is a ritual activity entailing man's encounter with death, and it is done by rigorous forms. The hero of this new dispensation is Pedro Romero, young bullfighter extraordinaire. In the descriptions of Romero's performance in the shadows of the monastery of Roncesvalles, we see the Hemingway ideals of "grace under pressure" and "purity of line," both of which describe writing (and love-making) as well. He embodies Hemingway's code.
4. There are sexual overtones to the bullfighter's "dance with death."

C. A reversal of the usual tale of the American abroad, Hemingway's story is about the corruption of this age-old tradition of bullfighting as a spiritual event. Lady Brett is inflamed by Romero, and she enlists Jake in her efforts to "have" him. We can compare this with Twain's *Innocents Abroad* and James's depictions of Americans in Europe.
1. Cohn, enraged with jealousy (he has also slept with Brett), accuses Jake of being a pimp. Cohn is right. He has his revenge physically on Romero.
2. Brett is one of Hemingway's triumphs of characterization. Her fiancé, Mike, calls her "an extraordinary wench," and her charm and beauty and inimitable Brit style add much to the book. In the end, she leaves Romero for fear that he would make her too "womanly," for fear of corrupting him; she takes pleasure in this renunciation and calls it her form of religion. Readers may not agree.
3. Jake, impotent, is kept "clean" by the plot, however implicated he may be otherwise.

D. Hemingway's original title was *Fiesta*. We need to think of "*carnaval*" and its attendant meanings of liberation, transformation, and play. Pamplona is indeed "another country."

Lecture Fifty-Nine—Transcript
The Sun Also Rises—Spiritual Quest

This is Lecture Fifty-Nine, and it's the second lecture that I'm giving on Hemingway's novel, *The Sun Also Rises*. You may remember that I closed the last lecture with a reference that might have surprised you a little bit, to Elliot's *The Waste Land*. In particular, I made the parallel that both authors, Elliot and Hemingway, are dealing with issues of sterility, issues of renewal. They're each searching for a new set of values. We've always known that about *The Waste Land;* it's easy to miss that dimension of Hemingway's novel. Yet, I do think this is a book about a spiritual quest—which is going to be the kind of central issue in this lecture—told in terms that are much more American than anything Elliot would have tried to do; in terms also of American innocence and in terms refracted through the kinds of characters that Hemingway has made immortal for us, the tight-lipped, stoic American hero who is Jake Barnes in this novel.

He is the classic, quintessential, Hemingway male. He's in control, he's savvy, he's a pro, he has a lot of savoir faire, he knows his way around Paris, he knows the restaurants, he knows the lingo, and he knows the French. He has a kind of mastery of all the codes, and it's crucial, I think, for us to get a sense of what kind of authority this figure has because there are also going to be areas where he has either no authority or where he is really surprisingly passive or—to take it to the full route, impotent—because he is impotent, he's been wounded. He's been wounded; he's been wounded sexually. He's been emasculated during the war and, therefore, he is obviously a kind of living symbolic figure such that he's a Hemingway version of the maimed or wounded or emasculated Fisher King.

How does he take to his wound? Well, of course, here you get a tonality that you wouldn't have in Elliot. He tries to be flippant about it. He tries to be hardboiled about it. He makes remarks to Brett that this was supposed to be funny. After all, people laugh at the notion that somebody is impotent or somebody's been wounded in the groin. He makes remarks such as, "Well, I never think about it." We know this, of course, to be completely false. He thinks about it all the time and [with] good reason to, because the whole book depends on the relationship between Jake and Brett, that they are wild about each other. They are sexually very drawn to each other. There's a great sense of desire that each has for the other. But Jake is unable to function. He's not able to perform.

Moreover, this book is very rich in its view of the hardboiled character because many people have felt that Hemingway is only hardboiled in appearance, only hardboiled in the daytime. That's essentially what Jake says, that he goes home and gets ready to go to bed and he makes the remark, that it's easy if you want to be hardboiled about everything in the daytime. But, as he says, at night it's another thing. That, of course, is an important feature of Hemingway, that there's nightlife, a nighttime side of thing. There's a vulnerability that comes into this text. Some people would argue it as mushiness, a softness that comes into this. If you wanted to gender it, that there's a woman who somehow cohabits with macho, tough man Hemingway.

We're going to see a lot of that in this book. It's also open to question, you know, exactly how impotent this guy is. Now, that's a kind of scurrilous remark, like the thing you might expect to find in the papers about checking out the exact sexual behavior of Jake. We know that, as I said, he cannot perform. There are a number of passages between Jake and Brett in the early part of the novel that are highly suggestive if we look at them very carefully. First of all, as I say, the two desire each other enormously. It makes them very unhappy, physically unhappy. We know that every time he kisses her, she will say that she turns into jelly. When he embraces her, the text will not fail to tell us that her hands are shaky or that she's shivering, and she's certainly not shivering because of the cold or anything like that.

The text insistently shows her to be sexually excited by this man at the slightest touch, but we are to realize that the fact that he can't perform has nothing to do with his desirability. That might be a very interesting equation in itself. Now, as I had said, it's also the case that there are scenes, one in particular, where we really might get the feeling that more is going on than meets the eye. It's a sequence between Brett and Jake, obviously. She has kissed him on the forehead, and they've told each other that they love each other. Then the prose goes like this: "Darling," she said. "Then: (and there's a colon) do you want me to send him away?" This is a scene between Jake and Brett and she's brought up the rich Greek Count and they've been joking and drinking, etc. "Do you want me to send him away?" He's not in the room now, but he's going to be coming in.

Well, what happened with that colon? "Darling," she said. "Then: Do you want me to send him away?" This is only my argument. Other critics have pointed out that perhaps there's something going on that she is arousing. That's what she's saying. "Do you want me to send him away?" That something is going to take place between Jake and Brett here. So we have their conversation where Jake is saying:

"Oh, no, no, no. He's nice. Don't."

"Yes, I must."

"But don't."

"Oh, you can't do that."

She is going to go and send the Count away and Jake lies down in bed. Hemingway's, again, clipped language; he tells us that he's not having a good time. He's having a bad time. She returns to the room and she strokes his head—the text says—and she calls him, "Poor old darling," and he asks about the Count—like, "What did you do? Where did you send him?" He's going to go and get champagne. Then we have another one of these phrases, about the "then" and with the colon. Again, then, later: Now what happens in that colon? "Then, later: Do you feel better, darling? Is the head any better?" And the remarkable answer, "It's better." So what has she done to him between, "Then: Do you feel better?" She has done something to make him feel better. That's what he says. "It's better." Again, without being too prurient, I think one is free to imagine that the two can, in some at least partial way, satisfy each other, perhaps some version of oral sex.

Some form of arousal is possible, and it's mutual, and it's something that they do for each other. Hemingway, in his extremely teasing fashion, is not going to describe that. Again, it's classic Hemingway performance in a dialogue, where it's what's in-between the words, it's the silences between the words; it's what's *not* said that is so fascinating in this text. I'll talk more about that in my next lecture. So, Jake comes across, then, as a figure that is both damaged and yet seductive. He arouses women. He arouses Brett, who is the kind of femme fatale of the book. The foil to Jake, Jake who knows everything, who is the insider, who is the kind of professional; Jake is Robert Cohn.

Robert Cohn is introduced in the first pages of this book as having been the middleweight boxing champion at Princeton. Hemingway hastens to say that that does not impress him but that it did impress Robert Cohn. Robert Cohn has the great misfortune in this novel of being Jewish, or "superior in Jewish," as the text says at one point, which is a way of saying, "he's not one of us." I'm using that phrase intentionally. It is the phrase of the text. It's a familiar phrase. "Not one of us." There is a very persistent, clubby dimension to Hemingway, that Cohn is going to be presented as the outsider, not only racially the outsider because he's a Jew, but he's exactly the opposite of Jake. He makes the wrong moves, his instincts are bad or, as the text is going to say, "he behaves badly."

He does a lot of things that are unforgivable in this text in terms of its own plot. He sleeps with Brett. That's a no-no. He's not supposed to be doing that. Now, of course, we know in real life, Harold Lobe and Dot Wiseman, in fact, did have a brief affair. So, Cohn sleeps with Brett even though she's engaged to Mike and even though she's in love with Jake. That's one "no-no," that's one transgression. Another one is—and this is probably worse in terms of the Hemingway pecking order—he also wants to go fishing with the boys. Well, he can't go fishing with the boys. The Jew can't go fishing with these boys. I mean—I'm exaggerating a point to make it—there is a real sense in which the book is going to punish Cohn. He may be the lightweight or middleweight boxing champion at Princeton, but the book is going to have its way with him and this comes unforgettably in Mike's putdown of Cohn. It's pretty vicious.

Cohn, of course, is mooning around and he's desperately jealous of the fact that Brett had this affair with him, went down to barites with him, but doesn't want to be with him anymore. Finally, Mike has had enough. He's, of course, in his cups. He's in his cups throughout this book, so he's half crocked when he says this. He says, "I know when I'm not wanted. Why don't you see when you're not wanted, Cohn? Go away. Go away, for God's sake." (And here comes the clincher.) "Take that sad Jewish face away." And that's just the most overt critique of Cohn along those lines. You get Mike comes at him over and over in the book, taunting him, going after him, reminding him that he is a Jew, that he's not one of them. He's not the insider the way the group is. He doesn't fit. It's the case, too, of course, using this same clubby view of things that, as it's put, Cohn misbehaves. This is between Brett and Jake and Mike.

"He's behaved very badly, damned badly. He had a chance to behave so well." There's a kind of British flavor to all of this, a sense of being in the right club, being in the right school, wearing the right tie, having the right manners, all of which, of course, Cohn fails to do. He had a chance to behave so well. Well, of course, he doesn't. However Cohn is disposed of, the boys will go fishing. It's Hemingway, after all. The text has to give us that. If I want to suggest to you that this book is about a spiritual quest, then the fishing expedition really is centrally located within that frame. Fishing, in Hemingway, has a kind of religious or spiritual dimension. This will be the escape from culture, from civilization, from women. This is where Jake and Bill will go fishing together, and it's a very lyrical passage in this book.

You've had all these other passages that detail the streets of Paris, the streets of Pamplona. But here, we finally have a natural setting and the text seems to remember Mark Twain's *Huckleberry Finn*. We know that Hemingway loved that book. He claimed that American fiction came out of that book. You have the walk of Jake and Bill as they go through the woods towards the river where they're going to go trout fishing. The trout fishing itself is conveyed with the same kind of seriousness, the same kind of solidity—and this is going to sound like an oxymoron—the same kind of luscious sobriety. It's serious business; and yet, there is something that is almost mouthwatering in the way Hemingway can describe how it feels to fish, how it feels to catch a fish, how it feels to pack the fish after you've caught them. So, in this sequence, Jake is catching a number of trout, and it's done in this same rigorous professional manner. After all, there's a way to fish right and there's a way to fish wrong.

We can assume that if Cohn had gone with them, he wouldn't have gotten it right. He wouldn't have known how to do it. Jake, of course, knows how, that it's a question of laying them out the right way, putting them down side-by-side, of course their heads have to all point the right way and then it's a question of pouring the cold water on them and, of course, you slit them and this, that and the other. You wash them in the water that is wonderfully called "cold and smoothly heavy." Then, of course, once you've cleaned them and washed them, you have to pack them. That's done, again, properly. This is ritual we're talking about. This has what Updike referred to as the *liturgical gravity* of Hemingway's style. That's a notion that I'll come back to in the next book of Hemingway's, *The Garden of Eden*.

Here we have the trout, which were properly packed with the ferns. Three trout on a layer of ferns, then we have another layer and then we have more trout. It's exactly the way—there's old recipes where you lay in the potatoes and then you lay in the meat and then you lay in the veggies and it's all done according to this very precise set of rules. Here, again, is the area of Jake's authority. Again, it's not like the text brags. It's rather that we see here something of the central values, the central kinds of skills that are important in this text, what it is a man is supposed to know. I said that this text remembers Twain. Of course, it also remembers an earlier Hemingway text, in particular, the story, "Big, Two Hearted River," which is part of *In*

Our Time. There we have the Nick Adams character, that is, in a sense, very parallel to Jake.

He is "shell-shocked" we come to realize, he is a wounded victim of the war. Jake has been emasculated. We come to understand that a fishing expedition is a form of spiritual healing. It's a form of therapy. That's also partly why it has these kinds of religious values. Nick seeks the same healing, he seeks the same wholeness, he seeks to immerse himself in these natural rhythms, much the way Jake and Bill do. They're joined at some point by Harris, a Brit. Harris, of course, as is characteristic in Hemingway's works, is wild about these two Americans, again, in his tight-lipped British fashion. He makes a remark about how much pleasure he has had with them in this fishing trip and it ushers in a sense of this war background, this sense of the great catastrophe of Europe that's behind this book, that shadows this book.

He says, "Really, you don't know how much it means. I've not had much fun since the war," and they assure him that they will meet with him anytime; they'll go fishing again. But, this is to get across, first of all, how *sympatique* and irresistible Jake and his cronies are, but also that they are wounded people, all of them. This pleasure that is found now is a kind of respite from the damage that has been meted out to them earlier. Then, of course, the friends separate.

Hemingway later writes that in a way that's pretty sappy. He can be sappy. As I said, there's a soft side that's always ready to surface and, particularly, it can surface between guys who are saying farewell to each other. So you hear an eloquent exchange such as this. "So long, fella," Bill said. "So long, kid. It was swell. I've had a swell time." (Then it closes,) "So long, old kid." This is the kind of mushy, sappy Hemingway and it's part of the picture. You don't have to love this. This is not hardboiled writing at all. It's the other side of the coin. After all, it's easy to be hardboiled during the daytime, but not so much at night, and perhaps not when the fishing trip is over, either.

This fishing trip, of course, is part of the great pilgrimage of this text, which is the pilgrimage to Spain. Spain is not France. For us, of course, in America, they may look just like two European countries. France has a very different resonance for Hemingway. It's a very different tonality. One of the lines in the text says, "Everything is in such a clear financial—or on such a clear financial basis in France." France is materialistic, France may be elegant, it may be a place of great etiquette; but Spain is spiritual, Spain is a different kind of world. This fishing trip is spiritual. They go to Roncesvalles—which is the famous place. There is the great monastery there. It's famous in Spanish history. It's famous in French history, *La Chanson de Roland,* "The Song of Roland," the great French medieval epic takes place at Roncesvalles. That's where Roland the French defeats the Saracens. This monastery dominates the setting and helps us to understand that these events are under the sign of a kind of religious history.

In Spain, particularly in Pamplona—which is where they're going—we meet a different kind of person. It's no longer even the Spanish per se; it's the Basques. The Basques are presented as different. I want to comment on that. I spent some 10 years of my life in the Basque country. We used to have a house there on the French side of the border. The Basques are different. They don't look like the French. They don't talk like the French— they sure don't talk like the French because Basque is a language that has no relation whatsoever to French. It sounds guttural to most people. There's certainly nothing romance in it. Some linguists have actually thought that it may have some relation to Japanese. Whichever, the Basques don't behave like the French. They're not very verbal in the same way that the French are. The reason that I'm making this comment on the Basque is that when Jake meets them, this text begins to show us something of what community would look like. The kind of backbiting, the one-upmanship, all of the kind of games that are played in Paris, those things are going to be put behind you here.

The Basques offer us an image of community. They share the food. They hand people food. Of course, their greatest gesture is they pass around these great big wine skins. Here, again, we are right in familiar Hemingway territory. That is to say these wine skins that have a lot of wine in them, you have to hold them out here [demonstrates] and squirt. It's quite an arc that the wine makes. The Basques are specialists at this. They love doing it. When they get in their cups, they still manage to hit. Can you imagine if you miss? It's not easy to hit your mouth with something that's that far away. Well, of course, needless to say, this is one of Jake's skills. He knows how to do this as well as anything else. But this is a sacramental scene. They're passing around bread and wine and all sharing one another's food. This is one way of signaling that we have shifted ground here. We're in a new kind of territory.

All of this, of course, leads to the great spiritual event that's going to be part of the pilgrimage, which is the bullfighting. The bullfighting has, as we know for Hemingway, a kind of religious value. This is man's encounter with death. This is the true test of courage. This is the true test of who you are. Jake, wounded though he is, is not a bullfighter. Hemingway credits Jake as having "Spanish," which means having passion. The way we know this, that Montoya, who is the hotel owner in Pamplona, treats Jake as one of the insiders, one of the initiated. No other Americans have this, of course. This, again, is a way of pointing to Jake's eminent status as insider, as hero, along Hemingway lines. He is an intimate of Montoya's.

Now, I would point out that this is the only passion he seems to have. He has a passion for bulls, but he, of course, to put it really crudely, cannot penetrate. He can't gore anyone. This text is going to do a lot with those notions of penetrator and penetratee. We are meant to respect Jake's savvy in this area and to realize that he is one of the rare Americans who has access to the people in Pamplona, the people who know the bullfighters and, of course, to the bullfighters themselves. So, it's through this that we meet arguably, the true hero of this novel. I said Jake is—and I don't want to really retract that—but in some sense, Jake is upstaged by the most attractive, seductive figure of the novel, which is the young bullfighter— very young bullfighter—Pedro Romero, who is named, in fact, after a real, or at least a legendary 18th century bullfighter.

Romero is precisely presented to us under the sign of a kind of stoic religious tradition. The setting in which we first encounter Romero is called "monastic." Romero is essentially just a boy, and he is described in very particular ways, the way his bullfighting manner speaks volumes for Hemingway's aesthetics, for Hemingway's ethics, for Hemingway's code. The terms are that Romero is one of the few bullfighters today that has a pure manner. It's straight and pure and natural in line. This is contrasted with the exaggerated contortions, corkscrew like moves that the other bullfighters make. They're melodramatic affectations versus Romero. Romero, his style is so pure that everything remains clean. The fake stuff turns bad, according to Hemingway. It doesn't last. But Romero's bullfighting gives real emotion. It's precisely because he keeps what Hemingway calls the "absolute purity of line." He holds that. He holds this purity of line. How does he hold it, in what conditions? Through the "maximum of exposure." Can you hear what aesthetic terms those are? Purity of line, maximum of exposure, that's a way of writing the clean style.

That's a way of living, of exposing yourself to danger, conceivably to death. It is something of an *ars poetica*. It's a living philosophy. I want to suggest that when we read the passages about Romero, it also seems to be a form of sexual husbanding. This man offers his body. Think about what bullfighters look like as they present their bodies, and these beautiful tight clothes, their capes, et cetera. They present their bodies to this rushing, maddened beast that wants to gore them. Of course, the challenge is to get as close as possible. So, the phrases that Hemingway uses over and over about Romero are that he offers the body. He offers it a little closer each time. But there are no tricks, Hemingway says. This creates a kind of longing, a kind of almost erotic dimension in the audience. Hemingway's term is that it "gave you a sudden ache inside." We learn that the crowds love this. They don't want it ever to be over. It sounds like a sexual performance or it sounds like foreplay. It sounds like the approach of a sexual performance.

All of this, then, is the kind of larger ramifications and the aura of bullfighting; that approaching contact that would be fatal if the bull did gore you, the dance with death, in some sense, the approach to a kind of permanent penetration. I want you to think of Romero as the foil to Jake. I said Robert Cohn is Jake's foil. But so, too, is Romero. This is the man whose life is about approaching a kind of lethal climax, a lethal penetration. Now, this story is really enlisted in the tradition of Americans abroad.

You'll recall that Twain wrote the book called, *The Innocents Abroad*, the great Jamesian theme that has to do with American innocents going abroad. Hemingway's going to reverse this theme; this story is going to be about these Americans who corrupt the Spanish, who in some sense desecrate the spiritual traditions that they are encountering, how are they going to go. It's not like this is a religious service—I don't want to overstate my case— there's plenty of drinking and carousing, but the bullfighting in Pamplona is spiritual. Of course, how would you corrupt that? One easy way: You corrupt the bullfighter. This young boy, Pedro Romero, he's going to be corrupted and he will be corrupted precisely because Brett sees him, she sees this extraordinary kind of seductive dance that he does as a bullfighter. She sees this offering of the body, that he performs, and she becomes madly sexually inflamed. She tells Jake that she's got to have him, that that's all there is to it.

She uses language that reminds me of the language of Catherine Barkley in *A Farewell to Arms*. "It's tearing me all up inside." Sexual desire can destroy you. She's got to have him. So, she's going to enlist Jake to get him. Jake will precisely play the role of pimp to get him. That will happen. It's a kind of remarkable scene where they are having a drink together, and Jake discreetly leaves. Hemingway never says that Jake is behaving like a traitor, but we know that. We know it partly through the looks people give him. Jake, as he leaves that room, says that it was pretty awful. It was a pretty terrible thing. It was not easy to do. Montoya, who runs the hotel—this is it; this is the transgression. These Americans have come—he has brought them because they are Jake's friends—and then this lady that they brought, Brett, has corrupted this Spanish spiritual hero. This is really one of the great crises of the novel; it sets off a number of things. First of all, it is the corruption that the Americans bring to the Spanish city of Pamplona. It also catalyzes the jealousy of this text. Cohn can't bear the fact, because he's still mooning for Brett, can't bear the fact, now that she's gone off with Romero. He calls Jake straight out. He says, "You're a pimp." Of course, he's right. Jake is a pimp. This is the turning point of the novel. She has her wild, mad fling with Romero. Cohn will eventually get his revenge. He will virtually annihilate Romero—because he's the middleweight boxing champion of Princeton—in a fight. But he can't beat him. He hits him, he hits him, and he virtually ruins him. Romero continues to get up. This doesn't last long—it won't surprise anyone—between Brett and Romero.

At one point, when she leaves him she says that, "He wanted me to let my hair grow out. He thought that would make a woman of me." Well, that's impossible, particularly in the Hemingway scheme of things. We're going to see women have to have short hair. She gives him up and she feels pretty good about it. She says that it's pretty good—not being a bitch—and that she's not going to be one of those people, she says, that ruins children. She also feels good about her little thing with Romero because, as she said, it wipes out Cohn. Interesting kind of sexual arithmetic. Cohn, the Jew, must have left a little dirty residue and then Romero has cleaned it up for her. She even talks about it being her form of religion, that for those of us who don't have God, perhaps. Jake, wisely I think, remarks on that, that some people do have God. It's as if Hemingway won't quite let her get away with this.

Brett, in some sense, is the text's Circe. Brett is the figure who turns everyone around her into swine. All of the men lust after her. The Basques start dancing around her. Jake is kept clean of this. It's going to "break her up all inside," she says—sexual desire. Jake has to be kept clear of this. The text wants him to. An interesting comment of Fitzgerald's on this text, which Hemingway wrote, that he couldn't really believe that Jake was fully impotent. He says he isn't like an impotent man. He's like a man in a moral chastity belt. It's as if there's something that Jake has to "be kept clean" is the point. Jake has to be kept free of the kind of torment, or of the kind of dirtying that sexual activity produces here. Well, as I say, Brett is the text's Circe. The text gives us this sphere versus bull—penetratee versus penetrator—philosophy that I think goes a long way in Hemingway's view of things. The bullfighting, and the entire carnival that we see in Pamplona, announces the great Hemingway theme of transformation, metamorphoses, of a world that is not only unlike France, but it's also unlike what it looks like on the page and it's that other dimension of this world in Pamplona that I'll want to look at in my last lecture.

Lecture Sixty
Ernest Hemingway—Wordsmith

Scope: Hemingway is justly famous for his crisp, clipped, clean style. Much of the verbiage and rhetoric of "English" is banished from American prose because of his initiatives—and many American readers cannot handle or enjoy complex language and syntax for the same reasons. "One true sentence" was Hemingway's mantra for getting past writer's block; likewise, he rejected the "big" words, which he blasted for being bogus and false to experience. The prose he tried to create was to be clean and yet dimensional, even to have "fourth and fifth dimensions," if one knew how to write it. Looking at *The Sun Also Rises* from the point of view of language can be exhilarating. The book is saturated with references to other writers, often coded as dirty jokes. The novel is also equipped with some remarkable puns and word play. Ultimately, Hemingway's interest in *double entendre* moves from the word to the psyche, as the book revels in innuendo, in suggestions of dual meanings and dual sexuality. Nothing is remotely as simple or stable as it first appears, and we may need to reconceive our view of the macho writer.

Objectives—Upon completion of this lecture, you should be able to:

1. Summarize the major characteristics of the "Hemingway style";

2. Give examples of Hemingway's use of literary allusion in *The Sun Also Rises*; and

3. Explain the importance of Hemingway's use of puns and innuendo in his construction of a worldview.

Outline

I. Hemingway is celebrated as a clean, simple stylist.

   A. In *A Moveable Feast*, Hemingway reveals his lifelong mantra for breaking writer's block: "One true sentence." Are sentences true?

   B. Consider a few examples of the clean style. It has a kind of heft and solidity that make you salivate.

C. In *A Farewell to Arms*, Frederick Henry delivers an impassioned critique of the "big" words as being obscene.

D. In *Green Hills of Africa*, Hemingway speaks of the "fourth and fifth dimensions" of prose, reachable only if you have done it exactly right.

E. One formula for "dimensionality" is to repress information. Hemingway often used this strategy, and it accounts for the brooding tone in some of his writing.

    1. The corollary to repression is the fear that "saying" something is tantamount to losing it.

    2. In this book, the presence of the Great War is often felt just behind the most idyllic scenes.

II. *The Sun Also Rises* is something of an echo chamber; it is larded with literary references.

    A. "Make it new" is the credo of modernism, but Hemingway also enjoyed replaying the old.

        1. Henry James makes several curtain calls in the novel. We hear echoes of Strether's famous advice to Little Bilham about "living all you can." In addition, James's experiments with American values being testing against French ones are present here. James can also be pleasantly mocked, and Hemingway is out to show that Strether's drama of sexual renunciation is nothing compared to Jake Barnes's.

        2. H. L. Mencken, the aging American arbiter of literary judgment, comes in for a scurrilous mention.

        3. And what about lesbianism and homosexuality? There is one snide reference to gays and little other overt mention of homosexuality. Yet consider the environment and friends of Hemingway: Gertrude Stein and Alice B. Toklas, Janet Flanner, Sylvia Beach, Natalie Barney and Djuna Barnes (at the Rue Jacob). Then rethink Jake Barnes, the man who cannot (will not?) "penetrate" women.

        4. Zelda Fitzgerald's belief that Ernest and Scott were lovers further heightens the fireworks behind the novel.

    B. The sexual innuendo of *The Sun Also Rises* is especially visible in the puns and word play.

        1. How does Romero get into those pants? "Pipe down."

2. Brett's short hair is arousing. Romero wants her to cut it, but she won't; the "boyish" girl in Hemingway is erotic.

3. Fiesta is introduced by "explosion"; these explosions happen to occur between people's legs.

4. The Count asks Brett the key question: Are you joking him (Jake)? Who is joking whom? Does "joking" suggest something else?

III. *The Sun Also Rises* may be thought of as "another country," a place unto itself, beyond even Paris and Pamplona.

A. Like all novels, it is a word-world; a world of verbal constructs, jokes, games, and codes. What does "*Vengo jueves*, Cohn" mean? Or "*globos illuminados*"? Or "joke" or "*festa*"? Or all the French and Spanish terms in this international text?

B. Hemingway's true target, beyond the word play, is the ambiguity and multiplicity of the psyche, especially as this informs vision. The most suggestive scene of the novel occurs when Jake is knocked out by Cohn (who calls him a "pimp"); this episode of literal trauma is presented as total strangeness of vision, of revisiting things we thought we knew. Here would be the "other country."

Lecture Sixty—Transcript
Ernest Hemingway—Wordsmith

This is Lecture Sixty. It's the third Hemingway lecture and it's the last lecture I want to give on *The Sun Also Rises*. I want to talk a lot about language in this lecture. I hope that's not going to seem dry to you. I don't think it's dry at all. Remember at the end of the last lecture I remarked that one of the titles that Hemingway was considering for this book was Fiesta? When they get to Pamplona one of the sentences, I think it's the first sentence of the chapter says, "The Fiesta began with an explosion." I used the word explosion in my own lecture. There's something explosive about this book, about its language, about what's being packed into its language. This affords me an opportunity to talk about the Hemingway style in general, and Hemingway has some very famous pronouncements about language.

In particular, In *A Moveable Feast*, he writes about the solutions that he had to develop whenever he experienced writer's block, which of course is what all writers periodically experience. He said this:

> I would stand and look out over the roofs of Paris and think, 'Do not worry. You have always written before and you will write now. All you have to do is write one true sentence. Write the truest sentence that you know.' So finally I would write one true sentence, and then go on from there. It was easy then because there was always one true sentence that I knew or had seen or had heard somebody say.

That is really one of the articles of belief in Hemingway's philosophy: one true sentence. Of course, this is that pared down style that doesn't want to fake, doesn't want to be phony. It's like Romero's' bull fighting: purity of line, absolutely nothing bogus. As an aside, the concept of "one true sentence" can lead you to suicide, and I think it's part of the reason that Hemingway did commit suicide, because it begs the question: "Is there such a thing as a true sentence?" A sentence is an arrangement of words. The most pared down sentence, the purest sentence with the most purity of line, is still a sentence, and it's still a linguistic construct. Language can't get beyond being language. I think that Hemingway, as he continued to grow older, found it harder and harder to summon that one true sentence. Other writers like Joyce for example move from simple sentences to more and more complex and parodic kinds of experiments because they know that language only can lead to more language. That's the evolution. I think Shakespeare does something of the same.

Well, Hemingway in *A Moveable Feast* does write these kinds of sentences that he's talking about. I'll read you a sample of it. This is the kind of sumptuous Hemingway prose that for me is just immortal. Listen how many of these words are monosyllabic.

> When we came back to Paris it was clear and cold and lovely. The city had accommodated itself to winter, there was good wood for sale at the wood and coal place across the street, and there were braziers outside of many of the good cafes so that you could keep warm on the terraces. Our own apartment was warm and cheerful. We burned *boules*, which were molded egg-shaped lumps of coal dust on the wood fire, and on the streets the winter light was beautiful. Now you were accustomed to see the bare trees against the sky and you walked on the fresh washed gravel paths through the Luxembourg gardens in the clear sharp wind. The trees were sculptured without their leaves when you were reconciled to them and the winter winds blew across the surfaces of the ponds and the fountains blew in the bright light.

This is a nostalgic remembrance of Paris. It's a man in his 50s thinking about his own 20s and the romantic city where he spent that time. That's the kind of language that Hemingway yearns for. It's the same kind of simple clean language that he uses in the description of Jake preparing the trout after he's caught them, putting them on the fern leaves three at a time then putting more fern leaves and then having a bulky group of them that he could then put in the shade. There is in Hemingway a very principled philosophical distrust of fancy words, of fancy language. There's a famous phrase or set of phrases from *A Farewell to Arms* where the protagonist Frederick Henry says the following,

> I was always embarrassed by the words sacred, glorious, and sacrifice and the expression in vain. We had heard them, sometimes standing in the rain almost out of earshot, so that only the shouted words came through, and had read them, on proclamations that were slapped up by billposters over other proclamations, now for a long time, and I had seen nothing sacred, and the things that were glorious had no glory and the sacrifices were like the stockyards at Chicago if nothing was done with the meat except to bury it. There were many words that you could not

stand to hear and finally only the names of places had dignity. Certain numbers were the same way and certain dates and these with the names of places were all you could say and have them mean anything.

So that's the kind of paring down. That's why it's happening; it's not just a kind of predisposition for clean language. It's ultimately a kind of linguistic bankruptcy, rhetorical bankruptcy. All of the $50 words, all of the high-faulting terms—particularly in so far as they throw us into a world that is bloated and inflated that talks about honor and glory and the like, when you have actually seen the carnage of war—these words are obscene. You can't use them. They don't correspond to anything. They utterly blind you to the truth of the situation.

Now there's a lot going on. Hemingway then settles for the clean simple words, but he wants his books to be resonant, to be "dimensional." That's the term he uses. I'm going to quote a passage, a famous description that comes out of the "Green Hills of Africa." "How far prose can be carried if one is serious enough and has luck." That's what he's looking for. "There is a fourth and fifth dimension that can be gotten." A fourth and fifth dimension that can be gotten? Well, how do you get it? His interlocutor says, "But that's poetry you're talking about." And he says, "No it is much more difficult than poetry. It is a prose that has never been written but it can be written without tricks and without cheating, with nothing that will go bad afterwards."

It's that same notion that the inflated bloated language will rot, will go bad. This is like the bogus bullfighters, the one's who pretend and they look melodramatic. They pretend they're in danger, and that's what doesn't last. It won't stay. With Romero, his purity of line is such that it stays with you forever, you can see; and I said then, this is also a kind of aesthetic philosophy. This is a way of viewing language and literature. I want you to think about those terms fourth and fifth dimensions because I love that language. I think that what he's trying to say is that the right kind of writing has magic in it because it somehow continues to speak, continues to signify and to resonate beyond the surface meaning.

Those are the extra dimensions. That's what I've been trying to get at in this book, *The Sun Also Rises*; it's packed, taught, condensed and at the same time it's echoing and resonant, and that it is achieving that kind of dimensionality. Part of this also is related to a kind of art of repression: of not saying too much one of conversation. Brett, at the end of the book, is talking to Jake and she's trying to tell him about how good she feels now that she has forsworn Romero and he says, "You'll lose it if you talk about it." And again, I think that's a writerly notion that too much said ruins everything; what you want is a book that is reader-intensive, not writer-intensive. That makes the reader come in and fulfill your task, or complete what you have started. So you want to convey a sense of doubleness, of ambiguity or ambivalence, mystery, and something beyond the words. That's partly—also the feeling that people had when they read this book.

When Edmond Wilson read this novel he thought there was a very peculiar consciousness in it. He said it:

> This particular consciousness does not arouse Hemingway to passionate violence but it poisons him, it makes him sick and thus invests with a singular quality, a quality perhaps new in fiction, the sunlight and the green summer landscapes of the sun also arises.

I alluded to that when I was talking about the presence, the looming, haunting presence of the war that is in this book, that's behind those idyllic fishing scenes, those notations that seemed to be unspoiled. I think that all of this is still part of an aesthetic, of a style of writing that aims precisely for you to feel this activity behind the surface.

I told you as well; sometimes this is really quite literal. Hemingway would literally write the passages out of his manuscript. He would probably do it with scissors. If I remove this, the reader will feel it as a loss, will feel that something is stirring here and that's the effect that I want to produce. There's more to it, what's unsaid is still present in some sense. Of course, this is the secret to those wonderful dialogues that he writes. So this leads me to the remark that this book is a kind of echo chamber in lots of different ways. It's a literary echo chamber. This book is literary to its fingernails and toenails, and that's not something Hemingway is ordinarily credited with. This book is studded with allusions. It's not quite as blatantly allusive as "The Waste Land" is which throws in six foreign languages. Nonetheless, it's a book that presents a lot of references to other kinds of writers.

For example, Henry James takes two curtain calls in this book—and you may or may not have sensed it. It's very similar to Eliot's technique in that there is a famous passage. I read it to you when I was lecturing on James in *The Ambassadors*. It's the great passage where Struther urges little Billhem to have his experience. It's the great summons to experience; and if you have missed that, you've missed everything. "Live all you can," James's character Struthers says, "Live all you can, it's a mistake not to. It doesn't so much matter what you do in particular, as long as you have had your life," Pardon me, "as long as you have your life"—if you haven't had that, what have you had?" That comes back in this novel in a way that I think most readers who know a lot of James pick up in the early conversation between Jake and Robert Cone, where Cone says, "Jake, don't you ever get the feeling that all your life is going by and you're not taking advantage of it? Do you realize you've lived nearly half the time you have to live already?" Now if that were the only thing in the text about James, you'd say well that's a pretty loose reworking of James. But James figures in, in still another way, and he's mocked in the text and then you know what the references are.

This is that really funny chitchat between Bill and Jake when they're fishing in Spain, and they're doing a lot of fun talk and parody talk, and Bill at one point says, "That's the thing that can't be spoken of. That's what you ought to work up into a mystery like Henry's bicycle." Now again, I'm pulling things out that most first time readers would never see. "Henry's bicycle" relates to Henry James. It relates in fact to an accident that Henry James had with a bicycle and that relates to another accident that James had which is the mysterious accident that many claim accounts for James celibacy. He received a kind of mysterious back injury at a certain point in his life. Hemingway has James on his mind here. James's character Strether urges Little Bilhem to live all you can, but Struther himself renounces love in that book. He's the one who renounces both Madame de Vionnet and Maria Gostrey in a way saying, "I can have nothing for myself at the end of this."

Hemingway read *The Ambassadors* as a book about sexual renunciation. You know what he said? He said, "James doesn't know anything about the subject. I'm the guy who can write that story. I'm going to write that story. That's what *The Sun Also Rises* is going to be." Now you might think that's a harsh thing to say, but I'm going to quote you something that Hemingway himself wrote precisely to Charles Scribner in 1949, so this is a long time after he had finished the book.

> For your information I started out trying to beat dead writers that I knew how good they were. (Excuse the vernacular.) I tried for Mr. Turgenev, but it wasn't too hard. Tried for Mr. Maupassant (He won't concede the de, de Maupassant, won't give him that) and it took four of the best stories to beat him. Mr. Henry James I would just thumb him once the first time he grabbed, and then hit him once where he had no balls and ask the referee to stop it.

So James had made sexual renunciation look like a kind of grand position in the Ambassadors, a kind of spiritual triumph. Struther will keep nothing for himself, but that's the only way Struther knows how to complete this. To remain clean, not going to be the case here. Jake is going to suffer and agonize and so will Brett because Jake can't give her what she needs.

I had mentioned at the beginning of my lectures, Hemingway slugs it out with everybody he knows, and a lot of people come in for a beating in this book, as well. For example, H.L. Mencken, who again was a kind of major literary avuncular figure by the time this book is written, he's nailed a couple of times. This is the economy of Hemingway, he wants to nail Robert Cone, and this is Jake bragging about how well he knows Paris. So Jake's talking about all the streets and which ones he likes and which ones you only walk down, other ones you ride down because different experience depending on how you do it. Then he thinks, "But maybe I'd only read about this street." Then he says:

> That was the way Robert Cone was about all of Paris. I wonder where Cone got that incapacity to enjoy Paris, possibly from Mencken. Mencken hates Paris I believe. So many young men get their likes and dislikes from Mencken.

Get Cone, get Mencken and get Jake all at the same time in a few sentences there. Well Mencken has a repeat performance, which you may not have picked up. It's in that same bantering conversation between Bill and Jake, and they're talking about utilizing this. They're utilizing a lot of wine at that time and turning the bottle upside down and everything into their mouths. At one point Bill says, "What shall we say brother?" And they've got the chicken that they've taken on their picnic lunch, the drumstick. "He pointed the drumstick at me and went on." And he has this long spiel and at the end he says, "Let us kneel and say, "Don't eat that lady,"" this drumstick, "that's Mencken." Now this is a lewd reference. It's called by the critics "Mencken's member." They're holding this drumstick there, "Don't eat that lady, that's Mencken." This is gratuitous, and it's amazing that he was able to get this through; that people didn't knock this stuff out of the book.

As I said James wrote a story of sexual renunciation. Hemingway's telling a story of sexual renunciation too, and Hemingway wants you to think that Brett is heaving and panting because she's been denied Jake. As I suggested in looking carefully at some of that material it's not clear that Jake and she are not, in fact, having something together. I remind you of the Fitzgerald comment that I quoted that Fitzgerald wrote him and said, "You know, something doesn't make sense in this book. I don't think he's impotent. He doesn't come across like a man who's impotent, he comes across like a man who has a moral straightjacket." I want to suggest that, that there is an incapacity there that's not just an accident of war. It's not just a physical inability or disability. It is a kind of working valid condition that Jake, unwilling, unable to penetrate women, as I said, is aligned to the figure of Romero who dances and teases the bull and gets as close as possible without being gored. I want to suggest that a man who cannot have sex with women has it's own resonance in this text.

In this text, I'm going to talk about other forms of sexuality. The text does not talk much about homosexuality. It has one or two references to gays and they're very distasteful references. You see men coming into the bar when Jake and friends were there, and they make some references to them. I want you to think about the Paris environment of which Hemingway is part. This is a little tendentious what I'm going to say, but I think it certainly helps prepare us for the next book we're going to talk about, which is that Paris in the '20s is a place of enormous sexual experimentation and gender bending.

This is Gertrude Stein and Alice B. Toklas. This is Syliva Beach, who was a lesbian. This is Jenny Pfeifer who was Pauline Pfeifer's sister. Pauline Pfeifer is Hemingway's second wife. It's the woman that, in fact, he is moving to in the '20s as he's leaving Hadley for Pauline. Pauline's sister Jenny is a practicing lesbian, and it turns out later that Pauline herself, after her marriage with Hemingway, will come to prefer women as partners. Janet Flanner was another well-known literary figure—lesbian—in Paris then. Hemingway had encountered lesbians before that. There is some scholarship that says that his mother, Grace, had had female friends, where there was a sexual dimension to their relationship. Then two of the most famous lesbians in Paris at the time that Hemingway is writing this book— here are the names here—Natalie Barney and Juna Barnes, and they are living at the *Rue Jacob*. This man's name is Jacob Barnes. So the people have said it is his dysfunctionality, as a kind of male stud figure.

The book is divided into bulls and steers. It talks about that. There is a bull/steer philosophy. You are the penetrator or you are the penetratee, one or the other. Jake can't be put easily in either of these camps because what Hemingway wants to do, I think, is to preserve the kind of ambivalence here that Jake is in all of these positions. I'm going to give you another really tendentious anecdote, which is the notion that some critics have—and that Zelda Fitzgerald had—that Hemingway and Fitzgerald were lovers. Now, we have read in *A Movable Feast* the way Hemingway puts down

Fitzgerald. It's called a matter of measurement and it's hysterically funny, but it's really malicious, where Fitzgerald has great sexual anxiety and wants Hemingway to check him out because he says that Zelda has told him that he's not equipped to make her happy.

So Hemingway, the superior man obviously, the expert, the savvy, the knowing man, checks him out and gives him all of this advise; talks to him about angles, about pillows, about all kinds of things, and says your wife is simply trying to geld you more or less is what he says. Well, that's what Hemingway wrote after Fitzgerald was dead. He was dead in 1940. In 1929, when there was a particular dinner party that Scott and Zelda had for Hemingway and Pauline—I'm quoting from one of the critics now:

> After they had been drinking at considerable length, the Fitzgerald's returned home and as Scott was getting into bed he drunkenly murmured, 'no more baby.' Zelda took out, (I'm quoting Kenneth Lin, the critic) took his words to mean that he was having a conversation in his mind with Hemingway, which may have been true. And from this conclusion she leapt to the conviction that the two men were lovers.

Zelda is famous for having thought that Hemingway's macho image was bogus. That's the word she used. She told Scott "He is bogus." I told you he's a colossus of a man. She described his muscular exhibitionism as "phony as a rubber check." And this is how she wrote about this event that she would list this suspicion that Scott and Ernest were lovers as one of the reasons of her own mental breakdown. She said, "We came back to the *Rue Palatine*, (she wrote this to her husband.) and you, in a drunken stupor, told me lots of things that I only half understood. But I did understand the dinner we had at Ernest's." And Fitzgerald denied it totally, and wrote her saying, "That the nearest I ever came to leaving you was when you told me you thought I was a fairy in the *Rue Palatine*." So a lot of this is innuendo, it's hearsay, but it's not entirely fabricated out of nothing.

All of it, I think, bears on the representation of Jake, and the way this book is written; I said, this is about language. There's an enormous amount of sexual innuendo in the novel. Brett, for example, when she sees the seductive, really inflammatory Pedro Romero as he's doing his act with the bull, she's inflamed. She keeps asking, "How does he get into those pants." You know what bullfighter's pants look like, they're very tight. "How does he get into his pants?" And the answer comes over twice or three times, "Pipe down," they say. "How does he get into his pants?" "Pipe down. Pipe down." Now you get it—you must get it, okay. The book is going to put this kind of material in there. Her short hair, which Romero wants her to cut, clearly is what makes her the masculine figure, the erotic figure that turns the men around her into swine. We're going to see how far that one goes later when we get to *The Garden of Eden*. The fiesta, which is an explosion that we have, a very fascinating description of the fireworks at the carnival, "That these fireworks that fell into the crowd and charged and chased, sputtering and cracking between the legs of people." It's a nice notation. That's where the fireworks are happening in this book is between the legs of people. One of the notations that comes off there is *globus illuminados*, and it comes up three times, four times: a collection of *globus illuminados*, which is referring to fire works and I would call that lit up balls, *globus illuminados*. Mike said, "a bunch of bloody *globus illuminados*." They really thrust it at you. You can't miss this kind of language. The joke lingo, "Are you joking him? Does he joke you? No I don't joke him."

I suggested that that too has its own allusion to something else; the way words are used in a kind of playful manner that takes them out of their ordinary meaning. Festa: "We're going to festa the English." "I'll festa them," Bill said. "We're going to festa the bloody English." They're talking about carnival—festa, but *fiesta*—it begins to become a verb of particular sorts here. The book, in key moments, will speak other languages. It will speak French, it will speak Spanish, but in English there are some astounding phrases. When Jake goes to Madrid to rescue Brett he goes to this hotel and Hemingway replicates the way the lady who runs the hotel speaks to him. He's worried about leaving his luggage downstairs and she says, "The personages of this establishment were rigidly selectioned." Again, I think, it suggests his castration and emasculation as well. "I was happy to hear of it, nevertheless I would welcome the upbringal of my bags." I mean no one writes like that.

There are passages where French is done the same way—not to mention all the French and Spanish that is actually in the text with the names of streets and places and festivals and things like that. This book is multilingual. I'm talking to you about Hemingway's style, Hemingway's language. It's a carnival of its own. One of the great lines in the book is when Cone sends him a telegram and it says, "Vingo Juevos Cone," Vingo Juevos Cone? I'm coming on Thursday, Cone, telegram. Mike reads it—or Bill, one of them— and says, "What does Cone mean?" I mean, he understands Vingo Juevos, which is "I'm coming on Thursday," but the book wants to write in languages, it wants to take its material and turn it into puns. "Is he joking you? Are you joking him?" Turn it into puns. "Could you fester them?" Turn it into *globus illuminados*. All of that, I think, is a kind of verbal equivalent of the double-ness, the twinships, the double sexuality, that plays out in this book.

I referred to Edmond Wilson's comment that he felt that Hemingway's consciousness has something disturbed and sick and decaying behind the brilliant summer light and the fishing scenes and the idyllic passages. I think that all of that is related to the argument that I'm making now, to somehow convey things and they are what they are and then also to suggest, but they're not that at all, something else is behind them. You're supposed to sense that. That is the other country. It's a phrase Hemingway uses: "another country." It's a world of the text that can have multiple spaces in it, dimensions, fourth and fifth dimensions of prose that you could achieve if you knew how to write it.

One of the most beautiful passages in the book is when Jake—you recall that Cone has called him a pimp—reacts, and Cone knocks him out because Cone is the great boxer of the text. Cone knocks him out and Jake is stunned and dazed, and Jake has this remarkable memory, he says, "Walking across the thick square to the hotel everything looked new and changed." And it looks new and changed because of the trauma Jake has received, a trauma that simply alters perception. This passage is doubled by memory of Jake returning to his hometown after a football game, walking the streets he'd walked all his life and not recognizing them.

"It was all strange," the text says. Only later do we learn that he had been kicked in the head early in the game. That's Hemingway's life story: to have been kicked in the head early in the game, to have been grievously wounded whether on the Italian front and then coming back home to Oak Park on crutches, or as Nick Adams comes home wounded in "Big Two Hearted River," or as Harold Crabbs comes home wounded psychically in *Soldier's Home*, or as Jake Barnes is sexually wounded in our novel here. That wound catalyzes a new vision of the world, a world that is strange, and a world where nothing stays itself. This is going to be the world of *The Garden of Eden*.

Lecture Sixty-One

Hemingway's *The Garden of Eden—*
Female Desire Unleashed

Scope: *The Garden of Eden*, published posthumously in 1986, is a fiercely edited version of a sprawling manuscript that Hemingway worked on from the late 1940s to 1958. In it, we finally see Hemingway fully address the explosive issues of sexual dynamics, androgyny, and gender-bending that one senses "behind the scenes" in so much of his other work. Here, at last, Hemingway offers us a female protagonist of staggering proportions. Catherine Bourne resembles her "sisters" in the Hemingway oeuvre, but she expresses her own subjectivity and her own sexual desire in draconian fashion. This leads to dazzling scenes of erotic play and metamorphosis in which the male protagonist, David Bourne (a writer), passively follows her lead. The project of sexual emancipation turns out to be artistic in nature as well. As such, it stands in sharp contrast to the male prerogatives to which Hemingway has accustomed us over the years. Female desire finally and fatefully comes out of the closet, commanding an authority and announcing a program of considerable reach.

Objectives—Upon completion of this lecture, you should be able to:

1. Summarize the ways in which *The Garden of Eden* is autobiographical;

2. Explain Hemingway's concept of Eden; and

3. Describe the role of sexual metamorphosis in *The Garden of Eden*.

Outline

I. The textual history of *The Garden of Eden* requires comment, given that what we are reading is a drastically edited version of what Hemingway wrote.

    A. In 1986 Scribner's brought out a 247-page volume entitled *The Garden of Eden*, which is what Tom Jenks, a Scribner's editor, had made of Hemingway's 1,500-page manuscript.

1. We know that Hemingway was working on this book between 1946 and 1958 and that he was experimenting with several endings, as well as commenting on the artistic scene in Paris during the 1920s.

2. Literary scholars have trouble viewing this text as "genuine" Hemingway, because we will never know if the author would have arranged the text in any way like Jenks did. There is also a price to pay for Jenks's excisions: The Sheldon subplot is gone, the rich commentary on artists and writers is largely gone, the fuller characterization of Marita has been sacrificed, and Catherine's own verbal poise has been diminished.

B. This novel, like all of Hemingway's work, is rich in biographical and autobiographical echoes.

1. This is a story of a young writer living (for a while) in a *ménage à trois* with two beautiful women—his rich and glamorous wife, who is later joined by the couple's beautiful new "friend." We can hardly miss seeing a key chapter of Hemingway's "evolution" away from Hadley toward Pauline. This shift from wife #1 to wife #2 (which possessed its own amount of androgynous sexual experiment) is further complicated by the fact that it is written 20 years after the events occurred by a writer who is himself moving from wife #3 to wife #4.

2. The crucial new interest in androgyny and lesbianism, kept in the background in *The Sun Also Rises*, is explosively out in the open in this book. We "know" that Pauline Pfeiffer's sister Jinny was an active lesbian, that Pauline herself preferred women mates after her divorce from Hemingway, and that lesbianism was part of Hemingway's personal background, as well as the Parisian setting in which he and Pauline lived.

3. Once again, Scott and Zelda Fitzgerald can also be seen in Hemingway's work. People were struck by the noticeable resemblance between Scott and Zelda—their golden hair and stylish good looks, their similar size, their propensity to dress alike—and Hemingway's book explores such "twinship." Moreover, Catherine Bourne's fierceness, her drive for power over her husband, and her economic and sexual power all parallel what we know Ernest thought about Zelda and her relationship to Scott. Yet, Hemingway seems to sense that this

"warfare" is also matched by a crucial kind of interdependence that "serves" the writer.

II. Hemingway's novel seeks to imagine and to chart the dimensions and whereabouts of Eden.

    A. One form of Eden is the immediacy of the good things in life, and Hemingway is unmatched in his talent for conveying the wonderful taste of food.

    B. The more compelling aspect of Eden, however, has to do with physical ease and sexual innocence, and it is here that the book's female protagonist, Catherine Bourne, stakes her claim.

        1. Catherine and David are young, in love, and beautiful and spend all their time eating, drinking, swimming, and making love. He is a successful writer; she has money. They are in the South of France.

        2. The first sign of impending trouble comes with a pedestrian ritual, the haircut. The project is ambitious: to sculpt the body, to see the body as the work of art.

        3. Consider the parade of short-haired women in Hemingway: The wife with cropped hair in "Cat in the Rain"; Brett in *The Sun Also Rises*, who refuses to let her hair grow long, even though Romero asks her to; and Maria, whose head was shaved by fascists in *For Whom the Bell Tolls* and whose short hair is caressed by Robert Jordan as his throat "thickens." The girl with short hair, the "boyish" girl, is highly erotic in Hemingway.

        4. Knowing Catherine's "sisters" still does not prepare us for the draconian lengths to which she goes to remake her identity. Here we deal squarely with androgyny and sexual metamorphosis.

        5. This theme is not new either, although it exists only in fragmented form in the earlier novels. It seems as if Hemingway's women were always tempted by androgyny, by a special "fusion" with the male lover, in which each one becomes the other and loses his or her "prior" markings. Is this fusion self-pleasure or love, sexual high or pure empathy?

        6. Whereas *The Sun Also Rises* labors under the sign of sexual impotence, *The Garden of Eden* explodes in sexual doing; Hemingway's style is perfectly suited to convey this.

7. The great theme of sexual metamorphosis is to be understood as both "fusion" and "confusion," of reconceiving gender roles and sexual conventions, of learning to approach sexuality "from the other side." The project sometimes seems like a desperate effort at self-recovery, as we saw in Hawthorne's bizarre tale, "Wakefield." At other times, it resembles a massive effort of reclamation, entailing markings of race and even species.

8. Hemingway's tale of sexual experiment and "alternative" sexual practices seems strangely familiar in post-1960s America, but we can trace this kind of situation further back, as well, to the pyrotechnics of the famous Rimbaud-Verlaine homosexual love affair. Moreover, the obsession with darkness and blondness harks back to the stereotypical models of blond and brunette that inhabit American literature (and male fantasies) in Cooper, Hawthorne, and Melville. Above all, Hemingway's morphological adventure calls to mind the pages of Proust and Joyce that are devoted to sexual transformation, as performance at once libidinal and verbal. One thinks of the primitivism of the early Picasso here; there is a comparable meditation about the constraints of civilization.

9. Hemingway takes his plot to the logical conclusion by providing a "swing figure," the beautiful Marita, who loves both David and Catherine, is bisexual and active with each, and functions as a weird "mirror" for all the parties.

10. The big question is: How does David—male, author—take to all this? He instigates nothing. Catherine is the female goddess and ruling shape-shifter of the text. And is Hemingway the writer?

Lecture Sixty-One—Transcript
Hemingway's *The Garden of Eden*—
Female Desire Unleashed

This is Lecture Sixty-One, and it's the first of two lectures on Hemingway's book, *The Garden of Eden*. This is going to be a real pleasure for me to present this text in this course. It's not a Hemingway text that most people know. It was published posthumously, in 1986. It's crazy Hemingway; it's a Hemingway like you've never seen before. I've obviously been alluding to it, and trying to build up to it, and prepare you for it. It's a book that I think is going to be fun to talk about; and, I think you're going to have fun when you work with this book.

It's a book that Hemingway never finished. We have a sprawling manuscript—some 1500 pages of it. It's a book that is kept at the Kennedy Library; apparently it's going to be eventually published in some scholar's edition. It's unwieldy. He wrote on it, as it were, between 1946 and 1958. He couldn't complete it. He couldn't finish it. In 1986, Scribner's brought it out in a very, very sleek volume of 246 pages, which was edited brilliantly, savagely, by their man, Tom Jenks.

This is the book in which the issues of female desire, or androgyny, of alternate sexuality, of sexual experiment—which I've been arguing are there in Hemingway in all the books—here they explode. As I said, Hemingway didn't finish it. Tom Jenks edited the book. We have this funny phenomenon where we have a book where every word we read in the book was written by Ernest Hemingway, and yet there's no reason at all to think that Hemingway would've ever gotten around to domesticating this material, wrapping it up the same way that Jenks did. There's a lot of suspicion in Hemingway circles as to the status of this book—if this is genuine Hemingway or not.

By the way, if you think of the work of editors like the well-known work of Max Perkins, who was at Scribner's and was an editor for both Hemingway, and Fitzgerald, and Thomas Wolfe—the amount of editing and cutting he did—in a sense, Jenks is following a long tradition; and, it may be that a lot of the books that we think of as canonical books have been very much shaped by editors rather than by authors. Any event, I said, Jenks was savage. He knocked out a good bit. There's a very big sub-plot in the original manuscript, of the couple of the Shelton's, a young artist couple who are living in Paris in the 1920s, who obviously resemble Ernest and Hadley. There's a whole lot of conversation—and some of it very sophisticated—about art and writing in the 1920s in Paris, the heyday of modernism.

That's not in the book that we have. We have a sleek, pared-down book. It's also a book that's unmistakably autobiographical. I'm going to draw some of our references here from Kenneth Lynn's very important biography of Hemingway. It's a story of a young writer who's living with, essentially, two women. His wife, and then afterwards, also—not instead of, but also—her beautiful new "friend." I put "friend" in quotation marks there, in a ménage a trois, a three person living arrangement. People have seen that this echoes Hemingway's own situation at a key point in his life, when he was beginning to move from Hadley to his second wife, Pauline Pfeiffer. In fact, people know that they really did live together, in some sense, the three of them for a while. If that angle isn't enough, given that Hemingway wrote this book between 1946 and 1958, he himself was on the move erotically, marriage-wise, shifting from wife three to wife four.

You've got a cubistic set of viewpoints here, and perspectives about marriage—depending on the passages in Hemingway's own life that are in the book—or the experiences of the writer when he was writing the book. As I said, the crucial new thing here—explosive new thing—is androgyny. You might want to think of it as lesbianism as well. Mostly, I'd call it androgyny. It hovers in the background of other books. I've tried to argue that there's experiment and sexual uneasiness in *The Sun Also Rises*, but it's in the open here.

I want to return to these biographical issues, or autobiographical issues. We know that Pauline Pfeiffer—his second wife—her sister Jinny was a well-known, active lesbian. We also know that Pauline herself chose women mates after she was divorced from Hemingway. It's been argued by Lynn and other critics that Hadley herself had possibly lesbian interests. We know that people actually reported having come to visit the Hemingways', and would find Ernest and Pauline and Hadley in the bed together. There are other echoes as well, that are not quite as of a sexual dimension, but they're equally interesting. The fortunes of this couple in this book remind us a great deal of what we know of Scott and Zelda Fitzgerald. Hemingway was obsessed with these two.

It's hard to know which one obsessed him more. I think Zelda did. They were recognized as beautiful young people. They took a certain pride in dressing alike. They looked alike, they were golden-haired, they were charming, they were elegant, they were godlike, and they were cultist. I think that this couple of David and Catherine Bourne is very much modeled on them as well. In particular, Catherine Bourne plays the same role that Hemingway accused Zelda of playing, which is the "bitch," the wife who both bankrolls and undermines or rivals with her husband, her male companion, threatening his writerly life, and enlisting him in her own projects of desire, and coming close to killing him: The Shrew. We have Francis Klein like that in *The Sun Also Rises*; she upbraids Robert Cohn.

Here we have it at the center of the book, not in the margins. I think that Zelda can be seen there—Zelda and Scott. Needless to say, this kind of issue—of a shrewish wife who rivals with her writer husband, and who bankrolls him—it is something that Hemingway may have felt that he knew all too much about himself. He did have his habit of marrying women who bankrolled him. Now, there are lots of ways to look at this. You can say, "Well, these are just details of Hemingway's life." Or, "These are accidents. This is just the way things happen to happen." We'd probably be closer to the mark if we recognized that Hemingway is drawn to women like this. Just as Hemingway is drawn to this kind of tug-of-war tension kind of filled plot of a wife who rivals with her husband.

When I say he's drawn to it, it's not like these are the inescapable facts only of his life. It's that, at some level as a writer, he elects these struggles, these conflicts, and this dynamic. What I'm saying is, it's good for him. He knows it too. He's drawn to it, because this is where he gets his mileage. These are the conflicts and issues that are at the core of his work. This is the combat zone, as it were, that he has covered all his life. I'm not thinking about his military experiences here. So there's a kind of interdependency, a kind of familiarity, and a kind of need, as well, that I think Hemingway recognized in himself, for the kind of marital arrangements that you have in this text.

The text is, in some sense, as the title suggests, a kind of meditation about Eden. What is Eden? What do we think Eden is? We could answer it theologically? We could talk about what Genesis tells us. Eden has to be a place of innocence, a place where pleasure itself might be innocent, where sexuality might innocent. A place that precedes consciousness. There are lots of definitions that have been given. I want us to remark on a passage that gives—at least for me—a very different interpretation of Eden. This is not something you'd find in the Bible at all.

This is a description of the way this young couple lives. In this description we find items such as the following: brioche, red raspberry preserves. We have a passage about boiled eggs, and pats of butter that melt. We have the salt and pepper that's ground on them. We have a memory of eating breakfast like that. Eggs that you dice up, it seems, with a spoon. There's a flow of butter that goes onto them, in order to moisten them. We hear about the texture, the early morning texture of a scene like this. We actually feel the bite, as it were, of those pepper grains that are ground on this. We hear about the hot coffee. We can virtually smell the chicory flavor bowl of café au lait. What I want to say is, that's Eden also. That's Eden in a different sense. A life of gustatory pleasures, the pleasures of the pallet. A life of physical ease. A life of a kind of enjoyment of pleasure, of the good things, the fruits of the earth.

In particular, there are things that you might find in France, on Riviera, because that's where this couple is. Catherine and David are young, in love, beautiful, and they spend all of their time in this book eating, drinking, swimming, and making love. They live on the Riviera. I mean, you couldn't have a more perfect formula, could you? It's a formula that'd either make people sick or that make them salivate, pretty much like that breakfast scene that I read to you. Moreover, he is a successful writer, and she has money. I said they're on the Riviera. They're also in le Grau du Roi and also in du Gard in the south of France. They travel a good bit in this text.

This couple is going to run into trouble in this story. The first sign of it comes with a haircut that Catherine gets. We learn that this hair is cut and cropped as short as a boy's. That leads to the following kinds of remarks that she makes. She tells David that now she's a girl. She's always been a girl, but she's also a boy. She's that, too. She says she can do "anything, and anything, and anything." That's what the text says, "anything, and anything, and anything." It's as if this close-cropped hair, that makes her look like a boy, is a kind of entry into a kind of freedom that she intends to explore. That's why she got her hair cut that way. She constantly asks David to put his hand over her head and to rub her head, that short, cropped hair, almost that butch hair cut, that *gemma* haircut. Now, there's a parade of shorthaired, desirable females in Hemingway. One remembers again, Brett, in *The Sun Also Rises*. Brett refuses to let her hair grow out, and one of the reasons for breaking up with Romero, who wants her to grow long hair and look like a woman. There are others as well. There's Maria, whose head was shaven by the Fascist in *For Whom the Bell Tolls,* and her short hair is constantly caressed by Robert Jordan in that book. Each time he caresses it, Hemingway writes that his throat "thickens." Most readers feel that it's not his throat that's thickening; it's some other part of his body.

What I'm getting at is, when the girl has short hair in Hemingway—when she is boy like, or *gemma*—she's maximum erotic. It's for us to imagine why this should be the case. Now, I want you to think too of that haircut scenario. It's an interesting remark that, when Catherine goes to have her hair cut, she then wants David to have his cut just like hers. That's the Scott and Zelda twin arrangements. The coiffeur tells David, he says, "You know, I'm an artist just the same way you are. Sculpting the hair, cutting the hair is a form of art. It's an artwork. It's crafting the human body." We know, for example, that Hemingway was much taken with certain sculptures of Rodin. Particularly sculptures that have a very clear lesbian dimension to them, of two women caressing each other. Those sculptures were part of the origin of this particular book. This view of the body, as a locus of pleasure, as a locus of control, as something that you sculpt, I want you to think of that in contrast to the Hemingway that we know.

Hemingway has told us about bodies that are constantly ravaged, that are exposed. Men's bodies are ripped apart by bullets, or beaten up by fists, or torn apart by gangrene. Women's bodies are cracked up, torn apart by childbirth. Here we have a different model, a model of pleasure, a model of mastery and control. Now, from the haircut scene that seems to announce a kind of freedom on Catherine's part, to the next scene that I'm going to read you, there's a long, long step—even though it comes one page later. It's a scene of erotic intimacy between the two of them. It's what, effectively, the short hair, the boy look, is supposed to lead to.

Hemingway tells us that David has his hands on Catherine. He's holding her where she's a girl. His hands on her breasts at this time. Hemingway writes about her breasts as having a hard, erect freshness. So, we know that she's aroused at this. She tells him that they are just her "dowry." It's a wonderful term. Her breasts are just her "dowry." What's new is a surprise, and she wants him to feel her hair, to feel the back of her neck. That's what's changed. She wants him to love her the way she is *now*—to understand her and love her the way she is now. I'll quote you one passage—which I think is vintage Hemingway—about this new kind of erotic intimacy, the kind of thing that becomes possible now that she has changed. You're going to see that we're dealing with metamorphosis here.

> He had shut his eyes and he could feel the long light weight of her on him and her breasts pressing against him and her lips on his. He

> lay there and felt something and then her hand, holding him and searching lower and he helped with his hands and then lay back in the dark and did not think at all and only felt the weight and the strangeness inside and she said, 'Now, you can't tell who is who...'

Notice the discretion of that scene. There's nothing pornographic. There are no details that are given. We don't know what aids are in play here. We do know that they're both changing roles. They are essentially having a kind of sexual encounter in which each has become the other's gender in some sense. This is the confusion, "Now you can't tell who is who." And she tells him that he is changing as well, she says, "Yes, you are! Of course, you are!" And she calls him, her "girl, Catherine." He becomes Catherine for her. She asks him, "Will you change?" She wants him to change. She wants him to be her girl. She wants him to allow her to take him as her girl. He tries to resist. He says, "Well, you're Catherine." She says, "No, no, no." She won't accept that. She calls herself, "Peter." She says he is "her Catherine." He is "her Catherine." "Beautiful Catherine. Lovely Catherine." She thanks him for being so good to change, and it closes with her promise to him that now they are going to make love. She is going to make love to him forever.

Well, the cat's out of the bag here. This is a kind of astounding passage, from my point of view, for Hemingway. As I say, I think one can argue it's been coming. I don't think it's brand new, but it's never quite been so explicit as it is in this sequence. I'm going to read you a couple of passages from earlier Hemingway where this has been right almost out in the open. Here's a passage from *For Whom the Bell Tolls*, and it's Robert Jordan and Maria making love, speaking to each other. She is telling him how they are so much alike now, "Can you not feel my heart be your heart?" And she talks about that, "neither one can tell that one of us is one and not the other."

> "And feel now, thou has no heart but mine. Nor any other legs, nor feet, nor of the body," he says.
>
> "But we are different," she said. "I would have us exactly the same."
>
> He says, "You do not mean that."
>
> "Yes, I do! I do," she says,
>
> "That is the thing I had to tell thee."

(He's pretty insistent.) "You do not mean that," he says.

"Perhaps, I do not. I wish to say it. Since we are different, I'm glad that thou are Roberto, and I, Maria. If thou should ever wish to change, I would be glad to change. I would be thee, because I love thee so."

Again, you notice that he's holding down the line. The male doesn't want this experiment. "I do not wish to change," he says. "It is better to be one. Each one to be the one he is." The male wants things to stay in place. This has happened as well even in a book like *A Farewell to Arms*, an earlier book, where in that case Catherine Barclay says, "I want what you want. There isn't me anymore. Just what you want." A kind of fantasy there. "I want us to be all mixed up," she has told Frederick Henry. "I want us to be all mixed up." That other passage I just quoted you, "I want what you want. There isn't any "me" anymore. Just what you want," that's probably a kind of male phantasm, or male fantasy, or sorts. The woman simply wants what you want. "I'm anything you want me to be."

That's not what I just read you in this book. Catherine Bourne is having what *she* wants. Not what David wants. She is taking the lead here. She is taking over the text in some sense. She is making it new. I want you to think about the kinds of adventure, the kinds of challenges that are involved in the passage that I read you, of the two of them changing sex together. It's presented as a kind of fusion. You can think of it as a high form of sexuality, even as a high of love itself. The male becomes the female; the female becomes the love. Each experiences sex from the other side. It also is a breaking down of the kinds of boundaries, and contours, and frontiers that not only define us, but also perhaps lock us in, and imprison us.

This has been present in this course. You think of the incestuous desires in Poe, or in Faulkner. You think of the *Fall of the House of Usher*—brother and sister—the whole house collapsing in on itself at the end of that story. There's a sense here in which there's a fusion. It's not like the fusion that we're going to later see in Tony Morrison. It's a clearly sexual fusion. It's one that really wants to annihilate the existing gender lines and contours that, up to now, have defined people. You can see it as a form of egomania. I think Catherine Bourne is an egomaniacal figure, but you can also see it as a form of generosity. You can see it as what drives human desire in the first place. That's why people are drawn to each other, is to, in some sense, become the other person. That's actually going to happen in a book like this.

If *The Sun Also Rises* is checked in under the sign of sexual impotency, this book explodes as a book about sexual *doing*. Once again, Hemingway's style is wonderfully suited for this. He can render sexual doing in ways that are really quite fine. It has a lot to do with his silences. It has to do with what he says, and what he doesn't say. It's not so easy to write about people making love. It's not the most obvious conversation to be able to convey. This is one of the ways it comes about in this text:

> "Please let's be slow, and slow, and slow."

> "Yes, slow."

> "Are you?"

> "Yes."

> "Are you really?"

> "Yes, if you want."

> "Oh, I want so much! And you are, and I have. Please be slow and let me keep it."

> "You have it."

> "Yes, I do! I do have it. Yes, I do, I do. Please come now with me. Please, can you now?"

I mean that's studded with silences. Nothing is specified. Nothing is spelled out. This is a very fine writer. He's conveying something of the interaction of this couple. We can feel the various phases and stages and thresholds of their coupling, of their lovemaking. A voyage, a trip. That's what ecstasy means. *Ex stasis*—to leave the space, to leave the person that you are—that's what climax is about. This is not so much climax, as desire. Desire, itself, being a voyage, a special kind of trip, that's one way Hemingway's language renders this. I'm going to read you another passage, which is a little bolder—a little more effrontery in this one. This is David and Catherine coming out of the shower, looking at their bodies, looking in the mirror at each other. Comparing how much suntan they've gotten. Who is the darkest, who's not. As they're looking in that mirror—they're both naked—Catherine says to him. "Oh you like us?" What a wonderful comment! "You like us." She can see on him that he likes looking at her. "That's nice. So do I. Touch here and see." So that, if he can join in the act here, he will see the alteration of her body, if he touches it in the right place.

I think this is done very decorous. I think there's nothing smutty in this at all. It's about desire. It's about two people's bodies being wonderfully attuned to each other. It's about the very rhythms of love. Not just sexual rhythms. Rhythms of attention. Rhythms of consideration. Rhythms of mutuality. All of that comes across in this novel. This is going to be his great project of fusion, of reconceiving gender roles, of reconceiving sexual conventions, of learning to do it, as it were, from the other side. In some sense, one has the feeling in this text, given that it's Catherine who initiates this—she has one line that she had always wanted to experience things like this when she was a girl, but she never dared to—you actually get a feeling that she is getting in touch—now think about this—with her own sexuality, via these gender changes—this gender bending—so that, when she asks David to be Catherine, and she says she's going to be Peter, it's a strange way of accessing herself.

When I put it like that, I have in mind one of the early texts we talked about in this course, which is "Wakefield" of Hawthorne. The story "Wakefield," of a man who leaves a marriage and spies on his own absence—ultimately in a kind of project of self-possession—to come into his own identity. I feel that there's something circuitous and homing in this book as well. Catherine is trying to access herself, in some strange sense. She says at one point, "It's not easy to be a girl if you are one." What an interesting remark. "It's not easy to be a girl if you are one." The only way you can possess yourself is to come at yourself from the other side, to experience yourself as the person that you're making love to—object as well as subject—so that kind of metamorphosis, that kind of transformation, that kind of malleability, that kind of fluidity, is what characterizes this text.

Sometimes it really has a kind of dimension of reclamation, or cultural reclamation. Not just gender, but issues of race. Catherine wants to be as dark as possible. At times, she says, she wants to look like a lion, because lions, too, she says, can be dark. She wants to look like an Indian. She wants to go to Africa. All of these are ways in which she wants to change. I'm talking about Africa, and lions, and India, because it's a sense in which she wants to leave that polite, white world behind her. I liken this text to the kind of primitivism of Picasso, of the early, again, of the '20s. It's an effort to get clear of the entire markings and constraints of polite European culture. I think this book wants to roll back the constraints of civilization itself. There is something very ambitious here it seems to me. It's very readable today. It's a text that's wonderfully readable by students today because, in our post '60s era of emancipated sexuality—and today's climate of alternative sexual practices—this book is right at home. This book shows us a Hemingway that we're hardly accustomed to. The censor seems to have left here.

I would like to link it as well to earlier kinds of revolutionary texts. I'm thinking of the explosive revolutionary relationship between the French poets, Rambo and Guerlain, the homosexual arrangement in which they try to reinvent love. That's their phrase, "L'amour doit avoir reinventé." "Love needs to be reinvented." An older man and a young boy celebrating their own passion together. I think of the kinds of constraints that have governed so much American thinking about women; the particular cliché dichotomy of the blonde and the brunette. If you think about Cooper, you think about Hawthorne, you think about Melville, you will find this. The blonde is usually pristine and virginal and innocent. She always wins out in these stories. The brunette is usually sensual, she's exotic, sometimes she's Jewish, and often the text arranges to have her killed. She represents threatening female sexuality. Hawthorne, in particular, is worried about these kinds of issues. James treats us to the same sorts of things.

I'd also like to refer to Hemingway's own peers—his very great peers, Proust and Joyce—who are very drawn to the issues of sexual transformation and sexual metamorphosis. The monumental shape-shifting that takes place in Joyce's *Ulysses*, in the chapter "Night Town," where Bloom changes sex, and becomes a female. Or in Proust's work, where all of the characters live under the sign of Sodom and Gomorrah, of having a sexual nightlife that nobody knows about, the kind of duality, duplicity All of that, I think, is something we've always known about Proust, we've known it about Joyce, but we've rarely thought it to be the case for Hemingway. He takes his place with his very great international peers here. He is an oneric writer. A dream writer. A writer about transformation. He's not the realist that we thought. He's not the macho writer that we've thought. This project is morphological. It's changing forms. It's shape shifting. It's ideological, too. It's a search for freedom, for a freedom beyond the constraints and forms that our culture, and that our bodies have given us.

The plot is relentless because, as this plot continues, they pick up a friend, Marita, the beautiful girl who loves them both. She seems to be bisexual. Catherine initiates her into their experiment. Again Hemingway indulges in his fine, I think, depictions of sexuality. These two, Marita and David are together. Hemingway will tell us that she has put her hand on him. He remarks that they're just riding in the car. She says that she can feel that he likes her. He answers to her, "Well, that doesn't mean anything." He's reliable in that way. But she says, "Well, yes, it does mean something." We know, of course, where she's touching him. This book is always about the response of the body. It has a kind of boldness and directness in that way that nothing else in Hemingway has.

One of the alternative titles for *The Sun Also Rises* that was considered was, *Fiesta*. Well, in this book they're constantly taking a "siesta." "Fiesta," you know, means carnival. What I want to say is that "siesta," sleeping, becomes "fiesta." Carnival time is in the bed. It's not going to be in Pamplona, it has nothing to do with bulls, at least in the obvious sense in this text. It is about explosions, it's about mirrors, and it's about reflections, it's about displacements, and it's about substitutions. I'm going to read you one of the splendid passages. I think it's strong medicine. It's not what you expect from Hemingway. This is not discreet, this passage. This is after Catherine has suggested that the three of them have group sex—the three of them do it together. "We could all just make siesta together." David again, the male, doesn't want this. He doesn't want that all. "Not siesta," is what David says. He's not interested in that. He's mad. Then Catherine comes into the room and he says, "To hell with her!" And Catherine explains to David that she was the one who wanted it to happen; moreover, Marita was ready to do it.

> "Fuck her!" David says.
>
> (The answer to that is) "Well, you have," she tells him.
>
> "That's not the point."
>
> "Go and talk with her, David. If you want to fuck her, then fuck her good for me."

Now you can say that's just gross language. Think about it for a moment. "Fuck her good for me." Freud once said—I'm going to probably misquote here—that, "every time two people get into bed, at least four people are involved." He's not talking about group sex. He's talking about the mind. He's probably talking about the genitals. He's talking about desire. He's talking substitutions and displacements that make sex exciting. "Fuck her for me." I think Hemingway is suggesting that we may be doing things like that all the time. Well, how does the male? You've seen him try to put this down. How is he going finally to assert himself in this arena? We'll see that in the next lecture.

Lecture Sixty-Two
The Garden of Eden—Combat Zone

Scope: The most pungent writing in Hemingway's novel depicts the gathering warfare between David and Catherine. Some of the withering attacks on David reveal Hemingway's profound sense of his own vulnerability. This war would seem to be inevitable. After all, if Catherine takes the lead sexually, what is David's arena? Where does he have authority? The answer is obvious: in his writing. Thus, we are witness to a struggle for control of the writing. Catherine wants David to write "their" story of sexual transformation, whereas David elects to write "African stories" about his childhood, his coming-of-age. David knows that writing is "his" terrain, but we gradually understand that his greatest African story, the tale of a fabled elephant hunt, is about the same issues of perception and fusion that were central to the sexual experiments: to see life from the other side. As the book reaches its fateful impasse, the reader is left uncertain about whether the warfare here is ultimately inimical or empowering. In putting this drama front and center, Hemingway gives us his boldest and frankest account of the warring yet interdependent forces of sexual experiment, androgyny, and creative writing that we will ever have.

Objectives—Upon completion of this lecture, you should be able to:

1. Summarize the role that writing plays in creating and destroying identity in *The Garden of Eden*;

2. Explain the source of the "war between the sexes" according to Hemingway; and

3. Describe Hemingway's ultimate judgment on Eden in the novel.

Outline

I. Hemingway sketches the dimensions of war, just as he does of Eden.

    A. The terrain of battle is often verbal, a kind of sparring that can be hilarious or hideous.

        1. David's vocabulary (Hemingway's manner!) is targeted.

    2.   In other scenes of combat, Catherine tells off David royally, essentially annihilating the entire Hemingway persona (which the author had taken a lifetime to construct).

B. Sometimes, the terrain is economic. Here, too, Hemingway knew all too much, given the bankrolling done by so many of his wives.

    1.   Catherine can be the consummate shrew, speaking words that must have been Hemingway's worst nightmare.

    2.   Catherine sweetly offers to organize and market David's work—which horrifies him—but only on the condition that he drop his African stories to write exclusively about himself and Catherine.

C. Other skirmishes entail no less than the whole Hemingway facade.

    1.   Superman can be dismantled, we see. There is an amazing form of self-criticism at work here.

    2.   We even learn that Mr. Savvy can't speak proper French. One senses, again and again, something confessional and purgative in this story, as if it all had to get said at least once.

II. David finally resists Catherine, because he knows he has no authority or initiative whatsoever in the sexual arena; hence, his field of "doing" has to be writing.

A. David's sense of being besieged can be offset only by turning to writing.

    1.   This is the only terrain he can control. Here he can make sense.

    2.   He elects to write the "hardest" story he can: about his own father.

    3.   Writing shores David up; it is indeed his core, the place in him where no division is possible.

B. David's artistic project consists of writing the African stories about his childhood. We see, as well, an account of the father, which calls to mind Hemingway himself, not the author's father.

    1.   Catherine cannot bear this "distraction."

    2.   Hemingway shows us, with great brilliance, that David is "living" in his writing. We watch the story-within-the-story start to take over, to become the real terrain of David's life.

    3.   Writing about his childhood also allows David to recreate himself, rather than letting Catherine do it in her sexual manner.

4. The story of the elephant hunt is the core of the African material. Hemingway is after big game here, in literary terms, as he rivals Melville's whale hunt and Faulkner's bear hunt.

5. The pursuit of the elephant is rich in moral and emotional truths. It represents Hemingway's feelings about betrayal, about the ways in which the hurting heart always gives us away, makes us targets for others.

6. In a magnificent passage, we see David brooding over his crucial discoveries and revelations in the elephant hunt, and the entire project of writing is illuminated here: How do we transform event into language? How do we recapture the past? How do we understand fields of vision that are not our own? How can we make art without cheating? Such is the grandeur of writing, *a la* Hemingway.

III. Ultimately, predictably, war breaks out between Catherine and David.

    A. Catherine does the intolerable. She goes beyond name-calling and destroys the *cahiers*, the notebooks where David's writing exists.

        1. David is unhinged; this is the cruelest blow of all.

        2. In a passage of rare male anger, David tells her he is ready to kill her.

        3. Catherine may be understood as the mad Zelda Fitzgerald, who wanted to wreck her man. Or she may be Hadley Hemingway, who lost the famous *cahiers* of her young husband at the *Gare de Lyon*, which may have been the greatest trauma of Ernest's life, greater even than the war injury he suffered in 1918.

        4. Finally, we may decide that the destruction of the writing is a kind of severe moral judgment meted out as punishment for precisely the sexual liberties and experiments of the story. We cannot live in the Garden of Eden. Sexual desire is understood by Hemingway to be awful, as well as irresistible.

        5. Yet, as we finish this book and reflect on it, Hemingway the author, the man who created both David and Catherine, comes across as a complex and full human being.

Essential Readings:

Hemingway, *The Garden of Eden* (MacMillan, 1987).

———, *The Sun Also Rises* (Scribner's, 1986).

Recommended Readings:

Hemingway, *A Farewell to Arms* (Scribner's, 1964).

———, *A Moveable Feast* (Scribner's, 1964).

Kazin, *An American Procession* (Vintage, 1985).

Weinstein, *Nobody's Home* (Oxford University Press, 1993).

Topics for Further Consideration:

1. Discuss *The Sun Also Rises* as a quest narrative modeled loosely on Eliot's "The Waste Land."

2. Describe how *The Garden of Eden* stages a war between the power of sexuality and the power of writing.

Lecture Sixty-Two—Transcript
The Garden of Eden—Combat Zone

This is Lecture Sixty-Two. It's the last lecture on Hemingway. It's also the last lecture on *The Garden of Eden*. In my first lecture on *The Garden of Eden*, I tried to unpack the issue of female desire or female sexuality, or also sexual transformation, because it's what's so shocking, and stunning, and new in the book. On the other hand, Hemingway is Hemingway, and you couldn't expect the book to stand exclusively on those lines. There will be a countermove in the book. After all, the male writer—who is David and who represents Hemingway—also has to take his stand or figure out how to manage what's happening to his life, what's happening to the plot.

Who's writing the plot of his own life? Is it his wife? Is it the other woman that he's living with? It's an interesting issue. I tried to deal with that issue of female desire as a cultural phenomenon, as a writerly phenomenon. I think we have to see it finally, too, as part of the complex makeup of Ernest Hemingway. He's not at all as simple as he has been thought to be. In a sense, these two lectures together on *The Garden of Eden*—the first a extending the argument about what Catherine Bourne is like and what that androgyny theme is like, and the second, to show how the male responds and how this gets folded into the writing enterprise—is what I want to be talking about in this lecture.

I think one can think of this as a combat zone. This is a novel about war, like so many of his books are. This is war on a different terrain, in a different key. One of the keys here—and the terrains is verbid—is that Catherine Bourne is going to take her husband apart verbally. We haven't seen much of this before in Hemingway, where they make fun of the male writer as a writer. For example, at one point David says to Catherine, "The sea was very good." That's a pretty typical Hemingway phrase. "You use such interesting adjectives," she said, "They make everything so vivid." This is interesting to me that this man, after all, knows your weak spots as well as you do. This book is auto-critical in a way that very little else in Hemingway has ever been. That's the Hemingway signature—good as an adjective—that's getting a little dirt thrown on it there.

There's another longer sequence—which is one of my favorite sequences in the book—which I want to treat you to. Let me show you how it starts; Catherine is waiting for David and Marita who have been swimming and have made love together and have come back. Part of what this book is about is about a sexual experiment that has to go sour, and that a ménage a trois can't last forever. Something is going to go wrong. People's vanity, their jealousy, their anxieties, and their insecurity, that's going to come into play. I'll have more to say about that at the end of the lecture.

Catherine is waiting for them—as David and Marita return—and David points out that he's been having a certain amount of exercise. The reader figures out what exercise that is. He takes a drink before lunch, and Catherine wonders about that. She points out that there was already an empty whiskey glass on the bar, and this is where the passage starts.

> "Yes," said David, "I had two whiskeys, actually."
>
> "Actually," she mimicked him, "You're very British today."
>
> "Really," he said, "I didn't feel very British. I felt sort of half-assed Tahitian."
>
> "It's just your way of speaking that irritates me," she said, "Your choice of words."
>
> "I see," he said, "Did you want a shot before they bring the chow?" [That's instead of saying, actually I had a second drink. "You want a shot before they bring the chow?"]
>
> "You don't have to be a clown," she says, "The best clowns don't talk. Nobody accused you of being the best of clowns," she said.
>
> "Yes, I'd like a drink if it isn't too much work for you to make it."
>
> He made three martinis, measuring them out, each separately and pouring them into the pitcher where there was a big chunk of ice and then stirring.

See, for me, that little passage is the same as measuring out the trout. This is Hemingway macho, knowingness. I can make the right martini, okay? This is the ritual that ordinarily pins down the world in Hemingway. This is the solidity, the authority of the Hemingway world.

> "Who was the third drink for?" she says.
>
> "Marita."
>
> "Your paramour?"
>
> "My what?"

"Your paramour."

"You really said it," David told her, "I never heard that word pronounced. I had absolutely no hope of ever hearing it in this life. You're really wonderful."

"It's a perfectly common word."

"It is at that," David said, "But to have the shear naked courage to use it in conversation. Devil be good now, couldn't you say your dusky paramour?"

So this book is making fun of the entire verbal project, about the languages of writing, the languages that we associate with the Hemingway male. This is where she's attacking him. She's going after him and then he's fighting back. So that's one of the terrains of the warfare, and it's one of the most interesting pungent terrains of the book. It can also be economic: Catherine the Shrew, Catherine the bankroller, and Catherine who represents again the Hemingway nightmare.

A line where she says, "She never interferes. I've only tried to make it economically possible for him to do the best work of which he is capable." I love that, "of which he is capable." Like, "He's not much, but I'm giving him enough money at least to get him up to the top level that he can attain." This is the language again, that Hemingway must have either heard or feared hearing all his life. It comes out in this book. Catherine, of course, goes much further than that. She also plans in this book to market David's book. She's going to organize it. She's going to show a manuscript that's not finished to publishers. All of these are heresy you've got to understand, within the male writer's scheme, within Hemingway's scheme. He has a totally, maniacally protective view of his own work, and there she is trying to take it from him.

She's got the money, she's going to get contracts, and this that and the other. She's going to hire artists who are going to make drawings for the work, etc. However, she has one condition, and this is a crucial condition, her condition is that the work that is to be published is the work that he writes about them—precisely, about their sexual education—about what they're going through here in the south of France. Whereas, what David wants to write about is something rather different. He wants to write about his own background, his own life story. I'll get into that a little bit later. I'm talking about the way in which the war between the two of them is carried out: economic, verbal. Sometimes you get a sense that it's really going after the entire Hemingway persona, not just writing, not just money, but also the entire manner of a certain figure that we know of as Ernest Hemingway.

For example, Catherine asks Marita, "Was he good today, Marita?" She doesn't mean morally good but "Did he perform well?" This is what she says: "Oh, I know he's a satisfactory lover. He's always that. That's just like his martinis or how he swims or skis or flew, probably. I never saw him in a plane. Everyone says he was marvelous. It's like acrobats, really, I suppose, and just as dull." So there he is. There's Mr. Macho, Mr. Proficiency, Mr. Man who can do every possible sport, who scores a hundred in all of these particular fields. She says it's just mechanical, it's dull, it's acrobatics, and it means nothing. It's amazing that he could be writing this. That's why I was suggesting earlier, there's interdependency here.

We're beginning to understand this is grist for his bills; somewhere behind all of this is Hemingway writing on the typewriter, writing this story. It's not like somebody else is coming in to tell the story about him. He realizes that he's got a book in this, that this is interesting. One of the lowest blows of all that she lands on him is that he can't speak French, and I love this one. There's Ernest, you know. Remember *The Sun Also Rises* trots out all the restaurants, the streets, Pernault? That's what this stuff is. She talks about the fact that his English is dreadful. He writes in these stupid little children's notebooks. Hemingway's fetish as a writer was these little blue notebooks that he's writes about religiously. He writes *about* them as well as writes *in* them.

> "Ridiculous child's notebooks," she says, "He doesn't even throw anything away, keeps it all. He makes mistakes in spelling and grammar, too. Did you know that, Marita? He doesn't really know grammar. Of course, his French is even worse. You've never seen him try to write it. He fakes it well enough in conversation, and he's amusing with his slang, but he's actually illiterate. Yeah, I thought he was wonderful until I found that he couldn't even write a simple note correctly, but then you'll be able to write in French for him."

And then the text says, "*ta quelle.*" This to me is one of the funniest things in this text. There is a slang French expression which is "*ta gueule.*" *Gueule* is the word in French for the mouth of an animal. *Halt's maul* is the German version of the same thing. Whenever you refer to people in animal terms in French, it's very offensive. So, *ta gueule* is what you tell the people when you say shut up, *"ta gueule."* It's misspelled. I don't know if it's intentionally misspelled or not, it's *ta quelle,* which doesn't exist. Of course, that's exactly her charge, that the guy doesn't know how to write, doesn't know how to spell. Even when he's doing this put-up thing—and he tries to get back at her, tells her to shut up in French—he gets it wrong. There's something really funny about this book, and I'd like to actually see the manuscript on that passage because I don't know what it looks like there, to check it out, it's funny. In any event, there's a purgative mood going on here. There's a lot of punishment being meted out here. It's a vicious attack that really can only be thought of as an inside job.

How does David resist this? The way he resists it, you know, is not a surprise. He resists it through his writing. His writing is what is going to anchor him. That's going to be his grounds of authority, his arena of doing, as opposed to the other arenas, like sexuality, where all the doing is coming from her. Writing is going to be his salvation. Although, as he puts it, "that's the place where he's going to make sense," that's his own language. You have to make sense there. You don't make any in this other. He's coming apart, he's being scripted, he's being molded and created by her, in bed, and in other arenas. Here, at least, he can do himself. He wants to write, he says, the hardest story he can, and it's going to be a story about his own past.

In this story, David is the son of a big game hunter, and he's going to write his African stories about his past in Africa with his father. The father is an interesting figure. The father comes through these stories, and he looks a lot like Hemingway—not like Hemingway's father—because Hemingway was the big game hunter as well. So it's an interesting portrait of himself, as a father, that comes across from Ernest's part. He knows that, in his writing, there's something fundamentally integral that cannot be divided; and that again is, that those are his terms. He "can't be rhythm" as he says, because he says the rest of him could be rhythm. In his writing, "there was an inter core which core which could not be split nor even marked nor scratched." That's what he wants to retreat back to, or to stand on. That's the way he can assert himself against her encroachments.

So he writes these African stories, and she can't stand it. Not only will she only want him to publish the stories about her work, she thinks that these stories are also indecent. There's a lot of interesting commentary there. She talks about these stories as really dreadful and obscene stories, about a lot of natives living in degrading circumstances. There's a lot of information here, that the father has sired black children. "Not knowing even which one of the little whores he had fathered," is what the text says, crawling around in these native huts, etc. She thinks the whole thing is obscene; it's a nightmare. She doesn't want any of that.

She obviously blasts that material as something that is unacceptable. She wants him to write about themselves, as I said. She says, "Someone has to show you that these stories," (these African stories) "are just your way of escaping your duty." His duty, according to her, is to write about the two of them. Of course, he is going to stay with the African stories. That is the area where he's going to try to make it. Now, all of this sounds like an attractive theory, like he's going to make it as a writer rather than in the sexual arena. What is quite wonderful about the book is that you see it happening. You see the writing becoming his life. In a number of passages Hemingway shows us David moving into his stories. The stories are becoming so vivid that he disappears from France and is in Africa. These are in single sentences. You'd think that Faulkner was writing some of these sentences, for all of a sudden, you're no longer in the present but you're in the past. You're no longer in France, but you're somewhere else entirely. Writing is called upon to save his life, and the best way to show us that, is that writing is going to become his life.

We begin to realize what the high stakes—the exciting promise, the ultimate reality of writing—is for David, and for Ernest Hemingway. Writing then about Africa, the other country, takes over the entire text. I'll paraphrase some of the passages there, because they're really quite, quite lovely. He's sitting down—this is in France—and the sun is not yet up. He's trying to write this story. It says that the words are now beginning to take him away into the other country. There we begin to get all the details of where he is, "then the sun rises up out of the sea, and in this place there are gray, dried, bitter lakes." His boots, we learn, are "white with crusted alkalis," and we learn that his shirt is wet, and the weight of the sun is there, and the sweat goes down his back, the sweat goes between his thighs, his shirt hangs away from his shoulders. Here he's crossing lakes, and he reaches rivers, and there are groves of trees, and the barks are green, and the barks are yellow, and the barks are heavy. The baboons are there, who have been eating wild figs, and there are baboon droppings, and there are broken figs on the ground. All of this comes to us as the text.

We're not in France anymore. We see this African terrain, we see this African home, and it is the home for this character. This is where he's going to be grounded. We have the stench of his place, with the baboon droppings. Then he stops the writing and goes to have lunch. You're beginning to get the picture that the writing is vehicular; the writing is an exit from this quagmire that he's in, of sexual experiment, sexual transformation metamorphosis. The writing is the opportunity for him, effectively, to establish a new ground for himself, or to return to his old ground. Here is David creating himself rather than being created by Catherine, by the woman. He's constructing his own life, that's why he's writing about his own past.

Of course, writing your past is the way to construct your life. He's writing about his childhood in Africa, the son of this powerful big game hunter. It's quite a story he writes. It's a story about an elephant hunt. In this story, "The Elephant Hunt," in my opinion, Hemingway is rivaling the greatest stories in American literature. He's rivaling the whale hunt of Melville and he's rivaling the bear hunt of Faulkner's "The Bear." This is the pursuit of legendary elephant, an elephant who was huge, and who has these enormous, oversized, and therefore invaluable, ivory tusks. That's the hunt that's going to be narrated in the stories that David is writing.

We're going to get those stories. They come through the text. The reason that this beast—this virtually legendary beast, like Old Ben, or Moby Dick—the reason this beast is being hunted is not just because of the tusks, but because David has seen this animal. He has seen this animal in the moonlight and has stupidly told his father, the professional hunter, about it. The father and his African friend, the guide Juma, take off after the elephant, and they bring the young David with them. That's what he's remembering, this experience as a child. They pursue this elephant. As you read about this story, the story has a considerable volume to it. As you read about this story, you learn that this elephant is on a particular trajectory, and they know it.

They figure this out because these are very seasoned hunters. They know that this elephant is going to the elephant burial ground. The elephant burial ground, in particular, is the place where this elephant's old friend—what the text calls his *ascari*, which is the African term for the elephant's soul mate—this elephant's friend is dead, dead because the guide had killed it many years earlier—Juma—and they know where that body is, and they know that's where the elephant is going. It's a rendezvous. It's a rendezvous of fidelity, of friendship, and of loyalty on the part of the elephant. So they are following him, and they know exactly how to get there.

It's a very suggestive plot, because this is the elephant's terrible secret, that's what the text calls it. This elephant will be killed, probably, because its own loyalty, its own heart is going to condemn it to death. They know where it's going; they know what its secret longings are. This is classic Hemingway. You remember I'd referred to it earlier, the expression in Hemingway, "friend or enema?" That is to say, keep you mouth shut, don't ever expose to people what's on the inside, because if you do, if you let the inside out, that's enema. If you let it out people will be able to track you, they'll be able to pursue you, and they'll be able to get you. This is the fundamental trauma in much of Hemingway.

The heart will betray you if others know it, and that's exactly what David realizes he has allowed his father and Juma to do. They pursue this elephant, and they shoot it twice. They shoot it once in the lungs and once in the gut. In the gut, all of this foul matter starts coming out, stench, and all of the red arterial blood is coming out through the lung shot. You've got this unbelievable scene of the heart leaving a trace, literally. They're following the blood that the creature is producing, and it's as if it's a script, it's as if it's a language. It's like the ink that is blood across the land, and that's what the two white pursuing hunters—or the white and the black man—are trying to trace. As I say, it's richly symbolic. We can't help but realize that there's a notion here, that you will be portrayed, pursued, trackable, punished if you reveal your heart.

That's what David learns. David understands that. In the story he says that he figures that out. "I'm going to keep everything a secret always. I'll never tell them anything again." It gets repeated in an obsessive way. "Never tell anyone anything ever," this is again "friend or enema?" Well, in a passage of extraordinary beauty, David, in Christian fashion, recaptures the past, and we see this extraordinary hunt becoming more and more almost hallucinatory in its reality for us. Writing is going to be David's access to this transcendent moment of his past.

I'd like you to hear how some of that works. David is looking at his own writing, about how he has delivered this story, and he realizes that he hasn't done it right. It's a very interesting piece of writing here. He hasn't told it quite right, and what is says is that he hadn't gotten some of the details quite right. He hasn't gotten, for example, the enormity of the skull quite right, as they had come into it, the skull of the other dead elephant. He hadn't gotten the tunnels underneath it in the earth that the beetles had made. That hadn't been quite done properly, because these tunnels were so big they looked like deserted galleries and catacombs when the elephant moved the skull of his ascari. Nor had he gotten quite right the huge link of the bones, the whitened bones of the other dead elephant, or the tracks, how they made tracks around the scene of the killing. None of this is delivered in quite the full scale that it really was when he saw it.

Then, in a passage that is one of the most perfect passages in the book, that he hadn't quite told them in his writing how, following them, he had been able to see the elephant as he moved, and then had been able to see what the elephant had seen. I want you to think about that. First, to see the elephant, that of course is the pursuit, as we know it. Second, is to see what the elephant sees. That's what this whole passage is about—is understanding the heart, the vision of the elephant—to put yourself in the position of the chased, pursued, legendary animal, to become that. Writing is the route into that. He tells the story in such a way that this chase and pursuit is his approach into the very field of vision of the great elephant. Can you see that this is a replay of the sexual experiments of the book? This is to see it from the other side. This is another fusion, another bridge, another "overpass," as Faulkner would call it. This is a way of understanding realities other than your own. All of the aggrandizing metaphors here, the catacombs, the deserted galleries, even the tracks that are now likened to the map of the metro in Paris—an astounding comparison.

He's talking about tracks in the jungle in Africa, and they now look like the metro in Paris. This is a very fine writer who's telling you that this African story has deep cultural echoes in history. This goes back to the Roman catacombs, it goes back to Paris. This is a tale about orientation, about finding your way. It's not just an exotic African tale at all. It has enormous resonance and scope. It's like the sighting of a new planet. It's about coming to understand the elephant. It's also about coming to understand his own father, making peace with his own father. It is a rite of passage, in the literal sense of the term. It is a passage through the jungle, through youth, and over to the reality of others. A passage from me to you, from David to the elephant, from David to his father. Literature makes that possible. Writing makes that possible.

When we read a text, that's what we do, we enter into a field of vision that is not our own. All of that is what the countermove of this text is about. This is the grandeur of writing. Hemingway comes to take its measure in this particular text, in a way that I have never seen him write about writing, in quite this way. We come to expect this from people like Virginia Wolff or James Joyce or William Faulkner, but we don't expect it from Hemingway. We know that he's a man who only wanted one true sentence, and spent X number of hours every day in front of a typewriter. We've never quite had from him this beautiful evocation of what the entire enterprise is about.

Well, what happens in this text? War breaks out. Catherine does the intolerable. She burns the notebooks. She has told him all along, "I don't want you to write about Africa. You're supposed to write about us, about me." She takes the notebooks and she burns them. It's an astonishing sequence, you don't see her do it. We only learn about it. He is unhinged. He says that the writing can never be reproduced. You can never do it again. If you had it right the first time, it never comes back. He's ready to kill her, that's what he tells her, that he is ready now. "All I want to do is kill you, and the only reason I don't do it is because you are crazy," which all may be true. Catherine is now the mad Zelda Fitzgerald. "You are crazy." She's the mad Zelda, who did lose her mind, who was put into an asylum, who did effectively go after her rival male husband writer and try to undo him, unhinge him.

Also Catherine has to stand in here for Hadley Hemingway, one of the most serious moments of Hemingway's life which, arguably, is a trauma greater than the wound he got in 1918, is the moment in the '20s at the Gare de Lyon when Hadley lost his *cahiers*, she lost his notebooks. This event that is, in this story, a replay of the great wound of his own life. He never got over it. The reason I say that is we have this text. He never got over it. He's rewriting it in this text. She, of course—I think—was never trying to hurt him, and she was deeply, deeply regretful.

He writes about this in *A Movable Feast.* He rushes back to Paris; she comes to visit him. They're in the Alps, she's bringing him a surprise, the notebooks of his writing, and she loses them in the Paris train station. He rushes back to Paris, he combs through the compartment, and he says in *A Movable Feast* that he doesn't care to recall the things that he did when he realized that they were gone forever. This is a wound, as I say, that is as great as any physical injury that he got.

Catherine Bourne's gesture there, of female desire, female freedom, female antagonism, is also melded into this terrible memory of loss, really a mutilation that he experienced himself. That's still another way to ground it. In closing this lecture, I'd like to suggest that there might still be a further way of understanding how this war comes to an end That this book of extraordinary experiment, of risk-taking, of sexual reinvention, of self-creation along line of sexuality, of the hedonism, of living in that totally pleasurable way in the south of France with money, with wine, with food, and with sex that finally has to pay the bills—that is to say, the bill comes—that's what's being punished, in my opinion, as well.

There's a moral punishment finally being meted out to what, in some part of his mind, Hemingway regards as the excesses of his life and of his story. There is a rectitude that is being reestablished here. He loses these notebooks partly because of the life they have led. Now the text isn't going to say that, but to me, that is the ultimate balance, the ultimate equilibrium of this book. It can't be as free and easy and permissible as it has been in this text. You can't take those chances. You can't make those transgressions. You can't break all the rules that this text has broken. The beauty, of course, of the text is that it does do all those things, and then, at the end, in comes the censor and the boom is lowered, the punishment is meted out. So as a result, what we have here is a book where everything is on show. All of it comes out into the open here. All of it is uncensored, along with the final censorship move of punishment. It's in that sense, the richest text that he wrote. It shows us the full Hemingway, and it's that full picture that really, I think, dwarfs the rather simplistic model, the simplistic image, clichéd image, that many of us have had of Ernest Hemingway.

Lecture Sixty-Three

William Faulkner's *The Sound and the Fury*— The Idiot's Tale

Scope: Of all modern American writers, William Faulkner occupies a place unto himself as a giant in the field of Western narrative. His greatest novels—*The Sound and the Fury, As I Lay Dying, Sanctuary, Light in August, Absalom, Absalom!, The Hamlet, Go Down, Moses*—appeared from 1929 to 1942. These works simply reinvent the form of the novel and deliver a testament to the dignity of the human enterprise. Faulkner is tirelessly experimental, beginning with the pyrotechnics of interior monologue a la Joyce, and moving on toward a rich, often baroque, Southern vernacular idiom that is capable of great power and passion. Faulkner's impact on modern fiction is enormous. He was the seminal writer for the Latin American boom and its spate of magic realists, and he profoundly influenced the shape of the European novel, as well. Faulkner's themes range from trauma and decay in the Old South to an increasingly complex engagement with issues of race, coming of age, and adaptation in a conflicted South that is living "the nightmare of history." Faulkner's books are not easy fare for modern readers, and he has fashioned an arsenal of narrative strategies for complicating our access and involvement with his stories. The upshot of these techniques, however, is a reading experience that can be unbearably intense and galvanizing, as we "enter" the writer's fictive precincts and attempt to process the violent moral and emotional crises at hand. Given the fact that Faulkner is "situated" as a white male writer in the American South in the early decades of the 20th century, we can hardly be surprised that his views on race and gender stick in the craw of many critics and readers today. Hence, Faulkner's "stock" is probably less exalted now than it was a few decades ago; but even on these issues, his books are prodigiously informative.

An overview of Faulkner's career shows us a writer who was active from the mid-1920s until his death in 1962, but his masterpieces date from the period when he was, in his own words, "hot": 1929–1942. The great breakthrough text, when Faulkner becomes Faulkner, is *The Sound and the Fury* (1929). This account of a Southern family's decline opens with the most famous piece of American prose in the 20th century—the idiot's monologue. In presenting the vision and voice of Benjy Compson, Faulkner fashions a prose of lyrical beauty and startling immediacy through which we, the jaded readers, recover something of the strangeness and violence of our world. Yet, Benjy is also an essential part of the novel's moral economy, in that Faulkner uses him to tell a simple but profound story about the loss of love. What is happening here is no less than the creation of a new kind of cogency, an affective logic of the senses and the feelings that turns out to be almost intolerably coherent, once we "enter" this field of vision. Perhaps this is the ultimate goal of art itself: to lend us eyes, to school our emotions, to lead us into worlds we cannot otherwise enter.

Objectives—Upon completion of this lecture, you should be able to:

1. Describe the general arc of Faulkner's career;
2. Give examples of how *The Sound and the Fury* breaks with the conventions of narrative prose; and
3. Explain how Benjy's narration explores the Faulknerian theme of inside/outside.

Outline

I. From 1929 to 1942, William Faulkner published six of the strongest novels written in English in this century; his career spans an even longer period of time.

    A. The early Faulkner is still a regionalist writer trying to find his way, although signs of his future themes can be seen.

        1. *Soldier's Pay* (1926), Faulkner's first novel, introduces the issues of trauma.

        2. *Mosquitoes* (1927) says much about Faulkner's views on writing, especially in connection with his "mentor," Sherwood Anderson.

        3. *Sartoris* (1929)—now known as *Flags in the Dust*—is the first rendition of Yoknapatawpha, that "postage stamp of soil" that Faulkner created and developed over the coming decades.

B. Then come the masterpieces, mixed with other ambitious but flawed and provocative texts.

   1. *The Sound and the Fury* (1929) is the true birth of Faulkner the novelist. It is a modernist explosion, incorporating interior monologue, tricks with time, play of memory, a saga of decay, and a rendition of lost love. Faulkner referred to it as his "heart's darling," and it remains that for many American readers as well.

   2. *As I Lay Dying* (1930) is the sister text to *The Sound and the Fury*. It consists exclusively of first-person vignettes recounting the astonishing events surrounding the death of Addie Bundren and the ensuing pilgrimage to get her body into the ground in Jefferson. This is Faulkner's most grotesque and philosophical story.

   3. *Sanctuary* (1931) is Faulkner's potboiler, a cold, nasty, and brilliant story of sexual violence and genteel pretensions. There is much misogyny on show here, including the famous corncob rape scene. Faulkner is now beginning to see the community itself as a party to rot and violence.

   4. *Light in August* (1932) is the first full entry into the problems of race, adding still more complexity to the constructs of identity and cultural scripts. This is Faulkner's "hottest" book, packed with considerable violence directed at women and blacks, yet seeking some kind of reprieve, some redemptive vision beyond the carnage at hand.

   5. *Absalom, Absalom!* (1936) is an epic of the Civil War, as Faulkner broadens and deepens his canvas, learns to see his familial stories as more echoing, more extended into the past, than first appeared. Here he revisits Quentin Compson of *The Sound and the Fury* and enlists him as co-narrator in an effort to make sense of the war. This is Faulkner's most baroque novel.

   6. *The Hamlet* (1940) is the most bucolic of the masterpieces, yet it too is saturated with violence and rage. This is Faulkner's first presentation of the Snopes family, the emblematic figures for the New South that he both fears and hates. Here also is Ratliff, Faulkner's mellowest and most endearing narrator.

   7. *Go Down, Moses* (1942) completes the string of pearls. Faulkner referred to these as his "nigger stories" and, although that term offends, we realize that it points to the continued growth of the writer: to depict—at long last—black subjectivity.

8. Faulkner produced many other works of interest, including *Pylon* and *The Wild Palms* in the 1930s, *The Town* and *The Mansion* as final installments in the Snopes saga, the bloated allegorical disaster of *A Fable* in the 1950s, and the fine, mellow final book of rites of passage, *The Reivers*.

C. Faulkner won the Nobel Prize in 1950, but it is fair to say that his critical reputation was created, in part, by the enthusiastic reception he received in France in the 1930s. Today, his reputation is the subject of considerable debate.

1. Race is one of Faulkner's great themes, but he is rarely polemical on this issue, and his best work—like that of Twain—succeeds largely in presenting black people as humans. Like all people, Faulkner was the product of his culture. In this case, that culture was in the midst of a growing debate on race matters in the South in the early decades of this century. Black readers may well have a different view of his novels, may be less disposed to accept his portraits of black people or of a culture that is inherently racist in its assumptions.

2. Gender is equally problematic for today's readers of Faulkner. One might argue that he never created a fully successful (or "acceptable") female character, although there are some unforgettable ones, including Caddy Compson, Temple Drake, Lena Grove, and Rosa Coldfield.

3. These are serious matters, and it is instructive to read Faulkner both "with" him and "against the grain" to question a number of issues that he presents as givens.

4. Of course "reading" Faulkner at all is the greatest of our obstacles and, perhaps, the sin for which he is least forgiven. In an age of immediate gratification via video games, film, and computers, reading Faulkner can seem like a form of exotic torture. He is perhaps most politically incorrect here, by demanding of us a kind of intellectual labor and engagement that not everyone—perhaps, not anyone—is willing to put forward.

II. *The Sound and the Fury* is Faulkner's first text that is nearly incoherent, and we need to understand how and why the story is presented in this manner.

A. In this novel, Faulkner breaks with all the familiar conventions of realist narrative prose (and thus makes us see them as conventions).

1. There is no omniscient voice—just voices. Here is perspective with a vengeance, and it tells us there can be no credible panoptic vision.

2. The plot of this novel does not go forward. The fictions of Hawthorne, Melville, and Twain may present problems, but they move in a linear direction. Here, past and present are a confusing jumble. Faulkner signals the shifts from one to the other using italics. We may detect Freud here, as well, in the sense that we are always working through materials of the past, materials that "inhabit" us and "speak." This view is bleak for meaningful projects or any kind of future.

3. This type of narrative is perfectly suited to the story Faulkner wants to tell of the decay of a family and the decline of the South. The novel is about a dysfunctional family, the Compsons.

4. Most acutely, Faulkner attends to the fate of the young. He tells the story of the three Compson brothers trying to cope with the great trauma of their lives: the defection of their spunky, willful sister, Caddy. In the novel, we meet Benjy, the youngest, who is an idiot; Quentin, the eldest, who goes to Harvard and commits suicide; and Jason, the pragmatist, who stays home to grow up and become ugly.

5. Faulkner's story is simple yet complex. It is a story of the loss of love and it will be told in an astonishing way.

B. The Benjy narrative is the novel's most extreme performance.

1. How does one process this kind of prose? Is Faulkner just attempting an experiment here? Why is the book written this way?

2. Consider the first page: "Waiting for Caddy." The text restores to us the immediacy of the world before we attach labels to it.

a. What does "through the fence" ultimately mean?

b. Why does the golf course become a pasture?

    c.   What do we know that Benjy doesn't? "Golf"? "Hitting"?

    d.   What does Benjy know that we don't?

    e.   Could "moaning" be a language?

    f.   Who or what is "caddie"?

3. Benjy is presented as our guide to key events and characters in the novel; there is nothing incoherent about this.

4. Benjy is also the conduit for pure sensory experiences that are then passed on "live" to us as readers, as in the narration of his drunkenness.

5. Above all, Benjy is rendering a story of excruciating *loss*. Faulkner's art consists in showing—in unprecedented graphic and economic fashion—what it is that Benjy has lost.

6. The gambit of the novel is that we readers end up on the "inside," with a full understanding of what Benjy is experiencing, while seeing that the "outside" public world can never know this. The essential project here is: "trying to say." This is Faulkner's signature.

Lecture Sixty-Three—Transcript
William Faulkner's *The Sound and the Fury*— The Idiot's Tale

This is Lecture Sixty-Three, and it's the first of six lectures on William Faulkner. Six lectures is a lot—and, of course, with this length—to spend on one author. Faulkner and Melville are the two figures to whom I am devoting this much attention, and the reasons are pretty obvious. I hold both of them to be the most distinguished writers in the American tradition. In the case of Melville, we know obviously what the book is; it's *Moby Dick*. In the case of Faulkner, I'm going to give three lectures on *The Sound and the Fury*—I think the early masterpiece—and then three lectures on *Absalom, Absalom!* which comes about eight years later during the great phase of Faulkner's work.

This first lecture is going to focus on Faulkner's career, the shape of the career, the curve of the life, and then to begin to look at the first infamous section of *The Sound and the Fury*, which is the idiot's monologue, the Benjy Section. Let me start by talking about Faulkner himself. Between 1929 and 1942 I would argue that he produced some five or six of the most distinguished pieces of writing, the most towering literary creations that we have in this country, and I would argue that we have in the English language in this century. This is not a judgment that everybody will agree with. It's not an accident that I am a white male, in my 50s, and from the South. Those are all biases—accidents—that have to do with the evaluation that I just indicated. I'm going to, in the course of these lectures, make it very clear where people would disagree with me and why, because Faulkner is a figure of considerable debate today.

Mind you too, I would recall the fact that, in 1929 and 1942—he starts writing before 1929, and he doesn't die until 1962, so we've got 20 years after that major phase that he is still writing books, and I'll talk about that too. The earliest books that we have, *Soldiers' Pay* and *Mosquitoes*, in particular, the first two novels are still the novels essentially of a regionalist who is trying to find his way. *Soldiers' Pay* is already, however, about trauma, someone coming back a soldier from World War I, published in 1926. I think trauma is here to stay for Faulkner. *Mosquitoes*, the second book, has a wealth of information of Faulkner's views about writing. It's not particularly a readable book. It's Faulkner's engagement with Sherwood Anderson, the older writer who was a kind of mentor for him. The third book begins to look recognizably "Faulkner," and that's *Sartorius*—we now know it as *Flags in the Dust*—and it's the first rendition of Yoknapatawpha, that postage stamp of soil that Faulkner created and developed over the coming decades.

After that—*Sartorius* was in 1920—another book published in 1929 is the beginning of the great phase, and that's *The Sound and the Fury*. That's the birth of Faulkner, the writer. That's the modernist explosion. That has the entire repertory of things that Faulkner's going to make famous in American fiction: interior monologue, tricks with time, jumbled narrative, play of memory, and also saga of decay of the decline of a southern family. This was the book that Faulkner himself loved the most. He has some very memorable statements about this book. He called this book really the one that was closest to his heart. It's where he found his vocation as a writer. It was dear to him in a sense that later books, which we might think of as equally accomplished, are seen by him to be somehow colder, more distant. This was the book for which he used the term "ecstasy," that there was a kind of a breakthrough of a really unique fashion; and, it's not an accident that this is also the book that many critics of Faulkner—critics in the sense of people who study Faulkner, not people who don't like him—also hold dearest.

After *The Sound and the Fury,* in 1930, he published *As I Lay Dying,* which is the really the sibling text of *The Sound and the Fury*, and it is like it in technique, in the sense that it is exclusively narrated in vignettes of stream of consciousness. It is the wryest, the funniest, the most grotesque, and the most speculative and philosophical of Faulkner's novels, I say it's a funny book—and yet its theme is burying the mother—and I think that this is the book that perhaps is the most underrated of Faulkner's great ones. Then he comes up with a novel called *Sanctuary* in 1931, which he himself referred to as a potboiler, a moneymaker. It's a cold, rather nasty, but stunning book. It has a good deal of misogyny in it, it has a good deal of violence, and it has this infamous corncob rape scene for which the book is known, although you have to read it very carefully to be able to find that rape, and it begins to sound the theme of Faulkner's indictment of the community itself.

Light in August, in 1932, in some ways is the most appealing or congenial book to start with in Faulkner. It's the first full entry into the problems and propulsions of race. It takes the kind of traumatized figures that you have in *As I Lay Dying* and *The Sound and the Fury,* and it inflects race and identity into that same problematic. It's also one of Faulkner's lushest books. It's a book that has a certain amount of virulence in it, directed against blacks, particularly directed against women, and yet it is also one of Faulkner's most reaching books. It gestures towards myth, towards a kind of symbolic realm, which might somehow redeem the story of carnage and destruction that is part of the realist plot.

In 1936, Faulkner writes *Absalom! Absalom*! It's hard to believe that this man could write this many staggering books in this sequence, in this few years. *Absalom! Absalom*! is his great epic of the Civil War. It's the first major book that returns to the old stories—the story now, as I say, of a century earlier of the Civil War—and in a kind of fascinating way what he does is he revisits *The Sound and the Fury*. He revisits his own two characters, Quentin Compson, the young Mississippian who's at Harvard and who's going to commit suicide at the end of *The Sound and the Fury*, and his Canadian roommate, Shreve. Now they're revisited in order for the two of them to tell a story, or to be involved in the creation of a story, that is focused on the war. It's focused on the Civil War. It's focused on an event many, many years—45 years—and prior to the events of their own narrative.

Here's the novel where Faulkner reconceives the family story of *The Sound and the Fury*, understands it to be ultimately a story about history, a story about an earlier time, a story really about the founding trauma of the United States, which is that war. It's also Faulkner's most baroque novel. It's the meditation on history. It's also a meditation on storytelling. Storytelling as a notion hardly exists in the early books. In *The Sound and the Fury* and *As I Lay Dying*, what's at stake is trying to save your life. By the time we get to *Absalom*, we begin to see that telling stories—uses of language—might be invoked for lifesaving purposes. It's an interesting kind of paradigm shift.

I'll refer to two more masterpieces. One of them is *The Hamlet*, published in 1940. It's Faulkner's most colorful account of the New South. In it we first encounter these memorable creatures that he calls the Snopes. You can even use a word like Snopsism. These are the figures that represent the new South in the wake of the Civil War. It's a South that's a little bit past carpetbaggers, but it's a scary South. It's a South that Faulkner doesn't like at all. He heaps it with contempt, but also with a kind of paralyzed fascination. This book has the same kind of sexual and racial grotesque events that you see in some of the earlier texts as well. It also has Faulkner's most appealing mature narrator, this man Ratliff, who sells sewing machines.

The last great text, in 1942, is *Go Down, Moses*. Faulkner referred to *Go Down, Moses* as his nigger stories, the "N" word, as they said at the O. J. Simpson trial. That word, of course, was in absolute currency in the 1920s and '30s and '40s and later still—'50s, when Faulkner was living in the South—and it's worth thinking about the term "nigger stories" because it's in *Go Down, Moses* that Faulkner finally succeeds in creating for us a kind of black subjectivity, a black character who would not simply be seen and perceived by white characters, but a black character who would have some agency of his own, and that's the figure of Lucas Beecham, and other blacks in that book as well. That's Faulkner's great effort also, to tell his final great version, of rites of passage, of growing up, of the evolution of the South. It's a meditation about ownership, ownership of the land and ownership of slaves.

He wrote other fascinating books during this same time. In the '30s, he wrote *Pylon and the Wild Palms* and then, in the '40s and '50s, he tried to make a trilogy out of *The Hamlet*. He added to it *The Town* and *The Mansion* that completed the Snopes story. These are all formidable kinds of novels. Then we have some formidable disasters, in my opinion. He writes *Requiem for a Nun*, a kind of remarkably unreadable dramatic version of *The Sanctuary*, which he goes back and revisits. He writes, in the mid '50s, a book called *A Fable*, which is a bloated allegorical disaster of a book. It's about the story of the Unknown Soldier. It's also the Unknown Soldier as Jesus in the trenches in World War I. It's the book that he got most attention for, and this was when Faulkner was canonized, more or less. He had won the Nobel Prize in 1950, so *Life* magazine goes down to Mississippi, takes pictures of Faulkner writing *A Fable*. You see all kinds of charts on the walls. All of this would be nice if the book was any good, but it's very, very hard to read.

His last good book is a book called *The Reivers*. It has a kind of wry humor. It's a kind of, I think, an appealing farewell to the Faulknerian themes of growing up and adventure. As I say, he won the Nobel Prize in 1950, and you'd think, well, that would establish his reputation for good, but things don't work that way. It's fair to say that his reputation is subject to very conflicting views today, in today's academy, and in today's literary climate, and the reasons for that are important. First of all, I don't think we'd have Faulkner at all if it weren't for the French.

It sounds like a crazy thing to say, but this Mississippi writer was not taken very seriously by American criticism when he wrote. He was thought to be a kind of minor local colorist, a creator of grotesque stories; and, in the '30s and particularly in the '40s, when his books were out of print in this country, they were being fiercely translated and talked about and written about and sold in France. Some of France's greatest intellectuals—I'm thinking of Jean Paul Sartre and Andre Malraux—wrote about Faulkner, wrote essays that are still immensely readable. There was a whole wave of French criticism of Faulkner, and then that wave comes back to the United States, and we recover Faulkner from the French over here. There's still, by the way, a great deal of very distinguished French criticism.

Now why would Faulkner's reputation be in jeopardy? Well, one of his great themes is race and, of course, race is one of our great themes today in the academy. We look at literature in terms of race and gender, in ways that we didn't before. Race, of course, becomes a major issue in Faulkner's work. Certainly, by the late '30s, it's an issue that he's dealing with in a very frontal way. He writes about the turmoil and the conflicts of his moment, a man who grew up in the early years of the 20th century in Mississippi and lived there. What I want to say here is that, like anyone else living in a culture, he is "of it" as well as being a critic of it; and, to expect him—or to expect any writer—to simply fly over, transcend, the assumptions and perspectives, often the unstated, often unarticulated, assumptions of a culture, is very naïve. So I think—you'll hear an edge in my voice on this—I think that readers who expect their writers to pass a kind of ideological litmus test are likely to be very disappointed in Faulkner. He will not necessarily come down on the right side of issues of race and gender in the way that readers today would want him to. He can be quite unappealing to black readers, for reasons again that I'm not going to quarrel with. If you were going to come across the word "nigger" page after page, and you're a black reader, you may not find that this is worth doing or particularly rewarding.

Gender is almost as problematic—in some ways *as* problematic—in his work as race is. It's not clear that he ever created a fully successful female character, although there are some very, very unforgettable ones. One thinks of Caddy Compson, whom I'm going to talk more about in these lectures on *The Sound and the Fury*; or Temple Drake, who was his flapper figure in *Sanctuary* who's quite a bitch; and there's a lot of misogyny in the avocation of Temple Drake; or Lena Grove, who comes to us as a kind of fertility goddess—that was something that came easily to him, to imagine women as fertility goddesses in *Light in August*—or Rosa Coldfield, whom we'll also deal with in the latter lectures on *Absalom*, who's a very vindictive, bitter spinster figure, and that type also, that sort of figure of a woman, comes to him very easily as well.

He once was asked, when he was teaching—he was a writer in residence at the end of his life in the late '50s at the University of Virginia—and an undergraduate asked him, "Sir, do you find it easier to create a female character in literature or a male character?" His answer is instructive it seems to me, "It's much more fun to try to write about women because I think women are marvelous. They're wonderful. And I know very little about them." And it's been pointed out, can you imagine him saying that about men, "Men are wonderful. Men are marvelous. I know very little about them?" Women appear frequently in Faulkner's work as entirely other, virtually as extraterrestrials coming from some other zone, some other space, having a kind of reality principle that has nothing to do with men and nothing to do with anything that this man really understands. I think you have to say that these are going to be at least potentially serious, perhaps fatal, liabilities for a writer, and you may wonder how on earth I can claim that he is the most distinguished writer in our century.

One of the things that I want to get at in these lectures, as we look at Faulkner, as I indulge in some sense in six lectures on the work of this writer, is a kind of double-pronged approach to be willing—because I think this is the only way to enter and to get something from his work—is to be willing to read him his way, to be willing to, at least provisionally; tentatively, vicariously, understand his values, his assumptions, his priorities; to see the books in the way we can assume he meant them to be read. But then, also, to read him against the grain, to read him—because we have to do this too—to read him through the lenses of race and class and gender; to see where he may come up short, to see where his possible flaws, or where his possible silences are; things that he cannot write about or things that he cannot write persuasively about. Now when I put it that way, I suggest that there are ideological issues in his work, having to do with race and gender, that will probably determine whether or not we read him, whether or not we like him. What I'd like to add to that is that, that's not the real problem. The real problem is the kind of cavalier remark I've been making all along, which is *reading* him.

Reading Faulkner is very, very difficult and arduous to do. Most people find that it isn't easy to negotiate a Faulknerian text. It wasn't easy a long time ago when these texts were first written, and it seems even more improbable, and perhaps quaint and esoteric today—in an age of video games for the young people and film, an age of media feedback, of immediate stimuli—

that Faulknerian texts can seem like a form of exotic torture. To ask high school or college students to read them—and believe me, you take a look at the subway and the buses and trains, you're not going to see many people thumbing through Faulkner—is quite, I think, a challenge. This may be what's most politically incorrect about his work, the amount of labor that he demands of us to negotiate his books. I'm not trying to say that as a drill sergeant, "Well, so we're just going to have to work hard." What I'm really saying is, "What kind of books are these?" What kind of literature is it that makes us work this hard? What are the conventions here that require the kind of somersaults and tricks and decoding and deciphering that is necessary to make sense of this work? Is that what literature is supposed to be? Is the payoff in any sense commensurate with the labor, if so, in what sense? What kind of patience do you need to read this? What kind of training do you need to read this? What kind of masochism do you need to read this?

As I said, *The Sound and the Fury* is his first breakthrough text. Equally, you could say it's his first incoherent text. It's the first text that makes you realize, "I don't understand that. What in the world is this all about?" It breaks all the conventions of realist narrative, the kind of story, the life story, that we're accustomed to reading in the 19th century. First of all, there is no omniscient voice in *The Sound and the Fury*, just voices in the plural. We're plunged into the interior. It's perspectival with a vengeance. It won't say it in print but I'm saying it, all of these voices tell us that there is no single right take on events. There's no objective view. God was not a novelist.

I'm going to quote Nietzsche on this because it's an interesting critique here, and it's similar, there is no panoptic, objective view of the world.

> Henceforth, (This is Nietzsche) my dear philosophers, let us be on guard against the dangerous old conceptual fiction that posited a 'pure, will-less, painless, timeless, knowing subject'; let us guard against the snares of [contradictory] such concepts as 'pure reason,' (He is obviously evoking Kant.) 'absolute spirituality,' 'knowledge in itself': these always demand that we should think of an eye that is completely unthinkable, an eye turned in no particular direction, (Most of the time we're looking at things; we are looking in a particular direction, and we're placed in a particular direction) in which the active and interpreting forces, through which alone seeing becomes seeing something, are supposed to be lacking; these always demand of the eye an

absurdity and a nonsense. (And here is the crucial point) There is only a perspective seeing, only a perspective 'knowing'; and the more affects we allow to speak about one thing, the more eyes, different eyes, we can use to observe one thing, the more complete will our 'concept' of this thing be, our 'objectivity'.

We circle around things. We have different takes, different vantage points. We all know that's true of life. Ask two or three people to comment on the same event and they'll give you different commentaries.

So this book then has something of that perspectival variety. Likewise, the plot doesn't go forward: Easy to say, hard to manage when you're reading it. Think back to the texts we've looked at in this course, famous novels like *The Scarlet Letter, Moby Dick, Huckleberry Finn, The Ambassadors*—the list could go on—even *The Sun Also Rises*. All of these are books that move apace, they move forward in a linear direction, they replicate the structure of the sentence; subject, verb, object, period, over next subject, verb, object, period. Not here. Past and present are going to be jumbled in this book, on the page just as they are in the human brain, just as they are in the mind, and that does not follow this linear sequence.

A Faulkner book is very difficult to negotiate. He tried to signal this wherever he could. When you're shifting back into the past, when you are moving from one time scheme or frame to another, he signals it by italics; he actually experimented with the idea and wrote his publisher about the possibility of using red-colored ink to signal it. This text is a kind of violent manifesto, of other ways to tell a story. Sartre, in one of his essays on *The Sound and the Fury*, compared the Faulknerian perspective to a man in a convertible, and the convertible is moving forward but the man is standing up looking backwards, and all he can see is an ever-growing past. That, I think, is true for Faulkner's work. At least it's true for the early work. The future, in Sartre's terms, is decapitated.

There is a mindset as well, of the South that Faulkner's trying to convey here. It doesn't have a sense of the future. *The Sound and the Fury* is about the decay of a family, the decline of a culture. It's about a dysfunctional southern family, the Compsons, and Faulkner's very, very much attuned in his early works to dysfunctional families, and above all, dysfunctional— suicidally dysfunctional—young men. His great early theme is trauma.

This story is about the Compson children. Quentin, the oldest, who was the great hope of the family, goes to Harvard and kills himself at the end of his first year. Candace, known as Caddy, the spunky, vital, irrepressible daughter, is promiscuous, ends up getting impregnated and has to flee the family, wants out. Her story can only be narrated through her absence. The book really is the three brothers—the other brothers I'm going to mention in a moment—take on her, their anguished sense of her loss. They are the narrators. Jason, the one who stayed home, the pragmatist, who is the most bilious character in all of Faulkner, and Benjy, the idiot son, who starts the book, the most victimized of all. You know, of course, that the title of the book comes from Shakespeare, comes from *Macbeth*, the "Out, out, brief candle!" passage, and it closes that passage, "A tale / Told by an idiot, full of sound and fury, / Signifying nothing." The idiot's tale is how we start the book, and it is, of course, the most radical challenge to us. How do we read it?

Faulkner once said: "Let the writer interested in technique take up bricklaying or surgery." It's an interesting line. This is a book that has always been cited as technically one of the most fascinating experiments in American literature. Faulkner didn't value technique. He thinks that surgeons and bricklayers are working with technique; writing is something different. The technical experiment here is not for technique alone. It's supposed to promote something else.

I would like to finish this lecture with some remarks about what is being promoted, what's happening here. The first page of this book gives us something of the vision of the idiot. We see him waiting for his sister to come home. "Through the fence, between the curling flower spaces, I could see them hitting." What we have in this first page is a description of people "hitting," and of "flags," and we don't know what it is all about. Soon enough we realize that this is probably a golf course, but the word golf is not going to be used in this passage. "Here Caddy," is written in this passage, "Here Caddy. He hit. They went away across the pasture." We realize that that word "pasture" has crept into this text, and so we wonder, "Why is this a pasture?" We thought it was a golf course, and we gradually understand that "Here Caddy" is the catalyst. That's the trigger, what makes it transform from a golf course to a pasture.

Now what's going on in this sequence? There are a lot of things. Most readers, when they negotiate this first page, they understand that Benjy doesn't have a cognitive sense of his world. He can't think golf course. What he can show us is "hit," and hitting is used four or five times—six times—in the passage. He can show us something of the violence of the word golf; but, when we supply terms like golf course, it demonstrates our own superiority over him. We know that. He doesn't know that. It's also useful to reflect on what he knows that we don't know. He knows, for example, that this golf course was a pasture. It was the Compson pasture. We will learn that this pasture was sold in order for Quentin to go to Harvard, where he only lasts for a year. It was what Benjy most loved. We will also learn that Caddy, who in any realist notation is the boy who follows the golfers and carries their bags, we're going to learn that Caddy, of course, is the name of his sister. "Here Caddy" is really the most succinct title of the novel you could imagine, because the tragedy of this story is that Caddy's not there, she's not here.

We see over and over in this text what Caddy meant to him. He's an idiot; he doesn't understand time. He hears those words, "Here Caddy" and he starts to moan, and the black person who is with him says, "Hush up that moanin'," and we as readers don't know why he's moaning. As the book goes on, we will understand he's moaning the loss of Caddy. Why does he moan her loss? He moans her loss because she has given him the only love that he ever had.

The story is about loss: The loss of Caddy. There are passages where we watch Caddy mother Benjy, because the mother in this family is entirely dysfunctional. We watch her hold him. We have scenes, for example, where Mrs. Compson says, "My poor baby," and then says, "Why don't you take him outside?" Caddy goes outside with him and she embraces him, and she says, "You're not a poor baby, are you? You've got your Caddy, don't you? You've got your Caddy." It's the same pathos as on the first page, "Here Caddy." He moans again because that's exactly what he doesn't have. He doesn't have his Caddy. The whole story is about Benjy waiting at that fence, for his sister to come with the only love that he ever knew.

The sequence reaches, I think, its crescendo—the Benjy Section—when at that fence one day he gets out, and the school girls are walking by it, and they forget to lock the gate and he gets out, and he rushes over to these girls, and they've all been sort of taunting each other, who's willing to go past this fence and past this idiot who's kept in there. What Faulkner writes as he reaches these girls, "I was trying to say, and I caught her trying to say, and she screamed, and I was trying to say and trying, and the bright shapes began to stop and tried to get out, I tried to get out, I tried to get it off my face."

"Trying to say" is the theme of this book. We see that his gestures with these girls are an effort to express love for the missing Caddy, who comes through that fence, used to. We see it. No one in the text can see it. That is our heavy burden in this book, to be witness to the inside picture of loss.

Timeline

1819	Birth of Herman Melville.
1819	Birth of Walt Whitman.
1821	Ralph Waldo Emerson graduates from Harvard.
1829	Emerson marries Ellen Tucker.
1830	Birth of Emily Dickinson.
1831	Emerson's wife dies.
1832	Spurred by his wife's death, Emerson resigns his ministry.
1835	Edgar Allan Poe writes "Berenice"; birth of Samuel Clemens (Mark Twain).
1836	Emerson publishes his essay "Nature"; Poe marries Virginia Clemm, his 14-year-old cousin.
1837	Emerson makes his famous speech at Harvard, "The American Scholar"; Nathaniel Hawthorne publishes his collection of stories entitled *Twice-Told Tales*.
1838	Poe pens "Ligeia."
1839	Poe publishes "The Fall of the House of Usher," considered the quintessential horror story, as well as Poe's masterwork. Poe also publishes "William Wilson" during this year.
1841	Emerson publishes several of his best-known essays, including "History," "Self-Reliance," and "Circles."; Poe publishes "The Murders in the Rue Morgue," considered one of the first detective stories, along with "Descent into the Maelstrom," an early science fiction story.

1842 .... Poe publishes "The Pit and the Pendulum."

1843 .... Poe publishes "The Black Cat" and "The Tell-Tale Heart"; birth of Henry James.

1844 .... Emerson publishes the essay "Experience"; Poe publishes "The Balloon-Hoax," a piece that could be considered science fiction.

1845 .... Poe publishes "The Raven," as well as "The Purloined Letter," considered one of the first detective stories, and "The Facts in the Case of M. Valdemar."

1846 .... Emerson publishes "The Poet," his chief statement about the literary agenda of the future; Henry David Thoreau spends one night in jail for his refusal to pay several years' poll tax as protest against the role of Massachusetts in perpetuating slavery; Poe's wife dies of consumption; Poe writes "The Philosophy of Composition, or How I Wrote 'The Raven,'" the famous account (perhaps spoofing) of his poetic practice; Poe publishes "The Cask of Amontillado"; Herman Melville publishes *Typee*.

1847 .... Melville publishes *Omoo*.

1848 .... Thoreau publishes his essay "Civil Disobedience"; attempted revolutions fail in several European nations.

1849 .... Poe publishes "The Bells," "Eldorado," and "Annabel Lee"; Melville publishes *Mardi*; death of Edgar Allan Poe.

1850 ....Hawthorne publishes *The Scarlet Letter*, perhaps his best-known work; Melville first encounters the work of Hawthorne and writes a now-well-known review; Melville publishes *White Jacket, or The World in a Man of War*; Karl Marx writes *The Communist Manifesto*; passage of the Fugitive Slave Act, which required Northerners to return runaway slaves to their former masters.

1851 ....Thoreau becomes active in the abolitionist movement; Melville meets Hawthorne in person. In this same year, he publishes his masterwork, *Moby Dick*.

1852 ....Harriet Beecher Stowe publishes *Uncle Tom's Cabin*.

1853 ....Melville publishes the short story "Bartleby, the Scrivener."

1854 ....Thoreau publishes his masterwork, *Walden*.

1855 ....Walt Whitman publishes the first version of *Leaves of Grass*.

1856 ....Whitman's poem "Crossing Brooklyn Ferry" published in a version of *Leaves of Grass*; Melville publishes the short story "Benito Cereno"; birth of Sigmund Freud.

1859 ....Thoreau reads publicly "A Plea for Captain John Brown"; Washington Irving dies; petroleum is discovered; Whitman writes "Out of the Cradle Endlessly Rocking."

1860 .... Whitman publishes the collections of poems *Children of Adam* and *Calamus*; birth of Charlotte Perkins Gilman.

1861 .... Start of the American Civil War.

1862 .... Death of Henry David Thoreau; Emily Dickinson has her literary exchange with noted critic Thomas Wentworth Higginson.

1864 .... Death of Nathaniel Hawthorne.

1865 .... Abraham Lincoln assassinated; Whitman writes "When Lilacs Last in the Dooryard Bloom'd," an elegy to Lincoln; end of the American Civil War.

1867 .... Mark Twain publishes the short story "The Celebrated Jumping Frog of Calaveras County."

1869 .... Twain publishes *Innocents Abroad*.

1871 .... Birth of Stephen Crane; Franco-Prussian War.

1874 .... Birth of Robert Frost.

1875 .... Public reburial and dedication of Poe's remains.

1876 .... Twain publishes The Adventures of Tom Sawyer.

1879 .... Henry James writes the first book on Nathaniel Hawthorne.

1881 .... James publishes *A Portrait of a Lady*.

1882 .... Death of Ralph Waldo Emerson.

1885 .... Twain publishes *Huckleberry Finn*, his acclaimed masterpiece, which was promptly banned by the Concord Public Library.

story "The Blue Hotel"; James publishes *The Turn of the Screw*; Gilman publishes *Women and Economics*.

1899 .... Crane publishes "The Monster"; birth of Ernest Hemingway.

1900 .... Whitman's wartime poem, "A Sight in Camp," published posthumously; death of Stephen Crane.

1902 .... James publishes *The Wings of the Dove*; birth of John Steinbeck.

1903 .... James publishes *The Ambassadors*.

1904 .... James publishes *The Golden Bowl*.

1910 .... Death of Mark Twain.

1911 .... Birth of Tennessee Williams.

1913 .... Gilman writes "Why I Wrote 'The Yellow Wallpaper'"; Frost publishes his first book of poems, *A Boy's Will*.

1914 .... Birth of Ralph Ellison.

1915 .... T. S. Eliot publishes "The Love Song of J. Alfred Prufrock"; birth of Arthur Miller.

1916 .... Death of Henry James.

1917 .... F. Scott Fitzgerald joins the army.

1920 .... Fitzgerald publishes his first novel, *This Side of Paradise*; Eugene O'Neill publishes *The Emperor Jones*.

1922 .... Eliot publishes his most influential poem, "The Wasteland"; Fitzgerald publishes The Beautiful and the Damned; O'Neill publishes *The Hairy Ape*.

1925 .... Eliot publishes "The Hollow Men";
Fitzgerald publishes his masterpiece,
The Great Gatsby; Ernest Hemingway
publishes his first major work, *In Our
Time*; O'Neill publishes *Desire Under
the Elms*.

1926 .... Hemingway publishes *The Sun Also
Rises*; William Faulkner publishes his
first novel, *Soldier's Pay*.

1927 .... Eliot becomes a British citizen;
Faulkner publishes *Mosquitoes*.

1929 .... Hemingway publishes *A Farewell to
Arms*; Faulkner publishes *Sartoris*, now
known as *Flags in the Dust*; Faulkner
publishes *The Sound and the Fury*,
considered to be his breakthrough text;
beginning of the Great Depression.

1930 .... Eliot publishes "Ash Wednesday";
Faulkner publishes *As I Lay Dying*, the
sister text to *The Sound and the Fury*.

1931 .... Faulkner publishes *Sanctuary*; O'Neill
publishes *Mourning Becomes Electra*;
birth of Toni Morrison.

1932 .... Hemingway publishes his treatise on
bullfighting, *Death in the Afternoon*;
Faulkner publishes *Light in August*.

1934 .... Fitzgerald publishes *Tender Is the
Night*.

1935 .... Death of Charlotte Perkins Gilman;
Hemingway publishes his treatise on
hunting, *Green Hills of Africa*; John
Steinbeck publishes *Tortilla Flat*.

1936 .... Faulkner publishes *Absalom, Absalom!*,
an epic of the Civil War; O'Neill wins
the Nobel Prize for Literature.

1938 .... Death of Sigmund Freud.

1939 .... Steinbeck publishes his masterpiece,
The Grapes of Wrath.

1940 .... Fitzgerald writes *The Last Tycoon*, left
unfinished at his death in the same year;
Hemingway publishes *For Whom the
Bell Tolls*; Faulkner publishes *The
Hamlet.*

1941 .... End of the Great Depression; the United
States enters World War II.

1942 .... Faulkner publishes *Go Down, Moses.*

1943 .... Eliot publishes the poem "Four
Quartets."

1945 .... Tennessee Williams publishes *The
Glass Menagerie.*

1946 .... O'Neill publishes *The Iceman Cometh.*

1947 .... Williams publishes *A Streetcar Named
Desire*; Eliot wins the Nobel Prize for
Literature; Arthur Miller publishes *All
My Sons.*

1949 .... Miller publishes *Death of a Salesman.*

1950 .... Faulkner wins the Nobel Prize for
Literature.

1951 .... Williams publishes *The Rose Tattoo.*

1952 .... Hemingway publishes *The Old Man
and the Sea*; Ralph Ellison publishes
Invisible Man.

1953 .... Ellison's *Invisible Man* receives the
National Book Award for fiction; death
of Eugene O'Neill; Miller publishes
The Crucible.

1954	Hemingway wins the Nobel Prize for Literature.
1955	The full body of Emily Dickinson's poetic works is published posthumously; Williams publishes *Cat on a Hot Tin Roof*; Miller publishes *A View From the Bridge*.
1956	O'Neill's *Long Day's Journey into Night*, which he had written in 1945, is published posthumously.
1957	Williams publishes *Orpheus Descending*.
1958	Williams publishes *Suddenly Last Summer*.
1959	Lionel Trilling pays homage to Robert Frost on his 85th birthday, saying that Frost belongs in the great iconoclastic tradition of American literature; Williams publishes *Sweet Bird of Youth*.
1961	Death of Ernest Hemingway; Williams publishes *Night of the Iguana*.
1962	Steinbeck wins the Nobel Prize for Literature; death of William Faulkner.
1963	Death of Robert Frost.
1964	Hemingway's *Moveable Feast* published posthumously.
1965	Death of T. S. Eliot.
1968	Death of John Steinbeck.
1970	Hemingway's *Islands in the Stream* published posthumously.
1974	Toni Morrison publishes *Sula*.

Glossary

aboriginal self: A concept defined by Ralph Waldo Emerson as an existing source of universal energy in which we all partake. This self is not in us, but rather, out in the world, and we must learn to move into it.

b'hoy: An American original character, one who challenges all niceties in pieties. The female counterpart is known as the g'hal (the gal).

boutade: French term meaning a joke, a spoof, or a setup that partially hides its true meaning.

Brahmins: Term coined in the mid-1800s by the American writer Oliver Wendell Holmes to describe a class of New England intellectuals determined on the basis of birth, education, and scholarly pursuits.

Calvinism: Christian theology of the French church reformer John Calvin. The central Calvinist tenets include belief in the absolute sovereignty of God and the doctrine of justification by faith alone.

Classic: A work of literature having lasting significance or generally recognized worth. The canonical tests of American literature stem out of vital, often unresolvable, conflicts from their own moments in history. They are bristling with ambiguities and insights that bid to challenge the reader, in their own time, in the present day, and even in the future.

coming of age: In American literature, an event or series of events that spurs a character to reach spiritual adulthood. These stories may or may not revolve around attainment of a character's physical adulthood.

cosmogony: Literally, the study of the universe's origin. In literature, the writer's personal theory of the universe, as reflected in his or her works.

cosmos: As defined by Walt Whitman, a brash young man, a jaunty fellow with a robust ego.

counterculture: A subculture, especially of young people, with values opposed to that of the established culture. Henry David Thoreau is often regarded as a major American counterculture hero.

Demiurge: The deity who fashions the world, a creative force. In literature, a character of such influential personality that he or she is an overpowering force in the story being told.

double entendre: A word or turn of phrase having double meaning, especially when the second meaning is risqué. Ernest Hemingway's works, for instance, revel in suggestions of dual meanings and dual sexuality.

dualism: The division of body from spirit. Whereas most religious traditions assert that spirit is superior to body, some American writers—particularly Walt Whitman—reversed that notion in their works, insisting on the naturalness and sanctity of the body.

dysfunction: Impaired or disorderly function of a cultural system, be it a family or a larger social group.

empowered self: Often regarded as one of America's worst gifts to modern culture, the concept that the individual is empowered to attain all he or she desires. Ralph Waldo Emerson presents the concept of the empowered, or "imperialistic," self in his essay "Self-Reliance."

epiphany: A sudden manifestation of the meaning or essence of something or a sudden intuitive realization or perception of reality.

Epistemology: A division of philosophy that investigates the nature and origin of knowledge.

Existentialism: A philosophy that emphasizes the uniqueness and isolation of the individual experience in a hostile or indifferent universe. A frequent theme in American literature, which often stresses freedom of choice and responsibility for the consequences of one's actions.

Expressionism: An artistic movement during the late 19th and early 20th centuries that emphasized subjective expression of the artist's inner experience. Stephen Crane and Emily Dickinson personify this approach to writing, reconfiguring the world we know by clothing it in images and metaphors.

Feminism: A doctrine advocating the same political and economic rights for women as granted to men. Charlotte Perkins Gilman was an early feminist writer, well known for "The Yellow Wallpaper."

fissured self: Essentially, an existential collapse, when all one knows of the world unravels.

Geworfenheit: German term meaning that we are thrust into a world not of our own making or choosing; a sense of alienation from the world around us.

Gothic: A style of fiction emphasizing the grotesque, mysterious, and desolate.

hagiography: A biography of saints. *Uncle Tom's Cabin*, though often criticized for being overly sentimental, became a black American hagiography that was part of opera and drama.

Impressionism: A movement in painting that originated in France in the late 19th century. Impressionist painters found many of their subjects around them rather than in history, which was then the accepted source of subject matter. Instead of painting an ideal of beauty that earlier artists had defined, the Impressionists tried to depict what they saw at a given moment. To achieve the appearance of spontaneity, Impressionist painters used broken brushstrokes of bright, often unmixed colors. The colors in Impressionist paintings have an overall luminosity because the painters avoided blacks and earth colors. The Impressionists also simplified their compositions, omitting detail to achieve a striking overall effect.

Individualism: The doctrine that society is an artificial device, existing only for the sake of its members as individuals and properly judged only according to criteria established by them as individuals.

Isolationism: A policy in which a nation's interests are best served if the nation secludes itself from other nations and avoids forming alliances with them. In literature, this concept often has been applied to individuals, as in Ralph Waldo Emerson's suggestion that we must "cultivate" our own earth, our own substance.

ludic: Playful in a way that is spontaneous and without any particular purpose.

malaise: A vague feeling of depression or illness.

manself: A term created by John Steinbeck to describe and celebrate the human species; used in place of *men* and *women*. This manself is always struggling to make a success of his or her life and will prevail, no matter how terrible circumstances are.

metaphor: A figure of speech in which a term is transferred from the object it ordinarily designates to an object it may designate only by implicit comparison or analogy. Metaphor allows the writer to yoke together diverse areas of experience and thought. Yet metaphor may also be suspected of falsely domesticating the world by substituting the poet's own projections and fantasies for the "hard facts."

Metaphysics: A branch of philosophy that systematically investigates the nature of first principles and problems of ultimate reality, including ontology and often cosmology. Also, critical or speculative philosophy.

Modernism: The 20th century saw the emergence of Modernism, which responded to the world's complexity by asserting that the individual had the potential to achieve a broader perspective than that offered by any one society or its history. At the beginning of the 19th century, American authors struggled to convince the world that they had a history; by the 20th century, American authors, like European authors, had to grapple with more than enough history.

modus operandi: A method of operating; a particular way of doing things.

motif: An important and sometimes recurring theme or idea in a work of literature. Also called *motive*.

Nantucketer: A uniquely American hero presented in Herman Melville's works. The Nantucketer is different from familiar examples of colonial character. Homespun in his manners, he is nonetheless ruler of the sea, hence, royalty in his own way.

Naturalism: A system of thought holding that all phenomena can be explained in terms of natural causes and laws without attributing supernatural significance to them. Also, the doctrine that all religious truths are derived from nature, not from revelation. In literature, Naturalism attempts to apply scientific theories to art.

Organicism: The concept that society is analogous to a biological organism, meaning that society's overall organization—not the functioning of its individual parts—plays the principal role in determining its processes and destiny.

oversoul: A spiritual essence or vital force in the universe that embraces all souls, thus transcending individual consciousness.

perspectival narration: The literary technique of viewing society from the outside. A writer may write about a historical period in retrospect, for instance, though his or her characters do not know what events are coming.

picaresque: A literary genre in which a rogue-hero's escapades are depicted in a context of sharp social satire. Mark Twain's Huckleberry Finn personifies such a character.

Poet of Babel: A term used to refer to poets who make us think that poetry could be nonsense, but rather, is the sound of the brain, the fabric of consciousness. Although poetry can be a description of the world, it can also be simply the representation of the experience of living with a brain and of sensing things, thinking things, and speaking things.

polysemy: The existence of several meanings for a single word or phrase.

Postmodernism: The literal meaning of *Postmodernism* is "after Modernism"; in many ways, Postmodernism constitutes an attack on Modernist claims about the existence of truth and value. In disputing past assumptions, Postmodernists generally display a preoccupation with the inadequacy of language as a mode of communication. Inaccessible ideas and impenetrable prose also characterize many Postmodern texts, although the difficulties in this case are often intentional and reflect specific claims about the nature of language and meaning.

Puritanism: Scrupulous moral sternness, especially aversions to social pleasures and indulgences. These attitudes and moral worldviews stem from the doctrines and practices of the Puritans.

Realism: In art and literature, an attempt to describe human behavior and surroundings or to represent figures and objects exactly as they act or appear in life. Though attempts at Realism have been made throughout history in all the arts, the term is generally restricted to a movement that began in the mid-19th century, in reaction to the highly subjective approach of Romanticism.

rite of passage: A genre in literature based on an anthropological concept concerning rituals that a young person goes through in growing up.

Romanticism: A movement in the literature of virtually every country of Europe, the United States, and Latin America that lasted from about 1750 to about 1870, characterized by reliance on the imagination and subjectivity of approach, freedom of thought and expression, and an idealization of nature.

self-made man: A classic hero in American literature and history, the self-made man is successful through his own actions. Benjamin Franklin personifies the concept of the wildly successful self-made man.

semiosis: The act of translating a word or visual signal into a cultural meaning, of taking language and turning it into meaning. In literature, the concept that words are signs of natural things, which in turn, are signs of spirit.

sentimentalism: A tendency to express obvious or powerful feelings or emotions without appealing to reason, especially self-indulgent or nostalgic writing or expression. The Sentimental tradition is the great popular literary form of the 19th century.

social contract: A voluntary agreement among people defining the relationship of individuals with one another and with government and, by this process, forming a distinct organized society. In the 17th and 18th centuries, the theory of a social compact among individuals of a society was linked with the doctrine of natural law.

stereotype: An oversimplified standardized image or idea held by one person or group concerning another. In literature, a character meant to typify or conform to an unvarying pattern or manner, lacking in any individuality or depth.

stream of consciousness: A fictional narrative technique, first used in the late 19th century to evince subjective as well as objective reality. It reveals the character's feelings, thoughts, and actions, often following an associative rather than a logical sequence, without commentary by the author.

symbolism: The use of symbols to invest things with a representative meaning, or to represent something abstract by something concrete.

Transcendentalism: In philosophy and literature, the belief that knowledge of reality is derived from intuitive sources, rather than from objective experience. Nearly all transcendentalist doctrines stem from the division of reality into a realm of spirit and a realm of matter. Such a division is made by many of the great religions of the world. Ralph Waldo Emerson and Henry David Thoreau are considered to embody what is known as *American Transcendentalism.*

trope: A word, phrase, expression, or image that is used in a figurative way, usually for rhetorical effect. Metaphor is the quintessential trope in all of poetry.

tuition: Learned knowledge, as opposed to *intuition*, innate or revealed knowledge.

un-naming: This term refers to the literary cleansing of customary labels to install fresh perception. Emily Dickinson's poetry typifies this sort of writing.

vagina dentata: The teethed womb that is a sexual nightmare for the male who is terrified of what it could mean to think literally about moving into the womb.

women's writing: Writing in a feminist vein that features language deemed to be closer to the body. Some characteristics of this kind of writing include fluidity rather than line, openness to affect and libido, suspicion of repressive order, and attention to the somatic.

Biographical Notes

Louis Armstrong (1901–1971): American jazz, cornet, and trumpet player, singer, bandleader, and popular entertainer. Armstrong overcame poverty, a lack of formal education, and racism to become one of the most innovative and influential musicians of the 20th century and one of the most beloved entertainers in the world. He is perhaps best known for helping to pioneer a style known as swing, which later formed the basis for most jazz and rhythm-and-blues (R&B) music. Armstrong's music had a profound influence on Ralph Ellison's *Invisible Man*.

Charles Baudelaire (1821–1867): A leading 19th-century French poet who seized on Edgar Allan Poe's work and career as the epitome of genius, becoming Poe's champion and translator in France. As the founder of Symbolism in poetry, Baudelaire ensured Poe's continued impact on poetic development.

Catherine Beecher (1800–1878): Sister to Harriet Beecher Stowe, Catherine Beecher wrote *A Treatise on Domestic Economy*, dedicated to "the women of America in whose hands rest the real destinies of the Republic."

Samuel Clemens: See **Mark Twain**.

Stephen Crane (1871–1900): American novelist and poet, one of the first American exponents of the naturalistic style of writing. Crane is known for his pessimistic and often brutal portrayals of the human condition, along with a sympathetic understanding of character.

Emily Dickinson (1830–1886): America's most well known female poet and one of the foremost authors in American literature. Dickinson's simply constructed, acutely intellectual writings examine issues vital to humanity: the agonies and ecstasies of love, sexuality, the unfathomable nature of death, the horrors of war, God and religious belief, the importance of humor, and musings on the significance of literature, music, and art.

Thomas Eakins (1844–1916): Regarded by most critics as the most outstanding American painter of the 19th century and, by many, as the greatest his country has yet produced, Eakins was an admirer of Walt Whitman. He was well known for his painting *The Swimming Hole*, as well as paintings of the male body and portraits of Whitman.

Jonathan Edwards (1703–1758): Often called the "last great Puritan," this theologian and intellectual authored such fierce sermons as "Sinners in the Hands of an Angry God."

T. S. Eliot (1888–1965): American-born writer regarded as one of the greatest poets of the 20th century. Eliot also wrote drama and literary criticism. In his plays, which use unrhymed verse, he attempted to revive poetic drama for the contemporary audience. Eliot won the Nobel Prize for literature in 1948.

Ralph Ellison (1914–1994): American author and educator, one of the most influential black American writers of the 20th century. Ellison uses rich, varied, and powerful language to portray the black experience in all its vitality and complexity. His best-known work, *Invisible Man*, expounds the theme that American society willfully ignores blacks and was one of the first works to describe modern racial problems in the United States from a black American point of view.

Ralph Waldo Emerson (1803–1882): Emerson, the guiding spirit of American Romanticism, lays the groundwork for a key tradition in American thinking and writing in his *Essays*, written from the 1830s through the middle of the century.

William Faulkner (1897–1962): American novelist, known for his epic portrayal, in some 20 novels, of the tragic conflict between the old and the new South. Although his intricate plots and complex narrative style alienated many readers of his early writings, Faulkner was a towering figure in American literature during the first half of the 20th century. With Ernest Hemingway, he is usually considered one of the two greatest American novelists of his era. Faulkner was particularly noted for the eloquent richness of his prose style and for the unique blend of tragedy and humor in his works.

F. Scott Fitzgerald (1896–1940): American writer whose novels and short stories chronicled changing social attitudes during the 1920s, a period dubbed the "Jazz Age" by the author. He is best known for his novels *The Great Gatsby* (1925) and *Tender Is the Night* (1934), both of which depict disillusion with the American dream of self-betterment, wealth, and success through hard work and perseverance.

Benjamin Franklin (1706–1790): Printer, scientist, statesman, and author in the early 18th century, Franklin personified the American concept of the "self-made man," particularly through his *Autobiography*. Franklin is particularly well known for his experiments in electricity; his launching of *Poor Richard's Almanac*, the first American periodical; and his role in the Revolutionary War. His is the great American story of tireless achievement, assertion, and adult responsibility in the difficult arenas of business, government, and politics.

Sigmund Freud (1856–1938): The father of psychoanalysis, Freud articulated the concepts of the unconscious and infantile sexuality and repression and proposed a tripartite account of the mind's structure, all as part of a then-radically new conceptual and therapeutic frame of reference for the understanding of human psychological development and the treatment of abnormal mental conditions. His conclusions affected the interpretation of much American literature during and after his lifetime.

Robert Frost (1874–1963): American poet who drew his images from the New England countryside and his language from New England speech. Although Frost's images and voice often seem familiar and old, his observations have an edge of skepticism and irony that make his work, upon rereading, never as old-fashioned, easy, or carefree as it first appears. In its embodiment of both tradition and skepticism, Frost's poetry helped provide a link between the American poetry of the 19th century and that of the 20th century.

Margaret Fuller (1810–1850): A 19th-century feminist writer and one of the great radical women among the Transcendentalists. Fuller was a journalist and edited *Dial Magazine*, working closely with Ralph Waldo Emerson. Nathaniel Hawthorne may have modeled aspects of Hester Prynne's character in *The Scarlet Letter* on Fuller.

Charlotte Perkins Gilman (1860–1935): American feminist and writer, best known for her book *Women and Economics* (1898), which has become a feminist classic. She was born Charlotte Anna Perkins in Hartford, Connecticut. She was educated at the Rhode Island School of Design and worked as a teacher and commercial artist before devoting herself to feminism.

Nathaniel Hawthorne (1804–1862): American novelist whose works are deeply concerned with the ethical problems of sin, punishment, and atonement. Hawthorne is considered America's first great classical writer and is particularly known for his novel *The Scarlet Letter*.

Ernest Hemingway (1899–1961): American novelist and short-story writer, whose style is brisk, terse, cleansed of adjectives, seemingly objective, and aimed at rendering the precise moment and feeling of experience. Hemingway's writings and his personal life exerted a profound influence on American writers of his time; in fact, Hemingway is usually considered one of the two greatest American novelists of his era (the other being William Faulkner). Many of his works are regarded as classics of American literature.

Thomas Wentworth Higginson (1823–1911): Unitarian minister, abolitionist, and well-known 19th-century literary critic with whom poet Emily Dickinson exchanged letters seeking critiques of her poems.

Washington Irving (1783–1859): Often called the father of the American short story, Irving is best known for two stories: "The Legend of Sleepy Hollow" and "Rip Van Winkle." His work is considered to precede early writings of the great Transcendentalists—Emerson, Thoreau, and Hawthorne.

Henry James (1843–1916): American expatriate writer whose masterly fiction juxtaposed American innocence and European experience in a series of intense, psychologically complex works. James's work is characterized by leisurely pacing and subtle delineation of character rather than by dramatic incidents or complicated plots. His major writings, highly sensitive examples of the objective psychological novel, deal with the world of leisure and sophistication he had grown to know intimately in Europe.

Toussaint L'Ouverture (1743–1803): Haitian general, now known as "the Precursor," and leader of the Haitian slave revolt, a 1791 black slave uprising against the French colonial regime. After France abolished slavery in the territory in 1794, Toussaint supported the French rulers of the country against British invaders and was made a general in 1795. In 1801, he succeeded, after many struggles, in liberating Saint-Domingue from French control and became president-for-life of a new republic.

Herman Melville (1819–1891): American novelist and major literary figure whose exploration of psychological and metaphysical themes foreshadowed 20th-century literary concerns. His works remained in obscurity until the 1920s, when his genius was finally recognized.

Arthur Miller (1915–): American dramatist whose works are concerned with the responsibility of each individual to other members of society. Simply and colloquially written, Miller's plays spring from his social conscience and from his compassion for those who are vulnerable to the false values imposed on them by society.

Toni Morrison (1931–): American writer whose works deal with the black experience and celebrate the black community. Morrison's work features mythic elements, sharp observation, compassion, and poetic language and is often concerned with the relationship between the individual and society. In 1993, she won the Nobel Prize in literature.

Eugene O'Neill (1888–1953): American playwright whose work dramatizes the plight of people driven by elemental passions, by memory and dream, and by an awareness of the forces that threaten to overwhelm them. His early plays (1916–1920) helped initiate American theater's shift away from elegant parlor dramas and toward gritty naturalistic plays.

Edgar Allan Poe (1809–1849): Best known for his poems and short fiction, Poe is credited with transforming the short story from anecdote to art. He virtually created the detective story and perfected the psychological thriller. He also produced some of the most influential literary criticism of his time—important theoretical statements on poetry and the short story.

Sir Walter Scott (1771–1832): Scottish novelist and poet considered to be the creator of the historical and the regional novel. He may have influenced the works of Nathaniel Hawthorne.

John Steinbeck (1902–1968): American writer and Nobel laureate, who described in his work the unremitting struggle of people who depend on the soil for their livelihood. Steinbeck's novels can all be classified as social novels dealing with the economic problems of rural labor, but there is also a streak of worship of the soil in his books, which does not always agree with his matter-of-fact sociological approach.

Wallace Stevens (1879–1955): American poet whose works deal mainly with the individual's interaction with the outside world. Stevens used sensuous, elaborate imagery and elevated, precise word choice to express subtle philosophical themes. He frequently contrasted the bleakness and monotony of modern industrialized life with the richness of nature.

Harriet Beecher Stowe (1811–1896): American author most famous for her anti-slavery novel, *Uncle Tom's Cabin*, one of the most influential American texts written by either man or woman and, possibly, the first American social protest novel.

Henry David Thoreau (1817–1862): American essayist, poet, and practical philosopher, renowned for having lived the doctrines of Transcendentalism, as recorded in his masterwork, *Walden*, and for having been a vigorous advocate of civil liberties, as evidenced in the essay "Civil Disobedience."

Lionel Trilling (1905–1975): American educator and influential literary critic. For most of his career, Trilling taught at Columbia University. In his books, he used psychological and sociological methods to elucidate cultural values. One of his major concerns was the relationship between the self and society. Trilling paid homage to poet Robert Frost on Frost's 85th birthday.

Nat Turner (1800–1831): American slave and leader of a black slave revolt in 1831. As a result of Nat Turner's revolt, southern legislatures imposed stricter control on slaves, and the movement to abolish slavery, which had previously enjoyed some support in the South, became a northern phenomenon.

Mark Twain (1835–1910): Pen name for Samuel Langhorne Clemens, American writer and humorist, whose best work is characterized by broad, often irreverent humor or biting social satire. Twain's writing is also known for realism of place and language, memorable characters, and hatred of hypocrisy and oppression.

Vincent Van Gogh (1853–1890): Dutch Post-Impressionist painter, generally considered the greatest Dutch painter and draughtsman after Rembrandt. He powerfully influenced the current of Expressionism in modern art. Among his masterpieces are numerous self-portraits and the well-known "Starry Night." An admirer of Whitman, Van Gogh corresponded with the American poet.

Booker T. Washington (1856–1915): American educator who urged blacks to attempt to uplift themselves through educational attainments and economic advancement.

Walt Whitman (1819–1892): American poet whose work boldly asserts the worth of the individual and the oneness of all humanity. Whitman's defiant break with traditional poetic concerns and style exerted a major influence on American thought and literature.

Tennessee Williams (1911–1983): American playwright and two-time Pulitzer Prize winner, whose works are set largely in the American South. As a playwright, fiction writer, poet, and essayist, Williams helped transform the contemporary idea of Southern literature. He not only paved the way for other writers but also helped the South find a strong voice, where before it had been heard only as a whisper.

Bibliography

Barbour, Brian M., ed. *Benjamin Franklin: Critical Views*. Englewood Cliffs, NJ: Prentice-Hall, 1979.

Bercovitch, Sacvan. *The Office of the Scarlet Letter*. Baltimore, MD: John Hopkins University Press, 1991.

Bloom, Harold. *Modern Critical Interpretations: Death of a Salesman*. New York: Chelsea House, 1988.

————. *Modern Critical Interpretations: Moby-Dick*. New York: Chelsea House.

————. *The Western Canon*. New York: Riverhead, 1994.

————. *William Faulkner's* Absalom, Absalom!. New York: Chelsea House, 1987.

————. *William Faulkner's* The Sound and the Fury. Philadelphia, PA: Chelsea House, 1998.

Bradbury, Malcolm. *The Modern American Novel*. New York: Oxford University Press, 1984.

Cox, C. B., and Arnold Hinchliffe, eds. *The Waste Land: A Collection of Critical Essays*. London: MacMillan, 1968.

Cox, James M. *Robert Frost: A Collection of Critical Essays*. Englewood Cliffs, NJ: Prentice-Hall, 1962.

Crane, Stephen. *Prose and Poetry*. New York: Library of America, 1984.

————. *The Red Badge of Courage*. New York: Norton Critical Edition, 1962.

Dickinson, Emily. *Final Harvest: Emily Dickinson's Poems*. Boston: Little Brown, 1961.

Eliot, T. S. *The Complete Poems and Plays*. New York: Harcourt, Brace & World, 1952.

————. "Tradition and the Individual Talent." In *Visions and Revisions in Modern American Literary Criticism*, edited by Bernard Oldsley and Arthur Lewis. New York: Dutton, 1962.

————. "*Ulysses*: Order and Myth." In *Forms of Modern Fiction*, edited by William Van O'Connor. Bloomington, IN: Indiana University Press, 1948.

Elliot, Emery, ed. *The Columbia History of the American Novel*. New York: Columbia University Press, 1991.

Ellison, Ralph. *Invisible Man*. New York: Vintage, 1989.

Emerson, Ralph Waldo. *Essays and Lectures*. New York: New American Library, 1983.

Faulkner, William. *Absalom, Absalom!*. New York: Vintage, 1986.

————. *As I Lay Dying*. New York: Random House, 1991.

————. *Go Down, Moses*. New York: Random House, 1991.

————. *Light in August*. New York: Random House, 1991.

————. *The Sound and the Fury*. New York: Vintage, 1986.

Fisher, Philip. *Hard Facts: Setting and Form in the American Novel*. New York: Oxford University Press, 1987.

Fitzgerald, F. S. *The Great Gatsby*. New York: Scribner's, 1960.

————. *Tender Is the Night*. New York: Simon and Schuster, 1995.

Franklin, Benjamin. *Writings*. New York: Library of America, 1987.

Frost, Robert. *Selected Poems of Robert Frost*. New York: Holt, Rinehart and Winston, 1963.

Gilbert, Sandra, and Susan Gubar. *The Madwoman in the Attic*. New Haven: Yale University Press, 1979.

Gilman, Charlotte Perkins. *The Yellow Wallpaper*. Thomas Erskine and Connie Richards, eds. New Brunswick, NJ: Rutgers University Press, 1993.

Hawthorne, Nathaniel. *Novels*. New York: Library of America, 1983.

————. *The Scarlet Letter*. New York: Norton Critical Edition, 1978).

————. *Tales and Sketches*. New York: Library of America, 1982.

Hemingway, Ernest. *A Farewell to Arms*. New York: Scribners, 1987.

————. *The Garden of Eden*. New York: MacMillan, 1987.

————. *Green Hills of Africa*. New York: Scribner's, 1987.

————. *A Moveable Feast*. New York: Scribner's, 1964.

————. *The Sun Also Rises*. New York: Scribner's, 1986.

Hoffman, Daniel. *Poe Poe Poe Poe Poe Poe Poe*. Garden City, NY: Doubleday, 1972.

Irving, Washington. *History, Tales and Sketches*. New York: Library of America, 1983.

James, Henry. *The Ambassadors*. New York: Norton Critical Edition, 1964.

————. *The Aspern Papers*. New York: Everyman's Library, 1994.

———. *The Beast in the Jungle and Other Stories*. New York: Dover, 1993.

———. *The Turn of the Screw*. New York: Norton Critical Edition, 1966.

Kaplan, Justin. *Walt Whitman: A Life*. New York: Simon and Schuster, 1980.

Kazin, Alfred. *An American Procession*. New York: Vintage, 1985.

———. *On Native Grounds*. New York: Harcourt, Brace & Co., 1942.

Kenner, Hugh. *A Homemade World: The American Modernist Writers*. New York: William Morrow, 1975.

Lawrence, D.H. *Studies in Classic American Literature*. New York: Viking, 1964.

Lee, A. Robert, ed. *Edgar Allan Poe: The Design of Order*. Totowa, NJ: Barnes and Noble, 1987.

Levin, Harry. *The Power of Blackness: Hawthorne, Poe, Melville*. New York: Vintage, 1958.

Lyne, William. "The Signifying Modernist: Ralph Ellison and the Limits of the Double Consciousness." *PMLA* (March 1992).

Lynn, Kenneth. *Hemingway*. New York: Simon and Schuster, 1987.

Matthieseen, F. O. *The Achievement of T. S. Eliot*. New York: Oxford University Press, 1958.

———. *American Renaissance*. New York: Oxford University Press, 1941.

Melville, Herman. *Billy Budd, Sailor and Other Stories*. New York: Penguin, 1967.

———. *Moby-Dick*. New York: Norton Critical Edition, 1967.

———. *Pierre, Israel Potter, The Confidence Man, Tales and Billy Budd*. New York: Library of America, 1984.

———. *Redburn, White-Jacket, Moby-Dick*. New York: Library of America, 1983.

Miller, Arthur. *The Crucible*. New York: Penguin, 1995.

———. *Death of a Salesman*. New York: Penguin, 1976.

Moorton, Richard F., ed. *Eugene O'Neill's Century*. New York: Greenwood, 1991.

Morrison, Toni. *Beloved*. New York: New American Library, 1988.

———. *The Song of Solomon*. New York: NAL-Dutton, 1993.

———. *Sula*. New York: NAL-Dutton, 1993.

Oberg, Barbara, and Harry Stout, eds. *Benjamin Franklin, Jonathan Edwards and the Representation of American Culture*. New York: Oxford University Press, 1993.

O'Meally, Robert, ed. *New Essays on Invisible Man*. Cambridge: Cambridge University Press, 1988.

O'Neill, Eugene. *Complete Plays: 1932-1943*. New York: Library of America, 1988.

———. *Long Day's Journey Into Night*. New Haven: Yale University Press, 1965.

Paglia, Camille. *Sexual Personae*. New York: Vintage, 1991.

Parker, R.B. *Twentieth Century Interpretations of* The Glass Menagerie. Englewood Cliffs, NJ: Prentice-Hall, 1983.

Poe, Edgar Allan. *Poetry and Tales*. New York: Library of America, 1984.

Poirier, Richard. Robert Frost: *The Work of Knowing*. Stanford, CA: Stanford University Press, 1990.

Porter, David. *Dickinson: The Modern Idiom*. Cambridge, MA: Harvard University Press, 1981.

Reynolds, David. *Beneath the American Renaissance*. Cambridge, MA: Harvard University Press, 1988.

Samuels, Charles. *The Ambiguity of Henry James*. Urbana: University of Illinois Press, 1971.

Steinbeck, John. *The Grapes of Wrath*. New York: Viking, 1958.

Stowe, Harriet Beecher. *Three Novels*. New York: Library of America, 1982.

Thompson, Judith. *Tennessee Williams' Plays: Memory, Myth and Symbol*. New York: Peter Lang, 1987.

Thoreau, Henry David. *A Week on the Concord and Merrimack Rivers, Walden; Or Life in the Woods, The Maine Woods, Cape Cod*. New York: Library of America, 1985.

Tompkins, Jane. "Sentimental Power: *Uncle Tom's Cabin* and the Politics of Literary History." In *The New Feminist Criticism*, edited by Elaine Showalter. New York: Pantheon, 1985.

Twain, Mark [Samuel Langhorne Clemens]. *Adventures of Huckleberry Finn*. New York: Norton Critical Edition, 1977.

———. *The Adventures of Tom Sawyer*. New York: Penguin, 1986.

———. *Mississippi Writings*. New York: Library of America, 1982.

———. *Pudd'nhead Wilson and Those Extraordinary Twins*. New York: Norton Critical Edition, 1980.

Warren, Robert Penn. *Faulkner: A Collection of Critical Essays*. Englewood Cliffs, NJ: Prentice-Hall, 1966.

Weinstein, Arnold. *The Fiction of Relationship*. Princeton, NJ: Princeton University Press, 1988.

———. *Nobody's Home: Speech, Self and Place in American Fiction from Hawthorne to DeLillo*. New York: Oxford University Press, 1993.

———. *Vision and Response in Modern Fiction*. Ithaca, NY: Cornell University Press, 1974.

Weinstein, Philip M. *Faulkner's Subject: A Cosmos Nobody Owns*. New York: Cambridge University Press, 1992.

———. *What Else But Love? The Ordeal of Race in Faulkner and Toni Morrison*. New York: Columbia University Press, 1997.

Whitman, Walt. *Complete Poetry and Collected Prose*. New York: Library of America, 1982.

Williams, Tennessee. *A Streetcar Named Desire and Other Plays*. London: Penguin, 1962.

Wyatt, David, ed. *New Essays on the Grapes of Wrath*. Cambridge: Cambridge University Press, 1990.

Young, Philip. "Fallen from Time: The Mythic Rip Van Winkle." In *Visions and Revisions in Modern American Literary Criticism*, edited by Bernard Oldsley and Lewis Arthur. New York: Dutton, 1962.

Credits

Notes

Notes

Notes